James Villas'
The *Town & Country* Cookbook

By the same author

American Taste

James Villas'

THE

Town & Country

Cookbook

Illustrations by Catherine Kanner

LITTLE, BROWN AND COMPANY
Boston · Toronto

FIRST EDITION

Library of Congress Cataloging in Publication Data
Villas, James.
  James Villas' The Town & country cookbook.
  Includes index.
  1. Cookery, American. I. Town & country (New York, N.Y.) II.
Title. III. Title: James Villas' The Town and country cookbook.
IV. Title: Town and country cookbook.
TX715.V625 1985   641.5   85-10315
ISBN 0-316-90301-9

H

Designed by Patricia Girvin Dunbar

*Published simultaneously in Canada
by Little, Brown & Company (Canada) Limited*

PRINTED IN THE UNITED STATES OF AMERICA

For
BRUNO and BRUNHILDE
BEAUREGARD and BESS

· CONTENTS ·

· A C K N O W L E D G M E N T S ·

I WISH TO EXTEND my warmest thanks to Patricia Brown, Marion Gorman, Leland Smith, and Paula Wolfert, all inimitable, indefatigable eaters who have shared my table so many times, tasted anything and everything, tolerated my often eccentric behavior in restaurants from one continent to the next, and provided the sort of unqualified support, understanding, and friendship that is as rare today as a bottle of Château Pétrus '61.

My thanks also to Mary Homi and Melissa Tardiff, both of whom have traveled the globe with me, eating, drinking, and plucking the cherries from my Bourbon Manhattans.

I owe a great deal to every member of the editorial staff at *Town & Country*, but most especially to Jean Barkhorn for reminding me from time to time of the difference between a teaspoon and a tablespoon, to Cathy Calvert for having turned my rough prose into poetry on more than one occasion, to Kim Waller for keeping a smile as she restructures still another article for the fifth time, and to Arnold Ehrlich for adding that touch of class to everything he edits.

Finally, words cannot express my appreciation to Frank Zachary, the last real editor's editor, the gentleman who has given so much to so many, the man without whose inspiration and guidance this book would have never seen the printer's ink.

· I N T R O D U C T I O N ·

EVER SINCE Frank Zachary offered me the food and wine editorship of
Town & Country shortly after he was brought in as editor in chief of the
magazine in 1972, my efforts have always involved not only exposing
readers to the fine cuisines, beverages, and restaurants of the world but
also providing plenty of tempting, sensible, workable recipes that illustrate both the great international traditions of the past and the culinary
innovations of the present. Reflecting on these twelve fascinating years, I
suppose what I pride myself on most at *T&C* is how, year after year, we've
managed to remain in the vanguard of everything that has happened in the
food and wine world. It's with no false modesty that I point out how (for
better or worse) we were one of the first to bring attention to many of the
famous new French chefs of the early seventies and their *nouvelle cuisine,*
the mounting popularity of northern Italian cooking, the gastronomic
advances in England and regional America, and, perhaps most important,
any number of those products that have been so instrumental in this
country's present food revolution: domestic caviar, cheeses, and wild
mushrooms; various new forms of pasta, smoked meats and fish, game,
and new types of herbs and chili peppers; and such obvious but neglected
items as root vegetables, cured country hams, chestnuts, and leeks. I
venture to say we were *the* first major publication to endorse and analyze
in depth the first great premium wines of California, and long before what
is now termed the New American Cuisine began to gather momentum we

were championing the cause of American cookery and trying to suggest ways it could be better understood and possibly redefined.

We have always zeroed in on trends when they appeared to exhibit worthwhile and lasting qualities, but never once have we allowed current fashion to affect our coverage of such fundamental issues as lobster, *cassoulet,* Bourbon whiskey, hash, breakfast, sandwiches, *foie gras,* truffles, asparagus, and postprandial liqueurs. Those who suffer the illusion that readers of *T&C* eat only beluga caviar and drink only vintage Taittinger were perhaps a little surprised when we ran full-length features (with recipes) on peanut butter, sardines, cheesecake, and the humble potato, and those same people would undoubtedly be even more amazed to know that our quality readership has responded to our coverage of Texas barbecue restaurants, Paris bistros, and San Francisco grills with the same interest and enthusiasm as to articles devoted to the famous three-star restaurants of France. If I've learned nothing else during my years at *Town & Country,* I've learned that the rich and successful love and respect a great hamburger as much as an elaborate fish baked in puff pastry.

This cookbook, therefore, is intended to reflect not only a certain attitude toward food that is at once personal and professional but also the many gustatory avenues we've opened up to readers over the past dozen years. The book should be useful to anyone who knows the fundamentals of the kitchen and is interested in producing primarily dishes that have new flair, that illustrate today's fascination with fresh native ingredients and modern cooking equipment, and that lend themselves to lots of individual interpretation and experiment. Rest assured that you'll find recipes here for such old-fashioned favorites as French onion soup, short ribs of beef, crab cakes, and pecan pie, classics that few of us ever tire of and that I want to see in the repertory for decades to come. But you'll also be introduced to duck *rillettes,* onion, feta cheese, and olive pizzas, johnnycakes with creamed shrimp and oysters, sautéed rabbit with anchovies and black olives, scrambled eggs with crabmeat and vermouth, strawberry-peach cobbler, and hundreds of other creative dishes meant to spark the appetite and inspire the imaginative cook. You'll also learn (especially in Parts Three and Four) how certain dishes can take on new dimension when conventional menu formulas are bypassed and engaging new options are suggested. Jellied country ham with parsley, sardines in aspic, and *oeufs aux crevettes grises,* for example, make excellent appetizers, but when preceded or followed by certain other dishes, they might also be served as main courses at brunch or lunch. Similarly, something like the classic Greek spinach and cheese pie known as *spanakopita* has always been considered a main course on any menu, but now professional and amateur cooks alike think nothing of serving a small portion of the dish as a tasty starter when more substantial fare is scheduled as a main course. If this sort of menu juggling sounds a bit unorthodox, it's because I do indeed tend to be unorthodox when it comes to making the eating experience more and more exciting. At *Town & Country,* we have never embraced novelty for novelty's sake, but when a new idea or concept that is sound and intelligent comes along, we're always ready to test it out.

Which brings me to the touchy topic of why you won't find in this cookbook many of the dishes commonly associated with the so-called *nouvelle* style of cooking. It is certainly no news to anyone who has followed my reportage over the past few years that I am no great admirer of either the French *nouvelle cuisine* or the embarrassing imitation in this country known as the New American Cuisine. As I stated above, *T&C* has always been willing to pay serious attention to any food trend that might contribute to the pleasure of great eating, and when, in the early seventies, there seemed to be impressive innovation taking place in France, I wasted no time planning a trip. Suffice it to say that I had nothing but praise for the initial efforts of Paul Bocuse, Roger Vergé, Jacques Manière, Pierre Troisgros, Paul Haeberlin, the young Georges Blanc, and a few other real pros who have made a very important and lasting impact on cooking styles everywhere. But the disgraceful abuses by amateurs that have followed, the attempts to discredit a classic cookery that took centuries to develop, and the almost total disregard for *la cuisine bourgeoise* in favor of what often turned out to be little more than manipulative, laboratory food gradually forced me to lose all sense of objectivity. That many young American chefs, untrained, a little overconfident and arrogant, and utterly infatuated with the French *nouvelle,* have managed to dupe so many and shove our wonderful regional dishes even further into oblivion by proclaiming a new style of cooking which is little more than the superficial application of tired *nouvelle* principles to native ingredients has hardly helped my attitude.

In any progressive, civilized culture, formalized cooking must indeed be allowed to evolve, as evidenced by numerous dishes included in this book. But the idea that old culinary concepts must be tossed in the fire to make way for unbridled, undisciplined invention, that traditional dishes do not merit at least serious reevaluation and possible refining, and that such age-old staples as salt, flour, butter, and cream should be automatically discarded all in the name of better health and our "new life-style" is contradictory to everything the art of gastronomy is about and to my own philosophy. I could belabor this point for hours, but no one hits upon the truth of the matter with more down-to-earth, trenchant accuracy than that witty, wise, perceptive amateur of the kitchen, Nora Ephron: "Anyone who believes for one second that the *nouvelle cuisine* has had any impact on the way Americans eat in their homes is crazy. It has nothing to do with anyone except possibly ten people who have chefs and are silly enough to think raspberries go with meat and kiwi with shrimp."

Although this cookbook includes virtually every tested dish that has appeared in *Town & Country* over the past twelve years, I decided to include also numerous recipes from my own personal files and from other sources. No matter where I travel, for instance, I collect recipes from restaurants the way others collect matchbooks, a rather demanding hobby, I must say, that keeps me hanging around kitchens for hours begging and pleading with chefs to reveal their most sacred secrets. Some of the recipes here were developed by professional chefs at my request; others come from close friends, long-time colleagues, and such charity events as the March of Dimes Gourmet Galas with which I've been closely involved; and still others were inspired by random recipes published elsewhere. Since I'm a firm believer in proper attribution when it comes to recipes, I've tried to the best of my ability throughout the book to give credit when credit is due in the headnotes. I'm certainly not one who sets out to "invent" recipes. I do, on the other hand, love to experiment with cooking, meaning I never hesitate to take a given recipe, develop and adjust it according to my own taste, and possibly call it my own. With most responsible food writers, the exact point where recipe modification assigns new identity to a dish is a sensitive topic that must be dealt with fairly and intelligently. If I have slighted anyone unintentionally, I offer my apologies.

Having fought these many years against the wrong type of snobbism so often associated with the name *Town & Country,* let me emphasize that very few of the dishes in this book utilize the sort of fancy, expensive ingredients that would frustrate most home cooks. Nor, in my opinion, is there a single recipe that could be considered beyond the scope of any chef with a grasp of kitchen basics. What I've tried to produce is a practical, sensible, self-contained cookbook that will appeal to those who are aiming toward a certain sophistication in their food preparation, menus, and eating habits, a book that addresses an American audience that is considerably more knowledgeable about food than just ten years ago and that loves to entertain and eat well like never before.

New York, February 1985

PART ONE

Appetizers

German Onion and Chive Pie

Serves 8

1 envelope active dry yeast
1 cup lukewarm milk
3 tsp. sugar
8 Tb. vegetable shortening, room
   temperature
3 eggs
1 Tb. salt
4 cups all-purpose flour, sifted

8 Tb. (1 stick) butter
5 medium onions (about 3 lbs.),
   well chopped
¼ cup sour cream
1 tsp. caraway seeds
Freshly ground pepper
3 Tb. chopped chives

Sprinkle yeast over ¼ cup of the milk in a small bowl, add 1 teaspoon of the sugar, stir, and let proof for 10 minutes or till mixture is bubbly.

Pour the yeast mixture into a large mixing bowl, add the remaining milk, the shortening, 1 egg, the salt, and 1 cup of the flour, and blend well with a pastry cutter. Add the remaining flour 1 cup at a time, stirring well with a wooden spoon. Transfer the dough to a lightly floured surface, wash, dry, and butter the bowl, and knead the dough till it is smooth and no longer sticky. Return dough to the bowl, turn it to grease all surfaces, cover with a towel, and let rise in a warm area for about 1 hour or till doubled in bulk.

Meanwhile, heat the 8 tablespoons of butter in a large, deep skillet, add the onions, sprinkle on the remaining sugar, and sauté over moderate heat, stirring, till golden. Transfer onions to a large bowl and let cool.

Preheat oven to 400°.

Punch the dough down, transfer to a lightly floured surface, and roll into a 12×16-inch rectangle. Fit the dough onto a lightly greased baking sheet about 12×16 inches in size and push sides of dough up to form a 1-inch border.

In a bowl, beat the remaining 2 eggs, add the sour cream, caraway seeds, and pepper to taste, and stir mixture into the cooled onions. Distribute the onion mixture evenly over the dough and bake for about 45 minutes or till edges of the dough are browned.

Sprinkle chopped chives over the top, cut pie into squares, and serve as a first course.

Dilled Lobster Mousse

Serves 4

1 cup cooked lobster meat
1 Tb. butter
1 Tb. flour
⅓ cup milk
Salt and freshly ground pepper

2 eggs, separated
⅓ cup heavy cream, whipped
1 Tb. finely chopped fresh dill
Sprigs of fresh dill for garnish

Preheat oven to 350°.

Place lobster meat in a blender or food processor and chop finely.

Heat the butter in a saucepan, add the flour, and whisk over low heat for about 2 minutes or till smooth. Increase heat to moderate, gradually add the milk, stirring, add salt and pepper to taste, and cook for 2 minutes.

In a small bowl, beat a spoonful of the hot sauce into the egg yolks, return mixture to the saucepan, cook for 1 minute, and remove pan from the heat. Stir in the chopped lobster, transfer mixture to a mixing bowl, and stir in the whipped cream and chopped dill.

Beat egg whites till stiff, fold into the lobster mixture, and spoon mixture into a buttered 5- or 6-cup mold. Place mold in a baking pan, pour in enough boiling water to reach halfway up the sides of the mold, and bake for 35 minutes.

To serve, run a sharp knife around edges of mousse, turn mousse out onto a platter, and garnish edges with sprigs of dill.

Chilled Country Ham Mousse

This is one of the best ways I know to utilize the fatty ends of a succulent country or Smithfield ham. If you don't like your ham flavor salty (I do), soak the ends in water for about 6 hours before preparing them for the meat grinder.

4 Tb. (½ stick) butter
¼ cup flour
1 cup milk, heated
1 Tb. Dijon mustard
¼ tsp. powdered sage
Cayenne
¼ cup Madeira
2 egg yolks

½ cup heavy cream
2 Tb. gelatin
½ cup Chicken Stock (p. 521)
1 lb. country ham, skinned,
    trimmed of all fat, and cut
    into chunks
Watercress for garnish

*H*eat butter in a heavy saucepan, stir in flour, and cook roux, stirring, over low heat for 2 minutes. Add hot milk gradually, stir well, and cook mixture over low heat till very thick. Add mustard, sage, cayenne to taste, and Madeira, and stir till very well blended.

In a small bowl, combine egg yolks with cream, whisk, and stir in a little of the hot sauce. Add mixture to the hot sauce and continue cooking sauce over low heat, stirring, till thickened.

In another small bowl, soften gelatin in chicken stock for 5 minutes and stir into hot sauce. Place ham in a meat grinder or food processor, grind finely, and stir into sauce.

Pour mixture into a 1-quart mold or 6–8 ramekins, chill for at least 6 hours, and unmold in center of a large serving dish or small salad plates. Garnish with watercress.

Onion Gougères

Serves 6 – 8

Classic French *gougères* do not contain onion, but after I once prepared these to accompany a huge lamb salad with fresh tomatoes and basil at a farmhouse in Bucks County, Pennsylvania, they became almost a regular feature at Saturday lunches. By themselves, they make a very nice, zesty appetizer.

1 cup water
8 Tb. (1 stick) butter, cut into
   pieces
1 tsp. salt
Pinch of nutmeg (preferably
   freshly grated)

1 cup flour
4 eggs
1 Tb. grated onion
8 oz. Gruyère cheese, shredded
Cayenne
1 egg yolk mixed with 1 Tb. water

Preheat oven to 450°.
    Combine water, butter, salt, and nutmeg in a large saucepan and bring to the boil. Reduce heat, add flour, and stir till dough forms a ball.

Remove pan from heat and beat in eggs one at a time. Add onion, cheese, and plenty of cayenne, and stir well. Drop dough by tablespoons onto a greased baking sheet, brush with egg wash, and bake for 20 minutes or till puffed and golden.

Slit side of each puff with a knife, return to oven with door ajar, and let dry for 10 minutes.

Mushrooms Tapenade

Serves 4 – 6

Made with capers, anchovies, garlic, and olive oil throughout southwest France and the Riviera, *tapenade* is a pungent mixture traditionally spread on toasted bread, cooked eggs, fish, or beef. I love also to stuff it into mushrooms, squash boats, cauliflower, and even scooped-out ripe tomatoes. Do not try to prepare *tapenade* in a blender or food processor unless you want a soupy texture.

4 Tb. capers, rinsed and dried
6 anchovies, drained
1 garlic clove, chopped
1 cup olive oil

¼ cup lemon juice
Freshly ground pepper
1 lb. large mushroom caps

*I*n a mortar or small bowl, pound 2 tablespoons of the capers, the anchovies, and the garlic to a paste, then scrape into a mixing bowl. Add oil very gradually, stirring. Add lemon juice and pepper to taste, stir thoroughly, and let stand in a covered container for at least 4 hours.

Wipe mushroom caps with a damp towel and divide evenly between 4 – 6 salad plates. Spoon equal amounts of *tapenade* into mushrooms and garnish plates with remaining capers.

Herbed Feta Cheese Ball

Serves 6 – 8

This ball is equally tasty made with fine aged cheddar, Stilton, or Double Gloucester. If you do substitute one of these cheeses, however, omit the oregano.

2 scallions (whites only), roughly
  chopped
1 garlic clove, chopped
1 8-oz. package cream cheese, cut
  into large pieces
1 Tb. sour cream
1 Tb. chopped fresh dill (or 1 tsp.
  dried dill)

½ tsp. oregano
¼ tsp. freshly ground pepper
1 lb. feta cheese, broken up
2 sprigs parsley, minced (or 2
  Tb. chopped chives)

*L*ine a 1½- or 2-cup bowl with plastic wrap.

Place scallions and garlic in a food processor and process for 3 seconds. Add all remaining ingredients but parsley, pulse machine 6 or 7 times, then process for 20 seconds or till completely smooth, stopping machine once to scrape sides. Spoon mixture into prepared bowl, cover with more plastic wrap, and chill for 4 – 5 hours.

To serve, remove ball from plastic wrap, set on a platter lined with lettuce or fresh spinach, sprinkle with parsley or chives, and surround with crudités and wheat crackers.

Skewered Snails and Mushrooms

Serves 6

2 7-oz. cans snails
¼ cup olive oil
2 Tb. lemon juice
¼ cup finely chopped shallots
½ tsp. salt
¼ tsp. freshly ground pepper
1 garlic clove, smashed

1 Tb. chopped parsley
6 slices bacon
24 fresh mushroom caps
½ cup bread crumbs
8 Tb. (1 stick) unsalted butter
6 lemon wedges
Watercress for garnish

Drain snails and place in a bowl. Whisk olive oil and lemon juice in a bowl till well blended, add shallots, salt, pepper, garlic, and parsley, and stir. Pour over snails, toss, and let stand for 2 hours.

Cut each bacon slice into 3 pieces and fold in half. On each of 6 long skewers alternate 3 snails, 3 folded bacon slices, and 4 mushroom caps, starting and finishing with mushrooms. Coat brochettes lightly with bread crumbs.

Heat butter in a skillet wide enough to fit brochettes and sauté brochettes over medium heat, turning, till golden brown. Serve on hot plates garnished with lemon wedges and watercress.

Marinated Chicken Wings Parmesan

Serves 4

12 whole chicken wings
½ cup plain yogurt
3 Tb. lemon juice
1 Tb. Dijon mustard
1 garlic clove, minced
½ tsp. oregano
½ tsp. salt

Freshly ground pepper
½ cup bread crumbs
½ cup freshly grated Parmesan
  cheese
1½ Tb. melted butter
Cayenne

Arrange chicken wings in a large, shallow baking dish. Combine yogurt, lemon juice, mustard, garlic, oregano, salt, and pepper to taste in a mixing bowl, stir well, pour over chicken, cover dish with plastic wrap, and marinate for 2 hours.

Preheat oven to 350°.

Combine bread crumbs and Parmesan in a large bowl and roll chicken wings in mixture. Arrange wings in another large baking dish, drizzle with butter, season with cayenne to taste, and bake for 45–50 minutes or till skin is crisp.

Leek Tart

Serves 4–6

Although leeks have been grown in this country for over two centuries, only now are we beginning to recognize them for some other quality than a flavoring agent for stocks and stews. Similar to but less sweet than onions, leeks have a unique, delectable savor — as illustrated in this modification of the classic Alsatian *tarte à l'oignon*. To prepare leeks for cooking, cut off root end and all but about an inch of the green top. Spread leaves as much as possible and rinse thoroughly under cold running water.

8 Tb. (1 stick) butter	2 tsp. sugar
1 Tb. peanut or vegetable oil	⅛ tsp. salt
12 leeks, trimmed, cleaned, and sliced thin	Pinch of mace
1 Tb. flour	Freshly ground pepper
4 eggs	Cayenne
1½ cups heavy cream	Pâte Brisée (p. 412)

*H*eat butter and oil in a large skillet, add sliced leeks, and sauté over low heat for 10 minutes. Sprinkle on flour, mix well, and continue cooking for 5 minutes longer.

Preheat oven to 350°.

In a bowl, combine eggs, cream, sugar, salt, mace, and pepper and cayenne to taste, whisk rapidly, and set aside.

Roll out dough ⅛ inch thick on a floured surface, line a 9- or 10-inch quiche or pie dish with dough, and set dish on a baking sheet.

Scatter the leeks over the crust, pour on egg mixture, and stir gently. Bake for 30 minutes or till tart is golden brown.

Serve tart very hot cut into wedges.

Rillettes de Canard
(Potted Duck)

Serves 8–10

French *rillettes* (especially those served in and about Tours) are generally made with only shredded pork and pork fat or a mixture of pork products and rabbit. So addicted am I to these earthy but silky concoctions that I've been known when traveling in France to make a complete meal of nothing but *rillettes* spread on toasted French bread, sour gherkins, a tart salad, and plenty of sturdy red wine. I've found that *rillettes* prepared with either duck or goose, however, are particularly flavorful and moist, and when served as an appetizer, they make a nice change from the overworked duck and goose pâtés. If you are obsessed about cholesterol, you might as well forget about making *rillettes,* since fat is what gives the dish much of its unctuous texture and subtle savor.

Note that the *rillettes* must be started at least one day in advance.

1 duck, quartered	Dry white wine
¾-lb. piece of boneless pork	Salt and freshly ground pepper
¼ lb. fresh pork fat, cut into slices	½ tsp. ground ginger
Herb bouquet (½ tsp. thyme, 1	½ tsp. ground allspice
cracked celery rib, 2 bay leaves,	Pinch of cinnamon
and 1 clove wrapped in	
cheesecloth)	

*I*n a large kettle, place duck, pork, pork fat, and the herb bouquet. Add wine to cover, bring liquid to the boil, lower heat, cover, and simmer for 1 hour or till meats are tender. Remove duck pieces, and when cool enough to handle, bone them and return meat to kettle. Continue simmering meats, uncovered, for about 3 hours or till liquid has evaporated and meats are cooking in the fat. Strain meats, discard the herb bouquet, remove and discard skin from duck, and reserve liquid fat.

Place meats in a food processor in batches, shred well, and transfer to a large mixing bowl. Add a little of the reserved fat and work mixture with a heavy fork till almost a heavy paste. Add salt and pepper to taste (plenty of pepper is essential) plus spices, blend well, and pack *rillettes* into small ramekins or a large crock, leaving ½ inch at top.

Heat remaining liquid fat, pour over *rillettes,* cover with wax paper secured with rubber bands, and refrigerate for at least 24 hours. Let sit for 1 hour at room temperature before serving with toast or toasted French bread.

Jalapeño Pie

Serves 4–6

One of the most memorable meals I've enjoyed anywhere was prepared in Brownsville, Texas, by Mary Yturria, considered by many to be one of the greatest experts on authentic Tex-Mex food in the region. The dinner included a large barbecued brisket of beef, cactus casserole, enchiladas made with Mexican chocolate, shrimp baked with lemon slices and filé powder, and congealed mango mousse, but for me the highlight was this simple, subtle pie that started off the feast in the form of finger food. Here the seeds have been removed from the chili peppers. For more assertive flavor, leave the seeds in and blanch the peppers briefly before adding to the pie.

7-oz. can jalapeño peppers,
drained, rinsed, and seeded
Basic Pie Pastry (p. 411)
½ lb. Monterey Jack cheese,
coarsely grated

4 eggs, beaten
Salt to taste
2 Tb. chopped fresh coriander
(also called cilantro and
Chinese parsley)

Preheat oven to 350°.
Cut peppers into thin long slices. Line bottom and sides of a 9-inch pie plate with pastry rolled out ⅛ inch thick, and arrange peppers on bottom and along sides of pastry. Sprinkle cheese over peppers and press down on mixture lightly with fingers.

Add salt to eggs, whisk, and pour over cheese and peppers. Bake for 25–30 minutes, let cool slightly, and cut into 4–6 wedges. Serve sprinkled with a little chopped coriander.

Escalopes de Foie de Canard à la Vinaigrette
(Duck Liver with Hot Vinaigrette Sauce)

Serves 4–6

I by no means agree with those who consider Fredy Girardet the greatest chef in the world, but I do concede that this sublime preparation of fresh duck liver, created by Fredy at his small, charming restaurant in Crissier, Switzerland, and now imitated by chefs all over, is one of the finest dishes ever conceived. At the restaurant, Fredy serves the liver with only parsley and fresh herbs, but it also looks nice nestled atop red-tipped lettuce.

Because they are totally different in size, texture, and flavor, do not substitute chicken livers in this recipe.

12 fresh duck livers, cut into 2 flat scallops each	2 Tb. finely chopped shallots
Salt and freshly ground pepper	¼ cup sherry wine vinegar (or red wine vinegar)
4 Tb. (½ stick) butter	¼ tsp. finely chopped parsley
4 Tb. walnut oil (or the best grade olive oil)	2 Tb. finely chopped chives
	1 Tb. finely chopped fresh chervil

Sprinkle duck liver scallops with salt and pepper to taste and set aside. Heat butter in a large skillet till quite hot, add livers, sauté for 2 minutes on each side, and transfer equal portions of liver to hot salad plates. Add oil to skillet, add shallots, shake skillet, add vinegar, and cook over high heat for 1 minute. Spoon sauce over livers and sprinkle with parsley, chives, and chervil.

Charleston Hobotee

Serves 6

I've yet to learn the origin of this delicious curried meat custard so indigenous to the Low Country of South Carolina and Georgia, but I can still hear my Georgian grandmother exclaiming from time to time, "My, but a little hobotee would sure hit the spot this noon." Cooks in Charleston will bake off these little ramekins even for breakfast, but I've found hobotee to be an ideal appetizer, especially when followed by a simple fish dish. In fine Low Country tradition, serve a small glass of dry sherry with the dish.

3 Tb. butter
1 medium onion, finely chopped
1 Tb. curry powder
1½ cups cooked beef, veal, or pork, finely chopped
1 slice bread, soaked in milk and squeezed
4 almonds, blanched and chopped

2 Tb. lemon juice
3 eggs
½ tsp. sugar
Salt
1 cup light cream
Dash of white pepper
Small bay leaves

Heat butter in a skillet, add onion, and sauté for about 2 minutes over low heat. Stir in curry powder and cook for 2 minutes longer. Transfer mixture to a mixing bowl, add meat, bread, almonds, lemon juice, 1 egg, sugar, and salt to taste, and blend thoroughly.

Butter six ½-cup ramekins and divide mixture among them. Preheat oven to 300°. In another bowl, combine cream, remaining 2 eggs, and white pepper and whisk well. Pour equal amounts of cream mixture into each ramekin, garnish tops with a bay leaf, and bake for 25 minutes.

Potato, Leek, and Carrot Terrine

Serves 6–8

10 large boiling potatoes
8 leeks, root ends trimmed and
    washed thoroughly
2 medium carrots, scraped and
    cut in rounds
2 envelopes unflavored gelatin,
    dissolved in ½ cup dry vermouth
¾ cup (1½ sticks) butter, melted

1 onion, minced
3 sprigs parsley, chopped
½ tsp. chervil
¼ tsp. ground fennel
1 cup plain yogurt
Salt and freshly ground pepper
1 cup mustard mayonnaise or cold
    Ravigote Sauce (p. 541)

*P*lace potatoes in a large saucepan or kettle with enough lightly salted water to cover, bring water to the boil, cover, reduce heat, and cook for about 30 minutes or till fork-tender. When cool enough to handle, peel potatoes, transfer to a large mixing bowl, and mash with a fork.

Place leeks in another large saucepan with water to cover, boil about 10 minutes or till soft, separate green leaves for molding the terrine, and set leaves aside. Slice remaining white part of leeks, return to saucepan along with the carrots, cover, and cook for about 30 minutes or till carrots are tender. Drain and mince both vegetables.

Grease a 9×5×3-inch terrine or loaf pan with a little of the melted butter and line the bottom and sides with three-quarters of the leek leaves. Add butter, minced leeks and carrots, and all remaining ingredients to the potatoes and beat till well blended and smooth. Pack mixture tightly into terrine, cover top with remaining leek leaves, cover with foil, and chill for 6 hours.

Serve in thick slices with a little sauce on the side of each portion.

Sardines à la Menthe

Serves 4

One evening at Le Bistrot de Mougins, located in a barrel-vaulted stone cave in the charming medieval town of Mougins above the French Riviera, I and some fellow gourmands managed to attack everything on Alain Ballatorc's menu from squash blossom fritters to a garlicky *timbale* of fresh cod to rabbit stuffed with chopped lamb's feet. The dish that astonished us most, however, was this highly original appetizer utilizing nothing but local ingredients. I suppose any small fish could be substituted here, but if you've never experienced the unique flavor of fresh sardines, you should make every effort to seek them out in better seafood markets.

8 large fresh sardines (or smelts)
1 lb. spinach
¼ cup finely chopped fresh mint
1 small onion, finely chopped
1 garlic clove, minced
¼ cup bread crumbs
Salt and freshly ground pepper
6 Tb. olive oil

Remove heads and tails of sardines, split down bottoms with a sharp paring knife, remove backbones, and rinse.

Drop spinach into boiling water for 1 minute, drain on paper towels, and chop fine. In a mixing bowl, combine chopped greens, mint, onions, garlic, bread crumbs, and salt and pepper to taste, and mix well.

Preheat oven to 400°.

Spread one sardine out flat, place part of the mixture at the head end, and roll carefully and snugly toward the tail (some of the mixture should stick out the sides of the roll). Repeat with remaining sardines, placing all rolls tightly together in a shallow baking dish. Drizzle olive oil over rolls and bake for 20 minutes, basting once.

Foie Gras with Grapes in Port Wine Sauce

Serves 8

This rich, rather expensive dish is intended for a truly grand occasion and should be followed by a simple main course. Although truffled *foie gras* can cost a great deal (especially the fresh variety often available around Christmas), the much cheaper and much less delectable *pâté de foie gras* should never be substituted in this recipe.

1 lb. seedless green grapes	*1 Tb. flour*
1 cup dry vermouth	*¼ cup Port*
8 Tb. (1 stick) butter	*10 oz. truffled foie gras*
8 slices French bread	

Place grapes in an enamel or stainless-steel bowl, add vermouth, and marinate for 30 minutes. Meanwhile, heat one-half the butter in a large skillet, add bread slices, and sauté on both sides over moderate heat till golden and slightly crisp. Drain on paper towels.

Pour grapes and vermouth into a large saucepan, bring liquid to the boil, lower heat, and simmer for 5 minutes. Heat remaining butter in another saucepan, add flour, and stir with a whisk over low heat till flour begins to brown. Drain liquid from grapes and stir into roux. Add Port and stir over moderate heat till sauce thickens.

Dipping knife regularly into a glass of water, cut *foie gras* into 8 slices and place one slice on each piece of bread. Place pieces in center of 8 salad plates, spoon sauce on top of each serving, and arrange equal amounts of grapes on the sides.

Steak Tartare and Caviar Canapés

Serves 4–6

2 lbs. sirloin or top round, cut into chunks	*1 tsp. freshly ground pepper*
3 small onions, finely chopped	*2 egg yolks*
2 Tb. finely chopped parsley	*2 Tb. Cognac*
2 tsp. Dijon mustard	*4–6 slices hard, thin pumpernickel*
6 anchovy fillets, finely chopped	*2 hard-boiled egg whites, chopped*
1 tsp. salt	*7-oz. tin fresh American sturgeon or salmon caviar*

Grind beef twice to a smooth consistency in a meat grinder (do not use a blender or food processor) and transfer to a large mixing bowl. Add onions, parsley, mustard, anchovies, salt, pepper to taste, egg yolks, and Cognac, and mix lightly but thoroughly.

Cut pumpernickel slices into strips, spread each strip liberally with steak tartare, sprinkle on a few chopped egg whites, and top each with 1 teaspoon of caviar. Serve strips on small salad plates with knives and forks.

Ramekins of Duck Liver and Walnut Pâté with Madeira

Serves 4–6

Note that this pâté must be made a day in advance.

½ lb. duck (or chicken) livers, trimmed of membranes and fat
2 Tb. melted butter
1 onion, chopped
Salt and freshly ground pepper
½ cup Madeira
1½ cups chopped walnuts
8 Tb. (1 stick) unsalted butter, softened and cut into pieces

¼ tsp. nutmeg
½ tsp. thyme
Pinch of powdered fennel
4–6 whole walnut halves for garnish
Toast, cut into strips

Dice livers and place on a broiler pan. Drizzle with butter, add onions, season to taste with salt and pepper, and toss livers to spread evenly over pan. Broil livers close to heat for 2 minutes, turn, and broil other sides for 2 minutes or till golden.

Pour one-half of the Madeira into a blender, turn blender on, add walnuts a few at a time, and blend till smooth. Add remaining Madeira plus the livers and blend to a smooth consistency, stopping machine once or twice and scraping sides of bowl. Add butter, nutmeg, thyme, and fennel, and blend thoroughly.

Pack pâté into small ramekins, top each with a walnut half, and chill overnight. Serve with toast.

Shrimp Pâté with Gin

Serves 4–6

1½ lbs. shrimp
½ lemon
3 Tb. gin
2 Tb. lemon juice
¼ tsp. dry mustard

⅛ tsp. mace
8 Tb. (1 stick) butter, softened
Salt and freshly ground pepper
Chopped parsley

Place shrimp and lemon in a large saucepan with enough water to cover, bring to the boil, remove from heat, let sit for 1 minute, and drain. When shrimp are cool enough to handle, peel, devein, and cut in half.

Combine shrimp, gin, lemon juice, mustard, and mace in a blender or food processor and run motor just long enough to chop shrimp coarsely. Transfer mixture to a large mixing bowl, add softened butter and salt and pepper to taste, and mix with a wooden spoon till shrimp mixture and butter are well blended. Pack mixture into small crocks or ramekins and chill for at least 2 hours.

When ready to serve, sprinkle tops with chopped parsley.

Herbed Wild Mushrooms on Pita

Serves 4

Although dried chanterelles can be used in this dish, it can hardly be said that they have the exquisite savor of the fresh mushroom. If substitution is necessary, however, soak 2 ounces of dried chanterelles in ½ cup of warm water for 30 minutes, rinse well, and slice before proceeding with the recipe.

3 Tb. butter
½ cup finely chopped shallots
1 garlic clove, minced
1 lb. fresh chanterelle mushrooms, sliced
½ tsp. thyme
½ tsp. chervil

½ tsp. dill
½ cup finely chopped parsley
Salt and freshly ground pepper
¾ cup heavy cream
2 4×4-inch pita bread, sliced in half and lightly toasted

*H*eat butter in a large skillet, add shallots and garlic, and sauté over low heat for 1 minute. Add mushrooms, stir, raise heat slightly, and simmer for about 5 minutes. Add thyme, chervil, dill, and parsley, toss well, and season to taste with salt and pepper.

Pour cream into a small saucepan, bring to the boil, and reduce by half. Add cream to mushrooms, stir, and heat thoroughly.

Open a pita half on each of 4 small warm plates and spoon equal amounts of mushroom mixture on top each.

Escabeche of Red Snapper

Serves 4–6

Escabeche refers to any number of "pickled" dishes found throughout Latin America. This is one culinary technique that lends itself to endless experimentation with both the item to be soused and the ingredients of the marinade. Try tuna, cod, striped bass, or salmon. Some chefs marinate the fish raw, but I find an initial light sauté adds not only more flavor but a better texture.

2 lbs. red snapper fillets, cut into narrow strips about 4 inches long
Salt and freshly ground pepper
Flour for dusting
1½ cups olive oil
2 onions, sliced
2 hot red peppers, seeded and cut into strips
2 garlic cloves, chopped

½ tsp. oregano
¼ tsp. thyme
2 whole cloves
1-inch piece of cinnamon
2 Tb. wine vinegar
2 Tb. lime juice
Fresh coriander (also called cilantro and Chinese parsley), chopped

*S*alt and pepper fish to taste and dust with flour. Heat one-half of the olive oil in a large skillet, add fish, and cook on both sides over moderate heat till golden. Transfer to paper towels to drain and cool.

Heat remaining oil in a large saucepan, add onions, peppers, garlic, herbs, and spices, and cook over low heat for 2 minutes. Pour in vinegar and lime juice and stir.

Arrange fish fillets in a shallow serving dish, pour marinade on top, and sprinkle with fresh coriander. Cover with plastic wrap, place in refrigerator, and let marinate for at least 10 hours.

Soused Chicken in Romaine Lettuce

Serves 4

This marinade also works well for boiled shrimp, raw scallops, oysters, steamed mussels, and even sweetbreads.

1½ lbs. boned chicken breasts
Salt and freshly ground pepper
Flour for dusting
4 Tb. (½ stick) butter
½ cup peanut oil
1 cup soy sauce
3 Tb. brown sugar
3 garlic cloves, smashed

1 Tb. grated ginger
2 Tb. sherry
4 large leaves romaine lettuce,
  blanched 1 minute and drained
Fresh coriander (also called
  cilantro and Chinese parsley),
  chopped
8 cherry tomatoes

Salt and pepper chicken breasts to taste and dust lightly with flour. Heat butter in a large skillet, add chicken breasts, and sauté over low heat for 3 minutes on each side or till golden. Drain on paper towels, cut into finger-width strips, and arrange strips in a shallow baking dish.

Combine peanut oil, soy sauce, sugar, garlic, ginger, and sherry in a bowl, whisk, till well blended, pour over chicken, and let marinate for 12 hours.

Lay leaves of blanched romaine on a flat surface and remove white stems. Arrange one-quarter of the chicken strips at the widest end of one leaf, sprinkle with chopped coriander, and roll chicken in leaf, tucking end of leaf under the bottom of the roll. Repeat with remaining 3 leaves. Arrange rolls in center of 4 small salad plates and garnish with cherry tomatoes.

Cold Creole Marinated Eggplant and Peppers

Serves 4

Try this also with squash, cauliflower, fresh bulb fennel, or broccoli.

4 Tb. (½ stick) butter
1 onion, finely chopped
1 large eggplant, peeled and cubed
1 large red bell pepper, roughly
*   chopped*
Salt and freshly ground pepper
2 Tb. lime juice
1 tsp. Creole mustard (available
*   in specialty food shops)*

¼ cup olive oil
½ tsp. sugar
1 Tb. chopped fresh basil
1 Tb. chopped fresh coriander
*   (also called cilantro and*
*   Chinese parsley)*
⅛ tsp. thyme
⅛ tsp. oregano
4 leaves Bibb lettuce or radicchio

*H*eat butter in a large skillet, add onions, and sauté over low heat for 2 minutes. Add eggplant and peppers, salt and pepper to taste, cover, and cook for 15–20 minutes, adding a little water if necessary. Transfer vegetables to a glass mixing bowl.

Combine lime juice and mustard in a bowl, whisk briskly, add olive oil and sugar, and whisk briskly again. Add herbs, whisk once more, pour over vegetables, and toss. Cover bowl with plastic wrap and refrigerate for at least 6 hours.

Place lettuce leaves on 4 small salad plates and mound equal amounts of vegetables in the center of each.

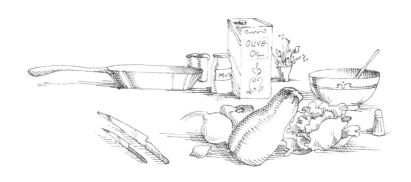

Deviled Scallops with Dill

Serves 4–6

3 Tb. butter
2 Tb. finely chopped scallions
2 Tb. finely chopped red bell pepper
2 Tb. finely chopped celery
1 pint scallops, chopped and liquor
  reserved
¼ cup dry vermouth or dry white
  wine

1 egg
½ tsp. dry mustard
1 sprig fresh dill, finely chopped
Tabasco
½ cup bread crumbs

*H*eat butter in a large skillet, add scallions, pepper, and celery, and sauté over low heat for 3 minutes. Add scallops, their liquor, and vermouth, stir, and cook over low heat for 2 minutes. Transfer mixture to a mixing bowl to cool slightly.

Preheat oven to 350°.

Crack egg into a small bowl, add mustard, dill, and Tabasco to taste, and beat with a whisk. Pour egg into scallop mixture, stir, add bread crumbs, and mix lightly but thoroughly (if necessary, add more bread crumbs to tighten mixture if it tends to be too liquid).

Spoon equal amounts of mixture into 4–6 seafood shells and bake for 20–25 minutes.

Crab Cakes with Mustard Sauce

Serves 8

Nothing is worse than heavy crab cakes bound with too much mayonnaise or bread crumbs and overloaded with onion, green pepper, and the like. These simple appetizer cakes are feather-light so long as you mix them very gently, and the light mustard sauce not only adds an interesting new dimension but precludes the need for salt.

*1 cup Blender Mayonnaise
  (p. 542)
1 egg white
1 Tb. lemon juice
3 Tb. very fine cracker crumbs
⅛ tsp. cayenne pepper*

*1 lb. lump crabmeat, picked for
  shell
¾ cup fine bread crumbs
4 Tb. (½ stick) butter
½ cup Mustard Sauce (p. 534)*

*I*n a large mixing bowl, blend mayonnaise, egg white, lemon juice, cracker crumbs, and cayenne. Add crabmeat and toss very gently. Divide mixture into 8 equal portions and gently shape each into a fairly thick patty. Spread bread crumbs on a cookie sheet and coat the patties lightly but securely. Chill at least 1 hour.

Heat butter in a large skillet, add crab cakes, and sauté over moderate heat for 3 minutes on each side or till golden brown. Serve one cake per person, with 1 tablespoon of mustard sauce over each cake.

Cold Zucchini Provençale

3 zucchini, brushed under running water and cut into ¼-inch rounds
Salt
1 onion, roughly chopped
3 tomatoes, peeled and diced
1 garlic clove, minced
1 celery rib, finely chopped
½ green pepper, finely chopped
¼ tsp. dried basil

¼ tsp. oregano
⅛ tsp. powdered fennel
½ tsp. crushed black peppercorns
½ tsp. chopped capers
½ cup olive oil
½ cup freshly grated Parmesan cheese
6 leaves red-tipped leaf lettuce
Chopped parsley

Sprinkle zucchini rounds with salt, place in a colander, weight down with a clean mixing bowl, and let stand for 1 hour. Rinse rounds well and dry with paper towels.

Preheat oven to 300°.

Arrange half the zucchini on the bottom of a medium baking dish and distribute the onion, tomatoes, garlic, celery, pepper, herbs, peppercorns, and capers evenly over top. Arrange another layer of remaining zucchini on top and sprinkle evenly with the olive oil. Cover dish tightly with foil and bake for 3 hours. Remove foil, sprinkle cheese on top, stir mixture with a fork, and continue baking for 30 minutes. Let stand at room temperature for 3 hours.

Arrange lettuce leaves on 6 small salad plates, spoon equal amounts of zucchini in the center of each, and sprinkle each portion with chopped parsley.

Deep-Fried New Potatoes with Golden Caviar

Serves 4–6

When Dafne Engstrom began producing her golden "Tsar Nicoulai" caviar from whitefish in San Francisco a few years ago, James Nassikas of the Stanford Court Hotel was impressed enough to create this unusual and delicious dish for his distinguished restaurant, Fournou's Ovens. It is a good example of what has become known as "California Cuisine."

12–14 very small red waxy potatoes (1 lb. or less)
4–5 cups rock salt

½ cup sour cream
Oil for deep-fat frying
3½–4 oz. golden caviar

Preheat oven to 450°.

Wash and dry potatoes, arrange on a bed of rock salt in a shallow baking pan, and bake for 30–35 minutes.

Remove potatoes from oven and slice in half. Scoop out pulp with a melon-ball cutter or small spoon, mash slightly in a small bowl, and keep warm.

Heat oil to 375° in a large saucepan, drop potato shells in oil, and fry till golden brown and crisp. Drain well on paper towels. Fill shells with mashed potato, top with a spoonful of sour cream, and add a teaspoon or more of caviar. Serve on thick salad plates atop hot rock salt.

Horseradish Flan with Fennel Sauce

Serves 4–6

This delectable appetizer utilizing fresh summer fennel is but one of the highly innovative creations of Jovan Trboyevic, owner of Les Nomades restaurant in Chicago and, in my opinion, the greatest restaurateur in America. If you happen to own small savarin molds, they make for a very elegant presentation, but should you use these molds, note that the baking time is no more than 8 minutes. At Les Nomades, the flan is served beautifully in miniature skillets.

3 eggs
1½ cups heavy cream
Salt and white pepper
Pinch of nutmeg
2 Tb. fresh grated horseradish
½ cup thinly sliced fennel bulb
⅓ stem fennel, including a few leaves, roughly chopped

3 Tb. roughly chopped onions
3 Tb. roughly chopped mushrooms
3 Tb. dry white wine
¾ cup Chicken Stock (p. 521)
1–2 Tb. butter
3 drops Pernod
Fennel leaves for garnish

Preheat oven to 325°.
In a large mixing bowl, whisk eggs lightly, add cream, stir, and strain through a sieve into another bowl. Add salt, pepper, nutmeg, and horseradish and stir.

Ladle batter into 4–6 buttered ramekins, stirring batter before each ladling. Place ramekins in a baking pan and add enough water to pan to rise halfway up sides of ramekins. Bake for 15 minutes or till slightly puffed, remove pan from oven, and let ramekins sit in water to keep warm.

Place vegetables in a medium skillet, add a little water, cover, and steam over moderate heat for 5 minutes. Add wine and reduce liquid slightly, uncovered. Add chicken stock and cook for about 5 minutes more. When vegetables are tender, transfer mixture to a blender or food processor, reduce to a puree, and strain into a clean skillet. Add butter plus Pernod and blend well.

Roll a film of sauce around bottom of 4–6 warmed plates and unmold flans into the center. Garnish sides with fennel leaves.

Flounder and Spinach Terrine with Prunes

Serves 10

This cold terrine lends itself to numerous combinations — such as striped bass, watercress, and dates. An ideal sauce is a little Red Bell Pepper Mayonnaise (p. 542) served on the side. Note that the terrine must be prepared a day in advance.

1 lb. fresh flounder fillets, cut into pieces
8 Tb. (1 stick) butter, softened
½ lb. fresh spinach, rinsed thoroughly, stems removed
1 cup bread crumbs
¼ cup heavy cream
2 egg yolks, beaten
¼ cup chopped shallots
¼ cup fresh chopped dill

1 tsp. salt
Cayenne
¼ cup minced scallions
1 lb. fresh salmon, skinless, boneless, and cut into strips
¼ cup dry white wine
10 prunes, pitted
1 tsp. mace
2 Tb. melted butter
Lettuce or watercress for garnish

*I*n a blender or food processor, puree flounder in batches and transfer to a large mixing bowl. Add all the butter except 2 tablespoons and mix thoroughly.

Bring 1 cup water to the boil in a large saucepan, add spinach, cover, and steam for 8 minutes. Drain spinach, let cool, and mince.

In another large bowl, moisten bread crumbs with cream and fold in egg yolks, minced spinach, shallots, dill, salt, and cayenne to taste. Combine fish and bread crumb mixtures and beat the forcemeat with a fork till fluffy.

Heat the remaining 2 tablespoons of butter in a large skillet, add scallions, and sauté over low heat for 2 minutes. Add salmon strips, white wine, and a pinch of salt and cook fish over moderate heat (tossing from time to time) for 3 minutes or till flaky. Transfer fish to a bowl or platter, reduce liquid in skillet to 3 tablespoons, and pour over fish.

Preheat oven to 300°.

Line bottom of a large terrine or loaf pan with ½-inch layer of forcemeat and arrange a layer of salmon strips on top. Season salmon with a pinch of mace and continue to fill terrine with alternate layers of forcemeat and salmon. When terrine is half filled, arrange a tight row of prunes down center and then continue filling with layers of forcemeat and salmon. Drizzle the top with melted butter, seal terrine tightly with foil, and set inside a larger baking pan. Pour enough boiling water into the baking pan to reach halfway up the sides of the terrine and bake for 55 – 60 minutes or till surface of pâté is firm and springy to the touch.

Remove terrine from the water, set a light weight (such as a can of soup or dog food) on top of foil, allow to cool to room temperature, and chill overnight in the refrigerator.

Unmold on a bed of lettuce or watercress and cut in thick slices.

Blue Cheese Beignets

Serves 4–6

Inspired by the yeasty doughnuts (beignets) prepared in the French Market of New Orleans, this delicious appetizer illustrates how one French-American concept can be radically modified to produce an imaginative dish with altogether different character. Other equally interesting fillings might be caramelized chopped onions, curried minced chicken, or even fresh horseradish. Serve the beignets with a spoonful of chutney on the side.

1 lb. blue cheese (or other blue-veined cheese), room temperature	*2 eggs*
	3 Tb. water
	Pinch of nutmeg
1 recipe of Brioche Dough (p. 414)	*Vegetable oil for frying*
¼ cup flour	*2 Tb. capers, rinsed and chopped*

Carefully form cheese into 2-inch balls and set aside.

On a floured surface, roll dough ¼ inch thick, cut into 2½-inch rounds, and arrange carefully in small stacks.

To assemble beignets, dust each cheese ball lightly with flour and place on a round of dough. In a small bowl, beat eggs with water, salt, and nutmeg and brush the edges of each round with this egg wash. Top with a second round of dough, press edges together to seal tightly, and place in refrigerator for 1 hour.

When ready to serve, bring 1 inch of oil to 400° in a large, heavy skillet or saucepan and fry beignets 4–5 minutes or till golden. Serve topped with chopped capers.

Mushrooms à la Daum

Serves 4

This is one of the most popular dishes at the "21" Club in New York. It is named for Earl Daum, an ex-vice-president of General Motors who first sampled the dish twenty years ago in a small restaurant outside Brussels, got the approximate recipe, and later asked the kitchen at "21" to try to reproduce it. The mushrooms can also be served over toast instead of around artichoke bottoms.

4 Tb. (½ stick) butter
4 Tb. flour
5 cups Beef Stock (p. 522) or bouillon
1 small onion, chopped
1 garlic clove, smashed
½ tsp. thyme
1 bay leaf
¼ tsp. Worcestershire

2 Tb. Madeira
Salt and freshly ground pepper
2 cups sliced mushrooms
1 cup minced onions
1 cup julienne of ham or tongue
3 Tb. butter
4 well-cleaned artichoke bottoms
4 whole mushroom caps

Heat butter in a saucepan, add flour, stir, and cook over moderate heat till slightly browned.

Preheat oven to 350°.

Pour stock into a heavy casserole, stir in flour mixture, and simmer for about 10 minutes or till stock begins to thicken. Add onion, garlic, thyme, bay leaf, and Worcestershire. Place uncovered casserole in oven and cook for 1½ hours. Strain sauce into a saucepan, add Madeira and salt and pepper to taste, stir, and keep warm.

In a large mixing bowl, combine sliced mushrooms, minced onions, ham, and salt and pepper to taste. Heat 3 tablespoons of butter in a large skillet, add mushroom mixture, and sauté over moderate heat for 5 minutes. Stir in brown sauce and heat for 1 minute longer.

Arrange artichoke bottoms in center of 4 heated salad plates, spoon equal amounts of mushrooms around each, and top each artichoke with a mushroom cap.

Bisteeya
(Spicy Chicken and Almond Pie)

Serves 12

I've sampled this classic Moroccan dish everywhere from Marrakesh to Paris to New York, but never have I found a more luscious example than the one perfected by my friend and colleague Paula Wolfert while living in North Africa. Her recipe is long but not difficult. *Phyllo* or Hungarian *streudel* leaves can be found in most specialty food shops and many supermarkets, and fresh coriander (also known as cilantro and Chinese parsley) is usually available in Mexican and Chinese markets. Remember that *phyllo* and *streudel* leaves dry out very quickly and must always be kept covered with a damp cloth while you are working.

4½ lbs. chicken thighs and legs
1 large onion, grated and
   squeezed in hand to exude
   moisture
Pinch of pulverized saffron
1 tsp. ground ginger
3 large cinnamon sticks, broken
   into 4-inch pieces
¼ cup chopped fresh coriander
¼ cup chopped parsley
8 Tb. (1 stick) unsalted butter
3 cups water
1 tsp. salt
1 tsp. freshly and finely ground
   pepper

¼ cup lemon juice
10 eggs, beaten
3 Tb. butter
1 lb. blanched almonds
1½ tsp. ground cinnamon
½ cup powdered sugar
5 Tb. unsalted butter
½ lb. phyllo or streudel leaves,
   kept under a damp towel
8 Tb. (1 stick) unsalted butter,
   melted
Powdered sugar for dusting
1½ tsp. or more powdered
   cinnamon

*R*emove excess fat from chicken parts and place parts in a large casserole with the onions, spices, herbs, 8 tablespoons butter, water, salt, and pepper. Bring liquid to the boil, reduce heat, cover, and simmer for 1¼ hours. Remove chicken pieces and cool.

Remove any bones and cinnamon sticks from casserole, bring liquid to the boil, and reduce to about 1 cup. Reduce heat, add lemon juice and eggs, cook over low heat till eggs are set, and set aside.

Remove meat from bones of reserved chicken, shred, set aside, and let cool.

Heat 3 tablespoons butter in a skillet, brown almonds, drain, and place in a food processor. Add ground cinnamon, powdered sugar, and unsalted butter and process a few seconds till well blended. Taste very carefully for ginger and black pepper, both of which should be pronounced.

Preheat over to 425°.

In a 10-inch round buttered cake pan, layer 6 leaves of *phyllo,* brushing each with melted butter before layering the next (leaves should cover bottom of pan and extend over sides). Spread shredded chicken in a layer at bottom of pan, cover with eggs, and top with almond mixture. Fold all extending layers over filling to enclose. Cover with 2 more layers of *phyllo,* brushing each sheet with butter. Tuck edges of *phyllo* hanging over sides underneath the pie to form a neat top, and brush entire surface with melted butter.

Bake for 20 minutes or till top is golden. Shake pan to loosen pie, running spatula around edges. Invert pie onto a large buttered baking sheet, return to oven, and continue baking for 15 minutes longer. Remove from oven and tilt to pour off excess butter. Invert pie onto a serving plate, dust top with powdered sugar, and run crisscrossing lines of powdered cinnamon over top. Serve piping hot.

Stuffed Snails in Puff Pastry

Serves 4

Note that this dish must be started two days in advance.

2 7-oz. cans snails
Cognac
¼ lemon, peeled and deseeded
1 garlic clove, chopped
¼ tsp. caraway seeds
8 raw shrimp, peeled and deveined

Dash of Pernod
¼ tsp. Dijon mustard
Salt and freshly ground pepper
½ lb. Quick Puff Pastry (p. 413)
1 egg, beaten

*P*lace snails in an enamel or stainless-steel bowl, add Cognac to cover, marinate for 2 days, and drain.

Place lemon, garlic, and caraway seeds in a food processor and pulse 6 or 7 times. Add shrimp and process mixture to a puree. Add Pernod, mustard, and salt and pepper to taste, and pulse machine to mix all ingredients thoroughly.

Scrape puree into a pastry bag with a fine-hole tip. Make incisions in tops of snails to form pockets and fill pockets with puree.

Preheat oven to 450°.

Roll out dough ¼ inch thick on a floured surface and cut into 24 strips. Place each snail on a strip of pastry, bring sides of pastry up to completely enclose snail, brush with egg, and bake on a cookie sheet for 15–20 minutes or till golden brown.

Spiced Oysters

Serves 2

3 Tb. butter
3 tsp. minced shallots
1 garlic clove, minced
2 tsp. minced green pepper
2 tsp. minced pimiento

⅛ tsp. curry powder
⅛ tsp. ground cloves
12 shucked oysters, liquor reserved
½ cup heavy cream
Salt and freshly ground pepper

*H*eat butter in a large skillet, add shallots, garlic, green pepper, and pimiento, and sauté over low heat for 3 minutes. Add curry powder and cloves and stir. Add oysters plus liquor and mix well. Add cream and salt and pepper to taste, raise heat to moderate, and poach oysters for 2 minutes or till firm and plump. With a slotted spoon, transfer oysters to each of two heated seafood shells or ramekins.

Reduce cream sauce over moderate heat till sauce just coats a spoon and spoon evenly over oysters.

Marinated Oysters

Serves 4

Note that this dish should be prepared two days in advance.

24 shucked oysters, liquor reserved
1/4 cup dry vermouth
1 large onion, sliced in thin rings
1 lemon, sliced thin
3/4 cup white wine vinegar
2 bay leaves
1/2 tsp. mustard seeds
1/2 tsp. cloves

1/2 tsp. dried ginger
1 tsp. salt
Freshly ground pepper
1/4 cup finely chopped parsley
1/4 cup olive oil
4 slices of toast, trimmed and cut
    into quarters

*I*n a large skillet, combine oysters, the reserved liquor, and vermouth, bring liquid to the boil, reduce heat to moderate, and poach oysters for 2 minutes or till firm and plump. Pour oysters into a sieve set over a large bowl, let drain, and reserve liquid.

Layer oysters in a glass dish and scatter onion and lemon over top.

Combine vinegar, reserved liquid, bay leaves, spices, and salt in a large enamel or stainless-steel saucepan. Bring liquid to the boil, reduce heat, and simmer for 8 minutes. Strain mixture through a fine sieve into a bowl, let liquid cool, and pour over oysters. Grind on pepper to taste, sprinkle with parsley and olive oil, cover dish with plastic wrap, and refrigerate for 2 days.

Serve oysters on toast points arranged on small salad plates.

Cervelas aux Fruits de Mer
(Seafood Sausages)

This is one of the more creditable creations to come out of the French *nouvelle cuisine*. You might choose to serve the sausages atop a thin pool of Beurre Blanc (p. 536); I prefer them sauceless, with perhaps a sprig of fresh coriander to nibble on. One small chopped black truffle makes an elegant (and very expensive) substitute for the olives, but in this dish I frankly find this a waste of fine truffle.

This dish should not be held, even overnight.

6 oz. scallops	1 egg
6 oz. boned salmon, cut into 2-inch pieces	¾ cup heavy cream, chilled
1 Tb. chopped fresh dill (or 1 tsp. dried dill)	4 oz. lump crabmeat, chopped
1 tsp. salt	6 black pitless olives, finely chopped
Freshly ground pepper	3 feet sausage casing, rinsed under running water
2 Tb. lemon juice	Fish Stock (p. 524) or Court Bouillon (p.524) for poaching
3 drops Tabasco	

Place scallops and salmon in a food processor, puree, and add dill, salt, pepper to taste, lemon juice, Tabasco, and egg. With machine running, add cream through tube, process for 30 seconds, scrape sides, and process for a few seconds longer. Transfer mixture to a bowl, add crabmeat and olives, stir well, and chill mousse for 1 hour.

Tie one end of casing with string. Spoon mousse into a pastry bag fitted with a 1-inch tip, slide casing onto tip, and squeeze mousse steadily into casing. When filled, tie off the other end with string, then twist and tie sausage at 4-inch intervals.

Place sausages in a large skillet, add stock to cover, and prick sausages at random with a pin. Bring liquid to a simmer, poach sausages for 15 minutes, and drain.

Serve while still warm.

Gâteaux de Carottes aux Fines Herbes
(Herbed Carrot Flans)

Serves 6

1½ lbs. carrots, peeled and sliced
  thin
3 cups Chicken Stock (p. 521)
4 eggs, beaten
1 Tb. olive oil
4 oz. finely chopped mushrooms,
  sautéed 2 minutes in 1 Tb.
  butter

8 oz. grated Gruyère cheese
½ tsp. salt
3 Tb. fresh chervil
Freshly ground pepper

FINES HERBES SAUCE:

1 cup Chicken Stock (p. 521)
1 shallot, chopped
2 cups heavy cream

2 Tb. butter, softened
1 tsp. each fresh minced chervil,
  chives, tarragon, and parsley

*P*lace carrots and stock in a large saucepan, bring liquid to the boil, lower heat, cover, and simmer for 30 minutes or till carrots are very tender. Transfer carrots and stock to a food processor, liquidize, and let cool slightly. Pour into a large mixing bowl, add eggs, olive oil, mushrooms, cheese, salt, chervil, and pepper to taste, and blend thoroughly.

Preheat oven to 350°.

Grease insides of 6 ramekins with a little butter, spoon equal amounts of mixture into each, and bake for 30 minutes.

In the meantime, make Fines Herbes Sauce. Pour stock into a large saucepan, add shallot, and reduce liquid over high heat by three-quarters. Add cream, bring to the boil, and strain into another saucepan to remove shallots. Stir in butter and herbs and keep warm.

Loosen gâteaux if necessary by running a small sharp knife dipped in water around the edges. Unmold onto 6 small plates, and spoon sauce on top of each.

Riñones con Romero
(Kidney Brochettes with Fresh Rosemary)

Serves 6

This sensational starter, created by chef Felipe Rojas-Lombardi at the New Ballroom restaurant in New York, is a good example of the Spanish appetizers known as *tapas*. Do not try to modify the recipe by simply sprinkling dried rosemary on kidneys, and by no means overcook the kidneys.

2 lbs. veal kidneys
Freshly ground pepper
18 fresh rosemary sprigs about 8
    inches long

6 slices lean bacon, cut into
    1-inch pieces
Olive oil

Clean kidneys thoroughly, cutting away hard cores and trimming off outer membranes. Slice kidneys into 1-inch pieces, drop pieces into a pot of cold salted water, let stand for 15 minutes, and drain.

Strip rosemary sprigs of all but about 1½ inches of leaves at tops and trim bases of sprigs to a sharp point with a paring knife. Thread 2 or 3 pieces of kidney onto each sprig, followed by 2 or 3 pieces bacon, and continue alternating kidneys and bacon till sprigs are filled.

Pour a thin film of olive oil into a large skillet, heat to moderate, add skewered kidneys, and grill for 4 minutes, turning brochettes 3 or 4 times.

Serve 3 brochettes per person, to be eaten with fingers.

· PART TWO ·

Soups

Pecos Bean Soup with Ham

Serves 6–8

This is one of the many delicious soups taught to students at the Culinary Institute of America at Hyde Park, New York, and served in the school's highly innovative American Bounty Restaurant. I like it also with a few chopped raw onions sprinkled on top, as well as with a piping-hot Corn Stick (p. 438).

1⅓ cups pinto beans, soaked in water overnight	2 tsp. chili powder
2 qts. Chicken Stock (p. 521)	¼ tsp. oregano
⅓ cup chopped onions	⅓ cup peeled, seeded, and diced green chili peppers
1 garlic clove, minced	Salt
½ lb. bacon, chopped	¼ cup diced lean cooked ham

Drain and rinse beans, place in a heavy pot or casserole, and add stock. Bring liquid to the boil, lower heat, cover, and simmer for 1 hour.

Add all remaining ingredients but salt and ham, bring soup back to the simmer, cover, and simmer for another hour. Add salt to taste and simmer for a third hour.

Puree one-quarter of the soup in a food processor, return puree to pot, and mix well. Heat thoroughly before serving in heavy soup bowls, and sprinkle diced ham over each serving.

Oyster and Spinach Stew

Serves 4

1 qt. shucked oysters
1 Tb. butter
1 Tb. finely grated onion
1 cup milk
½ cup minced celery
1 cup frozen chopped spinach,
   thawed

1 cup heavy cream
1 Tb. dry sherry
Salt and cayenne
Nutmeg
4 Tb. (½ stick) butter, softened

Strain liquor from oysters into a small saucepan, bring to the boil, skim off froth, and reserve.

Heat 1 tablespoon butter in another saucepan, add onion, and sauté over low heat for 2 minutes. Add oysters, simmer till oysters curl, and remove from heat.

Pour milk into another saucepan, add celery and spinach, and cook vegetables over moderate heat for 5 minutes. Stir in cream, bring almost to the boil, and remove pan from heat.

Add reserved oyster liquor, the oysters, sherry, salt, cayenne, and nutmeg to taste, and stir well. Ladle stew into wide soup bowls and top each serving with a little softened butter.

Saffroned Zucchini Soup

Serves 4–6

8 Tb. (1 stick) butter
¾ cup diced onions
¾ cup diced celery
2 cups diced zucchini
¾ cup peeled and diced potatoes
⅛ tsp. saffron, crushed and
   soaked 10 minutes in 2 Tb. of
   water

Pinch of dried thyme
Pinch of dried basil
2 cups Chicken Stock (p. 521)
1 cup heavy cream

*H*eat butter in a large skillet, add onions, celery, zucchini, and potatoes, and sauté over medium heat for 10 minutes. Add saffron, thyme, and basil, and continue cooking for about 5 minutes or till potatoes begin to stick to bottom of skillet.

Add chicken stock and bring liquid to the boil. Reduce heat and simmer till the starch from the potatoes thickens the stock. When soup is thickened to taste, remove from heat, stir in cream, and heat slightly again before serving.

Lime Glacé

Serves 4 – 6

I don't know how many times I worked with my friend Pearl Byrd Foster on this delicate, subtle soup, but once we had it perfected, nothing in the recipe ever changed. It's the perfect prelude to almost any elaborate meal, as well as a delightful summer soup.

6 cups Chicken Stock (p. 521)
1 medium onion, sliced
2 celery ribs (leaves included),
  chopped
5 garlic cloves, crushed
3 sprigs parsley

3 tsp. unflavored gelatin
½ cup fresh lime juice
3 or 4 drops Tabasco
1 cup heavy cream, whipped
2 Tb. candied ginger, chopped

*P*our chicken stock into a large saucepan or pot, add onion, celery, and garlic, bring liquid to the boil, reduce heat, and simmer for 1 hour.

Drop parsley to wilt in stock, transfer to a blender with 1 cup of the stock, blend well, and return contents of blender to saucepan. Stir mixture well, then pour through a fine sieve into a large bowl, pressing with back of a spoon to get all the liquid.

Dissolve gelatin in ¼ cup water, add to hot liquid, and stir till dissolved completely. Cool to room temperature, stir in lime juice and Tabasco, and chill till thickened.

Serve in icy-cold glass cups or bowls, topped with dollops of whipped cream and garnished with 1 teaspoon candied ginger.

Crab and Tomato Bisque

Serves 4–6

2 Tb. butter
1 onion, finely chopped
3 Tb. flour
1 Tb. tomato paste
2 tsp. curry powder
1 large ripe tomato, peeled,
    seeded, and chopped coarsely

2 cups dry white wine
1 cup half-and-half
1 lb. claw crabmeat, picked well
    for shell
1 tsp. salt
¼ tsp. cayenne

*H*eat butter in a large saucepan, add onion, and sauté over low heat for 3 minutes. Add flour and continue cooking for 2 minutes, stirring.

Add tomato paste, curry powder, and chopped tomato, and mix well. Increase heat to high, add wine very gradually, and cook, stirring constantly, till mixture comes to the boil and begins to thicken.

Reduce heat to moderate, add half-and-half, crabmeat, and seasonings, and stir well. Serve hot, or cool the soup, pour into a large bowl, cover with plastic wrap, refrigerate for at least 4 hours, and serve chilled.

Classic French Onion Soup

I've often wondered whether French onion soup fell out of favor in this country because of the low esteem in which it is held by what I call the laboratory *nouvelle* chefs or simply because so few people prepare it properly. I've championed the rich, sumptuous soup ever since my student days in France and never cease trying to perfect it. If you're not willing to spend time browning the onions, if you don't have excellent homemade beef stock, and if you're willing to settle for old onions and cheap wine, please don't add insult to injury by trying to make this legendary soup.

4 Tb. butter
1 Tb. olive oil
12 medium firm Spanish onions,
   thinly sliced
1 garlic clove, minced
1/8 tsp. sugar
Salt and freshly ground pepper
2 Tb. flour

5 cups homemade Beef Stock
   (p. 522)
4 cups water
1 cup fine white French burgundy
1/2 tsp. dried thyme
Pinch of nutmeg
6 toasted rounds of French bread
1 lb. Gruyère or Emmenthaler
   cheese, grated

*H*eat butter and oil in a large, heavy casserole (preferably enameled iron), add onions and garlic, cover, and sauté over moderate heat for 5 minutes, stirring. Add sugar, and salt and pepper to taste, stir, and continue cooking for 30 minutes, stirring and scraping frequently with a wooden spoon, or till onions are very brown and reduced in bulk by at least one-half.

Add the flour, stir, and cook for 2 minutes longer. Add 2 cups of stock, bring to the boil, and scrape bottom of casserole. Add remaining stock, the water, wine, thyme, and nutmeg, return to the boil, lower heat, cover, and simmer gently for 45 minutes, stirring frequently.

Preheat oven to 375°.

Divide soup evenly among 6 deep individual ovenproof soup bowls and place a round of toasted bread in center of each. Top each with generous sprinklings of cheese, place bowls on a baking sheet inside oven, and bake for 15 minutes or till cheese begins to brown.

Wild Mushroom Soup

Serves 6 – 8

2 oz. dried cèpe or morel mushrooms
1½ cups water
8 Tb. (1 stick) butter
3 Tb. minced shallots
⅓ cup flour

6 cups Chicken Stock (p. 521) or
  broth
Salt and freshly ground pepper
¾ cup heavy cream
3 egg yolks

Soak mushrooms for 30 minutes in 1½ cups warm water. Reserving soaking water, rinse mushrooms, picking for grit, and chop coarsely.

Heat butter in a large saucepan, add shallots, and stir over low heat for 3 minutes. Add mushrooms to the shallots, stirring for about 2 minutes.

Strain mushroom water through cheesecloth into shallot and mushroom mixture, bring liquid to the boil, lower heat to moderate, and simmer for about 15 minutes or till liquid is very concentrated. Add flour, lower heat, and cook mixture, stirring, for 2 minutes. Add chicken stock plus salt and pepper to taste, stir, bring to the boil, lower heat, and simmer soup for 30 minutes.

In a small bowl, combine cream and egg yolks, whisk rapidly, and add 1 cup of hot soup, whisking. Pour mixture into soup, stir, and heat, never allowing soup to boil.

Minted Tomato-Avocado Soup

Serves 6 – 8

This delightful summer soup should be prepared only when fresh tomatoes are beautifully ripe and full-flavored and when fresh mint is available.

10 large ripe tomatoes
4 Tb. (½ stick) butter
1 medium onion, chopped
6 cups Chicken Stock (p. 521) or
  broth

1 large ripe avocado
1 cup heavy cream
Salt and freshly ground pepper
10 mint leaves, chopped

Peel, seed, and chop 8 of the tomatoes. Heat one-half of the butter in a medium skillet, add onions, and sauté over medium heat for 2 minutes. Add tomatoes, raise heat, and cook for 5 minutes. Press mixture through a sieve, return mixture to skillet, and simmer gently till reduced to a paste.

Pour chicken stock into a deep saucepan, add tomato paste, and whisk till well blended.

Peel, seed, and chop remaining tomatoes. Heat remaining butter in skillet, add tomatoes, and cook over medium heat for 5 minutes. Add tomatoes to soup in saucepan.

Peel and pit avocado, chop flesh finely, and whisk into soup. Stir in cream, season with salt and pepper to taste, and stir in chopped mint. Serve piping hot or well chilled.

Stilton Soup with Port

Serves 4–6

2 cups Chicken Stock (p. 521) or broth
¾ cup minced celery
½ cup minced carrots
3 Tb. butter
2 Tb. minced onion

4 Tb. flour
2 cups milk
½ lb. Stilton cheese, finely crumbled
4–6 Tb. Port

Combine chicken stock, celery, and carrots in a saucepan, bring liquid to the boil, lower heat, and simmer vegetables for 10 minutes or till tender.

Heat butter in a large saucepan, add onion, and sauté over low heat for 3 minutes. Add flour and continue cooking, stirring, for 2 minutes. Gradually add chicken stock mixture and milk, raise heat to moderate, and cook, stirring constantly, till thickened and bubbly.

Remove saucepan from heat, add cheese, and stir till cheese is melted and well incorporated. Serve laced with a tablespoon of Port in each bowl.

Jellied Consommé with Caviar

Serves 6

This elegant but simple soup absolutely must be made with homemade consommé and not a commercially canned product. Don't be frightened by the amount of caviar, since the domestic kind is much less expensive than the imported variety.

1¼ envelopes unflavored gelatin
6 cups homemade Beef Consommé
   (p. 522)

6 tsp. American sturgeon or
   salmon caviar

*I*n a saucepan, soften gelatin in 1 cup of the consommé, heat slightly, and stir till gelatin is completely dissolved.

Pour into a 3-quart baking dish, add remaining consommé, stir thoroughly, and chill for 5–6 hours or till firm.

To serve, cut consommé into cubes, spoon into large crystal goblets, and top each portion with a teaspoon of caviar.

Crab Soup with Fennel

Serves 4

3 Tb. butter
1 Tb. flour
2 cups milk
2 cups heavy cream
1 lb. claw crabmeat, picked for shell
1 tsp. finely grated onion
1 tsp. finely grated lemon rind

½ tsp. Worcestershire
⅛ tsp. ground dried fennel
½ tsp. white pepper
4 Tb. dry sherry, heated
Paprika
Salt

*H*eat butter in a large saucepan, add flour, mix well, and cook the roux over low heat for 2 minutes, stirring with a whisk. Remove pan from heat and pour in milk and cream, stirring. Return to heat and stir till smooth. Increase heat, and add crabmeat, onion, lemon rind, Worcestershire, fennel, and pepper. Reduce heat and simmer for 20 minutes, stirring. Taste for salt.

Ladle soup into 4 warmed soup plates, lace each serving with 1 tablespoon sherry, and sprinkle a little paprika on top.

Cold Gingered Peach Soup

Serves 4–6

A popular favorite in the American South, this sweet-sour soup makes an ideal starter to a light, casual summer lunch. It might easily be followed by a Crabmeat and Mushroom Soufflé (p. 98), individual Prosciutto and Goat Cheese Pizzas (p. 102), or Cold Shrimp Curry (p. 120) using almonds and chutney.

3 cups sliced fresh peeled peaches	*3 Tb. Bourbon*
1½ cups water	*1½ Tb. cornstarch mixed in*
1½ cups dry white wine	*1½ Tb. cold water*
3 thin slices fresh peeled ginger	*3 tsp. grated lemon rind*
½ cup sugar	*¼ cup sour cream*

Set aside 4–6 peach slices for garnish.

Combine remaining peaches, water, white wine, and ginger in a large saucepan. Bring the liquid to the simmer, cover, and simmer for 15 minutes. Add sugar, Bourbon, and cornstarch, bring liquid to the boil, and stir well till thickened.

Transfer mixture in batches to a blender, add lemon rind and sour cream, and blend till smooth. Cool soup, then chill for at least 4 hours. Serve in chilled crystal soup bowls and top each serving with a reserved peach slice.

Chilled Carrot and Almond Soup

This soup has the quality of being both sweet and spicy, making it the ideal starter to a meal that might include Lamb Tajine (see Chicken Tajine, p. 235), Curried Turkey Hash Cakes (p. 255), or Singapore Chicken (p. 234). Try serving it with an Alsatian or California Gewürztraminer.

4 Tb. (½ stick) butter
2 medium onions, chopped
4 cups Chicken Stock (p. 521) or
  broth
6 medium carrots, scraped and
  cut into rounds

3 whole cloves
½ stick cinnamon
½ cup chopped blanched almonds
3 cups milk
Freshly ground pepper

Heat butter in a large saucepan, add onions, and sauté over low heat, turning, for 3 minutes. Add stock, carrots, cloves, and cinnamon, bring liquid to the boil, lower heat, cover, and simmer for 45 minutes or till carrots are soft.

Remove and discard cloves and cinnamon, pour mixture into a blender or food processor in batches, add almonds, and puree. Return mixture to saucepan, stir in milk and pepper to taste, and chill for at least 4 hours.

Cream of Scallop Soup with Chives

Serves 4

5 Tb. butter
3/4 cup sea scallops, chopped, plus 8
   whole scallops
3 medium potatoes, peeled and
   diced
2 onions, chopped
1 leek, trimmed of half the green
   tops and rinsed thoroughly and
   chopped

1 qt. water
2 cups Fish Stock (p. 524)
1/4 cup dry sherry
6 Tb. heavy cream
Salt and freshly ground pepper
3 Tb. chopped chives

*H*eat 2 tablespoons of the butter in a large skillet, add whole scallops, and sauté over low heat for 5 minutes, turning once. Add chopped scallops to skillet, and continue sautéing for 5 minutes more. Remove scallops and keep them warm.

Heat remaining butter in a large saucepan, add potatoes, onions, and leek, and stir over medium heat till leek has softened. Add water, fish stock, and sherry, bring liquid to the boil, lower heat, cover, and simmer for 20 minutes.

Pour contents of saucepan in several batches into a blender or food processor, add chopped scallops, and puree. Add cream to final batch. Pour soup back into saucepan, add salt and pepper to taste, and heat thoroughly.

Place two whole scallops in each of 4 warm soup plates, pour soup over them, and sprinkle each serving with chopped chives.

Chlodnik
(Cold Beet Soup)

Serves 8

Craig Claiborne game me his recipe for this colorful classic Eastern European cold soup when I had to whip up a quick luncheon one hot morning in East Hampton, but time and circumstances forced me to substitute buttermilk for the traditional sour cream and delete the veal broth in favor of doubling the chicken stock. Suffice it to say, it was one of the most successful soups I've ever prepared and one I've served many times since. Craig garnishes his version with chopped eggs and thin lemon slices; I choose to float a single whole shrimp in each bowl.

1 lb. raw beets
½ lb. beet tops
2 cups Chicken Stock (p. 521) or
*   broth*
1 cup water
¾ lb. fresh shrimp, cooked, peeled,
*   deveined, and all but 8 cut*
*   into thirds*
1 cup buttermilk

4 Tb. white wine vinegar
2 Tb. lemon juice
2 tsp. sugar
1 cup diced cucumber
1 cup chopped scallions (green
*   tops included)*
¼ cup finely chopped fresh dill
Salt and freshly ground pepper

Peel the beets, cut them into eights, and place in a large saucepan. Rinse the beet tops thoroughly, chop them coarsely, and add to the beets. Add 1 cup of the chicken stock and the water, bring to the boil, lower heat, cover, and simmer for 25 minutes. Drain the beets and reserve the cooking liquid.

Place the beets and tops into a blender or food processor and blend thoroughly. Scrape the mixture into a large bowl with a rubber spatula and add the reserved cooking liquid. Add the cut-up shrimp, buttermilk, vinegar, lemon juice, sugar, cucumber, scallions, dill, remaining chicken stock, and salt and pepper to taste. Stir to blend well, cover with plastic wrap, and chill thoroughly.

When ready to serve, garnish each bowl with one of the 8 reserved whole shrimps.

Cucumber Vichyssoise

Serves 6 – 8

5 cups Chicken Stock (p. 521)
3 cups peeled and sliced potatoes
2 Tb. butter
3 cups sliced white of leeks
1 small onion, sliced
1 large cucumber, peeled, seeded,
    and sliced

1½ cups heavy cream
¼ tsp. mace or nutmeg
Salt and white pepper
3 Tb. minced chives

*P*our stock into a large saucepan, add potatoes, bring liquid to the boil, reduce heat, cover, and simmer potatoes for 20 minutes or till tender.

Heat butter in a skillet, add leeks and onion, and sauté over low heat for 5 minutes.

In batches, combine vegetables and stock in a blender or food processor, add cucumbers, and puree. Pour mixture into a large bowl. Stir in cream, add mace or nutmeg and salt and pepper to taste, stir, and chill thoroughly. Serve in chilled soup bowls and garnish each portion with minced chives.

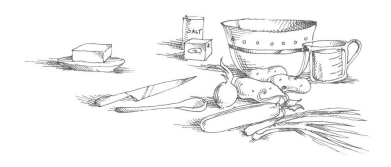

Sopa de Ajo
(Garlic Soup)

Serves 4–6

I first became hooked on garlic soup at a remote country inn in the Limousin region of France, then, shortly after, at a small restaurant outside Madrid. After each of these and every succeeding masochistic confrontation with this heady but sublime potage, most of the night was spent drinking Alka-Seltzer to assuage a hiatal hernia. You'll probably have no trouble digesting the soup so long as you don't overdo it, but be warned that it's addictive. The egg on top is strictly a Spanish custom. The French simply crust the top under the broiler.

4 Tb. olive oil
5 thin slices of French bread
4 large garlic cloves, chopped
5 cups hot Beef Consommé (p. 522)

¼ tsp. cumin
Salt
4–6 eggs

Heat one-half of the oil in a large skillet, add bread slices, and fry on both sides over moderate heat till golden. Drain on paper towels.

Pour any remaining oil from skillet into a large saucepan, add remaining 2 tablespoons of oil, add garlic, and sauté over low heat till golden.

Crumble bread slices slightly, add to garlic, and mix well. Add consommé and cumin, season with salt to taste, bring liquid to the simmer, and cook gently for 15 minutes.

Preheat oven to 400°.

Pour soup into 4–6 individual earthenware soup bowls, crack an egg into each bowl, and bake in oven for 10 minutes or till eggs are well set.

Senegalese Soup

Serves 4–6

This rich and creamy soup, similar to the classic example served at "21" Club and Mortimer's in New York, should be followed by a fairly simple main course.

2 Tb. butter
1 carrot, chopped
1 onion, chopped
1 celery rib, chopped
1 Tb. flour
1 Tb. curry powder
4–5 cups Chicken Stock (p. 521)

Paprika
½ Tb. almond paste
1 cinnamon stick
5 cloves
3 egg yolks, beaten
1 cup heavy cream, chilled
Chutney

*H*eat butter in a large saucepan, add carrot, onion, and celery, and sauté over low heat for 5 minutes. Add flour and curry powder and stir till well blended. Stir in chicken stock, bring liquid to the boil, reduce heat, and stir in paprika to taste. Add almond paste, cinnamon stick, and cloves, stir, and simmer for 30 minutes.

Gradually add a little of the mixture to the beaten egg yolks, stir, return egg mixture to saucepan, and stir till slightly thickened.

Strain soup through double cheesecloth into another saucepan or bowl, cool, then chill thoroughly. Before serving in chilled soup cups, taste for seasoning and blend in cream. Garnish each serving with a little chutney.

Chilled Mango Soup

Serves 4

1 Tb. butter
1 onion, minced
1 tsp. curry powder
2 cups Chicken Stock (p. 521) or broth
1 large mango, peeled, seeded, and chopped

½ cup plain yogurt
½ cup buttermilk
½ cup dry white wine
3 Tb. fresh lime juice
Salt and freshly ground pepper
Thin lime slices

*H*eat butter in a large stainless-steel saucepan, add onion, and sauté over low heat for 3 minutes. Add curry powder, stir, and continue sautéing for 1 minute. Add stock and mango, bring liquid to the boil, lower heat, cover, and simmer for 5 minutes or till mango is tender.

Transfer mixture to a blender or food processor in batches and puree. Pour into a large mixing bowl, stir in yogurt, buttermilk, wine, lime juice, and salt and pepper to taste, and let soup chill for at least 3 hours.

Ladle soup into chilled bowls and garnish each with lime slices.

Thai Shad Soup

Serves 4 – 6

2 lbs. boned shad (or red snapper)
2 Tb. dry sherry
1 scallion (white only), sliced in
    julienne strips
2 thin slices peeled fresh ginger
1 tsp. grated lemon rind
4 cups Fish Stock (p. 524)

3 Tb. red wine vinegar
2 Tb. sesame oil
Salt and freshly ground pepper
8 sprigs fresh coriander (also
    called cilantro and Chinese
    parsley), coarsely chopped

Cut fish into 4 – 6 equal chunks and place on a rack in a large saucepan or skillet with 1 inch water. Sprinkle fish with sherry, scatter scallions, ginger, and grated lemon rind on top. Cover and steam over moderate heat for 20 minutes.

Meanwhile, bring fish stock to a simmer in another large saucepan, add vinegar, oil, and salt and pepper to taste, cover, and simmer slightly.

Transfer fish and its stock to a soup tureen, pour on stock mixture, and scatter chopped coriander on top.

To serve, place a chunk of fish in each of 4 – 6 wide soup bowls and spoon equal amounts of stock on top.

Chilled Broccoli and Olive Soup

Serves 4 – 6

3 cups broccoli florets, rinsed
    (about 2 lbs. fresh broccoli)
1 cup water
2 Tb. butter
1 leek (some green top included),
    rinsed well and sliced

3 cups Chicken Stock (p. 521) or
    broth
¾ cup pimiento-stuffed green olives
Cayenne
1½ cups half-and-half

Combine broccoli and water in a large saucepan, bring water to the boil, lower heat, cover, and steam for 10 minutes or till tender.

In the meantime, heat butter in a small skillet, add leek, and sauté for 3 minutes.

Combine broccoli, cooking liquid, and leek in a blender or food processor, puree, and pour into a large saucepan. Add chicken stock and stir well.

Combine olives, cayenne, and half-and-half in blender or food processor, blend till smooth, add to broccoli mixture, and blend well with a whisk. Chill soup overnight.

Chicken Gazpacho

Serves 4–6

3 Tb. butter
1 chicken breast, split, skinned,
   boned, and pounded slightly
2 large ripe tomatoes, peeled and
   seeded
½ green bell pepper, seeded and
   sliced
1 onion, sliced
1 cucumber, peeled and sliced
1 garlic clove, halved
¼ cup mixed fresh herbs (1 Tb.
   each chopped coriander, basil,
   tarragon, and chives)

¼ cup olive oil
3 Tb. red wine vinegar
3 Tb. lime juice
¼ tsp. Tabasco
1½ tsp. salt
4 cups Beef Consommé (p. 522)
   or canned beef consommé
¼ cup chopped parsley

*H*eat butter in a skillet, add chicken breasts, and sauté over low heat for 5 minutes on each side. Drain on paper towels and chop into small cubes.

In a blender or food processor, combine three-quarters of the vegetables, the garlic, mixed herbs, olive oil, and vinegar, and puree (in batches if necessary). Transfer mixture to a large bowl, add lime juice, Tabasco, salt, consommé, and reserved chicken cubes, mix thoroughly, and chill soup for 1 hour.

Chop remaining vegetables and divide equally among 4–6 chilled soup bowls. Pour soup on top of vegetables and top each portion with a little chopped parsley.

Curried Fish Chowder

Serves 6 – 8

3 Tb. olive oil
1 onion, finely chopped
1 celery rib, finely chopped
1 garlic clove, minced
2 Tb. curry powder
3 Tb. flour
1 large ripe tomato, peeled and
   seeded

6 cups Fish Stock (p. 524)
⅛ tsp. chopped saffron
1 medium potato, peeled, boiled,
   and mashed
1½ lbs. fillets of striped bass,
     haddock, cod, or flounder
1 cup heavy cream

*H*eat oil in a large saucepan, add onion, celery, and garlic, and sauté over low heat for 2 minutes. Add curry powder and flour, stir well, and continue cooking for 2 minutes longer, stirring.

Add tomato, fish stock, saffron, and mashed potato, and stir till potato is well blended. Bring liquid to the boil, reduce heat, and simmer for 20 minutes.

Cut fish into 1-inch pieces, add to soup, and simmer for 10 minutes longer. Stir in cream, bring chowder to the boil, and serve in wide soup plates.

Chestnut Soup with Ginger

Serves 4–6

1 lb. chestnuts, shelled and peeled
1 small onion, finely chopped
1 tsp. sugar
2 tsp. grated lemon rind
½ tsp. salt
2½ cups Chicken Stock (p. 521)
   or broth

½ cup milk
½ cup heavy cream
Pinch of ground ginger
1 egg yolk, beaten
¼ cup sherry

*P*lace chestnuts in a large saucepan, cover with water, add onion, sugar, and salt, and bring liquid to the boil. Lower heat, cover, and simmer for about 35 minutes or till chestnuts are soft.

Transfer mixture to a blender or food processor, add the lemon rind, and blend to a puree. Transfer puree back to the saucepan, add chicken stock, milk, heavy cream, and ginger, bring to the boil, and stir.

Gradually stir a little of the soup into the beaten egg yolk, return mixture to the saucepan, add sherry, and reheat, making sure not to let the soup boil.

Pozole

Serves 6–8

In the Mexican province of Jalisco, this traditional soup-stew of chicken or tripe, pork, and hominy often includes a couple of pig's feet, which give the dish a nice gelatinous quality but also make it quite greasy. I think you'll find the pork shoulder and chicken suffice to produce one of the world's most unusual potages. Practically a meal-in-itself, the soup should be served with salad, bread, and full-bodied beer, followed perhaps by a little cheese.

THE SOUP:

1½ lbs. boneless pork shoulder, cut into 1-inch cubes
1 onion, roughly chopped
2 garlic cloves, chopped
2 qts. Chicken Stock (p. 521)

4 jalapeño or ancho chili peppers
3-lb. chicken, cut into serving pieces
Salt
1½ cups canned whole hominy

THE GARNISHES:

2 red onions, finely chopped
½ cup radishes, thinly sliced
½ lb. white Spanish cheese or Monterey Jack, grated

2 Tb. dried oregano
3 limes, cut into wedges

*P*lace pork, onion, and garlic in a large casserole and add chicken stock. Bring liquid to the boil, skim for scum, reduce heat, cover, and simmer for 1 hour.

In the meantime, remove and discard seeds from chilies, tear chilies into strips, and soak for 1 hour in 1 cup warm water. Drain chilies, place in a blender or food processor, and reduce to a puree.

Add chicken to casserole, bring liquid to the boil, and skim surface once again. Reduce heat, stir in pureed chilies plus salt to taste, and continue simmering for 1 hour longer. Stir in hominy, bring liquid to the boil, lower heat, and simmer for 15 minutes longer.

Place garnishes in individual small bowls and pass with soup.

Oyster Avgolemeno Soup

Serves 6

Having been raised in a part-Greek family, I've always been accustomed to numerous dishes prepared with the delectable lemon-egg sauce known as *avgolemeno*. Utilized mainly as the base for a traditional soup with Greek *orzo* pasta, *avgolemeno* adds an entirely new dimension to spinach, lamb, seafood, and even honeycomb tripe. For this rich soup, clams, lobster, or mussels could be substituted for the oysters. Do not, however, substitute ordinary white rice for the luscious *orzo*, available in specialty food shops.

4 egg yolks
Juice of 2 lemons
1½ pts. shucked oysters, drained, liquor reserved
4 cups Chicken Stock (p. 521) or broth

¼ cup orzo *pasta*
Salt and freshly ground pepper
Tabasco
2 sprigs parsley, chopped

Place egg yolks in a medium mixing bowl, whisk till creamy, add lemon juice, and whisk till well blended.

Combine reserved oyster liquor and chicken stock in a large saucepan, bring to the boil, and gradually add *orzo*. Reduce heat, cover, and simmer for 15 minutes or till pasta is tender. Add salt, pepper, and Tabasco to taste and stir.

Whisk ½ cup hot stock very gradually into egg mixture, add oysters to stock in saucepan, and gradually whisk egg mixture into stock. Heat well but do not boil soup, and stir in chopped parsley.

Tortilla Soup

2 Tb. corn oil
2 jalapeño chili peppers, seeded
  and chopped
1 onion, chopped
2 garlic cloves, finely chopped
2 large tomatoes, peeled, seeded,
  and chopped
3 cups Beef Stock (p. 522) or
  bouillon

1½ cups water
1½ cups tomato juice
1 tsp. chili powder
1 tsp. ground dried cumin
1 tsp. ground dried coriander
2 tsp. Worcestershire
Salt and freshly ground pepper
3 tortillas, cut into ½-inch strips
¼ cup shredded cheddar cheese

*H*eat oil in a large skillet, add chilies, onion, and garlic, and sauté over low heat for 3 minutes.

Transfer mixture to a casserole or large pot, add tomatoes, stock, water, tomato juice, chili powder, cumin, coriander, Worcestershire, and salt and pepper to taste, and stir thoroughly. Bring liquid to the boil, reduce heat, cover, and simmer for 1 hour.

When ready to serve, add tortilla strips and shredded cheese, stir, and simmer for 10 minutes.

Gulyás Leves
(Goulash Soup)

Although I've had memorable goulash soups in Germany and Austria, none can equal the various examples served throughout Hungary. You can use butter or lard instead of chicken fat to sauté the onions, but be warned that neither the flavor nor texture will be as rich and unctuous.

3 Tb. melted chicken fat	*1 Tb. tomato paste*
3 medium onions, chopped	*½ tsp. caraway seeds*
2 lbs. lean beef chuck, cut into	*1 garlic clove, minced*
1-inch cubes	*Salt and freshly ground pepper*
1 Tb. sweet paprika	*4 cups Beef Stock (p. 522)*
1 medium green bell pepper,	*3 cups water*
seeded and finely chopped	*Chopped parsley*
1 ripe tomato, peeled, seeded, and	
finely chopped	

*H*eat chicken fat in a large heavy skillet, add onions, and sauté over low heat for 2 minutes. Add beef and paprika, raise heat to moderate, and cook, stirring, till meat is browned.

Add bell pepper, tomato, tomato paste, caraway seeds, garlic, and salt and pepper to taste, and stir well. Add 3 cups of the beef stock plus the water and stir. Bring liquid to the boil, lower heat, cover, and simmer for about 1½ hours or till meat is tender.

Add remaining cup of beef stock, stir, and continue cooking for about 15 minutes. Taste for salt and pepper. Serve in heated soup bowls, and sprinkle each serving with chopped parsley.

Carolina Gumbo

Ever since the days of the great Carolina rice plantations, gumbo has been as much a staple in the coastal Low Country as in Louisiana. The big difference between this gumbo and the Creole version is that it's not conceived on a roux base and therefore has a totally different flavor.

4 slices bacon
4 chicken legs or thighs, boned
2 onions, diced
½ green bell pepper, diced
2 garlic cloves, finely chopped
⅛ tsp. thyme
Tabasco to taste
1 10-oz. package frozen okra, thawed
4 ripe tomatoes, seeded and chopped

2 lbs. fresh shrimp, shelled and deveined
1 pt. shucked oysters, liquor reserved
2 qts. Fish Stock (p. 524)
2 bay leaves
1 lemon, halved
1 Tb. butter
1 cup uncooked rice

Fry bacon till crisp in a large iron skillet, drain on paper towels, and crumble.

Add chicken to skillet, sauté on both sides over medium heat till just golden, and transfer to paper towels. When cool, shred chicken.

Add onions, bell pepper, garlic, thyme, and Tabasco to skillet, lower heat slightly, and sauté for about 3 minutes. Add okra, stir, and continue cooking for 3–4 minutes.

Combine bacon, chicken, and okra mixture in a large casserole and add tomatoes, shrimp, and oysters (plus their liquor). Add stock, bay leaves, and lemon halves, adding extra water to cover if necessary. Bring liquid to the boil, lower heat, cover, and simmer for 2 hours, stirring occasionally.

About 30 minutes before gumbo is finished, bring 2 cups salted water to the boil in a large saucepan and add 1 tablespoon of butter. Gradually stir in rice, reduce heat, cover, and simmer rice for 25 minutes. Uncover pan and cook 5 minutes longer, fluffing rice with a fork.

Remove and discard bay leaves and lemon from gumbo, divide rice equally among 6 wide soup dishes, and serve gumbo over rice.

Oxtail-Barley Soup

Serves 6

3 Tb. butter
2½ lbs. oxtails, cut up
1 large onion, chopped
1 carrot, chopped
2 celery ribs, chopped
1 garlic clove, minced
2 sprigs parsley
¼ tsp. dried thyme
¼ tsp. dried rosemary

¼ tsp. dried marjoram
1 tsp. salt
Freshly ground pepper
2 cups water
4 cups Beef Stock (p. 522) or broth
1 cup dry red wine
½ cup barley
¼ cup Madeira

*H*eat butter in a large skillet, add oxtails, and brown over moderate heat. Add vegetables, garlic, parsley, thyme, rosemary, marjoram, salt, and freshly ground pepper to taste, mix thoroughly, lower heat, cover, and continue cooking for 15 minutes.

Transfer mixture to a large casserole, deglaze skillet with water, and add this liquid plus beef stock and red wine to casserole. Bring to the boil, lower heat, cover, and simmer for 3 hours.

Strain mixture into a large saucepan and discard vegetables. Bone and chop meat, add to saucepan along with barley, and stir. Bring soup to the boil, reduce heat, and simmer for 30 minutes or till barley is tender. Skim fat from surface, add Madeira, stir thoroughly, and heat well before serving.

She-Crab Soup

She-crab soup, prepared for centuries in the Carolina Low Country with the delicate roe of blue female crabs, is, in my opinion, one of the truly great soups of the world and indeed one of the most subtle. For years I thought the best she-crab soup anywhere was that served at Henry's in Charleston, South Carolina. Then, one sultry summer evening at a remote restaurant up the coast at Murrel's Inlet called The Sea Captain, I found perfection. One of the secrets of this incomparable version, of course, is that the soup must be prepared entirely over boiling water.

4 Tb. (½ stick) butter
2 small onions, minced
3 Tb. flour
2 cups milk
2 cups heavy cream
1 tsp. mace
1 tsp. white pepper
2 tsp. salt

2 oz. Worcestershire
2 Tb. cornstarch
1 lb. fresh crabmeat, picked over
    carefully
½ cup crab roe (available in
    specialty food shops)
Sherry

Heat butter in top of a large double boiler over low direct stove heat, add onions, and sauté over low heat till just soft. Add flour gradually and stir over low heat till mixture thickens.

Place pan over bottom of double boiler half-filled with boiling water and slowly add 1½ cups of the milk, stirring. When milk is hot, add cream, mace, pepper, salt, and Worcestershire and cook for 5 minutes. Dissolve cornstarch in remaining ½ cup milk, remove pan from hot water, and stir in the cornstarch mixture.

Return pan to double boiler and cook mixture for 5 minutes longer or till hot. When ready to serve, add crabmeat and roe, heat soup thoroughly over boiling water, and lace with sherry to taste. Serve soup with additional sherry on the side.

Soupe de Moules la Caravelle

(Mussel Soup)

Serves 4

3 Tb. olive oil
1 onion, coarsely chopped
2 celery ribs, coarsely chopped
2 leeks (including half of green
    tops), cleaned thoroughly and
    coarsely chopped
½ garlic clove, crushed
2 sprigs parsley
2 tomatoes, peeled, seeded, and
    coarsely chopped
1 bay leaf

¼ tsp. dried thyme
¼ tsp. anise seed
Pinch of saffron
1 cup dry white wine
1 lb. fish bones, rinsed well
3 lbs. mussels, scrubbed well
1 cup water
1 cup Fish Stock (p. 524)
Salt and cayenne pepper
5 Tb. arrowroot, blended with
    3 Tb. water

*H*eat olive oil in a large saucepan or kettle, add onion, celery, leeks, garlic, and parsley, and sauté over low heat till leeks are wilted. Add tomatoes, bay leaf, thyme, anise seed, saffron, and white wine, and stir. Add mussels, fish bones, water, and fish stock. Bring liquid to the boil, lower heat, and simmer for 1 hour.

Season with salt and cayenne to taste, stir, and strain liquid through double cheesecloth into another saucepan. Remove mussels from open shells (discard any that are not open) and chop finely.

Thicken soup by stirring in arrowroot, add chopped mussels, and heat thoroughly.

Clam and Oyster Bisque with Orange Zest

Serves 4

8 Tb. (1 stick) butter
1 small onion, chopped
½ celery rib, chopped
2 sprigs parsley, chopped
12 fresh clams, shelled and chopped

12 fresh oysters, shucked and
  chopped
3 cups half-and-half
Salt and white pepper
1 Tb. chopped orange rind

*H*eat 2 tablespoons of the butter in a large saucepan, add onion, celery, and parsley, and sauté over low heat for 3 minutes. Add chopped clams and oysters, continue sautéing for about 5 minutes, stirring, and transfer contents to a blender or food processor.

Puree (in batches if necessary), add half-and-half, pour soup back into saucepan, and bring almost to the boil. Add salt and pepper to taste and remaining butter, and stir till butter is well blended with the cream.

Ladle bisque into soup plates and serve sprinkled with chopped orange rind.

Soupe de Poissons
Hôtel du Cap
(Provençal Fish Soup)

Serves 6

2 lbs. mixed saltwater white fish
    (sole, flounder, bass, haddock,
    or snapper), scaled and cleaned
4 Tb. olive oil
2 onions, chopped
1 leek (including half the green
    tops), rinsed thoroughly,
    trimmed, and chopped
½ bulb fresh fennel, chopped
    (or 2 tsp. ground dried fennel)
2 ripe tomatoes, chopped
3 garlic cloves, chopped

2 tsp. dried oregano
2 bay leaves
1 Tb. chopped orange rind
1 qt. water
1 qt. Fish Stock (p. 524)
Pinch of saffron, pounded in a
    mortar
Salt and freshly ground pepper
*Rouille (hot garlic mayonnaise)
Croutons
Grated Parmesan cheese

*W*ash fish well and cut into chunks. Heat olive oil in a large, heavy casserole, add onions, leek, and fennel, and sauté over low heat for about 5 minutes. Add fish, tomatoes, garlic, oregano, bay leaves, and orange rind and sauté over medium heat for 5 minutes. Add water, fish stock, pounded saffron, and salt and pepper to taste. Bring liquid to the boil, lower heat, cover, and simmer for 40 minutes.

Strain liquid into a large saucepan or another casserole, remove fish chunks from vegetables, discard heads, tails, and bones, and place flesh in a blender or food processor. Add vegetables to fish (in batches if necessary), puree, and return puree to liquid in saucepan.

Mix soup well, bring to the boil, and check seasoning. Serve in deep soup plates with *rouille*, croutons, and cheese on the side. (Traditionally a bowl of this soup is garnished with 2 floating croutons topped with a teaspoon of *rouille* and a liberal sprinkling of cheese.)

---

* *Rouille:* In a blender or food processor, puree 1 red chili pepper (seeds removed), 6 garlic cloves, 2 egg yolks, and a pinch of salt. With blades still turning, add ¼ cup olive oil very gradually in a fine stream, then blend in 2 tablespoons tomato paste.

Lobster Court Bouillon with Truffles

Serves 4 – 6

4 Tb. (½ stick) butter
1 onion, sliced
1 leek (white only), cleaned
    thoroughly and chopped
2 carrots, scraped, scored with the
    tines of a fork, and cut into
    thin rounds
2 sprigs parsley
1 bottle dry white wine

2 cups water
1 Tb. salt
10 black peppercorns
1 tsp. dried thyme
1 bay leaf
½ lemon
1- to 1¼-lb. live lobster
1 black truffle, thinly sliced

*M*elt butter in a large skillet, add onion and leek, and sauté over low heat for 2 minutes. Add carrots and parsley and sauté for 1 minute longer.

Transfer mixture to a large kettle, add wine, water, salt, peppercorns, thyme, bay leaf, and squeezed lemon half, and bring to the boil. Reduce heat, cover, and simmer for 20 minutes.

Pick out carrot rounds and set aside, return liquid to the boil, plunge in lobster headfirst, and cook for exactly 12 minutes. Remove lobster, and, when cool enough to handle, remove and discard dark intestinal vein running down the tail and the stomach sac in the head part. Remove meat, cut into small slices and chunks, and set aside. Return liquid to simmer.

Crush lobster shell, add to kettle, cover, and simmer for 20 minutes.

Strain court bouillon through double cheesecloth into a large saucepan and reheat. Pour into wide, heated soup plates, add a few lobster pieces to each plate, and float reserved carrot rounds and sliced truffles on top.

Shrimp and Corn Chowder

Serves 4 – 6

One of the most gifted natural chefs I ever knew was Pearl Byrd Foster, owner of the legendary Mr. & Mrs. Foster's Place in New York City and a pioneer of the new, innovative style of American cookery now so fashionable. Pearl guarded her recipes like gold, but one evening at the restaurant she finally agreed to "release" this one to me. I've never tasted a chowder quite like it.

6 cups strong Chicken Stock (p. 521)
3 lbs. shrimp, shelled and deveined
2 Tb. bacon grease
1 Tb. butter
1 onion, minced
2 celery ribs, minced
½ green bell pepper, minced
8 ears fresh corn
2 Tb. arrowroot dissolved in 1 cup cold milk

Salt, freshly ground pepper, and Tabasco
1 cup heavy cream
2 carrots, sliced paper-thin
½ sweet red pepper, cut into small cubes
4 slices of bacon, fried crisp and crumbled

*B*ring half of the chicken stock to the boil in a large, heavy saucepan. Add shrimp, return to the boil, cover, remove from heat, and let stand for 5 minutes.

Reserve 24 shrimp and cover with 1 cup of hot stock. Put remainder of shrimp through blender or food processor with remaining cold stock, then add liquefied shrimp to hot stock.

Heat bacon grease and butter in a skillet, add onion, celery, and green pepper and sauté over low heat for about 3 minutes or till vegetables are soft.

Slit the corn kernels by running the tip of a sharp knife down each row of kernels. With the back of a knife, scrape out pulp and juice into a bowl. Add corn pulp and juice to shrimp mixture and cook over medium heat for 1 minute, stirring. Add sautéed vegetables and arrowroot to mixture, bring to a brisk boil, and cook for 2 minutes. Remove from heat, add seasonings to taste, cover, and let stand for 30 minutes.

When ready to serve, bring chowder to the boil, add heavy cream, carrots, and red pepper cubes, and taste for seasoning. Pour into wide soup bowls and add 4–6 whole shrimp plus a sprinkling of crumbled bacon to each portion.

Philadelphia Pepper Pot

Serves 4–6

Legend has it that this all-American soup was first concocted by a Philadelphian cook serving under Washington at Valley Forge. That he had only tripe and scraps with which to feed the troops explains the major ingredients of the soup. If you've never learned to appreciate the unique texture of tripe, this is the best introduction I know to this highly neglected food. Serve this meal-in-itself with a tart salad and sturdy Zinfandel.

1 qt. water
1 qt. Chicken Stock (p. 521)
   or broth
1 lb. honeycomb tripe, cut into
   bite-size pieces
1 veal shank, sawed into 2 pieces
1 garlic clove, crushed
4 black peppercorns
1 dried hot red pepper
½ tsp. dried thyme

½ tsp. dried marjoram
1 tsp. salt
4 Tb. (½ stick) butter
1 cup finely chopped onions
½ cup finely chopped celery
½ cup finely chopped carrots
3 Tb. flour
1½ cups peeled potatoes cut into
   ½-inch cubes

Pour water and chicken broth into a large, heavy casserole and add tripe and veal shank, adding more water if necessary to cover by 2 inches. Bring liquid to the boil, remove scum, reduce heat, and add garlic, peppercorns, red pepper, thyme, marjoram, and salt. Stir well, cover, and simmer for 2 hours or till tripe is tender.

Transfer tripe and veal shank to a cutting board, remove meat from shank, and cut into bite-size pieces. Strain liquid into a bowl, reserve, and wash casserole.

Heat butter in the casserole over moderate heat, add vegetables, and sauté for 2 minutes. Add flour, stir well, add reserved liquid, raise heat, and cook over high heat till mixture thickens slightly. Add meats and potatoes, reduce heat to low, cover, and simmer for 1 hour.

Serve in wide soup bowls.

Shrimp, Oyster, and Mussel Gumbo

Serves 10–12

6 Tb. (¾ stick) butter
2 Tb. vegetable oil
1 onion, finely chopped
1 celery rib, finely chopped
½ green bell pepper, finely chopped
½ lb. fresh okra (or 10-oz. package frozen okra, defrosted), chopped
1 garlic clove, finely chopped
2 Tb. flour
4 cups Chicken Stock (p. 521)
4 ripe tomatoes, chopped (or 2 cups canned tomatoes)

½ tsp. dried thyme
1 bay leaf
2 tsp. salt
Freshly ground pepper
1 lb. fresh shrimp, shelled and deveined
12 oysters, shucked and liquor reserved
12 mussels, steamed open, shelled, and cleaned
2 tsp. Worcestershire
Tabasco
2 cups cooked rice

*H*eat butter and oil in a large, heavy casserole, add onion, celery, bell pepper, okra, and garlic, and sauté over low heat for about 5 minutes. Add flour and cook for 3 minutes, stirring. Slowly add chicken stock, stirring, then the tomatoes, thyme, bay leaf, salt, and pepper to taste. Bring liquid to the boil, lower heat, cover, and simmer for 45 minutes.

Add shrimp to gumbo and simmer for 5 minutes. Add oysters plus liquor and mussels and simmer for 3 minutes longer or till oysters curl. Add Worcestershire and Tabasco to taste, stir, check seasoning, and serve over small mounds of rice in warm soup bowls.

Chicken and Sausage Gumbo

Serves 6

This is but one of literally dozens of varieties of the aromatic Creole soup-stew that has been a veritable staple for centuries in New Orleans and the Louisiana bayou country. As I finally learned after once cooking for hours with the famous Cajun chef Paul Prudhomme, the secret of any great gumbo is the tricky cooking of the roux — the color must be just medium brown, never dark (or burnt). Although cooks in New Orleans use a delectable Creole smoked sausage, both Polish sausage and French garlic sausage make excellent substitutions. Filé, a powder made from dried sassafras leaves and used as both a flavoring and thickening agent in all gumbos, is generally available in specialty food shops.

2- to 2½-lb. chicken	¼ lb. baked or boiled ham, cubed
½ cup vegetable oil	2 bay leaves
⅓ cup flour	½ tsp. dried oregano
2 onions, chopped	½ tsp. dried thyme
½ green bell pepper, seeded and chopped	Cayenne
1 garlic clove, finely chopped	2 Tb. filé powder
½ lb. smoked sausage, thinly sliced	3 cups boiled rice

Place chicken in a large pot or kettle with enough water to cover, bring water to the boil, lower heat, cover, and simmer chicken for 30–40 minutes. Remove chicken, and when cool enough to handle, skin, bone, and shred. Strain cooking broth into another large pot and reserve.

Heat oil very hot in a large, heavy pot or casserole, add flour gradually, stirring constantly with a whisk, and cook roux over moderate heat, still stirring constantly, till medium brown but not dark in color.

Add onions, green pepper, garlic, sausage, and ham, mix thoroughly, and continue cooking for about 10 minutes. Add 2 cups of the reserved broth, the shredded chicken, bay leaves, oregano, thyme, and cayenne to taste and stir thoroughly.

Add 2 cups more of the broth, bring liquid to the boil, lower heat, and simmer mixture for 1 hour. Remove pot from heat, add filé powder, stir, and let stand for 10 minutes.

Distribute rice evenly in bottom of 6 soup bowls and ladle gumbo on top.

Fresh Tomato and Snapper Chowder

Serves 6

2 fillets of red snapper (or other
   firm-fleshed fish)
1 cup white wine
4 Tb. (½ stick) butter
1 onion, chopped
1 celery rib, leaves included,
   chopped
1 carrot, chopped

2 Tb. flour
1 Tb. chopped fresh basil
1 bay leaf
3 medium ripe tomatoes, peeled,
   seeded, and chopped
3 cups Fish Stock (p. 524)
Salt and freshly ground pepper
Fresh basil leaves

Place snapper fillets in a poacher or skillet, add wine and enough water to just cover, and poach for about 15 minutes or till fish begins to flake. Transfer fish to a platter, flake, and reserve cooking liquid.

Heat butter in a large saucepan, add onion, celery, and carrots, and sauté for 5 minutes over low heat. Stir in flour and add chopped basil, bay leaf, tomatoes, stock, and 1 cup of reserved cooking liquid. Bring liquid to the boil, lower heat, cover, and simmer for 30 minutes, stirring from time to time.

Press soup through a fine sieve or food mill into another saucepan, add flaked snapper, season with salt and pepper to taste, and heat thoroughly.

Ladle chowder into soup bowls or plates and garnish each with a basil leaf.

Soupe au Pistou Vencienne

Serves 6

This soup, chock-full of fresh vegetables and sparked with a *pommade* of garlic, basil, olive oil, and Parmesan cheese, is the very soul of the French and Italian Rivieras and a far cry from ordinary vegetable soup. This memorable version comes from the elegant Château du Domaine Saint-Martin, high above the French town of Vence.

5 Tb. olive oil
1 onion, minced
1 large carrot, diced
1 large leek, trimmed and chopped
1 qt. water
½ lb. dried white beans, soaked overnight and simmered 1 hour in water
¼ lb. shelled baby lima beans (or ½ cup frozen lima beans, defrosted)
¼ lb. shelled green peas (or ½ cup frozen green peas, defrosted)
1 medium potato, peeled and diced
¼ lb. green beans

¼ lb. shredded cabbage
1 ripe tomato, peeled, seeded, and chopped
1 celery rib, diced
1 zucchini, diced
1 turnip, diced
Herb bouquet (¼ tsp. each dried thyme and fennel, 1 bay leaf, and 2 sprigs of parsley wrapped in cheesecloth)
Salt and freshly ground pepper
6 garlic cloves
10 leaves fresh basil
3 Tb. olive oil
¼ lb. grated Parmesan cheese

Heat olive oil in a large pot or casserole, add onion, carrots, and leek, and sauté over low heat for 5 minutes. Add water and all remaining vegetables, add herb bouquet, and bring liquid to the boil. Season with salt and pepper to taste, lower heat, cover, and simmer for 45 minutes or till vegetables are tender.

Make *pistou* by combining garlic, basil, and olive oil in a mortar and pounding to a paste.

Remove herb bouquet from soup and stir in paste. Do not reheat soup after *pistou* has been added. Serve sprinkled with Parmesan cheese.

Cioppino

1 medium lobster, cleaned and
  hacked into serving pieces
1 lb. fresh shrimp, shelled and
  deveined
12 mussels, scrubbed thoroughly
12 clams, scrubbed thoroughly
3 lbs. firm white fish (striped
  bass, haddock, or cod), cut into
  serving pieces
½ cup olive oil
1 cup finely chopped onions
1 cup finely chopped green bell
  pepper

3 garlic cloves, chopped
6 ripe tomatoes, peeled, cored, and
  coarsely chopped
2 Tb. tomato paste
2 cups dry red or white wine
½ cup chopped parsley
Herb bouquet (¼ tsp. each dried
  thyme and fennel, 1 bay leaf,
  and 2 sprigs of parsley wrapped
  in cheesecloth)
Salt and freshly ground pepper

Pour 1 inch of water into a large kettle, add lobster, shrimp, mussels, and clams, bring water to the boil, cover kettle, and steam shellfish for about 10 minutes or till shells of mussels and clams open (discard any that remain closed). Remove shellfish, strain broth into a saucepan, and reserve.

Heat olive oil in a large casserole, add onions, bell pepper, and garlic and sauté for 3 minutes over low heat. Add tomatoes, tomato paste, wine, parsley, herb bouquet, salt and pepper to taste, and reserved broth, and simmer for 15 minutes. Add white fish and continue simmering for 10 minutes. Add shellfish, cover, and simmer for 15 minutes longer.

Serve seafood and broth in deep soup bowls.

Georgia Brunswick Stew

This meal-in-itself requires no accompaniments other than fresh coleslaw, Corn Sticks (p. 438) or hot biscuits, and ice-cold beer.

6 slices of bacon, chopped
3-lb. chicken, quartered
1 lb. boneless chuck, trimmed of
   fat and cut into chunks
1 cup chopped onions
1 cup chopped celery, including
   leaves
1 green bell pepper, chopped
1 medium ham hock, trimmed of
   fat and gristle
3 ripe tomatoes, cored and chopped
2 sprigs of parsley, chopped

1 small hot red pepper, seeded
   and minced
1 tsp. salt
½ tsp. each dried basil and thyme
2½ qts. water
1½ cups corn kernels (fresh, or
   frozen and thawed)
1½ cups sliced okra (fresh, or
   frozen and thawed)
1½ cups lima beans (fresh, or
   frozen and thawed)
1½ cups mashed potatoes

*I*n a large, heavy skillet, fry bacon till crisp, drain on paper towels, and crumble.

Add chicken to skillet, brown on all sides over moderate heat, and transfer to paper towels. Add chuck to skillet, brown on all sides, and transfer to paper towels.

Pour remaining fat from skillet into a large casserole, add onions, celery, and green pepper, and sauté for 3 minutes over low heat. Add chicken, chuck, ham hock, tomatoes, parsley, red pepper, salt, basil, thyme, and water, and stir thoroughly. Bring liquid to the boil, reduce heat, cover, and simmer for 45 minutes, skimming from time to time.

Remove chicken with a slotted spoon and continue to simmer stew for 1½ hours. When chicken has cooled, discard skin and bones, shred the meat, and set aside.

Bring casserole to the boil, add corn, okra, and lima beans, reduce heat, and cook for 30 minutes. Remove ham hock with slotted spoon, bone and shred meat, and return meat to casserole along with reserved shredded chicken and reserved crumbled bacon. Add mashed potatoes, stir well to thicken stew, and continue cooking for 15 minutes.

Serve stew in deep soup bowls.

Coach House Black Bean Soup

Serves at least 12

For years my home away from home has been the famous Coach House Restaurant in New York City, a veritable haven where this sumptuous soup has been on Leon Lianides' menu as long as anyone can remember. To attain ideal texture, the beans should be laboriously worked through a sieve as in the restaurant. I've used a blender (but never a food processor) on numerous occasions, however, and must say the result is quite acceptable. Since this soup is virtually pureed, it freezes very well.

2½ cups dried black beans
10 cups water
2 Tb. butter
1 cup chopped onions
½ cup chopped celery
7 cups Beef Stock (p. 522)
2 cups water

1 tsp. chopped fresh garlic
¼ cup sherry or Madeira
1 tsp. salt
½ tsp. freshly ground pepper
2 hard-boiled eggs, finely chopped
1 or 2 lemons, thinly sliced and
    dipped in minced fresh parsley

Soak beans in 10 cups water for at least 12 hours in refrigerator and drain well.

Heat butter in a large casserole, add onions and celery, and sauté over low heat for 3 minutes. Add beans, stock, 2 cups water, and garlic, bring liquid to the boil, reduce heat, and simmer for 2½ hours, stirring occasionally and adding water if needed to keep beans covered.

Transfer mixture in batches to a blender and blend till roughly pureed. Turn into a large saucepan, stir in sherry or Madeira, salt, and pepper, and place over moderate heat, stirring, till piping hot. Gently blend in chopped egg, ladle into warmed serving bowls, and garnish with lemon slices.

· PART THREE ·

Eggs

Spicy Cheese and Eggs

I was virtually raised on this breakfast dish created by my grandfather. When I serve it on a breakfast or brunch buffet with fried country ham, creamed spinach, sautéed apples, and hot biscuits, it never fails to bring exclamations from guests. The secret is the large amount of *very* sharp cheese — my mother would say nothing would do but New York State cheddar from the A&P.

8 Tb. (1 stick) butter
8 slices white bread, trimmed and
  cubed
2 cups milk
2 lbs. extra-sharp cheddar cheese,
  coarsely grated

1 small red chili pepper, seeded
  and minced
10 eggs, beaten
Salt and freshly ground pepper

*H*eat butter over moderate heat in a large, heavy skillet or sauté pan, add bread and milk, and mash thoroughly with a fork till mixture has the consistency of a soft roux.

Add cheese and chili pepper and continue mashing and stirring till cheese is well incorporated and mixture is smooth.

Add eggs and salt and pepper to taste and stir slowly and constantly with a large spoon till eggs are set and mixture is creamy (if mixture seems to be sticking to bottom of skillet, lower heat while stirring).

Serve in a chafing dish or large heated bowl.

Scrambled Eggs with Crabmeat and Vermouth

Serves 4–6

These silky-smooth eggs are lovely served with a puree of spinach, broccoli, or watercress. Alternatives for the crabmeat would be diced lobster or shrimp.

12 eggs
8 Tb. (1 stick) butter, softened
½ cup diced lump crabmeat

½ cup sweet vermouth, heated
Salt and freshly ground pepper
½ cup toasted slivered almonds

*B*reak eggs into a mixing bowl and beat with a whisk till whites and yolks are just blended.

Heat one-half of the butter in the top of a double boiler over simmering water, pour in eggs, and stir with a whisk till they just begin to set. Stir in remaining butter and the crabmeat and continue cooking for about 15 minutes or till eggs are creamy (do not overcook).

Remove pan from the heat and stir in vermouth and salt and pepper to taste. Spoon eggs immediately onto heated plates and sprinkle each serving with toasted almonds.

Scrambled Eggs with Chicken Livers in Brioche

Serves 6

I never tire of trying to figure out new ways to serve creamy scrambled eggs, and this is without doubt one of the most dramatic. You might also give thought to preparing the dish with chopped mushrooms or tomatoes, crumbled blue-veined cheese, diced country ham, or slivers of smoked salmon.

¾ cup (1½ sticks) butter	12 eggs
2 Tb. minced shallots	½ cup light cream
½ lb. chicken livers, cut into	Salt and freshly ground pepper
½-inch cubes	3 Tb. chopped fresh dill
2 Tb. Madeira	6 Brioches (p. 434)

*H*eat 3 tablespoons of the butter in a small skillet, add shallots, and sauté over low heat for 2 minutes. Add chicken livers, toss with shallots, and continue sautéing over low heat for 1 minute. Add Madeira, stir, raise heat, and cook for 1 minute longer.

In a mixing bowl, whisk eggs with the cream and salt and pepper to taste till well blended. Heat remaining butter in the top of a double boiler over simmering water, pour in eggs, and stir with a whisk till they begin to set. Add chicken livers and dill and continue stirring for about 15 minutes or till eggs are creamy (do not overcook).

Slice tops off the brioches, hollow out with a spoon, and fill shells with egg mixture. Replace brioche tops on mixture and serve immediately.

Country Ham and Tomato Frittata

The *frittata*, a substantial Italian omelet that is perfect for lunch with bread and salad, lends itself to literally dozens of fillings: sausage and mushrooms, spinach and potatoes, zucchini and prosciutto, artichoke hearts and peppers, and many more. I've watched Italian chefs flip *frittatas* with great ease and expertise; I've yet to try it without producing a disaster. Do note that *frittatas* are just as tasty cold as hot.

3 Tb. olive oil
1 large onion, diced
2 ripe tomatoes, peeled, seeded,
   and finely chopped
8 eggs
Freshly ground pepper
6 Tb. grated Romano cheese

1 cup diced lean fried country
   ham (see p. 213)
4 Tb. (½ stick) butter
1 Tb. olive oil
½ tsp. mixed dried herbs
   (oregano, basil, summer
   savory, or chervil)

Heat olive oil in a medium skillet, add onion, and sauté over low heat for 2 minutes. Add tomatoes, stir, and sauté for 2 minutes longer. Drain off excess liquid.

Break eggs into a mixing bowl, add salt and pepper to taste, and whisk till blended. Add one-half of the grated cheese and the ham and stir.

Heat the butter and 1 tablespoon olive oil over moderate heat in a 10-inch cast-iron skillet, add egg mixture, lower heat, sprinkle top of mixture with the herbs, and cook slowly for 15 – 20 minutes or till bottom is golden brown but top is still a little runny. Meanwhile, preheat the broiler.

Sprinkle top of *frittata* with remaining grated cheese and run skillet under the broiler for about 1 minute or till top is golden brown. Loosen *frittata* from skillet by running a knife around the edges, cool slightly, and cut into wedges.

Sigred's Spanish Omelet

Serves 4

One of my earliest memories was watching my Swedish grandmother whip up her Spanish omelets for the family at lunchtime. Where, in heaven's name, she ever tasted this fat omelet in the first place I don't know, but I've guarded the wonderful recipe these many years.

8 Tb. (1 stick) butter
2 cups chopped celery
1 cup chopped onion
2 ripe tomatoes, peeled and chopped
1 green bell pepper, chopped

1 cup frozen peas, thawed
Salt and freshly ground pepper
8 slices of bacon
8 jumbo eggs

*H*eat one-half of the butter in a large saucepan, add celery, onion, tomatoes, and bell pepper, stir slightly, cover, and simmer vegetables over low heat for about 30 minutes. Add peas, salt and pepper to taste, stir, cover, simmer for 10 minutes longer, and remove from heat.

Meanwhile, fry the bacon in a large skillet and drain on paper towels.

Break 2 eggs into a small bowl and beat. Heat 1 tablespoon of the remaining butter till sizzling in a medium omelet pan, add eggs, let set slightly, and spoon one-quarter of the vegetables over half the eggs. Flip other half over mixture and turn out omelet immediately onto a heated plate, making sure not to overcook. Repeat procedure with remaining eggs and vegetables.

Garnish top of each omelet with two strips of bacon and serve immediately.

Eggs à la Basquaise

Serves 6

1/4 cup olive oil
3 onions, sliced and separated
    into rings
1 garlic clove, minced
3 green bell peppers, seeded and
    cut into 1/8-inch strips
4 ripe tomatoes, peeled, seeded,
    and cut into 1/8-inch strips

1/4 tsp. oregano
Salt and freshly ground pepper
Tabasco
6 Tb. (3/4 stick) butter
4 oz. boiled ham, cut into julienne
12 eggs
1/2 cup half-and-half

*H*eat olive oil in a large skillet, add onions and garlic, and sauté over low heat for 2 minutes. Add the peppers, tomatoes, oregano, salt and pepper to taste, and Tabasco to taste, raise heat to moderate, and cook for 12 minutes or till vegetables are tender. Turn off heat and keep warm.

Heat 2 tablespoons of the butter in a small skillet, add ham, and sauté over moderate heat till lightly browned.

Break eggs into a mixing bowl, add half-and-half plus salt and pepper to taste, and whisk till well blended. Heat remaining butter in a large omelet pan or skillet, add eggs, and cook over low heat, whisking, till they are creamy.

Mound eggs in the center of a large heated oval sauté pan, surround them with the vegetable mixture, and scatter ham over vegetables.

Hot Curried Eggs with Tarragon

Serves 6

12 hard-boiled eggs, shelled
2 Tb. heavy cream
1 tsp. curry powder
1 tsp. grated onion
Salt and freshly ground pepper

2 Tb. flour
2 tsp. curry powder
3 Tb. melted butter
2 cups half-and-half
3 Tb. chopped fresh tarragon

Cut off in a sawtooth fashion the narrow white ends of the eggs and reserve. Trim the bases of the eggs so they stand upright.

Very carefully remove yolks, place in a bowl, and mash finely with a fork. Add cream, 1 teaspoon curry powder, onion, and salt and pepper to taste, and blend thoroughly. Spoon mixture into a pastry tube and press into egg cavities, allowing mixture to rise slightly above the tops of the cavities. Replace the reserved white ends on top of the mixture and arrange eggs upright in a shallow gratin dish.

In a saucepan, blend the flour and curry powder into the melted butter with a whisk over low heat and cook mixture for 2 minutes. Stir in half-and-half and salt and pepper to taste, raise heat, and cook, stirring constantly, till sauce thickens. Pour hot sauce around the room-temperature eggs and sprinkle the entire dish with chopped tarragon.

Oeufs Coque aux Crevettes Grises Troisgros
(Soft-Boiled Eggs with Shrimps)

Serves 4–8

Late one chilly fall morning after I accompanied Jean Troisgros to a farm outside Roanne, France, to see some beef cattle, the celebrated chef and I returned to his three-star restaurant where his brother, Pierre, whipped up this simple but elegant dish for breakfast. With it we ate earthy air-cured ham, crusty country bread layered with sweet butter, and fresh apricot preserves — all the while tossing ham fat and crumbs to their big Irish setter. The memory lingers.

½ lb. very small shrimp   *½ tsp. minced shallots*
   (preferably river shrimp)   *Salt and freshly ground pepper*
½ lemon   *8 large eggs*
2 Tb. unsalted butter   *Crusty day-old bread*

*P*lace shrimp in a saucepan with salted water to cover, squeeze lemon in water, bring water to the boil, and drain shrimp immediately. When cool enough to handle, peel and devein shrimp and cut into pieces.

Heat butter in a small skillet, add shallots, and sauté over low heat for 2 minutes. Add shrimp, toss, and remove from heat.

Bring a large saucepan of water to the boil, lower eggs into water, boil exactly 3 minutes, and drain. Grasping each egg with a cloth, cut off top quarter with a serrated knife, spoon out and discard white from lid, and replace with an equal amount of shrimp mixture. Set eggs upright inside egg cups or tiny ramekins and very quickly flip on lids without spilling shrimp.

Slice bread into 3-inch sticks and serve for dipping into eggs.

Eggs Commander's

I suppose I've tasted every egg dish ever created at Commander's Palace, probably the finest restaurant in New Orleans, but none ever impressed me as much as this rich, luscious masterpiece. The dish is a meal-in-itself and is traditionally served with a chilled bottle of rosé wine.

½ lb. veal, finely ground	12 eggs
½ lb. fatty pork, finely ground	6 Holland rusks or English
½ lb. beef chuck, finely ground	muffins, sliced in half
6 scallions, minced	3 cups Commander's Creole
½ tsp. ground fennel	Sauce (p. 533)
½ tsp. garlic powder	1½ cups Béarnaise Sauce (p.
½ tsp. grated nutmeg	527)
Pinch of dried thyme	Minced parsley
Salt and freshly ground pepper	

*I*n a large mixing bowl, combine ground meats, scallions, and all seasonings and blend well with hands or a wooden spoon. Transfer mixture to a 12-inch length of aluminum foil and wrap to form into a cylinder about 1½ inches in diameter. Chill cylinder in freezer for about 1 hour or till firm enough to slice without mashing. Remove foil, cut cylinder into 12 equal patties, and fry patties in a skillet till brown on both sides. Drain them on paper towels and keep warm.

Bring a kettle or large sauté pan of water to the boil and poach eggs carefully, about 2 minutes, draining on a clean towel as they are lifted from the water.

Arrange 2 halves of rusks or muffins on each of 6 plates and spoon 2 tablespoons of Creole sauce over each half. Place a poached egg on top of each sauced half and spoon 1 tablespoon of béarnaise sauce over each egg. Sprinkle eggs with minced parsley and serve with 2 sausage patties on each plate.

Poached Eggs in Potato Jackets
with Lobster Sauce

Serves 4

This is but one example of how the lowly spud serves as a dramatic setting for a classic combination. Served with no more than a light salad and crisp white wine, the dish makes an ideal luncheon main course.

4 large Idaho potatoes
6 Tb. (¾ stick) butter
2 Tb. milk
2 Tb. flour
Salt and cayenne pepper
½ cup half-and-half

½ cup heavy cream
4 Tb. Cognac
½ cup chopped cooked lobster meat
4 eggs
½ cup freshly grated Parmesan
   cheese

Preheat oven to 425°.
   Wash, scrub, and dry the potatoes, prick each with a fork, and bake for about 1 hour or till soft.

Slice off tops of potatoes lengthwise and discard or reserve skins to make Twice-Baked Potato Skins (p. 378) at another time. Scoop out most of the pulp into a large bowl and mash with a fork, reserving potato shells. Add 2 tablespoons of the butter plus the milk to the pulp, beat with an electric mixer till smooth, and spoon puree into a pastry bag.

Melt 2 tablespoons of the butter in a saucepan, remove from heat, and stir in flour and salt and pepper to taste. Add half-and-half, stir over low heat till cream comes almost to the boil, add heavy cream, Cognac, and lobster, and blend well. Stir in remaining butter, and simmer sauce gently for 2–3 minutes. Remove sauce from heat and keep warm.

Increase oven heat to broil.

Pipe a bed of potato puree on bottom of each potato shell. Poach eggs for exactly 3 minutes in simmering water, drain on a clean towel, and snip off any jagged white pieces. Fit one egg inside each potato shell and spoon sauce on top of each egg. Pipe potato puree around edges of eggs, sprinkle tops with grated Parmesan, and place under the broiler till golden brown.

Salmon-Stuffed Eggs with Herb Dressing

Serves 6

This makes a nice light luncheon dish served with pâté, fresh fruit, good French bread, and a simple wine. Substitutions for the salmon might include 4 tablespoons of chopped black olives, ¼ cup ground ham, 4 tablespoons of crumbled Stilton or blue cheese, or even a few tablespoons of fresh caviar.

6 jumbo hard-boiled eggs, cut in half lengthwise	*1 Tb. chopped capers*
	1 tsp. Dijon mustard
¼ cup finely chopped smoked salmon	*1 Tb. Fresh Mayonnaise (p. 541)*
	Freshly ground pepper
1 Tb. finely chopped fresh dill	*1 cup Herb Dressing (p. 544)*

*W*ork egg yolks through a sieve into a mixing bowl, add smoked salmon, dill, and capers, and mix well. Add mustard, mayonnaise, and pepper to taste, and blend well.

Fill egg cavities with the mixture, press halves together neatly and securely, and trim the broad bases of the eggs so they stand upright on a serving dish. Spoon herb dressing over eggs.

Sardine-Stuffed Eggs

Serves 6 as appetizer, 3 as main course

6 hard-boiled eggs, shelled
4-oz. can sardines, drained
1 Tb. vinegar or lemon juice
4 Tb. (½ stick) butter, room
  temperature
4 Tb. Fresh Mayonnaise (p. 541)

2 tsp. Dijon mustard
1 Tb. finely chopped fresh dill
1 Tb. finely chopped chives
Capers
6 strips pimiento

Cut a thin slice off the bottom of each egg, then cut off top third of each egg. Discard yolk scraps from tops, chop egg white scraps finely, and set aside.

Very carefully squeeze the yolks out of the eggs into a mixing bowl, add sardines to yolks, and mash to a puree with a fork. Add vinegar, butter, mayonnaise, and mustard, and blend well.

Fill white egg cases with the sardine mixture and smooth tops. Mix chopped dill, chives, and reserved chopped egg white scraps in a small bowl, roll stuffed eggs in mixture, and stand eggs on a serving platter. Place a few capers on top of each egg, arrange pimiento strips around capers in a circular, decorative fashion, and chill eggs till ready to serve.

Dilled Scotch Eggs

Serves 4

Served with baked tomato halves or a colorful vegetable puree, this dish makes for either an elaborate breakfast or an interesting brunch.

1½ lbs. pork sausage meat
1 onion, minced
1 Tb. fresh chopped dill (or 1 tsp.
  dried dill)
1 tsp. mace
1 Tb. Dijon mustard

Freshly ground pepper
4 large hard-boiled eggs, shelled
Flour
1½ cups fresh bread crumbs
1 egg, beaten
Peanut or vegetable oil for frying

Combine sausage meat, onion, dill, mace, mustard, and pepper to taste in a large mixing bowl and blend thoroughly with hands. Transfer mixture to a lightly floured surface, roll or pat into a ½-inch-thick square, and cut mixture into 4 equal squares.

Roll eggs in flour to coat lightly and wrap sausage squares evenly and securely around each egg. Roll sausage-covered eggs lightly in the beaten egg, then in the bread crumbs.

Heat 1 inch of oil in a heavy skillet over a moderate flame and fry the eggs, turning, till browned evenly (if sausage tends to burn, lower heat). Drain on paper towels, slice in half lengthwise, and serve warm or at room temperature.

Goat Cheese and Broccoli Soufflés

Serves 6

These simple individual luncheon soufflés (which can also be served as a first course to a more elaborate meal) never fail to produce oohs and ahs from guests. If smooth fresh cottage cheese is not available, try a little ricotta, and remember that the success of the dish depends on the strength of the goat cheese.

5 egg yolks, beaten	1 tsp. dried thyme
4 oz. strong goat cheese (chèvre or feta), finely crumbled	Dash of cayenne
2 oz. fresh cottage cheese	Pinch of nutmeg
6 broccoli florets, parboiled 5 minutes and finely chopped	Salt and freshly ground pepper
	10 egg whites

Combine egg yolks and cheeses in a large mixing bowl and whisk till well blended. Add chopped broccoli, thyme, cayenne, nutmeg, and salt and pepper to taste, and mix well.

Preheat oven to 450°.

In another large bowl whisk egg whites till almost stiff and fold gently into cheese mixture. Pour mixture into 6 well-buttered small soufflé dishes or 1-cup ramekins and bake for 15 minutes or till browned on top.

Jerusalem Artichoke Soufflé

Perhaps no vegetable is more neglected in this country than the Jerusalem artichoke, actually a knobby tuber that is native to the Western Hemisphere and that bears no relation to the globe artichoke. Although they are never so delicious as when sliced thinly and added to a salad, their unique savor (similar to water chestnuts) makes them an ideal ingredient for an imaginative luncheon soufflé.

2 lbs. Jerusalem artichokes	*Salt and freshly ground pepper*
4 Tb. heavy cream	*Pinch of nutmeg*
4 egg yolks, beaten	*5 egg whites*

Peel artichokes, place in a large saucepan, and cover with salted water. Bring water to the boil, cook artichokes for 15 – 20 minutes or till tender, and drain on paper towels. Cut artichokes into pieces, place in a food processor, reduce to a puree, and transfer puree to another large saucepan.

Add cream to puree, blend well, and cook over moderate heat, stirring for 3 minutes. Remove pan from heat, let cool slightly, then blend in beaten egg yolks gradually. Season with salt and pepper to taste and nutmeg and stir.

Preheat oven to 400°.

Place egg whites in a large mixing bowl and whisk to stiff peaks. Add puree to egg whites and gently fold into whites with a rubber spatula. Scrape mixture into a buttered 2-quart soufflé dish, attach a 3-inch aluminum collar around dish, and place in oven. Reduce heat immediately to 375° and bake for 25 minutes.

Corn and Bacon Soufflé

Serves 4

½ lb. bacon
8 Tb. (1 stick) butter
¼ cup grated Parmesan cheese
1 onion, finely chopped
1 cup whole kernel corn, fresh,
    canned, or frozen and thawed

3 Tb. flour
2 cups milk, heated just to the boil
4 egg yolks
6 egg whites
Salt and freshly ground pepper
Cayenne

*F*ry bacon in a large skillet, drain on paper towels, crumble, and reserve. Meanwhile, grease bottom and sides of a 1½-quart soufflé dish with 1 tablespoon of the butter, coat surfaces with one-half the grated cheese, and set aside.

Heat 4 tablespoons of the butter in a skillet, add onion and corn, and sauté over low heat for 3 minutes, stirring.

Preheat oven to 375°.

Heat remaining butter in a saucepan, stir in flour with a whisk, and cook over low heat, whisking, for 2–3 minutes or till golden. Remove saucepan from heat, add milk, and whisk till thickened and smooth. Cool mixture slightly.

One at a time beat in the egg yolks, then transfer mixture to a large bowl. Add corn mixture, reserved bacon, and salt, pepper, and cayenne to taste, and blend thoroughly.

Pour the egg whites into a large bowl, whisk till stiff, and gently fold into corn mixture. Scrape mixture into prepared soufflé dish, sprinkle top with remaining cheese, and bake for 30–35 minutes or till golden brown. Serve at once.

Crabmeat and Mushroom Soufflé

Serves 4 – 6

8 Tb. (1 stick) butter
1 small onion, minced
6 large mushrooms, diced
6 Tb. flour
2 cups milk, heated just to the boil

8 eggs, separated
½ tsp. dry mustard
Salt and Worcestershire
1½ cups lump crabmeat, broken up
1 Tb. chopped fresh dill

*H*eat 2 tablespoons of the butter in a small skillet, add onion and mushrooms, sauté over low heat for 2 minutes, and set aside. Preheat oven to 375°.

Heat remaining butter in a large saucepan, stir in the flour with a whisk, and cook over low heat, whisking, for 2 – 3 minutes or till golden. Remove saucepan from heat, add milk all at once, and whisk till thickened and smooth. Cool mixture slightly.

One at a time beat in the egg yolks, add mustard, season with salt and Worcestershire to taste, and stir. Add mushroom mixture, crabmeat, and dill, blend well, and transfer mixture to a large mixing bowl.

Pour egg whites into another large bowl and beat with a whisk or electric mixer till peaks are formed. Gently fold whites into the crabmeat mixture with a rubber spatula and scrape mixture into a buttered 2-quart soufflé dish. Place dish in oven and bake for 30 – 35 minutes or till golden brown. Serve at once.

PART FOUR

Luncheon Dishes

Stilton Puffs

Serves 6

This delightful concoction was inspired by a miniature cheese soufflé I was once served by Paul Bocuse as an accompaniment to a luscious lamb dish. Chopped broccoli, minced shrimp, or ground walnuts could also be added for greater novelty. Be sure to serve these puffs the second they are baked.

6 Tb. (¾ stick) butter
¾ cup water
1¼ cups flour
5 eggs, separated

1¾ cups Stilton cheese, finely
  crumbled
1 Tb. Port or Madeira
Pinch of mace

*P*reheat oven to 400°.
  Heat butter in a large saucepan, add water, and bring to the boil. Add flour and stir constantly with a whisk till batter is firm and smooth. Remove pan from heat, beat in egg yolks one at a time, add cheese, Port or Madeira, and mace, and blend thoroughly.

Pour egg whites into a large mixing bowl and whisk till stiff. Add half the egg whites to the batter and stir gently with the whisk. Add remaining whites and blend gently but thoroughly.

Scrape batter into 6 well-buttered ramekins and bake for 30 minutes or till a knife inserted into centers comes out dry.

Deep-Fried Roquefort Crêpes

Serves 6

2¼ cups Béchamel Sauce (p. 525)   2 eggs, beaten with 2 Tb. water
½ lb. Roquefort cheese, crumbled   2 cups fine bread crumbs
12 Basic Crêpes (p. 416)   Oil for frying

Pour béchamel sauce in a saucepan and reduce over moderate heat to 2 cups. Remove pan from heat and let sauce cool slightly. Stir in cheese, let sauce cool, cover, and refrigerate.

When crêpes have been made, spoon equal amounts of sauce on half of each crêpe, leaving a ½-inch border. Brush borders with egg wash, fold crêpes in half, and press edges together.

Heat oil to 375° in a deep-fat fryer or large saucepan.

Brush crêpes with egg wash, coat each with bread crumbs, and fry in oil, turning once, till golden. Drain on paper towels and serve hot.

Prosciutto and Goat Cheese Pizza

Serves 6

Wolfgang Puck, one of the most innovative young chefs in America, has added a whole new dimension to the art of pizza-making at his fashionable Spago restaurant in Los Angeles. The posh pizzas at Spago are topped with everything from sausage to grilled duck to Santa Barbara shrimp, but the one with prosciutto and goat cheese has always been the best seller. Strong buffalo mozzarella is often available at specialty food shops and Italian groceries and should be sought out with a vengeance.

1½ lbs. fresh mozzarella cheese   1 garlic clove, blanched 2 minutes
   (preferably buffalo mozzarella)   and chopped
½ lb. fontina cheese   2 red bell peppers, minced and
1 recipe of Basic Pizza Dough   sautéed 2 minutes in 2 Tb.
   (p. 415)   olive oil
¼ cup olive oil   6 oz. prosciutto, cut in fine julienne
2 Tb. chopped fresh basil   1 red onion, minced
10 plum tomatoes, sliced   ½ lb. fresh goat cheese

*P*reheat oven to 400°.
  Grate both cheeses into a bowl, toss, and set aside.

Divide dough into 6 equal parts, roll out or stretch into 6-inch circles, and fit on individual pizza pans or heavy-gauge baking sheets. Brush tops with olive oil and sprinkle each with fresh basil. Sprinkle cheese evenly over each circle and top each with equal amounts of tomatoes, garlic, peppers, prosciutto, and onion. Break off bits of goat cheese and arrange on top of each pizza.

Bake for 15 minutes or till dough is golden brown.

Onion, Feta Cheese, and Black Olive Pizzas

Serves 4

5 Tb. butter
3 onions, finely chopped
Salt
Cornmeal
1 recipe of Basic Pizza Dough
  (p. 415)

6 oz. feta cheese, crumbled
2 ripe plum tomatoes, cut in thin
  strips
18 black Greek olives in brine,
  pitted and chopped

*P*reheat oven to 425°.
  Heat butter in a large skillet, add onions, and sauté over low heat for 2 minutes. Add salt, cover, and continue to cook for 5 minutes.

Sprinkle a baking sheet with cornmeal, divide dough into 4 equal portions, roll out each portion on a floured working surface into a 6-inch circle, and place circles on a baking sheet.

Spread equal amounts of onions on each circle of dough, sprinkle equal parts of cheese on each, arrange tomato strips on tops, and sprinkle olives on top of tomatoes.

Bake for 20 minutes or till cheese has melted and serve immediately.

Eggplant and Bell Pepper Pita Pizzas

Serves 6

¼ cup olive oil
3 onions, chopped
1 large eggplant, peeled and cut
   into 1-inch cubes
1 red bell pepper, seeded and cut
   into thin julienne
2 Tb. chopped fresh coriander
   (also called cilantro and
   Chinese parsley)

1 tsp. oregano
3 Pita Bread (p. 424), halved
1 cup chopped black olives
1 cup freshly grated Parmesan

*H*eat oil in a large skillet, add onions, and sauté over low heat for 2 minutes. Increase heat to moderate, add eggplant and bell pepper, and cook, stirring, for about 8–10 minutes or till vegetables are tender. Stir in coriander and oregano, cook for 2 minutes more, and remove skillet from heat.

Preheat oven to 450°.

Place pita halves on a cookie sheet and sprinkle equal amounts of chopped olives on each half. Spoon equal amounts of eggplant mixture on each half, sprinkle each with cheese, and bake for 15 minutes or till cheese begins to brown.

Dilled Spanakopita
(Greek Spinach and Cheese Pie)

Serves 6–8

2 lbs. fresh spinach	3 eggs, beaten
3 Tb. olive oil	1 Tb. fresh chopped dill (or 1 tsp.
6 scallions, trimmed of all but 2	dried dill)
inches of green tops and chopped	Pinch of nutmeg
2 garlic cloves, minced	Freshly ground pepper
½ lb. strong feta cheese	12 sheets phyllo pastry
¼ cup chopped parsley	1 cup (2 sticks) melted butter

*R*emove stems from spinach and wash leaves very thoroughly under running water. Place spinach in a large saucepan or kettle with 1 inch of water, bring water to the boil, cover, and steam for 2–3 minutes or till spinach wilts. Drain, let cool, and chop coarsely.

Heat oil in a large skillet, add scallions and garlic, stir, and sauté over low heat for 2 minutes.

In a mixing bowl, crumble the feta cheese, add the spinach, scallions, parsley, eggs, dill, nutmeg, and pepper to taste, and mix thoroughly.

Preheat oven to 350°.

Line a large baking dish with a layer of *phyllo,* allowing edges of pastry to hang over sides, and brush with butter. Add 5 more layers of *phyllo,* letting edges hang over sides and brushing each layer with butter. Spoon on spinach mixture evenly and continue adding remaining sheets of *phyllo* as before. Trim off overhanging *phyllo* with a knife and bake pie for 35–40 minutes or till golden brown.

Snail Quiche

Serves 6

That some people are still squeamish about eating snails never ceases to amaze me. Long considered a great delicacy in France, edible snails are gradually finding their place in the new style of American cookery — and in ways other than simply baked in the shell with garlic butter. Snails are delicious, and particularly now that they are being produced commercially in California, there's no reason why we shouldn't make a greater effort to incorporate them into all sorts of dishes.

Basic Pie Pastry (p. 411)	*4 eggs*
2 Tb. butter	*Salt and freshly ground pepper*
3 Tb. finely chopped shallots	*1 cup heavy cream*
1 garlic clove, minced	*½ cup milk*
7-oz. can snails, drained	*Pinch of nutmeg*
1 tsp. finely chopped fresh dill	*¼ cup grated Parmesan cheese*

*P*reheat oven to 425°.
On a lightly floured surface, roll out pastry ⅛ inch thick and fit into a 9- or 10-inch quiche dish. Place a piece of wax paper over bottom of dish, scatter rice or beans over paper, place dish on a baking sheet, and bake pastry for 12–15 minutes or till shell browns evenly. Remove rice and let shell cool.

Heat the butter in a saucepan, add shallots and garlic, and sauté over low heat for 2 minutes. Add snails and dill, stir, and sauté for 1 minute longer. Remove mixture from heat and let cool.

Break eggs into a mixing bowl, add salt and pepper to taste, and whisk well. Add cream, milk, and nutmeg, and whisk. Add snail mixture and blend well.

Reduce oven to 350°.

Lift snails from mixture and arrange on bottom of pastry shell. Ladle cream mixture over snails, sprinkle top with grated cheese, and bake for 40–45 minutes or till golden.

Leek and Wild Mushroom Quiche

Serves 4 – 6

1½ oz. dried wild mushrooms
  (cèpes, chanterelles, or morels)
Basic Pie Pastry (p. 411)
3 Tb. butter
4 leeks (whites only), washed
  thoroughly and chopped

4 large eggs
1¼ cups half-and-half
¼ tsp. mixed dried herbs
Salt and freshly ground pepper
½ cup grated Gruyère cheese

Soak mushrooms in 1 cup warm water for about 20 minutes; then rinse, picking for grit, and chop.

Meanwhile, preheat oven to 425°.

On a lightly floured surface, roll out pastry ⅛ inch thick and fit into a buttered 10-inch quiche dish. Place a piece of wax paper over bottom of crust, scatter rice or beans over the wax paper, place dish on a baking sheet, and bake for 12 – 15 minutes or till shell browns evenly. Remove rice and let shell cool.

Heat butter in a medium skillet, add leeks, and sauté over low heat, stirring, for about 3 minutes. Add mushrooms, cook for 3 minutes longer, and transfer mixture to a bowl.

Reduce oven to 375°.

Break eggs into a bowl and beat with a whisk. Add half-and-half, herbs, and salt and pepper to taste, and whisk till well blended. Pour mixture into bowl with leeks and mushrooms and stir.

Pour mixture into prepared pie shell, sprinkle with the cheese, place quiche on a baking sheet, and bake for 45 minutes or till crust is browned and top is golden.

Authentic Chicago Deep-Dish Pizza

Yield: 1 14-inch pizza

If you've never tasted a genuine Chicago deep-dish pizza — which is a meal-in-itself and certainly unlike the other, lighter pizzas in this chapter — you haven't lived. This recipe is basically the same as the one guarded for years by my friend Ike Sewell, founder of the Windy City's now legendary Pizzerias Uno and Due. Note that at least one of the secrets of this pizza's wonderful flavor is the *fresh* basil.

THE DOUGH:

1½ packages active dry yeast	1 tsp. salt
½ cup warm water	½ cup yellow cornmeal
1 Tb. sugar	¼ cup vegetable oil
3½ cups unbleached flour	½ cup warm water

THE TOPPING:

28-oz. can Italian-style plum tomatoes, drained and crushed	¼ cup freshly grated Parmesan cheese
2 tsp. chopped fresh basil	½ lb. Italian sausage, casings removed
1 tsp. oregano	Olive oil
Salt to taste	
10 oz. mozzarella cheese, sliced thin	

*I*n a small bowl, dissolve yeast in the water, add sugar, and stir well. In a large mixing bowl, combine flour, salt, and cornmeal, and blend well. Make a well in the center of flour, add yeast mixture, vegetable oil, and water, and mix thoroughly till dough clears the sides of the bowl. Place dough on a well-floured work surface and knead for 5–6 minutes or till smooth and soft. Dust dough, place in a large mixing bowl, cover with plastic wrap and a towel, and let rise in a warm place for 1½ hours or till doubled in bulk.

Preheat oven to 475°.

Knead dough for 2 minutes more. Oil bottom and sides of a 14×2-inch round pizza pan, spread dough in bottom of pan with fingers and palms, and bring edges of dough up slightly to form a border all around pan.

Prick bottom with a fork, bake for 4 minutes, and brush crust lightly with olive oil.

Combine crushed tomatoes, basil, oregano, and salt in a large mixing bowl, mix well, and set aside.

Arrange slices of mozzarella over crust (but not up to the perimeter), spoon tomatoes over cheese, and sprinkle Parmesan over tomatoes. Flatten sausages with fingers, arrange on top of tomatoes, and drizzle olive oil on top.

Bake in lower third of the oven for 5 minutes, then transfer to the center oven rack, and continue baking for 30 minutes or till crust is lightly browned.

The Four Seasons' Steak Tartare

Serves 2

Raw ground sirloin mixed with numerous condiments is certainly nothing new to the gastronomic world, but the steak tartare served as a luncheon entree at The Four Seasons restaurant in New York is so elusive in flavor, so subtle in texture, so different from most mundane versions that I've actually come to think of the original concoction as having been conceived there. "The real secret to the texture," says co-owner Tom Margittai, "is the way we use the flat sides of two knives to work the meat and blend in the condiments. It takes a while to perfect, but it's the gentle mashing that gives the meat its character."

12 oz. bottom or top round sirloin, all fat removed, and ground	*2 Tb. chopped fresh chives or parsley*
	Olive oil
2 egg yolks	*1 tsp. Worcestershire*
4 anchovy fillets	*1 tsp. salt*
18 capers	*Freshly ground pepper*
¼ cup finely chopped onion	*1 Tb. spicy brown mustard*
	1 tsp. red wine vinegar

*P*lace meat on a large platter, shape into an oval, make two indentions in meat, and place an egg yolk in each indention.

On edge of the platter, mash anchovies to a paste with a fork and large spoon, mash capers in like manner, and, with two blunt knives, mix together the meat, egg yolks, anchovies, and capers. Mash onions lightly and add to meat, add chives or parsley plus a drop of olive oil, and combine lightly. Add remaining ingredients and blend well into meat, mashing lightly with the flat sides of the knives. Reshape meat into two ovals and score the tops with crisscross lines.

Hot Fruit Casserole

Serves 12–14

Rarely do I approve of using canned fruits when fresh are so readily available, but this is one time when cleaning cans from the cupboard can produce a very nice lunch dish. I've served it with country ham biscuits and a fine ripe cheese. Note that the dish should be started a day in advance.

16-oz. can sliced pineapple	*2 Tb. flour*
16-oz. can peach halves	*½ cup brown sugar*
16-oz. can pear halves	*¾ cup (1½ sticks) butter*
16-oz. can apricot halves	*1 cup sherry*

*D*rain all the fruits and cut pineapple slices in half. In a large 18×28-inch baking dish, arrange fruits in alternating layers.

Combine flour, sugar, butter, and sherry in the top of a double boiler over simmering water and cook, stirring, for about 10 minutes or till mixture is thickened and smooth. Pour mixture over fruit, cover with plastic wrap, and let stand in refrigerator overnight.

Preheat oven to 350°.

Place casserole in oven and bake for 20–30 minutes or till bubbly hot and slightly glazed on top.

Simca's Chilled Sardines in Aspic

Serves 8

I know of no recipe that better elevates the social status of the humble sardine than this one of Simone Beck, Julia Child's former associate and one of the most gifted chefs in France. I, like Simca and most of the French in general, have championed both canned and fresh sardines for years, incorporating them into one dish after another. Once you've tried this recipe, you'll agree canned sardines can be a great deal more than snack food.

5 4-oz. cans sardines, drained	3 cups cold chicken stock
2 Tb. butter, softened	1 cup dry sherry
3 hard-boiled eggs, sieved	Tabasco
¼ cup lemon juice	3 hard-boiled eggs, sliced
Freshly ground pepper	Leaves of Boston lettuce
2 envelopes unflavored gelatin	Chopped parsley

Place sardines and butter in a bowl or on a large plate and mash with a fork to a smooth puree. Add sieved eggs, lemon juice, and pepper to taste, and blend well.

In a small bowl, dissolve gelatin in three-quarters of the cold stock, stirring. Pour remaining stock plus the sherry into a saucepan, bring to the boil, remove from heat, and stir in dissolved gelatin. Add Tabasco to taste and stir.

Pour ¼ inch of jelly into each of 8 half-cup timbale molds or ramekins and place in refrigerator for a few minutes till jelly begins to set. Press a slice of egg into jelly and fill molds three-quarters full with the sardine mixture. Fill molds to the top with more jelly and place in refrigerator to set completely. Pour remaining jelly into a square dish and place in refrigerator to set completely.

When ready to serve, remove square dish of jelly from refrigerator, chop jelly, and place leaves of lettuce on chilled salad plates. Unmold aspics onto the lettuce by running a warm, wet, small knife around edges. Surround aspics with remaining sliced eggs and chopped aspic, sprinkle each with chopped parsley, and serve immediately.

Jellied Country Ham with Parsley

Serves 6–8

This is one of the most delightful ways I know to utilize the ends of a Smithfield or cured country ham. Basically, the dish is a classic Burgundian *jambon persillé* without all the tedious work involved producing an aspic with veal bones and pig's feet. It is important that the ham be as devoid of fat as possible. Also, if you insist on reducing the salty flavor, soak the ham in water for a couple of hours.

3 cups strong Chicken Stock (p. 521)	1 carrot, sliced
1 cup dry white wine	6 black peppercorns
2 lb. chunk of country ham, skinned, trimmed of all fat, and cut in half	¼ tsp. thyme
	1 bay leaf
	1 cup finely chopped parsley
1 onion, chopped	2 Tb. gelatin
1 celery rib, broken	2 Tb. tarragon vinegar

Pour stock and wine into a large saucepan or small casserole and add ham, onion, celery, peppercorns, thyme, and bay leaf. Bring liquid to the boil, lower heat, and simmer gently for about 30 minutes.

Lift out ham, transfer to a chopping board, and cut into small ½-inch cubes. Strain stock into a clean saucepan.

Rinse the inside of a medium glass bowl with cold water and dust sides thickly with one-half of the chopped parsley. Add ham cubes to bowl.

In a small bowl, soften gelatin in 4 tablespoons warm water for 5 minutes and stir into strained stock. Add remaining parsley and vinegar to stock and allow to cool till syrupy. Pour over ham, distributing cubes as evenly as possible with a fork and, if necessary, adding a little more wine to cover.

Cover bowl with plastic wrap and chill in refrigerator for a total of 12 hours, stirring once after slightly congealed (1–2 hours) to distribute ham evenly throughout. Unmold on a large, attractive round serving dish.

Marinated Tofu and Vegetable Brochettes
Grilled over Mesquite

Serves 6

Not till I was virtually forced by friends to taste this dish one afternoon at a remarkable Zen restaurant in San Francisco called Green's did I ever think I'd find myself actually loving vegetarian cookery. Mesquite charcoal (which imparts a very special flavor) can now be found in specialty food shops and many supermarkets around the country, and tofu is generally available at all Oriental food outlets. Vegetable possibilities other than those listed in the recipe are sweet peppers, chunks of winter squash, wedges of turnips, slices of yams or leeks, and whole button mushrooms. Remember to parboil all firm vegetables and to marinate the tofu one day in advance. Serve the brochettes over boiled rice or noodles.

1 oz. dried Oriental mushrooms	4 blocks of firm tofu, pressed to
1 cup red wine	remove excess water and cut
1 cup sherry vinegar (or red wine	into 1-inch cubes
vinegar)	24 cherry tomatoes
1 cup soy sauce	2 yellow squash, scrubbed, cut
1 cup olive oil	into 1-inch cubes, and
1 Tb. dried marjoram	parboiled 2 minutes
¼ tsp. ground cloves	24 tiny new potatoes, scrubbed
1 Tb. finely chopped garlic	and parboiled 5 minutes
1 tsp. salt	24 mushrooms caps
Freshly ground pepper	1 cup Vinaigrette Dressing (p. 542)

Place dried mushrooms in a large saucepan with 1½ cups water, bring water to the boil, lower heat, cover, and simmer mushrooms for 15–20 minutes. Add wine, vinegar, soy sauce, olive oil, marjoram, cloves, garlic, salt, and pepper to taste. Stir well, bring liquid to the boil, and remove from heat.

Place tofu in a shallow pan, pour hot marinade on top, and let cool. Cover pan with plastic wrap and refrigerate for 24 hours.

To assemble brochettes, thread alternately the tofu cubes and vegetables on twelve 8- or 10-inch skewers and brush each brochette with vinaigrette.

Grill brochettes over moderately hot mesquite coals for about 8 minutes or till vegetables are browned, turning frequently so that all sides are exposed to the heat. Serve 2 brochettes per person.

Vidalia Onions Stuffed with Ham and Mushrooms

Serves 6

Vidalia onions from Vidalia, Georgia, along with Wala Wallas from Washington State and Mauis from Hawaii, are some of the sweetest in the world and should be allowed to stand on their own merit as much as possible. I have substituted the Spanish giants in this dish when I couldn't find genuine Vidalias (which are sold in many specialty food shops and endorsed on the string sack by the Vidalia Chamber of Commerce for authenticity), and, while they were fully acceptable, I could tell the difference. These stuffed onions make a nice accompaniment to any pork dish.

6 large Vidalia onions (about 4 lbs.)
8 Tb. (1 stick) butter
4 medium scallions, trimmed of all but 2 inches of green tops and finely chopped
1 garlic clove
4 dashes Tabasco
3 cups finely chopped fresh mushrooms

2 cups finely chopped cooked ham
½ cup finely chopped parsley
Pinch of rubbed sage
Pinch of ground cinnamon
½ cup heavy cream
1 Tb. dry sherry
Salt and freshly ground pepper
1 cup dry red wine
1 cup beef broth
4 Tb. minced fresh parsley

*R*emove skin from each onion and cut off a thick slice from the stem end and discard. Scoop out the centers of each with a melon-ball scoop or sturdy spoon, leaving a ¼-inch shell. Finely chop enough of the centers to measure 1 cup.

Bring a kettle of salted water to the boil, add the onion shells, and cook over moderately high heat for 5 minutes. Invert the onions on paper towels and drain.

Preheat oven to 350°.

Heat one-half of the butter in a large skillet, add the chopped onions, scallions, garlic, and Tabasco, and sauté over low heat for 5 minutes, stirring. Add the remaining butter, mushrooms, ham, parsley, sage, and cinnamon, increase heat to moderate, and continue sautéing, stirring, for about 5 minutes or till mushrooms are soft. Add the cream, sherry, and salt and pepper to taste, stir well again, and let cook for 5 minutes.

Sprinkle the onion shells with salt and pepper to taste, arrange them open side up in a casserole or baking dish just large enough to hold them, and divide the stuffing among them, mounding it. Combine the wine and broth in a bowl, pour enough around the onions to reach 1 inch up the sides, cover with foil, and bake for 1 hour, basting once or twice.

Transfer the onions with a slotted spoon to a heated serving platter and sprinkle the tops with parsley.

Serve as a light luncheon dish or side vegetable.

Gratin of Oysters in Riesling

Serves 6

This simple luncheon dish — which could also be served as a dinner appetizer — is equally delicious made with shrimp or mussels.

8 Tb. (1 stick) butter	½ tsp. ground nutmeg
1½ cups heavy cream	Salt and freshly ground pepper
1 Tb. chopped fresh coriander (also called cilantro and Chinese parsley)	1 cup Riesling
	1 tsp. flour
	2 pts. fresh shucked oysters, drained
½ tsp. ground allspice	½ cup grated Parmesan

*H*eat butter in a large saucepan, add cream, coriander, allspice, nutmeg, and salt and pepper to taste, and bring almost to the boil. Add Riesling, stir, sprinkle on flour gradually, stirring, and cook over moderate heat till sauce is slightly thickened.

Preheat oven broiler.

Divide oysters among 6 small gratin dishes or ovenproof shells and spoon equal amounts of sauce over each portion. Sprinkle each with Parmesan, place dishes on a sturdy baking sheet, and place in broiler 6 inches from heat. Broil for 8 – 10 minutes or till puffy and cheese begins to brown.

Baked Oysters and Mushrooms with Mustard Sauce

Serves 6

2 cups Fresh Mayonnaise (p. 541)	½ lb. mushrooms, chopped
3 Tb. Dijon mustard	24 fresh large oysters, shucked
1 red hot pepper, seeded and minced	and drained
1 Tb. fresh lemon juice	1 cup freshly grated Parmesan
Salt and freshly ground pepper	cheese
10 strips of bacon	

*I*n a bowl, combine mayonnaise, mustard, minced pepper, lemon juice, and salt and pepper to taste, and set aside.

Fry bacon in a large skillet till crisp, drain, and crumble when cool. Pour off all but 2 tablespoons bacon grease from skillet, add mushrooms to skillet, and sauté over low heat for 2 minutes.

Preheat oven to 375°.

Butter the bottom and sides of 6 individual ramekins and place 4 oysters in each ramekin. Add equal amounts of mushrooms to each ramekin, then spoon on equal amounts of mayonnaise mixture. Add crumbled bacon, sprinkle with cheese, and bake ramekins for 12 – 15 minutes or till slightly puffy and cheese begins to brown.

Johnnycakes with Creamed Shrimp and Oysters

Serves 6

1 cup stone-ground cornmeal
½ tsp. salt
1¼ cups boiling water
5 Tb. butter
1¼ cups milk
2 onions, minced
½ cup dry white wine

18 fresh oysters, liquor reserved
1 cup heavy cream
1 celery rib, minced
1 lb. shrimp, shelled and deveined
1 Tb. sherry
Freshly ground pepper

*I*n a double boiler over simmering water, heat cornmeal and salt and add water in a thin stream, stirring constantly to avoid lumping. Stir for 10 minutes more, then add 2 tablespoons of the butter plus the milk, stirring.

Drop batter by the tablespoon on a greased hot griddle, cook cakes over low heat for 10 minutes, flip, cook till other side is golden, transfer cakes to a platter, and keep warm in a very low oven.

Combine one-half of the onions plus the white wine in a stainless-steel or enameled skillet and reduce wine over medium heat to about 1 tablespoon. Add reserved oyster liquor and reduce liquid by half. Add cream and reduce sauce till barely thick.

Heat remaining butter in another large stainless-steel or enameled skillet, add remaining onions plus the celery, and sauté for 3 minutes. Add oysters, shrimp, sherry, and pepper to taste, cover, and cook over medium heat for 2 minutes or till shrimp is fully pink but not tough. Pour juices from seafood mixture into the sauce, reduce till thick, add seafood mixture, and cook, stirring, till piping hot.

Arrange 3 johnnycakes on each of 6 heated plates and spoon seafood mixture over them.

Gratin of Shrimp and Artichokes

Serves 4

6 Tb. (¾ stick) butter
1 small onion, minced
2 9-oz. packages frozen artichoke hearts, cooked and drained
3 Tb. flour
1 cup light cream
¼ cup Madeira

½ tsp. dried tarragon
Salt and freshly ground pepper
2 tsp. Dijon mustard
1 cup freshly grated Parmesan cheese
1½ lbs. fresh shrimp, shelled, deveined, and coarsely chopped

*H*eat one-half of the butter in a large skillet, add onion, and sauté over low heat for 2 minutes. Add artichoke hearts, stir, continue sautéing for 1 minute, and remove from heat.

Melt remaining butter in a large saucepan, add flour, and cook over low heat, stirring with a whisk, for 3 minutes. Add cream and Madeira gradually, stirring. Add tarragon and salt and pepper to taste, increase heat, stir, and simmer sauce for 3 minutes. Remove skillet from heat, stir in mustard and one-half the cheese, and let sit for 2 minutes.

Preheat oven to 375°.

Divide artichoke and onion mixture among 4 greased gratin dishes, top each with equal amounts of chopped shrimp, spoon sauce over shrimp, and sprinkle with remaining cheese. Bake for 20–30 minutes or till bubbling and golden on top.

Cold Shrimp Curry with Pumpkin Seeds

Serves 4–6

What to do with all those seeds scooped from pumpkins or acorn squash? Roast them, of course, and sprinkle on all types of spicy cold dishes and salads. I've found these nutritious, crunchy seeds go especially well with curry dishes.

1 cup pumpkin or acorn squash seeds	1 Tb. curry powder
2 Tb. melted unsalted butter	1 Tb. chopped fresh dill (or 1 tsp. dried dill)
Salt	Cayenne
2 lbs. shrimp	Freshly ground pepper
½ lemon	Curly endive leaves (chicory)
1½ cups Blender Mayonnaise (p. 542)	Chutney

*P*reheat oven to 300°.

Wash seeds well under running water, pat dry with paper towels, scatter on a cookie sheet, and roast for 2 hours or till crunchy. Drizzle with butter, sprinkle with salt to taste, and toss lightly.

Meanwhile, place shrimp in a large saucepan with enough salted water to cover and squeeze lemon into water. Bring to the boil, cover, remove from heat, let sit for 1 minute, and drain. When cool enough to handle, shell and devein shrimp and place in a mixing bowl.

In another bowl, combine the mayonnaise with the curry powder, dill, cayenne and pepper to taste, and blend thoroughly. Spoon dressing over shrimp, toss to coat well, cover, and chill for 1 hour.

When ready to serve, mound shrimp atop leaves of curly endive on plates, sprinkle each portion with pumpkin seeds, and garnish each plate with a spoonful of chutney.

Stir-Fried Shrimp with Ham and Straw Mushrooms

Serves 4–6

This delicate Cantonese dish can be on the luncheon table or buffet within minutes once you've marinated the shrimp and boiled the smoked knuckle. The shrimp might also be prepared with broccoli florets and cucumber or peas and sliced asparagus.

1 smoked pig's knuckle
2 lbs. small shrimp
1 Tb. sherry
1 Tb. light soy sauce
Freshly ground pepper
2 egg whites, beaten slightly
2 Tb. cornstarch
4 Tb. peanut or vegetable oil
1 lb. canned straw mushrooms,
   drained and rinsed

2 slices peeled ginger, minced
1 Tb. sherry
2 tsp. salt
1 Tb. chopped fresh coriander
   (also called cilantro and
   Chinese parsley)
3 Tb. sesame oil

Place knuckle in a large saucepan with water to cover, bring to the boil, lower heat, cover, and simmer for 1½ hours or till meat is very tender. Drain, remove excess fat, coarsely chop enough meat to yield 1 cup, and reserve.

Meanwhile, shell and devein shrimp and place in a bowl. Add sherry, soy sauce, pepper to taste, egg whites, cornstarch, and 2 tablespoons of the oil, stir till shrimp are well coated, cover, and refrigerate for 1 hour.

Heat remaining oil in a wok or large heavy skillet till very hot but not smoking. Add mushrooms and ginger and quickly stir-fry for a few seconds. Add sherry and salt and stir rapidly. Add shrimp and continue stirring rapidly till shrimp turn pink. Add the chopped meat and coriander, toss, then drizzle on the sesame oil and continue stir-frying for about 30 minutes.

Spoon equal amounts of mixture on individual plates and serve immediately.

Baked Acorn Squash Stuffed with Curried Chicken

Serves 6

I owe this unusual and sumptuous recipe to my Southern friend Jean Anderson, one of the most respected food writers in the U.S. and one of our most inventive cooks. The dish is perfect illustration of how the finest curries are made without the use of commercial curry powder. If you like your curry hot, add more pepper flakes.

4 Tb. (½ stick) clarified unsalted butter
4 large chicken breasts, skinned, boned, and cut into 1½-inch strips
1 large onion, chopped
1 small red bell pepper, cut into ¼-inch strips
1 garlic clove, crushed
½ tsp. turmeric
¼ tsp. each ground cinnamon, cardamom, cumin, coriander, and hot pepper flakes

Pinch of ground cloves
½ cup Chicken Stock (p. 521) or broth
½ cup apple juice or cider
1 Tb. tomato paste
3 small acorn squash
1 small butternut squash
½ cup heavy cream
½ tsp. salt
Freshly ground pepper

Preheat oven to 350°

Heat 2 tablespoons of the butter in a large heavy skillet, add chicken, and stir-fry over high heat for 5 minutes. Transfer chicken to a bowl.

Add another tablespoon of butter to skillet, reduce heat to moderate, add onion, bell pepper, and garlic, and stir-fry for 5 minutes. Add spices and hot pepper flakes and cook, stirring, for 2 minutes. Stir in chicken broth, apple juice, and tomato paste, add reserved chicken, cover, and simmer mixture for 45 minutes.

Place acorn and butternut squashes in a baking dish and bake for 20 minutes. Turn squashes and bake for 20 minutes longer or till they are tender. Cool, cut butternut squash in half, scoop out seeds and strings, peel, and cut flesh into ¾-inch cubes. Add butternut squash and the cream to chicken, add salt and pepper to taste, and stir well.

Cut each acorn squash in half, scoop out seeds and strings, and brush cut surfaces with remaining butter. Place acorn squash, cut side up, in a large shallow baking dish, mound equal amounts of chicken mixture inside each half, cover loosely with foil, and bake for 30 minutes or till squash is tender.

Escabeche of Chicken with Lime and Orange Zest

Serves 8

When I once told my friend and colleague Paula Wolfert about the merits of soaking chicken in milk before frying it Southern style, she proceeded to develop any number of new dishes applying the principle. Traditionally, Colombian *escabeche* is made with fried fish, but Paula's chicken substitution makes for one of the most luscious luncheon or picnic dishes I've ever tasted. The dish must be prepared one day in advance.

8 boned chicken breasts, split
⅔ cup buttermilk
1 tsp. coarse salt
Pinches of grated nutmeg,
  ground cloves, ginger, and
  cinnamon
½ cup all-purpose flour
½ cup whole wheat flour
Vegetable or peanut oil for frying
⅔ cup Spanish olive oil

3 onions, sliced
3 carrots, sliced
1 green bell pepper, chopped
2 bay leaves
½ cup cider vinegar
½ cup lime juice
Lime slices and orange rind for
  garnish
Fresh basil leaves

In a large bowl, marinate chicken in buttermilk seasoned with salt and spices for 3 hours.

Combine flours, remove chicken from marinade, and roll in flour mixture. Pour 1 inch of vegetable oil in a large cast-iron skillet, add chicken, fry on both sides till golden, drain on paper towels, and set aside.

Heat olive oil in a large enameled cast-iron skillet and add vegetables, bay leaves, vinegar, and pinches of spices. Bring to the boil, reduce heat to moderate, and cook for 15 minutes. Slip in the chicken and cook for 10 minutes more. Add lime juice, cover, cool, then let marinate in refrigerator 24 hours.

Serve topped with lime slices and orange rind in a large glass bowl partially lined with basil leaves.

Toasted Brie with Almonds on Chicken Sandwich

Serves 1

Although at first glance this main-course sandwich combination might appear a bit strange, it makes sense texturally to present the crunch of almonds against Brie running sensually over tender chicken breast. The sandwich is especially delicious when complimented with something like fresh peach chutney on a bed of chopped roasted red bell pepper, and a good ale.

1 slice of black bread
Tarragon Mayonnaise (p. 542)
1 boned, cooked chicken breast,
  shredded

3-oz. wedge of Brie cheese
1 Tb. sliced almonds
2 Tb. melted butter

*P*reheat oven broiler.
　　Spread mayonnaise evenly over one side of the bread and arrange chicken on bread. Carefully slice Brie in half lengthwise and place the two slices on the chicken. Cover top of cheese with a layer of almonds and drizzle with melted butter.
　　Place sandwich on a baking sheet, place sheet 6 inches below the broiler, and broil sandwich slowly till almonds brown slightly and the cheese begins to run.

Peanut Butter with Kiwi on Raisin Bread

Serves 6

This unorthodox open-face sandwich caused quite a sensation when it was featured in *Town & Country* — despite my worst fears! For months after the recipe appeared, readers wrote in to relate all sorts of variations they'd tried: cashew butter with sliced figs, walnut butter with chopped mango, even pecan butter with chutney. So we've come a long way from that classic comfort combination of youth called the peanut butter and jelly sandwich. And just for the record: Yes, I am indeed addicted to peanut butter.

6 slices of thin raisin bread,   *6 kiwi fruit*
*   crusts trimmed*   *1 cup finely chopped pecans*
Smooth peanut butter

Spread a thick layer of peanut butter on each slice of bread. Peel kiwi fruit, cut each into thin slices, and arrange overlapping slices in 2 rows over peanut butter.

Sprinkle chopped pecans over each sandwich and serve with knives and forks.

Belegtes Brot
(Open-Face Bavarian Sandwich)

Serves 4

5 cups shredded cabbage   *2 onions, thinly sliced*
1½ cups heavy cream   *4 slices of pumpernickel*
2 tsp. caraway seeds, crushed   *German mustard*
1 Tb. capers   *4 large slices of smoked pork butt*
Salt and freshly ground pepper   * or ham*
3 Tb. butter   *4 slices of Münster cheese*

In a large, heavy skillet, combine cabbage, cream, caraway seeds, capers, and salt and pepper to taste, stir, and cook over moderate heat for about 20 minutes or till all the cream has been absorbed.

Heat butter in another skillet, add onions, sauté over low heat for 2 minutes, and drain on paper towels.

Preheat oven broiler.

Toast pumpernickel, spread one side of the slices generously with mustard, and arrange equal amounts of onion slices on each piece of bread. Top onions with a slice of pork butt, mound equal amounts of cabbage on top of pork, and lay a slice of cheese over cabbage.

Broil sandwiches till cheese begins to melt and serve with knives and forks.

Hot Curried Fish Sandwich

Serves 6

Maurice Moore-Betty, an Englishman by birth and one of the most illustrious cooking teachers in New York, was no doubt inspired by that wonderful British fish and rice concoction known as kedgeree when he came up with this highly imaginative sandwich. On more than one occasion I've also spooned a little chutney into the pita pocket.

¾ lb. smoked fish fillets
1 cup milk
3 cups hot cooked rice
4 Tb. (½ stick) unsalted butter,
*   melted*
4 hard-boiled eggs, shelled and
*   chopped*

½ cup pine nuts
¾ tsp. imported curry powder
2 Tb. flour
Salt and freshly ground pepper
6 Pita Bread (p. 424), heated
*   and cut into half-moons*

Place fish in a small skillet, pour on milk, bring milk to the simmer, cover, and poach fish for about 8 minutes. Remove fish from liquid, reserving milk, and flake.

In a large mixing bowl, combine the fish and rice, stir in 2 tablespoons of the butter, the eggs, and the pine nuts, and set aside.

Pour remaining butter into a small skillet, stir in curry powder, and cook over low heat for 2 minutes. Add flour, stir, and cook for 3 minutes longer, stirring. Add reserved milk, raise heat slightly, and simmer for 3 minutes longer. Add salt and pepper to taste and stir.

Add sauce to the fish mixture, stir to blend well, and spoon equal amounts of fish mixture into the pockets of the pita.

Greek Keftedes Sandwich

Serves 6

1 cup milk
½ cup fine bread crumbs
8 Tb. (1 stick) butter
1 large onion, minced
½ lb. ground beef
½ lb. ground pork or lamb
1 egg, beaten

1 garlic clove, minced
¼ tsp. ground allspice
1 tsp. ground cinnamon
1 tsp. minced fresh mint
Salt and freshly ground pepper
2 Tb. olive oil
6 hard oblong rolls

*I*n a small bowl, soak bread crumbs in the milk for 10 minutes. Meanwhile, heat 3 tablespoons of the butter in a small skillet, add onions, and sauté over low heat for 2 minutes.

In a large mixing bowl, combine soaked bread crumbs, onions, and meats, and mix well. Stir in the egg, garlic, allspice, cinnamon, mint, and salt and pepper to taste, and mix thoroughly. Roll mixture with hands into 1-inch balls and flatten slightly.

Heat remaining butter plus the olive oil in a large skillet, add meatballs, and fry over moderate heat till they are browned all over, adding a little more oil if necessary.

While meatballs are cooking, cut rolls three-quarters open and remove and discard a little of the soft center. Place an equal number of meatballs in each roll, pour a little of the pan drippings over each sandwich, and serve with knives and forks.

Pastrami Reuben on Onion Bread

Serves 4

Sandwich aficionados know that the toasted corned beef – sauerkraut – Swiss cheese – on-rye beauty known as the Reuben was conceived decades ago in New York at Reuben's delicatessen on Madison Avenue at 59th Street, but is it true (as James Beard once told me) that the original actually involved corned beef, turkey breast, Swiss cheese, coleslaw, and Russian dressing on pumpernickel and was *not* toasted? No matter, for this wonderful meal-in-itself sandwich lends itself to multiple interpretations.

8 slices of onion rye bread
1 cup Russian dressing
8 oz. lean pastrami, sliced very thin
4 oz. uncooked sauerkraut,
    drained

8 slices of Gruyère cheese
4 Tb. (½ stick) butter

Spread dressing over one side of each bread slice and arrange equal amounts of pastrami on each of four dressed sides. Top pastrami with equal amounts of sauerkraut, arrange cheese slices on top of sauerkraut, and cover with remaining bread slices, dressing side down.

Heat butter over moderate heat in a large heavy skillet or griddle and brown sandwiches on both sides till golden and cheese begins to melt.

Sardine Club Sandwich

Serves 4

There's no sandwich I love and prepare more regularly than the classic all-American Club made with chicken, bacon, tomato, lettuce, and mayonnaise on white toast. The origins of our most celebrated triple-decker have been identified with any number of bars, restaurants, and country clubs, but I have it from reliable sources that the Club was easily the favorite sandwich in the plush club cars of such legendary crack trains as the *Twentieth Century Limited*. Whatever, I enjoy experimenting with this sandwich and find this sardine variation particularly delightful — albeit an unorthodox double-decker.

4 Kaiser rolls, sliced in half
Anchovy butter (½ tsp. anchovy
    paste, ½ tsp. minced parsley,
    and a few drops lemon juice
    worked into 4 Tb. [½ stick]
    softened butter)

2 4-oz. cans sardines, drained
    and sliced in half
Capers
8 raw onion slices
4 sprigs of watercress, stems
    removed

Spread anchovy butter evenly over interior of rolls and cover bottom halves with equal amounts of sardines interspersed with capers to taste. Place 2 onion slices on each half, add a sprig of watercress, and complete each with top halves of rolls.

Mediterranean Sandwich

Serves 4

2 long, narrow loaves of French
    or Italian bread
½ cup olive oil
½ lb. feta cheese, sliced as thinly
    as possible
2 4-oz. cans sardines, drained
    and sliced in half

Oregano
4 ripe tomatoes, sliced
4 onions, sliced and separated
    into rings
24 salt-cured Greek or Italian
    olives, pitted and halved
Salt and freshly ground pepper

Slice loaves in half lengthwise and brush interior surfaces with olive oil. Arrange on each half a layer of feta topped with a layer of sardine halves. Sprinkle surface lightly with oregano, then add a layer of tomatoes topped with a layer of onion rings. Scatter equal amounts of olives on each sandwich and season with salt and pepper to taste. Serve sandwiches with a knife and fork.

Creole Croque Monsieur

Serves 4

8 thin slices of dry French or
    Italian bread
Creole mustard (available in
    specialty food shops)
12 oz. grated Gruyère cheese
4 slices of lean ham or Canadian
    bacon

1 tsp. oregano
Nutmeg
Freshly ground pepper
4 eggs beaten with 3 Tb. water in
    a wide bowl
4 Tb. butter

Spread mustard evenly over one side of each bread slice and sprinkle half the grated cheese evenly over 4 slices. Add ham to the 4 cheese-sprinkled slices, sprinkle remaining cheese over ham slices, season each with pinches of oregano and nutmeg and pepper to taste, and top with remaining four bread slices.

Heat butter over moderate heat in a large heavy skillet or griddle. Carefully dip both sides of sandwiches in the prepared egg wash and brown sandwiches for about 3 minutes on each side or till golden brown and the cheese begins to melt, turning carefully with a spatula and fork.

Club Cheeseburger in Pita

Serves 6

12 slices of bacon
2 lbs. ground beef round
1 cup crumbled blue cheese
2 Tb. prepared horseradish
2 garlic cloves, minced
Salt and freshly ground pepper
4 Tb. (½ stick) butter

4 Tb. peanut or vegetable oil
1 cup chopped onions
1 cup chopped mushrooms
6 Pita Bread (p. 424), sliced
   three-quarters around
Mayonnaise (Fresh, p. 541, or
   commercial)

Fry bacon in a large skillet till crisp, drain on paper towels, and crumble.

In a large mixing bowl, combine the beef, blue cheese, horseradish, garlic, and salt and pepper to taste, mix gently but thoroughly with hands, and shape into six 5-inch patties.

Heat 1 tablespoon of the butter and 2 tablespoons of the oil in each of two large skillets till hot but not smoking, add the patties, and sear about 4 minutes on each side. Reduce heat and continue cooking for about 3 minutes per side for medium rare.

While burgers are cooking, heat remaining butter in a medium skillet, add onions and mushrooms, and sauté over low heat, stirring, for about 3 minutes.

Spread interior of pitas with mayonnaise and fit a burger into each pocket. Sprinkle crumbled bacon over each burger, then spoon on each equal amounts of the onions and mushrooms.

Crab and Guacamole Burgers

Serves 4

3 ripe avocados
1 ripe tomato, peeled, seeded,
   chopped, and patted dry
2 tsp. finely chopped scallions
1 tsp. chili powder
1 Tb. chopped fresh coriander
   (also called cilantro and
   Chinese parsley)

Salt and freshly ground pepper
1 tsp. olive oil
2 tsp. lime juice
4 large sesame buns, split
1 lb. king crab legs, cut into small
   chunks

Peel and pit avocados, place in a large mixing bowl, and mash with a fork. Add chopped tomato, scallions, chili powder, coriander, salt and pepper to taste, olive oil, and lime juice, and mix thoroughly with the mashed avocados to make guacamole.

Toast the buns. Spread guacamole generously over tops and bottoms of the buns, add equal amounts of crab to bun bottoms, and cover with bun tops.

Chinese Burgers

This is but one way to add an international flair to the all-American burger. For Mexican burgers, you might stuff the double patties with minced green pepper and onion, chili powder, and some chopped fresh coriander, and for Italian burgers, try a combination of minced onion and garlic, crumbled basil and oregano, mozzarella slices, and sliced tomato.

2 lbs. ground beef round
¾ cup soy sauce
1 tsp. ground ginger
Freshly ground pepper
6 Tb. drained bean sprouts

5-oz. can water chestnuts,
    drained and chopped
¼ cup scallions (whites only),
    chopped
3 sesame buns, halved and toasted

In a large mixing bowl, combine meat, ¼ cup of the soy sauce, ginger, and pepper to taste, and toss lightly with a fork till well blended. Shape into twelve 3-inch patties, handling meat as little as possible, and set aside. Preheat oven broiler.

In another bowl, combine bean sprouts, water chestnuts, scallions, and ½ cup of the soy sauce, and toss well. Spoon equal amounts of mixture on six of the reserved patties, cover with other six patties, and seal burgers by pressing edges of meat together.

Place burgers on the rack of a broiling pan, brush each with some of the remaining soy sauce, and broil for 3 – 4 minutes on each side, basting with remaining soy sauce.

Serve burgers atop bun halves with knives and forks.

PART FIVE

Salads

Red-Tipped Lettuce and Endive with Pears

Serves 6

6 leaves red-tipped lettuce
1 head Belgium endive
6 bosc pears
1 Tb. sherry vinegar (or red wine
    vinegar)

1½ tsp. Dijon mustard
Salt and freshly ground pepper
3 Tb. hazelnut oil

*R*inse lettuce leaves under cold running water and pat dry with paper towels. Separate endive leaves, wash well for grit under running water, pat dry, and cut into thin julienne strips. Core pears, peel, and slice each into eighths.

Combine vinegar and mustard in a mixing bowl and whisk briskly till well blended. Add salt and pepper to taste, add oil, and whisk briskly till thoroughly blended.

Arrange a leaf of lettuce on each of 6 iced glass salad plates and drop equal amounts of endive strips on each lettuce leaf. Arrange pears in star pattern around lettuce and spoon dressing over endives.

Pears à la Ritz

Serves 4

Lunching in the Edwardian splendor of the main dining room at the Ritz-Carlton overlooking the Public Garden in Boston has got to be one of the last truly civilized experiences left in this country. This simple but elegant salad, created years ago at the hotel, has been on the menu for as long as I can remember.

2 cups currant, guava, or Bar-le-
   Duc jelly
2 Tb. lemon juice
8 ripe Bartlett pears, chilled

2 3-oz. packages cream cheese
4 leaves Boston lettuce
½ cup blanched slivered almonds

*I*n a saucepan, melt the jelly, stir in lemon juice, and let cool. Place sauce in refrigerator to thicken slightly while preparing pears.

Peel pears and level bottoms so they stand upright. Remove stems and cores with an apple corer, fill cavities with cream cheese, and set 2 pears on a lettuce leaf arranged on each of 4 glass salad plates.

When ready to serve, pour jelly sauce over pears and coat each pear with slivered almonds.

Pasta Salad with Tuna, Broccoli, and Tomatoes

Serves 6

1 large head broccoli
1 cup Basic Vinaigrette (p. 542)
1 lb. rigatoni *or* bucatini *pasta*
4 tomatoes, seeded and cut into
   ½-inch strips

1 tsp. oregano
3 6½- or 7-oz. cans solid white
   tuna, drained and broken up
Salt and freshly ground pepper

*R*emove stems from broccoli and discard or reserve for another use. Separate broccoli florets and wash thoroughly. Place florets in a large saucepan with 1 inch of water, bring water to the boil, lower heat to moderate, cover, and steam for 10–15 minutes. Drain florets in a colander, run under cold water, and pat dry with paper towels. Place florets in a large serving bowl with one-half of the vinaigrette, toss, and set aside.

Bring 4–5 quarts of salted water to the boil, add pasta, and cook for 4–5 minutes or till pasta is just *al dente*. Drain in a colander and let cool.

Add pasta, tomatoes, oregano, and remaining dressing to bowl with broccoli, and toss. Add tuna and salt and pepper to taste, toss gently, and chill salad for at least 2 hours before serving.

Arugula Fettucine, Prosciutto, and Goat Cheese Salad

Serves 6

½ cup (pressed down) arugula leaves	1½ tsp. salt
3 large eggs	Flour
2¼ cups unbleached all-purpose flour	½ lb. goat cheese
1 Tb. vegetable oil	¼ lb. prosciutto, cut into thin 1-inch strips
	½ cup Basic Vinaigrette (p. 542)

Place arugula in a food processor and pulse about a dozen times. With machine running, add 1 egg and process for 10–15 seconds. Add remaining eggs, flour, oil, and salt, process till dough forms a ball, adding extra flour if too sticky, and continue processing for 1 minute to knead dough. Remove from machine, wrap in plastic, and let stand at room temperature at least 30 minutes.

Lightly flour 2 baking sheets and set aside.

Divide dough into 6 portions and shape each into 4-inch cylinders. One at a time, roll out each cylinder on a lightly floured surface to form a rectangle ¹⁄₁₆ inch thick. Carefully cut pasta at ¼-inch intervals, transfer strips to a baking sheet, and sprinkle lightly with flour. Let stand for 15 minutes.

Bring 4–5 quarts salted water to the boil in an 8-quart pot and add fettucine. Cover till water returns to a roaring boil, remove cover, cook pasta 1–1½ minutes, and drain in a colander.

Place pasta in a large serving bowl, crumble goat cheese on top, add prosciutto strips, pour on vinaigrette, and toss lightly.

Smoked Sturgeon Pasta Salad with Capers

Serves 4–6

1 cup light olive oil
6 Tb. lemon juice
2 Tb. heavy cream
1 tsp. salt
Freshly ground pepper

1 lb. linguine, fresh or dried
1 Tb. grated lemon rind
10 oz. smoked sturgeon, cut into
    bite-size pieces
4–6 Tb. capers

*I*n a small bowl, whisk together the oil and lemon juice, add heavy cream, salt, and pepper to taste, whisk till well blended, and set sauce aside.

Bring a large kettle of salted water to the boil. If linguine is fresh, add pasta to water, bring back to the boil, and cook for 1 minute longer; if dried, cook according to package directions. Drain pasta, rinse under cold running water, and drain well.

Place pasta in a large serving bowl, add sauce plus lemon rind, and toss well.

Serve salad at room temperature. Place mounds of pasta on 4–6 individual serving plates, add portions of smoked sturgeon, and top each with 1 tablespoon of capers.

Lentil Salad with Spicy Sausages

Serves 4–6

To celebrate the grape harvest in Burgundy each year, Lalou Bize-Leroy, owner of the legendary Romanée-Conti and other prestige vineyards, invites one hundred guests worldwide to the Domaine d'Auvernay near Nuits-St.-Georges to sample old and new wines and partake of some of the best home-cooked food in France. It's a feast not to be forgotten, and her lentil salad is one of the more memorable dishes. It was prepared with those succulent garlic sausages you find all over France, but a good Polish sausage also works very well.

1 lb. lentils, rinsed, picked over, and soaked overnight	2 Tb. Dijon mustard
8 cups water	2 egg yolks
2 onions, halved	1 tsp. salt
2 carrots, halved	Freshly ground pepper
1 bay leaf	1 cup equal parts olive oil and
¾ cup wine vinegar	safflower oil
	2 garlic sausages, sliced in rounds

*D*rain lentils and place in a large saucepan with water, onions, carrots, bay leaf, and ¼ cup of the vinegar. Bring liquid to the boil, lower heat, cover, and simmer for 45 minutes, stirring occasionally. Drain, discard onions, carrots, and bay leaf, and let lentils cool in a large mixing bowl.

In another mixing bowl, whisk remaining vinegar with the mustard, whisk in egg yolks, salt, and pepper to taste, then gradually whisk in oils. Combine vinaigrette with the lentils, toss well, and serve in mounds surrounded by sausage rounds.

Shrimp and Pea Salad with Pork Cracklings

Serves 4–6

One scorching July day at the Carolina shore when I didn't feel much like cooking, I spotted in the refrigerator the two-pound bag of fat blue shrimp I hadn't been able to resist buying right on the dock the previous afternoon. There were also fresh peas we'd shelled while having cocktails before dinner, as well as some beautiful pork fat I'd cut from a loin and reserved to make a pâté or possibly some good country sausage. A few hours later guests were eagerly finishing off this salad, as well as some homemade dill bread, leftover cold peach cobbler with nectarine sherbet, and a chilled chablis. It proves how truly wonderful a cold seafood salad can be when a little imagination is applied to fine, fresh ingredients.

2 cups diced fresh pork fat
2 lbs. fresh medium shrimp
½ lemon
2½ cups cooked peas
2 small dill pickles, diced
1 cup Blender Mayonnaise (p. 542)
3 Tb. lemon juice

3 Tb. heavy cream
1 tsp. horseradish
Salt and freshly ground pepper
Leaves of curly endive (chicory)
2 tomatoes, quartered
3 hard-boiled eggs, shelled and quartered

*I*n a large heavy skillet, render diced pork fat over moderate heat for about 45 minutes or till crisp and golden brown, watching carefully and reducing heat if fat threatens to burn. Drain cracklings on paper towels and set aside.

Place shrimp and squeezed lemon half in a large saucepan with enough salted water to cover, bring to the boil, and drain. When shrimp are cool enough to handle, shell, devein, and place in a large mixing bowl. Add peas and diced pickles, mix, and chill for 1 hour, covered with plastic wrap.

In a small bowl, whisk together the mayonnaise, lemon juice, heavy cream, horseradish, and salt and pepper to taste. Add dressing to shrimp and pea mixture and toss well.

Line a large salad bowl with the curly endive, mound salad in the middle, sprinkle top with cracklings, and garnish sides with tomatoes and eggs.

Soused Shrimp and Avocado Salad

Serves 6

This salad is equally delicious made with soused mussels, lobster chunks, or sea scallops. Note that the preparation should begin a day in advance.

2 cups white vinegar	2 lbs. large shrimp, shelled and
2 onions, sliced	deveined
1 celery rib, broken in half	2 avocados
1 Tb. sugar	3 Tb. capers
10 cloves	6 leaves Boston lettuce
1 Tb. salt	2 Tb. chopped chives
1 tsp. cracked peppercorns	

*I*n a large enameled or stainless-steel saucepan, combine vinegar, onions, celery, sugar, cloves, salt, and peppercorns, bring to the boil, lower heat, and simmer for 15 minutes. Add shrimp, return vinegar mixture to the boil, lower heat, cover, and simmer shrimp for 1 minute. Remove pan from the heat and let shrimp cool in the liquid. Pour mixture into a large glass bowl, cover with plastic wrap, and chill in refrigerator overnight.

At serving time, peel and pit the avocados, cut into 1-inch cubes, add cubes to the shrimp, add capers, and toss gently.

Place a leaf of lettuce on each of 6 salad plates, spoon equal amounts of shrimp, avocado, and capers on each leaf, and sprinkle each with chopped chives.

Curried Potato and Shrimp Salad
on Avocado

Serves 4

4 medium boiling potatoes	1 tsp. curry powder
2 lbs. shrimp	¾ cup olive oil
1 onion, minced	Salt and freshly ground pepper
¼ cup parsley	2 large avocados
¼ cup white wine vinegar	4 large red cabbage leaves

Place potatoes in a large saucepan with enough salted water to cover. Bring water to the boil, lower heat, cover, and boil for about 30 minutes or till potatoes are tender. Drain and, when cool enough to handle, peel and cut into 1-inch cubes.

Place shrimp in a large saucepan with enough salted water to cover, bring to the boil, drain in a colander, and, when cool enough to handle, shell and devein. Chop one-half of the shrimp into small pieces and leave other half whole.

In a large mixing bowl, combine warm potato cubes, the cut-up shrimp pieces, onion, and parsley, and toss lightly.

Pour vinegar into another bowl, add curry powder, oil, and salt and pepper to taste, and whisk vigorously till dressing is well blended. Pour half the dressing over potato mixture and toss lightly. Add whole shrimp to remaining dressing and let marinate for 1 hour.

Peel, pit, and slice avocados in half. Arrange cabbage leaves on 4 serving plates, place an avocado half in the middle of each leaf, mound equal amounts of potato salad on and about each avocado, and garnish each serving with the marinated whole shrimp.

Lobster and Mushroom Salad with Capers

Serves 6

2 cups cooked lobster meat, cut into 1-inch pieces
½ cup sliced mushrooms
1 cucumber, peeled, seeded, and finely diced
½ cup Fresh Mayonnaise (p. 541)

Lobster tomalley and coral (if available), sieved into a bowl
6 leaves romaine
2 ripe tomatoes, cored and cut into wedges
Capers

*I*n a large mixing bowl, combine lobster meat, mushrooms, and cucumber, add mayonnaise, and toss well. Add tomalley and coral, and mix gently but thoroughly.

Arrange romaine leaves on each of 6 chilled salad plates, top each leaf with equal amounts of salad, garnish edges with tomato wedges, and sprinkle capers over salad.

Mussel, Eggplant, and Walnut Salad

Serves 4–6

2 qts. mussels, washed and
   scrubbed thoroughly
1 lb. eggplant, peeled and diced
½ cup olive oil
½ tsp. dried thyme
¼ tsp. dried summer savory
Salt and freshly ground pepper

4 Tb. lemon juice
1½ tsp. anchovy paste
1 tsp. minced garlic
1 red onion, minced
½ cup chopped walnuts
4–6 leaves Bibb lettuce
Parsley, minced

*I*n a large pot, steam mussels in 1 inch of boiling water till shells open (discard any that do not), detach mollusks from shells, remove and discard black rims, and chill mussels in a covered bowl.

Preheat oven to 400°.

In a medium baking dish, combine eggplant, olive oil, herbs, and salt and pepper to taste, mix well, bake for 30 minutes, and cool.

In a large salad bowl, combine lemon juice, anchovy paste, and garlic, and mix well. Add mussels, eggplant, onion, and walnuts, toss well, cover, and chill for at least 4 hours.

Arrange lettuce leaves on a platter, mound salad in the middle, and sprinkle with minced parsley.

Lobster and Grapefruit Salad with Nutmeg

Serves 4–6

1½ lbs. cooked lobster meat
2 grapefruits
1 cup finely chopped celery
2 scallions (including some green
   tops), finely chopped

2 sprigs parsley, chopped
½ cup Fresh Mayonnaise (p. 541)
Salt and freshly ground pepper
Leaves of Belgium endive
Fresh nutmeg

*P*lace lobster meat in a large mixing bowl.

Peel grapefruits, remove all exterior skin and membrane, cut in half, and cut out sections with a citrus knife, avoiding as much membrane as possible. Add grapefruit sections to lobster, as well as the celery, scallions, and parsley, and toss gently. Add mayonnaise and salt and pepper to taste and toss just enough to bind ingredients.

Line a serving platter with endive leaves, arrange salad in center, and grate nutmeg very sparingly on top.

Herbed Salmon Rice Salad

Serves 4–6

Chervil is one of the most interesting herbs, but it is hard to come by. It really adds a flair to this particular salad, but if it is unavailable, fresh basil is an acceptable substitute.

3 salmon steaks, 1 inch thick	*2 Tb. equal parts of chopped fresh*
½ lemon	*dill, tarragon, chervil, and*
1 sprig fresh dill (or 1 tsp. dried	*parsley*
dill)	*3 Tb. Fresh Mayonnaise (p. 541)*
3 cups cooked rice, cooled	*¾ cup chopped green bell pepper*
2 Tb. lemon juice	*¾ cup chopped cucumber*
½ tsp. Dijon mustard	*3 Tb. chopped scallions*
Freshly ground pepper	*4–6 leaves romaine*
6 Tb. olive oil	*Cherry tomatoes*

*I*n a heavy skillet, poach salmon in 1 inch of salted water with juice of half lemon and the sprig of dill for about 10 minutes. Drain, cool, remove skin and bones, and flake into 1-inch pieces.

Place rice in a large mixing bowl. In a small bowl, combine lemon juice, mustard, and pepper to taste. Add olive oil in a stream, beating well, then stir in mixed herbs. Pour dressing over rice, add mayonnaise, and toss well. Add flaked salmon, green pepper, cucumber, and scallions, combine mixture thoroughly, and chill.

Arrange lettuce leaves on 4–6 individual serving plates, place a mound of salad on top each leaf, and garnish each plate with cherry tomatoes.

Seviche Salad with Avocado

Serves 4 – 6

1 lb. shrimp
1 lb. bay scallops
½ lb. red snapper or striped bass
    fillets, cut into ½-inch strips
¾ cup lime juice
¼ cup sliced scallions
1 ripe tomato, cored, seeded, and
    chopped
2 hot green chili peppers, cored,
    seeded, and cut into thin strips

1 garlic clove, minced
1 Tb. chopped fresh coriander
    (also called cilantro and
    Chinese parsley)
⅓ cup olive oil
Salt and freshly ground pepper
2 avocados, peeled, seeded, and
    cut into bite-size pieces
Red-tipped lettuce

Place shrimp in a medium saucepan with salted water to cover, bring to the boil, immediately drain in a colander, and, when cool enough to handle, shell and devein.

Place shrimp, scallops, and fish strips in a shallow glass dish, cover with lime juice, cover with plastic wrap, and let chill for 6 hours.

Drain and transfer seafood to a large glass mixing bowl. Add all remaining ingredients except the lettuce, toss lightly but thoroughly, and chill well.

When ready to serve, place a leaf of lettuce in each of 4 – 6 large serving shells and mound equal amounts of salad on top each.

Artichokes Stuffed with Curried Crab and Corn Salad

Serves 6

6 artichokes
½ lemon
3 Tb. olive oil
2 tsp. lemon juice
½ tsp. salt
2 cups lump crabmeat

2 cups canned kernel corn
½ cup sour cream
1 tsp. grated onion
½ tsp. salt
½ tsp. imported curry powder
White pepper

Slice off 1 inch from tops of artichokes, cut stems to make level bases, snip off tips of leaves, and rub all cut surfaces with lemon to prevent discoloring.

Pour 2 inches of water into a kettle, add oil, lemon juice, and salt, and bring to the boil. Add artichokes, cover, and cook over moderate heat for about 30 minutes or till bases are easily pierced with a knife. Drain upside down, spread leaves, remove fuzzy chokes with a spoon, cover artichokes, and chill thoroughly.

In a large bowl, combine crabmeat and corn. In a small bowl, combine sour cream, onion, salt, curry powder, and pepper to taste. Spoon dressing over crabmeat and corn mixture and toss gently.

Fill artichokes with salad and serve on colorful plates.

Crabmeat Salad Louis

Serves 4

This modern version of the Crab Louis served at the opulent old Palace Court in San Francisco is certainly as good if not better than the original. Classic Louis dressing is believed by some to have been first concocted at the Bohemian Hotel in Portland, by others at either Solari's Restaurant or the St. Francis Hotel in San Francisco. Ideally, Pacific Dungeness crab (often available now in larger city markets) should be used in this salad. Shrimp or lobster served in this manner are just as delicious as crabmeat.

8 leaves Bibb lettuce
4 large slices of ripe tomato
8 fresh artichoke bottoms (or 8 frozen artichoke bottoms, defrosted)
1 lb. Dungeness crabmeat (or lump crabmeat, picked for shell)

1 lemon, halved
1 cup Louis Dressing (p. 546)
2 hard-boiled eggs, shelled and chopped
8 pimiento strips

*P*ut artichoke bottoms in a large saucepan containing 1 inch of boiling salted water. Cover and steam over moderate heat for 8 minutes or till tender. Drain on paper towels and let cool.

Arrange 2 lettuce leaves on each of 4 salad plates, add a tomato slice to each, and arrange 2 artichoke bottoms on top of each tomato slice.

Cover artichokes with crabmeat, squeeze on a little lemon juice, spoon dressing over each portion, and garnish tops with chopped eggs and 2 pimiento strips each.

Creole Crab Imperial

Serves 4

Although I have modified the recipe slightly over the years, this is basically the same Crab Imperial that was developed by Paul Prudhomme when he was head chef at Commander's Palace in New Orleans and the one still served in this great restaurant. At first I was shocked by Paul's use of garlic powder (which he adds to most of his seasoning mixes), but when he showed how this commercial product actually added more balance than fresh garlic to the rather complex salad, I no longer demurred.

4 Tb. (½ stick) butter
1 cup minced scallions (green tops included)
4 Tb. minced green pepper
4 Tb. minced celery
2 tsp. garlic powder
Salt and freshly ground pepper
1½ cups Blender Mayonnaise (p. 542)
½ cup Creole mustard (available in specialty food shops)

Tabasco
1½ Tb. Worcestershire
1 cup well-drained and minced pimiento
1 lb. lump crabmeat, picked for shell
4 leaves red cabbage
4 Tb. chopped parsley

*H*eat butter in a large skillet, add scallions, green pepper, celery, garlic powder, and salt and pepper to taste, and sauté over low heat for about 10 minutes.

Transfer mixture to a large mixing bowl and let cool slightly. Add mayonnaise, mustard, Tabasco to taste, Worcestershire, and pimiento, mix lightly, and let cool further.

Place crabmeat in another large mixing bowl, add mayonnaise, and mix gently to coat crabmeat without breaking up lumps. Chill for 1 hour.

Spoon crabmeat onto the red cabbage leaves arranged on 4 salad plates, and sprinkle each serving with chopped parsley.

Crabmeat and Coconut Salad with Pink Grapefruit

Serves 4–6

1 lb. lump crabmeat, picked for
    shell
1 shallot, finely chopped
1 small tomato, seeded and cut
    into thin strips
1 small celery rib, halved and cut
    into thin strips
¼ cup shredded fresh coconut
½ Tb. chopped chives

Salt and freshly ground pepper
4 leaves curly endive (chicory),
    shredded into pieces
1 cup Walnut Oil Dressing
    (p. 545)
4–6 leaves red-tipped lettuce
2 pink grapefruits, segments
    separated

In a large salad bowl, combine crabmeat, shallot, tomato, celery, coconut, chives, and salt and pepper to taste, and toss gently. Add shredded curly endive and salad dressing, toss thoroughly but gently, and chill briefly.

Cut grapefruits in half and remove sections with a grapefruit knife, avoiding as much membrane as possible.

Arrange lettuce leaves on 4–6 salad plates, place equal amounts of salad in middle, and garnish edges with grapefruit sections.

Mixed Seafood Salad

Serves 4–6

24 mussels, washed and scrubbed
24 littleneck clams, washed and
   scrubbed
½ lb. fresh shrimp
½ lemon
2 Tb. vinegar
1 onion, peeled
½ lb. squid, cut into thin rings
1 celery rib, finely diced
1 red bell pepper, blanched 2
   minutes and sliced into thin
   strips

12 black olives, quartered
1 garlic clove, crushed
⅛ tsp. oregano
Salt and freshly ground pepper
¼ cup lemon juice
¼ cup olive oil
4–6 leaves Boston lettuce
2 ripe tomatoes, quartered

In separate covered pots, steam mussels and clams in 1 inch of water till shells open (discard any that do not). Detach mollusks from shells, remove and discard tough rims, place mussels and clams in a bowl, and set aside.

Clean pots. In one pot, place shrimp in salted water to cover with the squeezed lemon half, bring to the boil, drain immediately, and cool. Shell and devein shrimp, place in a bowl, and set aside.

In the other pot, place 3 cups water plus vinegar and onion, bring to the boil, add squid, boil for 20 minutes or till tender, drain, cool, and set aside.

In a large mixing bowl, combine seafood, add celery, bell pepper, olives, garlic, oregano, salt and pepper to taste, and mix well. Add lemon juice and olive oil, toss till ingredients are well coated, cover with plastic wrap, and let chill in refrigerator for at least 2 hours. Retrieve garlic and discard.

Line a shallow serving dish with lettuce leaves, mound salad in center, and garnish with quartered tomatoes.

Chicken Salad with Mushrooms, Ginger, and Fresh Kumquats

Serves 4

This recipe was inspired one Christmas season when, just as I was about to compose one of my many chicken salads, there arrived a veritable crate of citrus fruits including tiny fresh kumquats from friends in Florida. Although in mainland China miniature potted kumquat plants are in such abundance that they are placed about the house for Chinese New Year, our supply of these midget oranges is fairly limited, often resulting in high prices. If during the winter, however, you spot a small basket, grab it. Because kumquats tend to be excessively tart, you might prefer to remove about half the skin before using—though this will affect the color of the salad.

4 chicken breasts
4 Tb. (½ stick) melted butter
Salt and freshly ground pepper
¼ cup sherry vinegar
¼ cup soy sauce
2 tsp. Dijon mustard
Freshly ground pepper
3 Tb. sesame oil

3 Tb. peanut oil
½ lb. mushrooms, thinly sliced
1 bunch watercress, rinsed
*   thoroughly and shaken dry*
3 Tb. chopped chives
2 pieces ginger root, peeled and
*   cut into julienne strips*
16 tiny kumquats, halved

*P*reheat broiler.

Brush chicken breasts with butter, season with salt and pepper to taste, and broil 6 inches from the heat for about 12 minutes. Turn chicken over, brush with a little more butter, and continue broiling for about 5 minutes or till cooked but still juicy. When cool enough to handle, skin and bone chicken and shred it into long strips.

In a bowl, combine vinegar, soy sauce, mustard, and pepper to taste, and whisk briskly till well blended. Add oils and continue whisking till well blended. Set dressing aside.

Place chicken strips in a large salad bowl and add mushrooms, watercress, chives, ginger root, and kumquats. Pour dressing over salad, grind on a little more pepper, and toss lightly but thoroughly.

Chicken Salad with Avocado and Hot Bacon Dressing

Serves 6

1½ cups shredded spinach
1½ cups shredded escarole
4 cups cubed cooked chicken breast
2 small avocados, peeled, pitted, and cubed
2 hard-boiled eggs, shelled and cut into large dice

1 tsp. lemon juice
Salt and freshly ground pepper
1 cup Hot Bacon Salad Dressing (p. 546)
2 oranges, sections separated

*I*n a large mixing bowl, combine greens, chicken, avocados, eggs, lemon juice, and salt and pepper to taste, and toss.

Cut oranges in half and remove sections with a grapefruit knife, avoiding as much membrane as possible.

When ready to serve, add hot dressing, toss to blend thoroughly, and divide salad equally on 6 salad plates. Garnish edges of each salad with orange sections.

Crisp Mandarin Chicken Salad

Serves 8

3½-lb. frying chicken, cut up
½ cup powdered water chestnuts
    (available in Chinese markets)
    or cornstarch
Peanut or vegetable oil for frying
½ cup peanut or vegetable oil
2 tsp. Chinese mustard
2 tsp. 5-spice powder (available in
    Chinese markets)
1 Tb. salt

½ tsp. sesame oil
½ head iceberg lettuce, shredded
¼ cup chopped fresh coriander
    (also called cilantro and
    Chinese parsley)
3 scallions (whites only), shredded
2 cups cashew nuts, minced
¼ cup toasted sesame seeds
8 leaves of romaine

Place chicken pieces in a large kettle and add water to cover. Bring water to the boil, lower heat, cover, and simmer for 20 minutes. Remove chicken from water. When cool enough to handle, dust with water chestnut powder or cornstarch, rubbing in by hand.

Heat 1½ inches frying oil in a large heavy skillet, add chicken (in batches, if necessary), deep-fry for 10 minutes, and drain on paper towels.

Place chicken on a cutting board and bone. Flatten meat, skin with the side of a cleaver, and shred.

In a large mixing bowl, combine the ½ cup of oil, mustard, 5-spice powder, and salt, and whisk briskly. Add shredded chicken to bowl and toss to coat. Add sesame oil, lettuce, coriander, scallions, nuts, and sesame seeds, and toss well.

Arrange romaine leaves on a large serving platter or 8 individual salad plates and place salad in middle of platter or divide equally among the plates.

Turkey Salad with Poppyseed Dressing

Serves 4

6 leaves escarole
3 cups iceberg lettuce, cut into
  small chunks
4 tomato slices
4 hard-boiled egg slices
2 cups cubed cooked turkey
8 fresh pea pods
2 cups bean sprouts
½ cup slivered carrots
½ cup slivered green onions
  (whites only)

6 slices cucumber, cut ¼ inch
  thick, scored, and halved
¼ cup thinly sliced water chestnuts
8 leaves fresh coriander (also
  called cilantro and Chinese
  parsley)
1 cup Poppy Seed Dressing
  (p. 547)

Line a large serving platter with escarole leaves and fill with a bed of iceberg lettuce. Arrange tomato slices at the two ends, and top each with an egg slice.

Spread turkey across center and place pea pods in outer quarters of the platter. Top the turkey with the sprouts, then the carrots and onions. Scatter cucumber slices and water chestnuts around the platter, arrange coriander leaves above pea pods, and drizzle dressing over entire salad.

James Beard's Turkey and Chutney Salad

Over the years I suppose I sampled each of the many chicken and turkey salads Jim Beard concocted for one occasion or another at his townhouse in Greenwich Village, but without doubt this one he composed once while we were photographing him for the magazine is the most unusual. Green grapes also make a nice addition to the salad.

4 cups diced turkey	*2 heads Boston lettuce*
¾ cup chutney, finely chopped	*¾ cup toasted filberts*
½ cup olive oil	*3 Tb. chopped parsley*
2 Tb. wine vinegar	*¾ cup Basic Vinaigrette (p. 542)*
Salt and freshly ground pepper	

*I*n a large ceramic or stainless-steel bowl, combine turkey, chutney, oil, vinegar, and salt and pepper to taste. Toss briskly, cover with plastic wrap, and chill for about 2 hours.

Tear lettuce into a large salad bowl, add turkey mixture, filberts, parsley, and vinaigrette, and toss to coat ingredients well with the dressing.

Duck and Rice Salad

4 cups salted water	*12 – 14 small salt-cured black*
Pinch of saffron	*olives, pitted and halved*
1 cup long-grain rice	*Salt and freshly ground pepper*
1 cup fresh shelled or frozen peas	*¾ cup Walnut Oil Dressing*
1 whole duck breast	*(p. 545)*
2 Tb. butter	

*B*ring water to the boil in a saucepan, add saffron, and stir. Add rice, boil for 15 minutes, drain well, place in a large salad bowl, and fluff with a fork.

Meanwhile, place peas in another saucepan with enough salted water to cover, bring to the boil, lower heat to moderate, and cook for 10 minutes or till tender but still firm. Drain well and add to the rice.

Skin, bone, and cut duck breast into thin julienne strips. Heat butter in a medium skillet, add duck strips, sauté over moderate heat for 3 minutes, turning, and drain on paper towels.

When duck strips have cooled, add to rice and pea mixture. Add olives, season with pepper, pour on dressing, and toss well with two forks.

Beef and New Potato Salad with Capers

Serves 6

6 small new potatoes
1 head romaine
3 leaves curly endive (chicory)
4 cups cold roast beef, cut into 1-
inch cubes
6 hard-boiled eggs, shelled and
cut in half
20 cherry tomatoes

2 onions, sliced and separated
into thin rings
1 Tb. capers
¾ cup thinly sliced mushrooms
2 Tb. chopped parsley
Salt and freshly ground pepper
1 Tb. prepared horseradish
1 cup Basic Vinaigrette (p. 542)

Scrub potatoes thoroughly and place in a medium saucepan with enough salted water to cover. Bring to the boil, lower heat to moderate, cover and cook for 10 minutes. Drain, cool, and slice in half.

Remove leaves from romaine, snap off white stems and discard, wash leaves thoroughly, pat dry, and place in a large salad bowl. Wash curly endive leaves thoroughly, pat dry, and add to bowl. Tear greens with fingers into bite-size pieces.

Add potatoes and all remaining ingredients but the horseradish and vinaigrette, and toss well. Add horseradish and vinaigrette, toss thoroughly, and serve on 6 individual salad plates.

Lamb Coleslaw with Poppy Seed Dressing

Serves 4–6

I love coleslaw and find it sad that we don't utilize it more as the base for any number of compelling main-course salads. All sorts of meat, poultry, fish, and vegetables can be folded into the chopped or shredded cabbage, not to mention such tasty additions as chopped fresh dill or basil, celery seeds, chopped pickles, and diced olives.

1 medium-size cabbage, trimmed,
cored, and cut into chunks
1 onion, finely grated
1 carrot, scraped and grated
2 cups cubed cooked lamb

Freshly ground pepper
1½ cups Poppy Seed Dressing
(p. 547)
4–6 leaves red cabbage

Place cabbage chunks in a food processor and chop finely. Transfer cabbage to a mixing bowl, add onion, carrot, lamb, and pepper to taste, and toss well. Add dressing and mix thoroughly.

Arrange red cabbage leaves on 4–6 serving plates and mound equal amounts of coleslaw on top each leaf.

Ham, Fennel, and Olive Aspic

Serves 6 as a first course or 4 as part of light lunch

1 envelope unflavored gelatin
1½ cups chicken broth
2 tsp. Dijon mustard
2 Tb. minced onion
5 Tb. minced bulb fennel

5 Tb. chopped green olives
1 cup chopped cooked ham
½ cup sour cream
1 bunch watercress, rinsed

Soften gelatin in ½ cup of the chicken broth, bring remaining cup of broth to the boil in a saucepan, add gelatin, and stir till gelatin is dissolved. Remove pan from heat, stir in mustard, and let cool.

Pour mixture into a mixing bowl, add onion, fennel, olives, and ham, and stir well to distribute ingredients. Fold in the sour cream.

Turn mixture into a lightly oiled 1-quart ring mold and place in refrigerator. After about 15 minutes, stir mixture again to distribute ingredients evenly, return to refrigerator, and chill for 2 hours or till mold is firm.

Unmold on a large colorful serving platter and fill center of mold with watercress.

Ham, Sweet Potato, and Grapefruit Salad

Serves 6

2 cups lean cooked ham cut into
  julienne strips
2 cups diced cooked sweet potatoes
2 cups grapefruit sections,
  membranes removed

½ cup macadamia nuts
½ cup Fresh Mayonnaise (p. 541)
1 Tb. Dijon mustard
Freshly ground pepper
6 leaves romaine

Combine ham, sweet potatoes, grapefruit, and nuts in a large mixing bowl and toss. In a small bowl, combine mayonnaise with the mustard, add dressing to the ham mixture, season with pepper to taste, and mix lightly but thoroughly.

Serve salad in a chilled salad bowl lined with romaine leaves.

Sardine, Sausage, and Bean Salad

Serves 6–8

5 cups Great Northern white beans
1 garlic clove, cut in half
1 cup Basic Vinaigrette (p. 542)
1 cup lean corned beef cut into julienne
2 hard-boiled eggs, shelled and chopped
½ cup finely chopped scallions

2 4-oz. cans boneless, skinless sardines, drained and broken up
1 Tb. minced chives
1 Tb. chopped fresh basil or summer savory
¼ cup chopped parsley
Freshly ground pepper
Olive oil and red wine vinegar

*P*lace beans in a large saucepan, cover with water, bring water to the boil, and let cook for 3 minutes. Remove pan from heat, cover beans, and let soak for 1 hour. Add more water to cover, if necessary, return to the boil, lower heat, and simmer for about 30 minutes or till just tender. Drain beans and let cool to room temperature.

Rub sides of a large glass serving bowl with the garlic halves, pressing down hard with fingers, and add beans to bowl. Pour vinaigrette over beans, toss lightly, and let sit for 15 minutes. Add corned beef, chopped eggs, scallions, sardines, chives, basil, parsley, and pepper to taste, and toss again lightly. If necessary, add more olive oil and vinegar to taste, toss again lightly, cover salad with plastic wrap, and chill slightly.

Haringsla
(Herring and Veal Salad with Apple)

Serves 4–6

This intriguing main-course salad hails from Estonia, the northernmost of the Baltic republics and a region known for its salted herring. I've also made the hefty salad with chicken or sweetbreads in place of the veal, with gratifying results. Note that the herrings must be soaked a day in advance.

6 salted herrings, soaked
   overnight in about 1 qt. milk
2 fresh beets, stems removed
2 large boiling potatoes
10 Granny Smith apples, peeled,
   cored, and chopped
6 hard-boiled eggs, shelled and
   chopped

½ lb. cooked veal, chopped
2 Tb. olive oil
2 Tb. vinegar
Freshly ground pepper
Lettuce leaves

Place beets in a small saucepan with enough water to cover, bring water to the boil, lower heat, cover, and simmer for about 30 minutes or till beets are tender. Drain and chop.

At the same time beets are cooking, place potatoes in another saucepan with enough water to cover, bring water to the boil, lower heat to moderate, cover, and cook for about 30 minutes or till potatoes are tender. When cool enough to handle, peel potatoes and mash with a fork or ricer in a large mixing bowl.

Bone the soaked herrings, cut the flesh into thin strips, and add to the mashed potatoes. Add chopped beets, apples, eggs, and veal, and mix well. Add oil, vinegar, and pepper to taste, and blend thoroughly.

Transfer mixture to a deep basin or bowl and press it down fairly tightly with a rubber spatula. Line a large serving platter with lettuce leaves and unmold salad in middle of leaves.

Sweetbreads and Wild Rice Salad with Grapes and Coriander

Serves 6

1 lb. sweetbreads
1 cup wild rice
3 cups water
Salt
1 cup seedless green grapes
2 small onions, finely diced

3 Tb. red wine vinegar
½ cup olive oil
Freshly ground pepper
3 Tb. snipped fresh coriander
  (also called cilantro and
  Chinese parsley)

Soak sweetbreads in cold water in the refrigerator for 2 hours, changing the water three times, and drain.

Place sweetbreads in a saucepan with enough salted water to cover, bring to the boil, lower heat, simmer for exactly 5 minutes, and drain. Place sweetbreads on a cake rack, cover with another rack covered with foil, and weight down with cans of soup for 2 hours.

With a sharp knife, remove and discard excess membranes and filaments from sweetbreads, cut sweetbreads into 1-inch pieces, and either set aside or place in the refrigerator, covered.

Combine wild rice, water, and salt to taste in a heavy saucepan, bring water to the boil, reduce heat, cover, and simmer rice for 35–45 minutes or till water is absorbed and rice is fluffy. Remove from heat, stir, transfer to a large salad bowl, and let cool.

When rice is cool, add sweetbreads, grapes, onion, vinegar, olive oil, and pepper to taste, and toss well. Add coriander and toss no more than two or three times.

Watercress, Apple, and Pecan Salad

Serves 4–6

2 bunches of watercress
2 large apples, cored and diced
1 red onion, thinly sliced

½ cup chopped pecans
1 cup Basic Vinaigrette (p. 542)

*R*emove and discard stems from watercress, rinse leaves thoroughly under cold running water, and pat dry with paper towels. Tear watercress into pieces and place in a large salad bowl. Add apples, onion, and pecans, and toss lightly. Add vinaigrette and toss salad thoroughly to coat ingredients well.

Serve salad at room temperature.

Caesar Salad with Bulb Fennel

Created during the 1920s by Caesar Cardini at his restaurant in Tijuana, this classic salad has been subjected to more abuse than perhaps any other American original. I'm as guilty as the next cook, but I must say that various experiments such as this recipe have led to some mighty interesting eating. Serve the salad either as a first course, an accompaniment to a juicy steak, or as a main luncheon dish.

2 heads romaine lettuce
1 small fennel bulb
2 garlic cloves
¾ cup olive oil
2 cups unseasoned croutons
    (packaged will do)
1 lemon, cut in half and pitted

4 anchovy fillets, drained
Worcestershire
Salt and freshly ground pepper
2 eggs
½ cup freshly grated Parmesan
    cheese

Strip leaves from romaine and rinse them well under cold running water. Shake the leaves dry, wrap in paper towels, and crisp in the refrigerator. Cut off top stalks and feathery leaves from fennel and remove and discard any discolored outer ribs from bulb. Cut each rib lengthwise into ¼-inch strips, rinse under cold running water, wrap in paper towels, and place in refrigerator.

Place garlic in a mortar or small bowl with 4 teaspoons of the oil and mash to a smooth paste. Scrape paste into a small skillet and heat gently over very low heat. Add croutons, toss for 1 – 2 minutes or till well coated, and set pan aside.

Pour remaining oil into a large salad bowl, squeeze lemon halves on top, and whisk till foamy. Add anchovies and mash with a wooden spoon till well incorporated into the dressing. Add Worcestershire, salt and pepper to taste, and blend well into dressing.

To prepare salad, tear romaine into bite-size pieces, add to salad bowl along with the fennel, and toss till well coated with dressing. Break eggs over salad and toss again to coat leaves further. Add croutons and cheese, toss once again, and taste a leaf of romaine for seasoning. Serve immediately.

Spinach, Radicchio, and Endive Salad with Avocado

Serves 4–6

1 medium avocado
2 Tb. lemon juice
½ lb. spinach, ends trimmed
½ lb. radicchio, ends trimmed

1 Belgium endive
3 scallions, finely chopped
1 cup Yogurt Dressing (p. 548)

*P*eel and pit avocado, cut flesh into ½-inch cubes, place in a glass bowl with the lemon juice, and toss lightly.

Rinse spinach and radicchio leaves under cold running water, pat dry with paper towels, tear into bite-size pieces, and place in a large salad bowl. Separate endive leaves, rinse thoroughly, pat dry, and add to the spinach and radicchio. Add avocado cubes, scallions, and yogurt dressing, and toss well.

Marinated Vegetable Salad

Serves 4–6

5 carrots, scraped, halved
   lengthwise, and cut into julienne
½ lb. green beans
1 head cauliflower, separated into
   stemmed florets
1 small eggplant, halved
   lengthwise and cut into julienne

12 mushroom caps, cut in half
2 cups Marinade for Vegetables
   (p. 550)
1 head red-tipped leaf lettuce
1 cup Herb Dressing I (p. 544)

*A*rrange all vegetables in a steamer or on a rack in a large skillet with 1 inch of water. Bring water to the boil, lower heat, cover, and steam for 5–7 minutes.

Transfer hot vegetables to a large shallow glass baking dish, pour marinade over top, cover with plastic wrap, and let marinate at room temperature for at least 2 hours, turning once.

When ready to serve, rinse lettuce leaves under cold running water, pat dry with paper towels, tear into bite-size pieces, and place in a large salad bowl. Add marinated vegetables to lettuce, pour on dressing, and toss well.

Spiral Pasta and Ham Salad with Pesto Sauce

Serves 6

1 lb. dried fusilli or tortiglione
    pasta
1¾ cups coarsely diced smoked ham
1 cup sliced mushrooms
1 cup coarsely chopped fresh basil
¾ cup coarsely chopped Italian
    parsley

1 tsp. oregano
3 garlic cloves, chopped
¾ cup toasted pine nuts
¾ cup olive oil
½ cup freshly grated Parmesan
    cheese
Salt and freshly ground pepper

Bring 4 quarts of salted water to the boil in a kettle, add pasta, stir, return to the boil, and cook for 5 – 6 minutes or till *al dente*. Drain in a colander, rinse under cold running water, and drain well.

Combine pasta, ham, and mushrooms in a large serving bowl. Combine basil, parsley, oregano, garlic, and pine nuts in a food processor and reduce to a puree. Add olive oil, continue processing till smooth, scrape sauce onto pasta mixture, and mix well. Chill salad briefly.

When ready to serve, add cheese and salt and pepper to taste, and toss well again.

Wheel Pasta and Vegetable Salad
with Smoked Trout

Serves 6

For years, I've felt that The American Restaurant at Crown Center in Kansas City serves some of the finest, most creative food in the country, and once you've sampled the exotic array of cold pasta salads featured each day on the luncheon buffet, you'll understand why I begged the chef for this recipe.

½ lb. dried ruote (or rotelli) pasta
2 smoked trout, about 10 oz. each
4 scallions, trimmed of most
   green leaves and cut ⅛ inch
   thick on the bias
1 red onion, thinly sliced
1 medium zucchini, halved and
   cut into thin julienne
1 medium red bell pepper, seeded
   and cut into thin julienne

2 medium heads cauliflower,
   stems removed and florets
   blanched 2 minutes
1 Tb. chopped fresh tarragon (or
   1 tsp. dried tarragon)
Juice of 4 lemons
1 tsp. dry mustard
½ cup tarragon vinegar
Salt and freshly ground pepper

*B*ring 2 quarts of salted water to the boil in a kettle, add pasta, stir, return to the boil, and cook for 5 – 6 minutes or till *al dente*. Drain in a colander, rinse under cold running water, and drain well.

Remove and discard skin from trout, pull off meat in large chunks, and reserve.

Combine pasta and vegetables in a large serving bowl. Combine tarragon, lemon juice, mustard, and vinegar in a bowl, whisk till well blended, pour over pasta and vegetables, and toss well. Add the trout and toss lightly, taking care not to break up chunks. Chill salad for about 15 minutes before serving.

Sausage-Filled Carrot Tortellini Salad with Bulb Fennel

Serves 4 – 6

Quite often now you can find frozen meat-filled *tortellini* in specialty food shops and even supermarkets, which would reduce the work time for this attractive pasta salad. If, on the other hand, you want to add color and a bit more flavor, you should learn to make your own fresh pasta. The carrots produce a very light pink pasta; for more heightened color, substitute diced cooked beets.

¾ cup peanut or vegetable oil
2 Tb. mixed minced herbs,
    including: fresh dill, tarragon,
    and basil
1 Tb. minced chives
1 tsp. minced parsley
Salt and freshly ground pepper
¼ cup wine vinegar
½ lb. Italian sweet sausages,
    casings removed

12-oz. can diced carrots, drained
1 large egg
2½ cups all-purpose flour
½ tsp. salt
1 tsp. olive oil
1 head red-tipped lettuce, rinsed,
    dried, and torn into bite-size
    pieces
1 fennel bulb, trimmed of stalks
    and feathery tops, and sliced

In a bowl, combine oil, mixed herbs, chives, parsley, and salt and pepper to taste, and whisk till well blended. Add vinegar, continue whisking till oil and vinegar are well incorporated, cover, and let stand while preparing sausage and pasta.

Crumble sausage finely into a small skillet, fry till well cooked, drain on paper towels, and set aside.

Place carrots and egg in a blender or food processor and reduce to a puree. Combine flour and ½ teaspoon salt in a mixing bowl, make a well in the center, add carrot mixture and olive oil to the well, and blend thoroughly with a wooden spoon. Turn dough out onto a lightly floured surface, knead for about 10 minutes or till smooth, cover, and let rest for 10 minutes.

Divide dough into 4 portions and roll each portion very thin (about ¹⁄₁₆ inch thick). Cut out 1½-inch circles with a round cutter, place a small amount of sausage in the center of each circle, fold circle in half, and press edges together securely. Bring one corner of half-moon up to meet the next and press ends to secure. Let *tortellini* rest for 5 minutes.

Bring 4 quarts of salted water to the boil in a kettle, add pasta, return to the boil, and cook for 7–8 minutes or till *al dente*. Drain in a colander, rinse under cold running water, and drain well.

Place lettuce in a large serving bowl, add sliced fennel, *tortellini,* and dressing, toss lightly but thoroughly, and chill for about 15 minutes before serving.

Japanese Soba Salad with Crabmeat and Mushrooms

Serves 4–6

2 Tb. vegetable oil
8 large shiitake *mushrooms,*
    rinsed and thinly sliced
½ lb. soba (*Japanese buckwheat*
    noodles, available in Oriental
    food shops)
¼ cup Oriental sesame oil

¼ cup wine vinegar
¼ cup soy sauce
3 Tb. minced scallions
1 lb. lump crabmeat
1 Tb. finely chopped fresh
    coriander (also called cilantro
    and Chinese parsley)

Heat oil in a small skillet, add mushrooms, sauté over low heat for 5 minutes, and set aside.

Bring 2 quarts of water to the boil in a kettle, add noodles, stir, return to the boil, and cook for 4–5 minutes or till *al dente*. Drain in a colander, rinse under cold running water, drain well, and place in a large serving bowl.

In a bowl, whisk together the sesame oil and vinegar till well blended, add soy sauce, whisk again, add sauce and scallions to the noodles, and toss. Add reserved mushrooms, crabmeat, and coriander, toss again gently but thoroughly, cover, and chill for about 15 minutes before serving.

Cellophane Noodle, Shrimp, and Asparagus Salad with Ginger Dressing

Serves 4–6

12 oz. cellophane noodles (Chinese
   vermicelli, available in
   Oriental food shops)
1 lb. small fresh shrimp
½ lemon
½ lb. fresh asparagus tips
¼ cup minced scallions with some
   green tops

¼ cup peanut oil
¼ cup wine vinegar
3 Tb. soy sauce
¼ tsp. freshly grated ginger
Freshly ground pepper

*P*lace noodles in a large mixing bowl, add enough boiling water to cover, and let soak for 20 minutes or till soft. Drain noodles, rinse under cold running water, drain well, and place in a large serving bowl.

While noodles are soaking, place shrimp in a large saucepan with enough salted water to cover and squeeze juice from lemon into water. Cover pan, bring to the boil, and drain shrimp immediately. When cool enough to handle, shell and devein shrimp.

Drop asparagus into another large saucepan half full of boiling water, blanch 2 minutes, and drain.

Add shrimp, asparagus, and scallions to bowl with the noodles and toss. In another bowl, whisk together the oil and vinegar till well blended, add soy sauce and ginger, whisk again, and add dressing to the noodles. Season with pepper to taste, toss salad well, and chill briefly before serving.

Curried Quill Pasta Salad with Chicken and Cashews

Serves 6

1 lb. dried penne *pasta*
1 *large head Boston or Bibb
lettuce, torn into bite-size pieces*
1 *green bell pepper, seeded and
cut into thin julienne*
1 *cup cooked chicken breast, cut
into ½-inch cubes*

½ *cup whole cashew nuts*
¼ *cup peanut or vegetable oil*
3 *Tb. wine vinegar*
1 *Tb. sugar*
1½ *tsp. curry powder*
Salt and freshly ground pepper

*B*ring 4 quarts of salted water to the boil in a kettle, add pasta, stir, return to the boil, and cook for 5 – 6 minutes or till *al dente*. Drain in a colander, rinse under cold running water, and drain well. Place lettuce in a large serving bowl, scatter on green pepper strips, chicken cubes, and nuts; add pasta, and toss.

In a bowl, whisk together the oil, vinegar, and sugar till well blended. Add the curry powder and salt and pepper to taste, whisk well again, and pour dressing over salad. Toss thoroughly and chill briefly before serving.

Vegetable Salad with Yogurt Dressing

Serves 4

4 leaves romaine
4 leaves escarole
4 leaves curly endive (chicory)
2 large cucumbers, cut into
    ⅛-inch slices
8 rings green bell pepper
2 carrots, scraped and shredded

8 small canned beets, shredded
8 mushrooms, sliced
8 radishes, sliced
½ cup chopped celery
½ cup roughly grated bulb fennel
16 cherry tomatoes
1 cup Yogurt Dressing (p. 548)

Tear greens into bite-size pieces and arrange equal amounts on 4 large dinner plates. At each of 4 corners on each plate, place 2 slices of cucumber, and on the center of the greens place 2 rings of bell pepper. On one ring, arrange some of the shredded carrots and on the other some of the shredded beets. Building toward the center of each plate, add equal amounts of mushrooms, radishes, celery, and grated fennel, and garnish each plate with 4 cherry tomatoes. Pour dressing over each portion.

· PART SIX ·

Meat

Beef Rump Roast Braised in Ale

Serves 8

4-lb. boneless beef rump roast
Salt and freshly ground pepper
4 Tb. vegetable oil
1 onion, chopped
1 carrot, chopped
1 celery rib, chopped

3 bottles imported ale
1 garlic clove, crushed
½ tsp. dried thyme
1 bay leaf, crumbled
1 Tb. tomato paste
2 Tb. arrowroot

*P*reheat oven to 350°.
Season meat all over with salt and pepper to taste. Heat the oil in a large heavy casserole over moderate heat, add meat, and brown evenly on all sides. Add vegetables, sauté for 2 minutes, then pour 2 bottles of the ale over the meat. Add garlic, thyme, bay leaf, and tomato paste, stir well, cover, and braise for 2 hours or till meat is cooked medium-rare, adding part or all of the third bottle of ale as cooking liquid reduces.

Transfer roast to a heated platter and let stand for 15 minutes. When ready to serve, strain cooking liquid into a saucepan, add arrowroot, bring liquid to the boil, and reduce sauce till slightly thickened.

Serve meat in slices with sauce on the side.

Barbecued Brisket of Beef

After years of steady failure, I've just stopped trying to reproduce the authentic barbecued brisket Texans smoke in huge pits over mesquite, just as I'd never attempt to produce the hickory-smoked pork barbecue I travel hundreds of miles every year to eat in North Carolina. Second best, however, is this brisket barbecued in the oven, which allows the meat to cook slowly a long time in order to absorb the sauce.

1 Tb. salt
1 Tb. freshly ground pepper
1 Tb. dry mustard
1 Tb. paprika
4-lb. brisket of beef
8 Tb. (1 stick) butter

2 Tb. vegetable oil
¼ cup Worcestershire
1½ cups white vinegar
1 tsp. sugar
Tabasco

Preheat oven to 300°.

Combine salt, pepper, dry mustard, and paprika in a small bowl, mix well, and rub mixture thoroughly and evenly into both sides of the meat.

Heat one-half of the butter and the oil in a large heavy skillet till very hot, add meat, and sear quickly on both sides. Transfer meat to a large roasting pan lined with enough foil to fold completely over meat.

While meat is searing, combine remaining butter, the Worcestershire, vinegar, sugar, and plenty of Tabasco in a saucepan, bring to the boil, lower heat, and simmer for 5–10 minutes, stirring.

Pour sauce over meat, fold foil snugly around meat, place pan in the oven, and cook for 4 hours. Remove pan from oven, fold foil back and tuck around the sides of the pan, return pan to the oven, and cook meat for 1 hour longer, adding a little water if sauce dries up and basting meat from time to time with the liquid.

Serve brisket in thick slices with plenty of fresh cole slaw, sliced onions, Jalapeño Cornbread (p. 436), and ice-cold beer.

Short Ribs of Beef with Olives

Serves 4–6

Unless you're lucky enough to have a butcher who will custom-cut large, meaty, short ribs, you will almost have to live in the South to prepare this earthy dish. Frankly, the anemic ribs found in most supermarkets throughout the rest of the U.S. are nothing less than a disgrace. And by large, meaty short ribs, I mean ribs at least 4 inches wide and 3 inches thick. Serve these succulent beauties with a Squash Soufflé (p. 360), tart salad with chunks of feta cheese, and plenty of fresh biscuits.

6 meaty short ribs of beef
Salt and freshly ground pepper
12 small whole onions
10 small red potatoes, peeled

4-oz. jar green olives
1 large can whole tomatoes
Beef Stock (p. 522)

Place short ribs in a large saucepan with enough water to cover and add salt and pepper to taste. Bring water to the boil, lower heat, cover, and simmer for 3 hours, adding more water if necessary. During the last hour of simmering, add onions. During the last 30 minutes, add potatoes and olives.

Preheat oven to 375°.

Transfer meat to a shallow baking dish with a slotted spoon, place onions, potatoes, and olives around meat, and add tomatoes and their juices. If juice does not fill baking dish by three-quarters, add a little beef stock. Salt and pepper the dish to taste and bake for about 45 minutes, basting.

Picadillo
(Caribbean Beef Stew)

What *boeuf bourguignonne* is to France and Lancaster Hot Pot is to England, *picadillo* is to Mexico and the Caribbean islands. The character of the spicy stew varies from island to island, but one of the best I've encountered was served on St. Lucia.

3 Tb. vegetable oil	*3 tomatoes, coarsely chopped*
2 lbs. lean beef chuck, cut into	*½ cup raisins*
1-inch cubes	*¼ tsp. ground cloves*
2 medium onions, chopped	*¼ tsp. ground cinnamon*
2 garlic cloves, finely chopped	*1 hot chili pepper, seeded and*
1 large green bell pepper, chopped	*finely chopped*
Salt and freshly ground pepper	
4-oz. jar stuffed green olives,	
rinsed	

*H*eat oil in a large casserole, add beef, and brown on all sides over moderate heat. Add onions, garlic, green pepper, and salt and pepper to taste, stir, and continue cooking till vegetables are soft. Add water to cover, bring liquid to the boil, lower heat, cover, and simmer for 1 hour.

Add olives, tomatoes, raisins, cloves, cinnamon, and hot pepper to casserole, stir well, cover, and continue simmering for 30 minutes longer, stirring occasionally. Taste for salt.

Serve stew with hot cooked rice.

Paupiettes de Boeuf à la Moutarde
(Beef Rolls with Mustard Sauce)

Serves 6–8

2 Tb. butter

2 large onions, one finely chopped,
   the other sliced

⅓ lb. lean ground veal

⅓ lb. ground pork

¼ lb. fresh pork fat, finely chopped

1 egg, beaten

1 garlic clove, minced

⅓ cup finely chopped parsley

Pinch each of dried thyme and
   allspice

Salt and freshly ground pepper

3-lb. top round roast, trimmed of
   all fat

2 Tb. vegetable oil

1 carrot, sliced

3 Tb. flour

1½ cups bouillon

1 cup dry white wine

Herb bouquet (8 sprigs parsley, 1
   bay leaf, ½ tsp. dried thyme,
   and 2 garlic cloves tied in
   cheesecloth)

1 Tb. Dijon mustard

½ cup heavy cream

Chopped parsley for garnish

*H*eat 1 tablespoon of the butter in a small skillet, add the chopped onion, and sauté over low heat for 2 minutes. Transfer onion to a mixing bowl, add veal, pork, pork fat, egg, garlic, parsley, thyme, allspice, and salt and pepper to taste, and blend stuffing thoroughly.

Cut roast into 12–16 slices, place slices between wax paper, and flatten with a mallet. Season slices with salt and pepper to taste, spread equal amounts of stuffing on each slice, roll up slices, and tie rolls with string.

Preheat oven to 325°.

Heat remaining tablespoon of butter plus the oil in a large ovenproof casserole, add beef rolls in batches, brown on all sides over high heat, and transfer to a platter. Reduce heat to low, add remaining sliced onion and the carrot to the casserole, and sauté for 5 minutes. Increase heat to moderate, add flour, stir, and cook mixture till browned, stirring constantly. Add bouillon, wine, and herb bouquet, and stir. Add the beef rolls, and, if necessary, enough water to just cover. Bring to the boil, cover casserole, transfer to the oven, and bake *paupiettes* for about 1½ hours or till tender.

Transfer *paupiettes* to a heated platter and remove strings. Strain liquid from casserole into a saucepan, bring to the boil, and reduce to about 1½ cups. Remove saucepan from heat, add mustard, cream, and pepper to taste, and stir till well blended. Reheat sauce, pour over *paupiettes,* garnish tops with chopped parsley, and serve immediately.

Bourbon Beef and Oyster Pot

Serves 6–8

This is but one of the highly original dishes created by Pearl Byrd Foster, past owner of the lamented Mr. and Mrs. Foster's Place in New York and the lady who taught me so much about American cookery. My only contribution to this dish is that I was the one who named it during a memorable lunch in mid-Atlantic aboard the *Queen Elizabeth 2* when Pearl and I were sharing a Lancaster Hot Pot and discussing how it could be varied. Serve the dish with simple boiled new potatoes.

4 lbs. beef chuck, top or bottom
   round roast, cut into 1½-inch
   cubes
2 Tb. lemon juice
Salt and freshly ground pepper
4 Tb. vegetable oil
2 Tb. butter
4 oz. Bourbon
4 cups boiling Beef Stock (p. 522)
4 cups boiling water
1 large carrot, scraped and cut
   into 1-inch pieces
2 celery ribs, cut into 1-inch pieces
1 large potato, peeled and cut in
   half

1 medium onion, studded with 2
   cloves
2 Tb. tomato paste
1 small bay leaf
1 garlic clove, crushed
¼ tsp. ground thyme
Tabasco and Worcestershire
36 fresh shucked oysters
   (including their liquor), picked
   for shell
1 oz. Bourbon
½ cup freshly grated horseradish

*D*ry meat thoroughly with paper towels, sprinkle on lemon juice, and let stand for 15 minutes. Season with salt and pepper to taste.

Heat the oil and butter in a large skillet, add the meat in batches, and sauté over moderate heat till golden brown on all sides, transferring each browned batch to a large casserole. Pour the 4 ounces of Bourbon over the browned meat and ignite. When flames die out, pour boiling beef stock and water over beef, discard grease from skillet, deglaze it with a little water, and scrape all browned bits into the meat pot. Add the vegetables, tomato paste, bay leaf, garlic, and thyme, and stir to blend well. Bring liquid to the boil, reduce heat, cover, and simmer for about 3 hours or till meat is tender.

Transfer meat to a platter, pour liquid and vegetables into a blender (in batches, if necessary), and reduce to a puree. If too thick, add extra beef stock. Season sauce with salt, pepper, Tabasco, and Worcestershire to taste, return to the pot, add meat, and stir.

When ready to serve, heat beef till bubbly, add oysters plus their liquor, and heat just till edges of oysters curl. Warm the 1 ounce of Bourbon, pour over beef, and flame. Serve with the grated horseradish on the side.

Meat Loaf with Piquant Mushroom Sauce

Nothing is more delicious (or underestimated) than a well-prepared meat loaf, especially one enhanced by a good sauce made from scratch. Since I've found that the standard mixture of ground beef round, pork, and veal produces a loaf much too dry and bland for my taste, I always use nothing but ground chuck and sausage for both moist texture and zesty flavor. (If you grind your own pork sausage as I do, be sure to add a little ground fennel.) Yes, this combination produces lots of fat, which should be discarded. Do not substitute tomato paste for the catsup since it's the vinegar in the catsup that gives the sauce its piquancy.

2 lbs. ground beef chuck
¾ lb. spicy pork sausage or
    Italian sweet sausage links
    (casings removed)
1 onion, finely chopped
1 celery rib, finely chopped
1 large garlic clove, minced
½ tsp. dried thyme
½ tsp. dried crushed bay leaf
1 Tb. chopped fresh dill

¼ cup tomato catsup
2 eggs
2 slices of white bread, toasted
1 tsp. salt
Tabasco and freshly ground pepper
2 cups Beef Stock (p. 522)
3 Tb. tomato catsup
1 cup finely chopped mushrooms
Watercress for garnish

*P*reheat oven to 375°.
    Combine chuck, sausage, onion, and celery in a large mixing bowl and mix lightly with hands. Add garlic, herbs, the ¼ cup catsup, and eggs and mix again thoroughly. Crumble toast finely over mixture, add salt and Tabasco and pepper to taste, and continue mixing till all ingredients are well blended.

Pack mixture tightly into a 1½-quart loaf dish and bake for 1½ hours or till nicely browned on top.

Shortly before loaf is finished baking, bring stock to the boil in a saucepan, add the 3 tablespoons catsup, stir, and reduce slightly. Add mushrooms, reduce heat to moderate, and cook for about 5 minutes or till sauce is reduced to desired consistency.

To serve, transfer meat loaf from dish to paper towels to drain momentarily, then place loaf on a heated serving platter garnished with watercress. Serve meat loaf sliced, with sauce on the side.

Frikadellar
(Swedish Meat Balls with Dilled Sour Cream Sauce)

Serves 6

Although my Swedish grandmother saw to it that *frikadellar* played as important a role in my childhood diet as country ham and Greek beans, I must say her meat balls were not on the same level as these savory morsels prepared by Mr. and Mrs. Jack Rees at a March of Dimes Gourmet Gala in Kansas City, where I served as a food judge. The bone marrow does add delectable flavor and moisture, but if you don't have a butcher who's willing to split a few marrow bones, I've found that two slices of finely diced bacon makes an interesting substitution. These are great served with buttered noodles and an exotic composed salad.

2 Tb. bread crumbs	Salt and freshly ground pepper
½ cup half-and-half	2 eggs, beaten
½ lb. beef chuck	3 Tb. butter
½ lb. lean pork	2 Tb. vegetable oil
½ lb. lean veal	2 Tb. flour
4 Tb. finely diced beef marrow	1 cup Beef Stock (p. 522) or
2 Tb. butter	canned bouillon
½ cup finely chopped onions	½ cup sour cream
1 Tb. finely chopped shallots	2 Tb. finely chopped fresh dill
½ tsp. finely chopped garlic	¼ tsp. lemon juice
1 tsp. grated lemon rind	⅛ tsp. cayenne
2 Tb. finely chopped parsley	Chopped fresh dill for garnish
½ tsp. dried thyme	

*P*lace bread crumbs in a small bowl with the half-and-half and let soak while grinding the meats.

Grind meats together twice in a meat grinder (do not use a food processor) or chop very finely by hand and place in a large mixing bowl. Add soaked bread crumbs and marrow and mix thoroughly.

Heat the 2 tablespoons of butter in a small skillet, add onions, shallots, and garlic, sauté over low heat for 5 minutes, and add to the meat mixture. Add lemon rind, parsley, thyme, salt and pepper to taste, and eggs, and mix thoroughly with hands or a wooden spoon till meat loses its granular texture. In the palms of your hands, form meat into 1½-inch balls, place on a large platter lined with wax paper, cover with another sheet of paper, and chill for 1 hour.

Heat the 3 tablespoons of butter and the oil in a large heavy skillet over high heat, and when fat begins to sputter, drop in enough meat balls to cover about three-quarters of the bottom of the skillet. At once, slide the pan back and forth so the meat balls brown evenly, reduce heat to moderate, and cook for 6 – 7 minutes or till balls are cooked through completely and nicely browned. Transfer balls to paper towels and continue cooking remaining balls in like manner. When drained, transfer balls to a heated serving casserole.

Pour all but 3 tablespoons of fat from skillet, reduce heat to low, stir in the flour with a whisk, and cook the roux slowly for 2 minutes, stirring constantly. Add stock, raise heat to moderate, stir with the whisk, and cook till sauce is thickened and smooth. Add sour cream a tablespoon at a time, continuing to stir. Add dill, lemon juice, salt and pepper to taste, and cayenne, stir, and pour hot sauce over meat balls in the casserole. Sprinkle the top with chopped dill and serve immediately.

Bourbon Burgers with Wild Mushrooms

Serves 4

1 oz. dried Boletus mushrooms
   (cèpes or porcini)
8 Tb. (1 stick) butter
2 slices white bread, crusts removed
3 Tb. milk
3 onions, finely chopped
1 garlic clove, finely chopped
1½ lbs. ground beef sirloin

2 eggs
Salt and freshly ground pepper
½ cup bread crumbs
2 ripe tomatoes, cored, seeded,
   and chopped
3 Tb. Bourbon
Pinch of dried thyme
Tabasco

Soak dried mushrooms in 1 cup of warm water for 30 minutes, pick for grit, rinse, pat dry, and chop coarsely. Strain mushroom liquor through triple cheesecloth and set aside.

Heat 2 tablespoons of the butter in a heavy skillet, add mushrooms, sauté over moderate heat for about 10 minutes, and transfer to a plate.

Place bread and milk in a bowl and let stand.

Heat another tablespoon of the butter in the same skillet, add one-third of the onions and all the garlic, sauté for 3 minutes over moderate heat, stirring, and mix into softened bread. Transfer mixture to a large bowl, add ground beef, 1 egg, and salt and pepper to taste, and mix thoroughly.

Divide meat into 4 balls, make a hole in the center of each, fill holes with equal amounts of chopped mushrooms, fold meat over stuffing, and carefully press meat down into oval burgers. Beat second egg with 1 teaspoon of water, brush egg glaze over each burger, and coat burgers with bread crumbs.

Heat another 2 tablespoons of butter in the skillet, add remaining onions, tomatoes, Bourbon, thyme, Tabasco to taste, and 3 tablespoons of the mushroom liquor, and sauté over moderate heat till only a little liquid remains.

Heat remaining butter in a large, heavy skillet, add burgers, and sauté over moderate heat on both sides till crusts are golden brown. Transfer burgers to a heated serving platter and top with the sauce.

Alsatian Baeckeffe
(Mixed Meat Stew)

Serves 6

This husky stew can be made without marinating the ingredients a full day, but believe me, it will not taste half as good. If you can't locate a pig's foot, double the amount of oxtail.

1 lb. pork butt, trimmed
1 lb. beef shoulder, trimmed
1 lb. lamb shoulder, trimmed
½ lb. chorizo *or Polish kielbasa sausage, sliced thick*
1 pig's foot
Herb bouquet (¼ tsp. each dried thyme and rosemary, 1 bay leaf, and 2 sprigs parsley wrapped in cheesecloth)

2 whites of leeks, sliced lengthwise and washed thoroughly
2 medium onions, chopped
Salt and freshly ground pepper
1 bottle Riesling wine
1 Tb. red wine vinegar
5 all-purpose potatoes, sliced ¼ inch thick and soaked in cold water

Combine all the meats in a large stainless-steel or glass mixing bowl. Add herb bouquet, leeks, and onions, season with salt and pepper to taste, and mix ingredients together with hands. Add wine, vinegar, and enough water to cover, cover with plastic wrap, and let marinate in the refrigerator for at least 24 hours.

Preheat oven to 350°.

Layer one-half of the potatoes in a large casserole, arrange meats and vegetables on top, then layer remaining potatoes. Cover casserole tightly and bake for 3½ hours.

To serve, place helpings of potatoes in wide soup bowls, carve meats and distribute over potatoes, then add more potatoes and a little of the broth to each bowl. Serve stew with fresh horseradish, Belgium endives vinaigrette, and either chilled Riesling or Gewürztraminer.

Stuffed Saddle of Veal

This is a ceremonial, expensive dish intended to be presented on a festive buffet. The stuffed saddle should be allowed to rest a good fifteen minutes before carving. The roast is also delicious served cold.

8 Tb. (1 stick) butter
¼ lb. lean veal shoulder, cubed
¼ lb. lean pork shoulder, cubed
1 onion, sliced
½ lb. mushrooms, sliced
1 lb. fresh spinach, trimmed and washed thoroughly
2 garlic cloves, crushed

¼ tsp. thyme
Salt and freshly ground pepper
2 eggs, beaten
1½ cups bread crumbs
1 saddle of veal, boned (ordered in advance from butcher)
1 large piece of caul fat (available at butcher shops)

*H*eat 4 tablespoons of the butter in a large, heavy skillet, add cubed veal and pork, sauté on all sides over moderate heat for about 5 minutes, and transfer to a plate. Add 2 more tablespoons of the butter to the skillet, add onion and mushrooms, reduce heat, sauté for 2 minutes, and add onion and mushrooms to sautéed meats. Add remaining butter to the skillet, add spinach and garlic, and sauté till spinach is completely wilted.

Preheat oven to 400°.

Pass all sautéed ingredients through the fine blade of a meat grinder into a large mixing bowl, add thyme, salt and pepper to taste, eggs, and bread crumbs, and mix well. Stuff mixture into the saddle of veal, tie securely with butcher's twine, wrap roast in caul fat, place saddle in a large roasting pan, and roast for 1¼ hours.

Medallions of Veal with Black Caviar

Serves 4

This elegant dish was created specially for *Town & Country* by chef Larry Forgione, owner of An American Place in New York, when I did a feature introducing domestic caviar to our readers. Domestic sturgeon caviar is a fraction of the price of imported Russian or Iranian and can be equally as delicate. At even less cost, you could substitute domestic red salmon caviar. Personally, I prefer to reduce the amount of cream to 1½ cups.

8 Tb. (1 stick) unsalted butter
1 medium onion, sliced thick
½ tsp. freshly ground pepper
2 oz. white wine vinegar
6 oz. dry white wine
2 cups Veal Stock (p. 523) or
*   Chicken Stock (p. 521)*

2 cups heavy cream
1 loin of veal, well-trimmed and
*   cut into 8 3-oz. medallions*
About ¼ cup sour cream, room
*   temperature*
4 oz. domestic sturgeon caviar
½ bunch chopped parsley

Heat one-third of the butter in a stainless-steel or enameled skillet, add onion, and sauté over low heat for 2 minutes. Add the pepper and vinegar, increase heat to moderate, and reduce slightly. Add wine, reduce by half, add stock, and reduce to a syrup. Add cream and reduce till just thickened. Strain sauce through a fine sieve and keep hot.

In another skillet, heat remaining butter, add veal medallions, and sauté over moderate heat for 4 – 5 minutes on each side. Transfer 2 medallions to each of 4 hot serving plates, pour equal amounts of sauce over each medallion, and grind on a little pepper to taste.

To serve, top each medallion first with a teaspoon of sour cream, then with ½ ounce of caviar. Sprinkle tops with chopped parsley and serve immediately.

Veal Birds

As a youngster in France, I thought these little roll-ups quaintly called *oiseaux sans tête* ("headless birds") were the ultimate in French cuisine. I'd like to believe my culinary education has progressed a bit since those innocent, mythical days, but from time to time I still fix these "birds" and enjoy them as much as ever. This dish can be baked in advance and reheated.

½ lb. bulk sausage
1 cup finely chopped onions
2 garlic cloves, minced
1 tsp. dried thyme
½ tsp. ground dried fennel
½ tsp. crushed dried rosemary
1 cup bread crumbs
2 eggs, beaten
2 Tb. chopped parsley
Salt and freshly ground pepper

4 Tb. (½ stick) butter
2 ripe tomatoes
1 cup finely chopped mushrooms
1½ cups Beef Stock (p. 522) or bouillon
1 bay leaf
6 veal cutlets (about 1½ lbs.)
¼ cup dry white wine
Chopped parsley for garnish

*F*ry sausage in a small skillet till brown, breaking up with a fork, drain on paper towels, and place in a mixing bowl. Add half the onions, half the garlic, half the thyme, the fennel, rosemary, bread crumbs, eggs, parsley, and salt and pepper to taste. Mix all ingredients thoroughly and set filling aside.

Heat half the butter in another skillet, add remaining onions and garlic, and sauté over low heat for 2 minutes. Add remaining thyme, the tomatoes, mushrooms, stock, and bay leaf, increase heat slightly, and simmer sauce, stirring, for 10 – 15 minutes.

Preheat oven to 350°.

Meanwhile, place cutlets between sheets of wax paper and pound lightly with a mallet till quite thin. Spread cutlets on a flat surface, add equal amounts of filling to the center of each, roll meat over filling, tucking in edges, and tie birds with string.

Heat remaining butter in a large, enameled baking dish, add birds, and brown on all sides over moderate heat. Add wine and sauce, cover dish with foil, and bake for 1 hour.

When ready to serve, remove string and sprinkle tops of birds with chopped parsley.

Grilled Veal Chops with Basil Cream and Mustard Sauce

Serves 4

The Remington in Houston is not only one of the finest hotels in the country but also boasts a very innovative grill room. When I was served this veal chop flanked by fresh oyster mushrooms one day at lunch, I waited around for two hours to get the recipe. I suppose standard button mushrooms could be used, but since both oyster and *shiitake* mushrooms are more and more readily available at specialty food markets and green grocers, you really should try to find them.

8 Tb. (1 stick) butter
2 Tb. finely chopped shallots
2 cups dry white wine
1 bunch fresh basil, leaves pureed
   in a food processor
½ cup Veal Stock (p. 523)
Salt and freshly ground pepper
2 Tb. brandy

1 Tb. Dijon mustard
1 cup heavy cream
2 Tb. olive oil
4 thick veal chops
2 scallions (whites only), minced
½ lb. fresh oyster or shiitake
   mushrooms
4 fresh basil leaves for garnish

*H*eat 1 tablespoon of the butter in a medium skillet, add shallots, and sauté over moderate heat for 1 minute. Add wine and basil and cook till basil begins to darken. Add veal stock, stir, increase heat, and reduce to about ½ cup. Strain liquid through a fine sieve into a saucepan, add salt and pepper to taste, brandy, mustard, and cream, and cook, stirring, over moderate heat till sauce is slightly thickened and smooth. Add 2 tablespoons of the butter, whisk till well incorporated, and keep sauce warm.

Heat olive oil in a large heavy skillet till hot, add chops, and sauté for about 6 minutes on each side. Transfer to a heated platter.

While chops are cooking, heat 1 tablespoon of the butter in a small skillet, add scallions, and sauté over low heat, stirring, for about 2 minutes. Heat remaining butter in a medium skillet, add mushrooms, and sauté over moderate heat for 5–7 minutes, stirring steadily so they don't burn.

Spoon equal amounts of the sauce on the bottom of 4 heated serving plates, place a chop in the center of each, and sprinkle equal amounts of the sautéed scallions over each chop. Add equal amounts of the mushrooms to one side of each plate, arrange a basil leaf on top of each chop, and serve immediately.

Stuffed Veal Cutlets with Mustard Sauce

Serves 4

Nothing could be more stylish yet simple to prepare than these thin, zesty cutlets which, if necessary, can be stuffed in advance. Serve with Artichoke Pilaf (p. 396) and broiled tomato halves topped with fresh chopped herbs.

8 thin veal cutlets (about 1 lb.)	Salt and freshly ground pepper
8 Tb. (1 stick) butter	1 Tb. vegetable oil
1 small onion, minced	2 Tb. Cognac
1 lb. mushrooms, minced	1 cup heavy cream
¼ tsp. dried summer savory	1 Tb. Dijon mustard

*P*lace cutlets between sheets of wax paper and flatten with a mallet till very thin.

Heat one-half of the butter in a skillet, add onion, and sauté over low heat for 2 minutes. Increase heat to moderate, add mushrooms, summer savory, and salt and pepper to taste, and sauté, stirring, till mushrooms are almost golden.

Spoon equal amounts of the mushroom mixture onto the centers of the cutlets and fold edges of cutlets snugly over mixture. Heat remaining butter plus the oil in a large skillet, add stuffed cutlets, and sauté over moderate heat for 2–3 minutes on each side or till golden. Transfer cutlets to a heated serving platter and keep warm.

Add the Cognac to the skillet and ignite. When flames subside, scrape brown bits from sides and bottom of skillet into the brandy, then pour mixture into a saucepan. Add cream and mustard, heat to moderate, and beat mixture with a whisk for 7–8 minutes or till cream is reduced and thick.

Taste sauce for salt and pepper, pour over cutlets, and serve immediately.

Veal Cutlets with Pumpkin Sauce

Serves 6

6-lb. pumpkin
2 Tb. melted butter
Salt
4 Tb. (½ stick) butter
1 shallot, minced

1 garlic clove, minced
6 medium veal cutlets
¾ cup heavy cream
Freshly ground pepper

Preheat oven to 350°.
Cut pumpkin in half, scoop out seeds and membrane, wash and dry seeds, and discard membrane. Place pumpkin in a large baking dish, scatter seeds on a baking sheet, and bake both for about 1½ hours or till pumpkin is tender and seeds are crunchy. Drizzle seeds with the 2 tablespoons of melted butter, sprinkle with salt to taste, toss lightly, and set aside. Spoon pulp from pumpkin, place in a food processor, reduce to a puree, and set aside.

Heat 2 tablespoons of the butter in a large skillet, add shallot and garlic, and sauté over low heat for 2 minutes. Pound veal cutlets slightly between wax paper while vegetables are sautéing, add 3 cutlets to the skillet, increase heat to moderate, sauté cutlets for 2 minutes on each side or till golden, and transfer to a heated platter. Add remaining butter to skillet, sauté remaining cutlets, and transfer to the platter.

Add 1 cup of the pumpkin puree to the skillet, scrape bottom and sides of skillet with a wooden spoon, and reserve remaining puree for another use. Add cream to puree in skillet, season with pepper to taste, stir, bring sauce almost to the boil, and strain through a sieve over the cutlets.

Sprinkle ½ cup of the pumpkin seeds over sauced cutlets and reserve remaining seeds for another use.

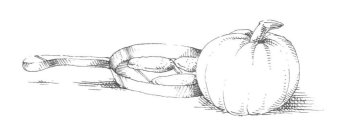

Braised Veal Fillets with Onion Sauce

Serves 4

One of this country's more advanced centers of culinary learning is located at Johnson & Wales College in Providence, Rhode Island, and one of the more interesting testing grounds for the new creative style of American cookery is the college's Plantations Room restaurant. For this elegant dish, the students use the exceptionally sweet Vidalia onion from Georgia, but I've found that the large white Bermuda works perfectly well.

1 lb. white Bermuda onions,
* finely diced*
1 pt. half-and-half
6 Tb. (¾ stick) butter
4 Tb. flour
Salt and freshly ground pepper
¼ cup brown sugar
¼ cup finely chopped shallots
1 cup Veal Stock (p. 523)

1 cup Port
12 2½-oz. veal tenderloin fillets
12 strips bacon
1 cup flour mixed with salt and
* freshly ground pepper to taste*
3 Tb. vegetable oil
¼ cup Port
4 small bunches red grapes for
* garnish*

Combine onions and half-and-half in a saucepan, bring almost to the boil, lower heat, and poach onions for about 5 minutes. Transfer mixture to a blender and reduce to a puree. Heat 4 tablespoons of the butter in another saucepan, add flour, and cook over moderate heat, whisking for 3 minutes. Add onion mixture, stir, bring to the boil, and season with salt and pepper to taste. Keep warm.

Heat remaining butter in a saucepan, add brown sugar, stir, and cook over moderate heat till sugar has caramelized. Add shallots, stock, and wine, bring to the boil, reduce heat, and simmer for 15 minutes. Keep wine sauce warm.

Preheat oven to 400°.

Wrap veal fillets with bacon, secure with toothpicks, and dredge lightly in the seasoned flour. Heat oil in a large skillet, add fillets, and fry till bacon is crisped. Transfer fillets to a large casserole, remove toothpicks, and pour grease from skillet. Deglaze skillet with the ¼ cup Port wine, add the wine sauce, stir, and pour mixture over fillets. Place casserole in the oven and braise fillets for 10 minutes.

Coat 4 heated dinner plates with the onion sauce, place 3 fillets on top of sauce in each plate, and top each fillet with a little of the wine sauce in which meat was braised. Garnish each plate with a small bunch of grapes and serve immediately.

Coach House Rack of Lamb

Serves 2

Although I must have consumed more racks of lamb in my travels than any other main course, I've yet to come across one that equals the simple seven-rib beauty served for decades at The Coach House in New York. The rack must be trimmed completely of all fat, and by no means decide to coat it in bread crumbs. The real secret (which most other restaurants have yet to learn) is that the meat is roasted very quickly at very high temperature. If you have room in the oven, the recipe can be easily doubled.

1 rack of baby lamb (6 or 7 ribs)   *Salt and freshly ground pepper*
1 tsp. fresh lemon juice   *2 tsp. minced fresh parsley*
1 tsp. olive oil   *¼ lemon*
1 garlic clove, crushed   *Watercress for garnish*
1 tsp. crushed dried rosemary

*H*ave the butcher crack the chine bone of rack, remove all fat from the meat, and French-cut the bones (removing about 1 inch of meat from the end of the ribs).

Preheat oven to 500°.

Rub the rack all over with lemon juice and oil, rub with crushed garlic (discarding garlic when finished), then rub lightly with rosemary.

Heat a large, heavy skillet till very hot, add rack, and sear quickly on both sides.

Transfer rack to a large roasting pan, season with salt and pepper to taste, rub well with the parsley, and roast for 10 minutes. Turn meat over and continue roasting for 5 – 7 minutes or till lamb is crusty brown on the outside but still rare and juicy inside.

Transfer rack to a heated serving platter and squeeze lemon half over meat. Carve into chops of 1 or 2 bones each, and garnish platter with watercress. Serve with Potatoes and Squash Anna (p. 380) or Vegetable Ragout (p. 362).

Assyrian Rack of Lamb

Serves 4 or 5

One of the few times I ever set foot into a health food store was to purchase pomegranate juice in order to reproduce this delicious rack of lamb served at Narsai's in Kensington, California. The pomegranate juice is truly what gives the dish its unique flavor, but if you have no access to a health food store or Middle Eastern market, you can obtain somewhat similar results by using another cup of red wine and a few strips of lemon peel. Note that the lamb first must be marinated at least six hours.

2 racks of lamb (8 or 9 ribs apiece)	*½ tsp. salt*
2 large onions, coarsely chopped	*½ tsp. freshly ground pepper*
6 garlic cloves, peeled	*1 cup pomegranate juice*
2 tsp, finely chopped fresh basil leaves	*½ cup dry red wine*

*H*ave the butcher remove the flap meat from the racks, French-cut the rib bones, and trim off all but a very thin layer of fat.

Place onions, garlic, basil, salt, and pepper in a food processor and reduce to a puree. Add pomegranate juice and wine, and run machine just long enough to blend all ingredients.

Place lamb in a shallow glass dish or enameled pan, rub well with the pomegranate marinade, pour remaining marinade over the meat, and let marinate at cool room temperature for 6 – 8 hours.

Preheat oven to 450°.

Wipe excess marinade off lamb, place racks in a large shallow roasting pan, and roast for 15 minutes for rare lamb.

Lamb Steaks with Dilled Cream Sauce

Serves 6 – 8

8 Tb. (1 stick) butter
4 cups sliced mushroom stems
3 bay leaves, crushed
2 tsp. Worcestershire
½ cup brandy
2 cups heavy cream

Salt and freshly ground pepper
3-lb. loin of lamb, cut into 12 4-
  oz. steaks
¼ cup dry white wine
2 Tb. chopped fresh dill

*H*eat one-half of the butter in a large skillet, add mushrooms and bay leaves, and sauté over moderate heat till mushrooms begin to darken. Add Worcestershire and stir.

Warm brandy, pour over mushrooms, and ignite, shaking pan constantly till flames subside. Add cream, increase heat, and boil, stirring, till cream has reduced slightly. Strain sauce into a saucepan, discard mushrooms, season sauce with salt and pepper to taste, and keep warm.

Heat remaining butter in another large skillet, add steaks, and cook over moderate heat for 3 minutes on each side. Transfer steaks to a plate as they cook.

Add wine to skillet and deglaze over high heat, stirring and scraping brown bits from the bottom. Add the cream sauce to the pan juices, add dill, stir, and heat thoroughly. Add steaks to sauce to heat through, transfer steaks to a heated serving platter, and pour sauce on top.

Barbara Kafka's Lamb Medallions with Mint and Tomatoes

Serves 4–6

Although my friend and colleague Barbara Kafka is perhaps best known as one of this country's most respected and talented food and restaurant consultants, she also happens to be a very creative chef who champions the cause of refined American cookery with intelligence and sobriety. Serve these easy-to-prepare, juicy medallions with fresh noodles and the finest vintage cabernet you can find.

2 racks of lamb
4 Tb. (½ stick) unsalted butter
2 tsp. finely chopped garlic
2 Tb. finely chopped shallots
1 cup peeled, seeded, and coarsely chopped ripe tomatoes

14 fresh mint leaves
2 Tb. fresh lemon juice
2 tsp. coarse salt
Freshly ground pepper

Cut the center "eyes" from the racks so you have 2 long cylinders of lamb. Cut each cylinder into 4 equal pieces about 1 inch thick and refrigerate while preparing stock.

Trim and discard the fat from the bones and place bones and any meat trimmings in a kettle. Add water to cover, bring to the boil, lower heat, and simmer for 1 hour, skimming as needed. Strain stock into a large saucepan, bring to the boil, and reduce by half.

Heat the butter in a large skillet, add garlic and shallots, and sauté over moderate heat for 30 seconds. Add lamb medallions in a single layer and cook till lightly browned on both sides. Add tomatoes and cook for 1–2 minutes. Add mint leaves and cook for another minute. Add lemon juice, salt, pepper to taste, and ½ cup of the lamb stock, and cook for 2–3 minutes longer.

Serve immediately.

Badami Josh
(Lamb with Coconut and Almonds)

Serves 6

This subtle mélange, which I first sampled at Shezan restaurant in London, has got to be one of the most enticing lamb dishes in the entire North Indian repertory. Note that the lamb must be marinated overnight. I've also prepared this recipe with lean bottom round of beef.

2 lbs. boned lamb shoulder
1 lemon, halved and seeded
Salt and freshly ground pepper
1 tsp. saffron threads, steeped 15
    minutes in 1 cup boiling water
1 cup plain yogurt
¼ cup peanut or vegetable oil
2 medium onions, thinly sliced
2 garlic cloves, minced
1 green chili pepper, minced
6 whole cardamom pods, crushed

8 cloves, crushed
2 Tb. ground coriander
1 Tb. ground cumin
½ tsp. ground turmeric
2-inch stick of cinnamon
1 Tb. finely chopped fresh coconut
3 Tb. tomato paste
1 cup canned unsweetened
    coconut milk
¼ cup blanched almonds

Trim lamb of all fat, cut into 1-inch cubes, and place in a large glass or stainless-steel bowl. Squeeze juice from lemon halves over the lamb, season with salt and pepper to taste, and toss well.

Combine the saffron, saffron water, and yogurt in a bowl, mix well, pour over lamb, toss again, cover, and let marinate in the refrigerator overnight.

Heat the oil in a large heavy saucepan, lift lamb from the marinade with a slotted spoon and add to saucepan, and brown on all sides over moderate heat. Add onions and garlic, stir, and continue cooking for 2–3 minutes. Add chili pepper, spices, tomato paste, and coconut, stir well, and cook for 5 minutes longer. Add the marinade and coconut milk, stir well, bring to the boil, lower heat, and simmer for 30 minutes or till lamb is tender.

Add the blanched almonds, stir well, and cook stew for 5 minutes longer. Serve over boiled dry rice.

Arni Kapama

(Spicy Greek Lamb Stew)

Serves 4 – 6

8 Tb. (1 stick) butter
2 medium onions, chopped
2 garlic cloves, minced
1 Tb. olive oil
2 lbs. lean boneless lamb, cut into
    1-inch cubes
Salt and freshly ground pepper
2 bay leaves

1 stick cinnamon, broken in half
3 cloves
½ tsp. dried rosemary
8-oz. can tomato sauce
16-oz. can whole tomatoes
1 cup white wine
1 lb. macaroni
½ lb. feta cheese

*H*eat 2 tablespoons of the butter in a large, heavy skillet, add onions and garlic, and sauté over low heat for 2 minutes. Add 2 more tablespoons of the butter plus the oil to the skillet and increase heat to moderate. Season lamb cubes with salt and pepper to taste, add to skillet, and sauté for 3 minutes, turning.

Add bay leaves, cinnamon, cloves, rosemary, tomato sauce, tomatoes, and white wine, and stir well. Cover skillet, reduce heat, and simmer for 1 hour or till lamb is tender, adding water to cover if necessary.

Boil macaroni according to package directions, drain in a colander, and arrange half on a heated platter. Crumble a little feta on top, add remaining macaroni, and crumble on a little more cheese.

Melt remaining butter in a small saucepan, pour over macaroni, then arrange lamb with its juices on top, crumbling on the remaining cheese or to taste.

Crown Roast of Pork with Sausage, Apricot, and Prune Stuffing

Serves at least 10

9-lb. crown of pork, rib ends only
1 Tb. ground sage
1 Tb. dried thyme
3 garlic cloves, crushed
2 Tb. flour

½ cup dry white wine
½ cup Chicken Stock (p. 521)
1 cup heavy cream
1 Tb. Dijon mustard
Freshly ground pepper

STUFFING:

2 lbs. bulk sausage
½ cup diced onions
½ cup diced celery
2 garlic cloves, minced
½ cup chopped pitted prunes
1 cup soft bread crumbs
2 Tb. light brown sugar

½ cup chopped parsley
½ tsp. ground sage
½ tsp. ground cinnamon
1½ tsp. salt
Freshly ground pepper to taste
1 egg, beaten
¼ cup chopped dried apricots

Have a butcher French-cut the bones (removing about 1 inch of meat from end of ribs) and score the fat in diamonds on the crown of pork.

Preheat oven to 400°.

Wrap tips of bones in foil, rub meat with the sage, thyme, and garlic, and set crown on a rack in a large roasting pan. Roast for 20 minutes, reduce heat to 325°, and continue roasting for 1¼ hours.

Meanwhile prepare the stuffing:

In a large skillet, fry sausage till brown, breaking up with a fork, drain on paper towels, and pour all but 3 tablespoons of fat from skillet. Add onions, celery, and garlic to skillet, reduce heat, and sauté for 3 minutes, stirring. Place sausage, onions, celery, and garlic in a large mixing bowl, add remaining stuffing ingredients, and mix thoroughly.

Remove crown from oven and fill with the stuffing. Return to oven and continue roasting for 1 hour longer, increasing heat to 450° for the last 20 minutes. Transfer roast to a large round serving tray and remove foil from ends of chops, replacing with decorative paper frills.

Pour all but 2 tablespoons of fat from the roasting pan, add flour to pan, and cook over moderate heat for 3 minutes, stirring. Add wine, increase heat, and reduce liquid to about 2 tablespoons. Add stock, cream, mustard, and pepper to taste, stir thoroughly, and continue cooking till gravy is smooth.

To serve, carve 1 chop per person, spoon a little dressing on the plate, and serve sauce separately in a gravy boat.

Pork Tonnato with Capers

Serves 6

Utilizing pork to reproduce the classic Italian *vitello tonnato* (veal with tuna sauce) not only yields a more flavorful and less expensive dish but also is a good way to use up a large pork roast. Remember to slice the pork very thin and to serve the dish at room temperature. A great summer dish.

2 lbs. cold roast loin of pork	*1 cup white wine*
7-oz. can tuna	*1 Tb. water*
5 anchovies, drained	*1 tsp. white vinegar*
1 small onion, minced	*Virgin olive oil*
1 large carrot, scraped and	*Capers*
* finely chopped*	

Slice pork very thin, stack slices on a platter, and set aside while preparing sauce.

In a blender or food processor, combine the tuna, anchovies, onion, carrot, wine, water, and vinegar, and reduce to a puree. With machine running, gradually add enough olive oil to make a smooth paste of desired consistency.

Cover the bottom of an attractive serving platter with half the paste, arrange pork slices over the paste, and spread remaining paste on top of pork. Sprinkle capers over the top.

Pork Chops Stuffed with Wild Mushrooms

Serves 4 – 6

½ oz. dried Boletus mushrooms
(cèpes or porcini)
4 Tb. (½ stick) butter
1 onion, finely chopped
1 small celery rib, finely chopped
1 garlic clove, finely chopped
Pinch of dried sage

1 cup dry bread crumbs
2 sprigs fresh parsley, finely chopped
½ tsp. salt
Freshly ground pepper
4 – 6 loin pork chops, 2 inches thick
3 Tb. vegetable oil
1 cup heavy cream

Soak dried mushrooms in 1 cup of warm water for 30 minutes, pick for grit, rinse, pat dry, and chop finely. Strain mushroom liquor through triple cheesecloth and set aside.

Heat 2 tablespoons of the butter in a large skillet, add mushrooms, and sauté over low heat for about 20 minutes. Add remaining butter to the skillet, add onion, celery, garlic, and sage, and continue sautéing for 5 minutes longer. Stir in the bread crumbs, parsley, salt, and pepper to taste, and mix well.

Cut a deep pocket in fat side of each pork chop, stuff each chop loosely with equal amounts of the mushroom mixture, and secure edges horizontally with small metal skewers. Heat oil in another large skillet, add chops, and brown on both sides over moderately high heat. Add mushroom liquor, bring to the boil, reduce heat to simmer, cover, and cook chops for about 35 minutes or till tender.

Transfer chops to a hot platter, skim fat from skillet, add cream, increase heat, and cook down till slightly thick. Pour sauce over chops and serve immediately.

Pork Chops with Onion and Apple Puree

Serves 4–6

One late fall I traveled to England for the sole purpose of illustrating to readers exactly why this country is anything but a gastronomic desert when it comes to native cookery. One of my most interesting discoveries was Plumber Manor in Dorset, an elegant country house that the Prideaux-Brune family now maintains as a public inn. This is but one of the delectable dishes I was served in the magnificent dining room.

1 onion, chopped
2 cooking apples, peeled, cored,
  and chopped
¼ cup water
Salt and freshly ground pepper

4 Tb. (½ stick) unsalted butter
12 boned pork chops
⅓ cup dry white wine
1 cup Veal Stock (p. 523)
1 cup heavy cream

Combine onion and apples in a large stainless-steel sauce pan and add water. Bring liquid to the boil, lower heat, cover, and simmer for 10 minutes. Pour mixture into a sieve, mash to a puree with the back of a spoon into a bowl, season with salt and pepper to taste, and stir.

Preheat oven to 450°.

Heat one-half of the butter in a large skillet over high heat, add half the pork chops, and brown well on both sides. Repeat with remaining butter and chops, transferring browned chops to a large enameled baking dish. Spoon a thin layer of puree over each chop and bake uncovered, for 10 minutes. Transfer chops to a warm platter and cover.

Add wine to baking dish, deglaze dish over moderate heat, and reduce wine by half. Add stock, bring to the boil, and reduce liquid to about ½ cup. Add cream and cook till sauce begins to thicken.

Spoon a thin layer of sauce on the bottoms of 4–6 heated plates and arrange 2 or 3 chops in the middle of each plate.

Barbecued Pork Ribs

Serves 4 – 6

What makes these ribs a bit different (and gives them a slightly Oriental overtone) is the addition of honey, ginger, and fresh coriander to the marinade. For full flavor, the ribs should be marinated for at least 6 hours, so plan accordingly.

2 medium onions, finely chopped
3 garlic cloves, minced
1 green bell pepper, finely chopped
4 medium ripe tomatoes, chopped
2 cups red wine vinegar
¼ cup honey
½ tsp. dry mustard
½ tsp. ground ginger

¼ cup chopped fresh coriander
(also called cilantro and
Chinese parsley)
Salt, freshly ground pepper, and
Tabasco to taste
4 racks (about 4 lbs.) pork ribs
(spareribs)

*I*n a large stainless-steel saucepan, combine onions, garlic, bell pepper, tomatoes with their juices, and vinegar. Bring to the boil, lower heat, cover, and simmer for 15 minutes. Add all remaining ingredients but the ribs, stir well, and let sit till cooled.

Place ribs in a large glass or stainless-steel container, pour on the marinade, cover with plastic wrap, and let marinate in the refrigerator for 6 – 8 hours, turning and spooning marinade over meat at intervals.

If grilling outdoors, set grill about 5 inches over coals that have turned gray and barbecue the ribs for about 1 hour, turning at intervals. If roasting in the oven, preheat oven to 450°, place ribs on racks in 2 roasting pans, and roast for about 40 minutes or till meat is very tender. (If oven is not large enough to hold 2 pans, roast 2 racks of ribs at a time, wrap first set in foil, and reheat shortly before second set has finished cooking.)

Remove ribs from oven, separate racks into individual ribs with a sharp knife, and serve piping hot.

Pork Hash with Sautéed Apples

Serves 4

3 slices of bacon
1 medium onion, minced
1 garlic clove, crushed
2 tomatoes, peeled, seeded, and
    chopped
1 hot red pepper, seeded and
    chopped
1½ lbs. lean pork, chopped
½ lb. smoked pork sausage,
    casings removed and chopped

3 Tb. lemon juice
Pinch of ground cloves
1 hard-boiled egg, white chopped,
    yolk sieved
2 apples
2 Tb. butter
Shaved roasted almonds

*F*ry bacon in a large, heavy skillet till crisp, drain on paper towels, and crumble.

Pour off all but 2 tablespoons of fat from the skillet, add onion and garlic, and sauté over low heat for 2 minutes. Add tomatoes and red pepper, increase heat slightly, and simmer for about 5 minutes or till mixture is thick. Add pork, sausage, crumbled bacon, lemon juice, and cloves, and continue cooking for about 30 minutes, stirring. During the final 5 minutes, preheat oven broiler.

Brown hash under broiler till slightly crusty on top, transfer to a large heated serving platter, sprinkle with chopped egg white and sieved yolk, and keep warm.

Core apples and slice into rings. Heat butter in a large skillet, add apples, and sauté on both sides over low heat till slightly golden.

Arrange apples around edges of hash, sprinkle dish with shaved almonds, and serve immediately.

Tourtière Québecoise
(Canadian Meat Pie)

Serves 6

I've sampled this earthy dish all over eastern Canada and have yet to find two cooks who prepare it alike. To be authentic, it must contain pork and potatoes, but you could also add chicken, rabbit, or cubes of salt pork. This is great cold-weather food meant for eating with plenty of tart salad or crisp vegetables and bottles of sturdy red wine — preferably before the fire in a rustic farmhouse.

3 strips of bacon, cut into 1-inch pieces
1 lb. lean pork, cut into 1-inch cubes
1 onion, chopped
1 garlic clove, minced
½ tsp. salt
Freshly ground pepper

¼ tsp. nutmeg
¼ tsp. ground cloves
¼ tsp. celery seeds
1½ tsp. cornstarch
1 cup water
1 cup cubed potatoes
A double recipe of Pâte Brisée (p. 412)

Fry bacon in a large, heavy saucepan for 1 minute, lower heat, add pork, onion, and garlic, and cook with bacon for 3 minutes, stirring. Add seasonings, cornstarch, and water, bring liquid to the boil, lower heat, cover, and simmer for 30 minutes. Uncover, add potatoes, and cook for 5 minutes longer.

Preheat oven to 425°.

Line a 9-inch pie pan with pastry, pour in pork mixture, and cover with remaining pastry. Press edges together and prick top of pie with a fork. Bake for 10 minutes, reduce heat to 350°, and bake for 30 minutes longer.

Pork Chili with Corn

Serves 6–8

When I go on about how the new young chefs in this country should stop imitating foreign dishes (all in the name of the New American Cuisine) and begin reinterpreting any number of our glorious regional specialties, chili is but one example of what I'm talking about. *Pace* Texas, I do indeed love old-fashioned beef chili with plenty of tender beans, but why not make the dish also with pork, and why not substitute something like corn for the kidney beans? Since chili is such a personal matter, feel free to add or subtract ingredients and change quantities, but at least once do try this chili with the beer

3-lb. boned pork loin
¼ cup vegetable oil
3 medium onions, finely chopped
1 green bell pepper, seeded and
   finely chopped
4 garlic cloves, finely chopped
3 Tb. chili powder
2 tsp. ground cumin

2 tsp. oregano
Salt and freshly ground pepper
Tabasco
3 cups canned tomatoes
1 cup beef bouillon
2 cups beer
2 12-oz. cans whole-kernel corn,
   drained

Remove and discard all fat from loin, cut loin into chunks, and cut chunks into ½-inch cubes.

Heat the oil in a large, heavy casserole, add pork cubes, and brown over moderate heat, stirring. Add onions, bell pepper, and garlic, stir well, and continue cooking, stirring, for about 5 minutes or till vegetables are soft. Add the chili powder, cumin, oregano, and salt, pepper, and Tabasco to taste, stir mixture well, and continue cooking for 2 minutes.

Add the tomatoes, bouillon, and beer, and stir well. Bring liquid to the boil, reduce heat, cover, and simmer for 1 hour.

Add the corn, stir, return chili to the simmer, and cook for 30 minutes longer or till chili has the desired consistency.

Serve piping hot with Corn Sticks (p. 438).

Cervelas aux Cèpes

(Poached Lyons Sausages with Wild Mushrooms)

Serves 4–6

Anyone who has spent time in the simple bistros of Lyons in France —
especially the legendary Léon de Lyons — can't help but have tasted these
fat savory sausages. Serve them with a nice steamed green vegetable and
plenty of Pommes à l'Huile (p. 370). The sausages should be prepared at
least one day in advance.

4 feet large pork sausage casings	*½ lb. fat bacon*
(available in butcher shops)	*2 Tb. Cognac*
1 oz. dried Boletus mushrooms	*1 Tb. salt*
(cèpes or porcini)	*Freshly ground pepper*
2 Tb. butter	*¼ tsp. ground fennel*
1½ lbs. lean boneless pork shoulder	*½ garlic clove, crushed*

Rinse casings under cold running water, soak for 1 hour in a bowl of
cold water, rinse again, and drain. At the same time, place mushrooms in a small bowl of warm water, soak for about 20 minutes, pick for
grit, and drain on paper towels.

Heat butter in a small skillet, add mushrooms, sauté for 10 minutes
over low heat, turning. Chop mushrooms finely.

Cut pork and bacon into cubes, place in a mixing bowl, add the mushrooms, Cognac, salt, pepper to taste, fennel, and garlic, and mix thoroughly. Put mixture through the coarsest blade of a meat grinder. Shape 1
tablespoon of the mixture into a patty, fry over medium heat on both sides
till browned, and taste for seasoning.

To stuff sausage, gather all but 2 inches of the casing up over the mouth
of a sausage funnel or a meat grinder, tie knot in free end, force mixture
through funnel into casing, and tie knot in top end. Twist and tie sausage
at 6-inch intervals with heavy thread, working out air pockets with fingers,
and refrigerate for at least 24 hours.

To poach sausages, place in a large heavy skillet with enough water to
cover, bring to the boil, lower heat, cover, and simmer for 30 minutes.

Baked Country Ham

This is the basic method of preparing a Smithfield, dry-cured country, York, or other specialty ham that requires cooking (the more aged a ham, the less cooking it needs). Soaking time can be doubled for those who prefer no salty flavor, but remember that the more you soak a country ham, the more of its distinctive flavor you lose. Remember also that nothing is better than ½-inch-thick slices of country ham simply fried 3 – 4 minutes per side and topped with red-eye gravy made by deglazing the skillet with a little water or hot coffee.

12- to 15-lb. dry-cured specialty   *1 cup dark brown sugar*
   ham   *10 – 12 cloves, ground*

Scrub ham thoroughly with a stiff brush under running water and place in a large oval roasting pan. Add cool water to cover and let soak for 12 hours, changing water twice.

Scrub again with a stiff brush under running water to remove all traces of mold and pepper and return ham to roasting pan. Add fresh water to cover, bring water very gradually to a gentle simmer, cover pan, and simmer very gently for 15 minutes per pound, adding more water to keep ham covered.

Preheat oven to 425°.

Remove skin from ham and trim off all but ¼ inch of the fat. Score in diamonds, cover with brown sugar and ground cloves, and rub seasonings well into ham. Place in roasting pan fat side up and bake for 15 minutes.

Carve into thin slices with an electric or serrated knife.

Country Ham Simmered in Cider and Molasses

Serves at least 10

12- to 15-lb. country or
  Smithfield ham
1 cup molasses
1 cup light brown sugar
1 gal. cider

3 onions, chopped
3 carrots, chopped
2 cups bread crumbs mixed with
  2 cups light brown sugar

Soak ham according to directions for Baked Country Ham (p. 213). Rinse well the roasting pan in which ham has been soaking, return ham to pan, and add enough water to come halfway up the sides. Add molasses and brown sugar to water, stir as well as possible, and add enough cider to just cover ham. Add onions and carrots, bring liquid to a very low simmer, cover partially, and simmer for 15 minutes per pound. Let ham cool completely in liquid.

Preheat oven to 425°.

Place ham on a working surface, remove skin and all but ¼ inch of the fat, and score in diamonds. Rinse roasting pan well after discarding contents, place ham fat side up in pan on a rack, and coat with bread crumb and sugar mixture, pressing down with fingers. Bake, uncovered, for 20 minutes or till crumbs are browned.

To serve, carve ham into thin slices with an electric or serrated knife.

Baked Ham Stuffed with Greens and Apricots

Serves at least 10

4 slices of bacon
½ cup finely chopped scallions,
    including 2 inches of green tops
¼ cup finely chopped celery
¼ cup chopped parsley
1 cup chopped turnip greens,
    mustard greens, or kale
1 cup chopped spinach

1 cup chopped dried apricots
1 tsp. dry mustard
¼ tsp. dried marjoram
1 tsp. crushed dried hot red pepper
Freshly ground pepper
12-lb. ham
2 cups (½ fifth) Bourbon
Sprigs of watercress

Fry bacon in a large skillet till crisp, drain on paper towels, crumble, and pour all but 4 tablespoons of fat from skillet. Add scallions and celery, and sauté over low heat for 3 minutes. Add crumbled bacon, parsley, greens, spinach, apricots, mustard, marjoram, hot pepper, and freshly ground pepper to taste. Toss mixture, cover, reduce heat, and cook for about 20 minutes or till greens are soft. Transfer mixture to a large bowl and mix well.

Preheat oven to 350°.

Trim all but ¼ inch of fat from ham. With a sharp paring knife, cut about 10 deep X-shaped incisions over surface of ham, spread incisions apart, and, using fingers, force stuffing deeply into each pocket.

Wrap ham in a large piece of cotton cheesecloth and tie edges securely. Place in a large oval roasting pan, pour Bourbon over ham, cover, and bake for 2 hours, basting occasionally and adding a little water to pan if necessary. Remove ham from oven, remove and discard cheesecloth, return ham to oven, and continue baking for 30–45 minutes or till top is nicely glazed.

Place ham on a ham rack or large serving platter surrounded by sprigs of watercress and carve in thick slices.

Smithfield Ham in Pastry with Port Sauce

Serves at least 10

12-lb. Smithfield ham
½ cup peach jam
1 cup brown sugar
1 Tb. dry mustard
⅛ tsp. ground cloves
¼ cup Port
1 cup bread crumbs
1 recipe of Quick Puff Pastry
   (p. 413)

1 egg, beaten with 2 Tb. water
2 cups Beef Stock (p. 522) or
   bouillon
2 Tb. arrowroot dissolved in 3 Tb.
   water
⅓ cup Port
½ cup heavy cream

*P*lace ham in a large oval roasting pan, add cool water to cover, and let soak for 12 hours, changing water twice.

Scrub ham with a stiff brush under running water to remove all traces of mold and pepper, and return to roasting pan. Add fresh water to cover, bring water very gradually to a gentle simmer, cover pan, and simmer for no more than 1 hour.

In a small saucepan, heat the jam till melted and pour into a bowl. Add the brown sugar, mustard, cloves, and ¼ cup Port, mix thoroughly, and set aside.

Preheat oven to 425°.

Remove skin from ham and trim off all but ¼ inch of the fat. Rinse well the roasting pan in which ham was simmered, place ham fat side up in the pan, and brush well with peach glaze. Sprinkle bread crumbs over ham, pressing them with fingers, and bake for 25 minutes. Let ham cool for 1 hour, transfer to a working surface, and rinse roasting pan.

On a floured surface, roll out dough about ¼ inch thick, wrap around a rolling pin, and drape over ham. Press dough securely all around ham, wrapping ham completely and closing dough with a bottom seam. Brush pastry with egg wash. Roll out strips from dough trimmings, fashion strips decoratively into ovals, leaves, stems, flowers, etc., secure them to the pastry-covered ham, and brush with egg wash.

Return ham to roasting pan, reduce oven heat to 375°, and bake, uncovered, for 45 minutes or till pastry is golden. Transfer ham to a warm serving platter, cut crust all the way around bottom, and lift off pastry lid.

Carve ham horizontally toward the shank in thin pieces with an electric or serrated knife and, leaving slices in place, replace pastry lid.

Pour stock into a saucepan, bring to the boil, and reduce to about 1¼ cups. Add arrowroot, stir, and continue cooking over moderate heat till reduced to about 1 cup. Add the ⅓ cup Port, bring to the boil, and remove from heat.

Pour cream into another saucepan, reduce over moderate heat by half, add to Port sauce, and stir.

To serve, remove crust from ham at the table and serve slices with a little crust and sauce on the side.

Stuffed Country Ham Braised in Sherry

7- to 10-lb. boned country ham, tied securely
1½ cups bread crumbs
1 tsp. ground cinnamon
½ tsp. ground nutmeg
½ tsp. ground cloves
¾ cup finely chopped pecans
6 pitted prunes, chopped
3 dates, chopped
¼ cup sweet sherry
½ cup brown sugar
4 cups (1 fifth) sweet sherry
Watercress for garnish

Soak and simmer ham according to directions for Baked Country Ham (p. 213).

Combine bread crumbs, spices, pecans, prunes, dates, and ¼ cup sherry in a large mixing bowl and mix thoroughly with hands to make a compact stuffing.

Trim all but ¼ inch of fat from ham. With a larding needle or apple corer, make 8–10 deep incisions in ham, turning utensil so that small pockets are made. Force stuffing into pockets with fingers, pushing firmly so that stuffing is as compact as possible.

Preheat oven to 350°.

Rub ham well with brown sugar, pressing down with fingers. Place in a large shallow baking pan and add 4 cups sherry. Cover pan with foil, seal ends partially, and bake for 15 minutes per pound, basting occasionally and adding more sherry or a little water if necessary.

Let ham cool in liquid for 1 hour, then place on a serving platter with sprigs of watercress and carve into thin slices with an electric or serrated knife.

Jambon en Saupiquet
(Ham in Vinegar-Cream Sauce)

Serves 4–6

3 Tb. bacon grease
⅓ cup chopped shallots
2 Tb. flour
2 cups hot bouillon
1 cup red wine vinegar
2 peppercorns, crushed

2 juniper berries
1 cup heavy cream
4 Tb. (½ stick) unsalted butter,
   cut into pieces
4–6 slices lean ham, ½ inch thick
Chopped parsley

*H*eat bacon grease in a large skillet, add shallots, and sauté over moderate heat for 2 minutes. Sprinkle with flour, stir, and cook the roux, stirring, for 3–4 minutes or till very brown.

Remove skillet from heat, add bouillon in a stream, then add the vinegar, crushed peppercorns, and juniper berries, stirring. Return skillet to moderate heat and cook till liquid is reduced by half. Strain through a fine sieve into a saucepan, add cream and butter, stir slowly with a whisk till smooth, and keep warm.

Place ham slices in one or more large skillets and brown slightly on both sides over moderate heat. Transfer slices to hot dinner plates, spoon sauce on top, and sprinkle each slice with chopped parsley.

Ham and Sweet Potato Hash

Serves 4

Some colleagues at *Town & Country* were a little shocked when I suggested running a feature upgrading the social status of hash, but never did readers respond with so much interest. "No matter what pseudosophisticates care to think," I wrote when including this recipe in *American Taste,* "a platter of well-made hash is as satisfying to the appetite and gratifying to the soul as a steaming pot of savory stew, a bowl of genuine chili or chowder, and a juicy hamburger." My conviction stands firm. Serve this hash with steamed buttered fresh asparagus and pickled peaches.

1 lb. cooked lean ham, cut into
   ½-inch cubes
1½ cups diced cooked sweet
   potatoes (slightly firm in
   texture)
2 medium onions, minced
½ large green bell pepper, cored,
   seeded, and finely chopped

1 Tb. chopped fresh basil
Salt and freshly ground pepper
¾ cup heavy cream
4 Tb. (½ stick) butter
4 eggs
Minced fresh parsley

*I*n a mixing bowl, combine ham, potatoes, onions, green pepper, basil, salt and pepper to taste, and cream, mix lightly, and form as well as possible into a large cake.

Heat one-half of the butter in a large heavy skillet over moderately high heat, add the ham mixture, and press down evenly with a spatula to form a compact oval cake. Reduce heat to moderate and cook hash for 5 minutes or till underside is browned and crusty. Loosen hash with the spatula and invert onto a plate. Add remaining butter to the skillet and increase heat slightly. Slide other side of hash into skillet, reduce heat to moderate, and cook for 5 minutes longer or till other side is browned and crusty. Transfer hash to a heated platter and keep warm.

Break eggs into 1 or 2 saucepans of boiling water, poach for 2 minutes, and transfer with a slotted spoon to a clean cloth to drain. Top hash with the poached eggs and sprinkle with minced parsley.

Sautéed Sweetbreads with Tarragon-Butter Sauce

Serves 4

During my tenure as an undercover captain at Le Perroquet in Chicago (a mission undertaken for the purpose of learning what *really* goes on behind the scenes at a luxury restaurant), this was one of the most popular dishes I served. After snitching numerous bites from the orders I'd prepare at the serving tables, I too fell in love with the glorious dish.

1½ lbs. sweetbreads	1 cup (2 sticks) butter, softened
2 Tb. white vinegar	Salt and freshly ground pepper
3 Tb. lemon juice	½ tsp. dried tarragon
⅓ cup white wine vinegar	¼ cup flour
⅓ cup dry white wine	4 Tb. (½ stick) butter
3 scallions (whites only), minced	2 lemons, cut into large wedges

*P*lace sweetbreads in a large bowl with enough water to cover, add 2 tablespoons of the vinegar, and soak for 2 hours. Drain and add fresh water to cover plus remaining ⅓ cup of vinegar and soak for an additional hour.

Drain sweetbreads and carefully trim off and discard all fat and membrane with a sharp knife. Cut sweetbreads into ½-inch slices, place in a shallow dish, sprinkle with the lemon juice, and let sit while preparing the sauce.

Combine the white wine vinegar, wine, and scallions in a small saucepan, bring to the boil, and reduce liquid to about 2 tablespoons. Remove pan from heat, cool slightly, and whisk in butter a tablespoon at a time. Return pan to low heat, continue whisking till sauce is thick and smooth, season with salt and pepper to taste plus the tarragon, stir, and keep warm.

Drain sweetbreads and dredge lightly in the flour. Heat the 4 tablespoons of butter in a skillet and sauté sweetbreads over moderate heat for about 3 minutes on each side or till golden brown. Arrange on a heated platter, spoon sauce over the top, and surround with the lemon wedges.

Sweetbread and Spinach Sausage

Serves 6

Once, when Pierre Franey and I were judging dishes at one of the four or five March of Dimes Gourmet Galas we work together each year, the famous chef mentioned to me this delightful sausage recipe he'd created. You can also substitute chicken for the sweetbreads with good results. Pierre likes to serve the sausage with a Beurre Blanc (p. 536). Note that the preparation must be started a day in advance.

5 feet large sausage casings
(available in butcher shops)
1 lb. sweetbreads, trimmed of all
membrane and soaked in
water overnight
1 lb. fresh spinach
½ lb. lean pork
½ lb. lean veal
½ lb. pork fat

2 shallots, chopped
½ tsp. ground nutmeg
½ tsp. ground coriander
¼ tsp. ground allspice
Salt and cayenne
2 eggs
1 cup heavy cream
Butter

Rinse casings under cold running water, soak for 1 hour in a bowl of cold water, rinse again, and drain.

Meanwhile, place sweetbreads in a large saucepan with enough salted water to cover, bring to the boil, lower heat, and simmer for 5 minutes. Transfer sweetbreads to a clean towel, wrap tightly, squeeze well to extract moisture, and chill for 1 hour.

Remove stems from spinach and wash leaves well. Place leaves in a large saucepan, cover, and cook over low heat till wilted. Transfer to another clean towel and squeeze well to extract moisture.

Cut pork, veal, pork fat, and chilled sweetbreads into 1-inch cubes and chop spinach coarsely. Combine meats, shallots, seasonings, and eggs in a food processor (in batches, if necessary), and process for 15–20 seconds. Add cream and process for 15 seconds longer or till mixture is smooth. Transfer mixture to a mixing bowl, add spinach, and mix well with a wooden spoon.

To make sausages, gather all but 2 inches of casing up over the mouth of a sausage funnel or a meat grinder, force mixture through funnel into casing, and tie knot at top end. Twist and tie sausage at 4-inch intervals with white thread, working out air pockets with fingers.

To poach, place sausage in a large kettle with enough salted water to cover, bring liquid to the boil, lower heat, and simmer for 15 minutes. Remove from heat, let stand for 15 minutes, and drain sausage on paper towels.

To serve, grill sausages in butter, turning, till golden on all sides.

Sautéed Rabbit with Anchovies and Black Olives

Serves 2 or 3

Leave it again to my friend Paula Wolfert to take a dish we've shared in our travels around the globe (this time a chicken stew with anchovies and black olives in southern France) and transform it into something even more exciting. Rabbit can be found not only in many butcher shops but also frozen and cut up in supermarkets. For those who are still unenlightened or squeamish, young rabbit, which resembles chicken in texture, is one of the most delectable meats on earth. This recipe can be easily doubled.

2½-lb. young rabbit (fresh or frozen), cut into 8 pieces, liver reserved
2 Tb. Dijon mustard
12 Tb. (1½ cups) olive oil
2 Tb. unsalted butter
1 small onion, finely chopped
1 garlic clove, sliced
½ tsp. dried rosemary, crumbled
½ cup dry white wine
1 ripe tomato, peeled, seeded, and cut into ½-inch dice

Pinch of sugar
1½ cups Chicken Stock (p. 521)
1 Tb. red wine vinegar
1 oz. (½ can) anchovy fillets, rinsed and patted dry
6 – 9 slices French or Italian bread ½-inch thick
1 garlic clove, cut in half
12 salt-cured black olives, pitted and coarsely chopped
½ cup chopped parsley
Salt and freshly ground pepper

Wipe rabbit pieces dry with paper towels. In a large bowl, whisk mustard and 1 tablespoon of the oil till well blended, add rabbit, turn to coat, cover with plastic wrap, and refrigerate for at least 3 hours.

Heat 2 tablespoons of the oil and the butter in a large enameled or stainless-steel skillet, add rabbit, and sauté over moderate heat for 5 minutes, turning, till golden brown. Add onion, sliced garlic, and rosemary, and sauté for 2 minutes longer. Carefully pour all but 1 tablespoon of the fat from skillet, add wine, increase heat, and cook for 2 minutes or till wine is reduced to a glaze. Add tomato, sugar, and chicken stock, bring liquid to the boil, reduce heat, cover, and simmer for 10 minutes.

Meanwhile, heat 2 tablespoons of the oil in a small skillet, add reserved liver, and sauté over moderate heat for 2 minutes on each side. Transfer liver plus another tablespoon of oil to a blender or food processor, add vinegar and anchovies, and blend to a smooth puree.

Heat remaining oil in a large, heavy skillet, add bread slices, and sauté both sides over moderate heat till golden brown. Drain slices on paper towels, rub with cut garlic, and keep croutons warm.

Stir liver-anchovy mixture into rabbit, add olives, parsley, and salt and pepper to taste, stir well, and heat for 5 minutes.

Transfer rabbit pieces to a warmed serving platter, spoon on a little sauce, and pass remaining sauce separately. Surround rabbit with croutons and serve immediately.

Roast Saddle of Venison with Black Pepper Sauce

Serves 6 – 8

Today, most venison on the market is young, meaning you can avoid marinating the meat and simply lard it with fresh pork fat or bard it with salt pork or bacon. An older, prime piece, however, must be marinated for 2 – 3 days and turned every 6 hours, and I find marinating even the most tender meat a short while gives it much better flavor. This is a magnificent cut of meat which should be ordered from a butcher well in advance.

6- to 7-lb. saddle of venison
A double recipe of Wild Game
   Marinade (p. 549)
1 large garlic clove, cut in half
2 Tb. butter, softened

1 Tb. crushed dried thyme
Freshly ground pepper
Salt
Black Pepper Sauce (p. 530)

Place venison in a large stainless-steel or glass container, pour on marinade, cover with plastic wrap, and let marinate in the refrigerator for 6 hours, turning once.

Preheat oven to 500°.

Remove venison from the marinade, pat dry with paper towels, and rub thoroughly with garlic, butter, thyme, and pepper to taste.

Place meat on a rack in a shallow roasting pan and roast for 30 minutes, basting frequently. Reduce heat to 350° and continue roasting till meat thermometer placed into the thickest part of the meat registers 130°. Remove meat from oven, salt to taste, and let stand for 15 minutes on a hot serving plate before carving.

Carve meat in long, thin slices parallel to the spinal column and serve with black pepper sauce on the side.

Venison Steaks with Stuffed Pears

Serves 6

Inspired by an elegant preparation of Montana elk at The American Restaurant in Kansas City, this dish is one of the simplest and best ways I know to serve venison. If the meat is young and tender and has been hung a couple of weeks (ask your butcher), it need be marinated only long enough — about 6 hours — to take on additional flavor.

6 venison steaks	¼ cup dry white wine
1 recipe of Wild Game Marinade	½ cup Beef Stock (p. 522)
(p. 549)	2 Tb. fine brandy
3 Tb. butter	½ cup heavy cream
2 Tb. peanut or vegetable oil	3 large ripe pears
Salt and freshly ground pepper	6 Tb. red currant jelly

*A*rrange steaks in a large, shallow glass baking dish, pour marinade over top, cover, and let marinate for 24 hours.

Remove steaks from marinade, pat dry with paper towels, and strain ¼ cup of the marinade into a measuring cup.

Heat the butter and oil in a large skillet, add steaks (in batches, if necessary), and brown over moderate-high heat for about 6 minutes per side for medium-rare. Transfer steaks to a heated platter, season with salt and pepper to taste, and keep warm.

Add wine to skillet, increase heat, and reduce to dry. Add reserved ¼ cup marinade and reduce by two-thirds. Add stock, reduce heat, and simmer for 10 minutes. Add brandy and cream, stir well, and cook for 5 minutes longer or till sauce is smooth. Keep warm.

Peel, slice in half, and core pears, making a pocket in the center of each half. Fill each pocket with a tablespoon of jelly.

Pour sauce over the steaks, garnish the platter with the stuffed pears, and serve immediately.

Venison Ragout

Serves 4–6

Although aged venison seems to be more and more available each year during the cold months, you almost have to know a good butcher (or have a good friend who hunts) in order to lay hands on cuts other than the tenderloin, rack, and various steaks. If, however, you care to savor the ultimate meat stew, you'll go out of your way to obtain such less-choice venison cuts as shoulder, round, rump, and shank for the sole purpose of stewing. Serve the ragout with wild rice or buttered noodles and a good bottle of Zinfandel.

2½ lbs. boneless venison stew
   meat, trimmed and cut into
   1½-inch pieces
1 cup flour mixed with salt,
   cayenne, and freshly ground
   pepper to taste
8 Tb. (1 stick) butter
1 cup sweet vermouth
2 cups Beef Stock (p. 522)
2 celery ribs (leaves included),
   chopped

½ tsp. dried thyme
½ tsp. dried rosemary
1 bay leaf
6 medium onions, each studded
   with 1 clove
3 medium carrots, scraped and
   cut into 2-inch pieces
12 small new potatoes, scrubbed
¼ lb. mushrooms, sliced in half

Dredge venison pieces in the seasoned flour.
   Heat butter in a large, heavy casserole, add venison, and brown on all sides over moderate heat. Add vermouth, increase heat, and cook for 3 minutes. Add stock, celery, thyme, rosemary, bay leaf, and more salt and pepper to taste, bring to the boil, reduce heat, cover, and simmer for 1 hour.

Add onions, carrots, and potatoes, return to simmer, cover, and continue simmering for 30–45 minutes or till vegetables are tender. During the final 15 minutes of simmering, add mushrooms to ragout, adding more stock if liquid has become too thick.

When ready to serve, transfer ragout to a large tureen or deep serving platter.

PART SEVEN

Poultry

Dilled Chicken

I also make this simple chicken dish with a tablespoon of fresh chopped coriander or a teaspoon of freshly grated ginger. Whatever seasoning you use, remember that the chicken is also very good chilled about 2 hours and served cold.

3½-lb. chicken	1½ cups Chicken Stock (p. 521)
1 cup flour	¼ cup dry white wine
Salt and freshly ground pepper	1 Tb. chopped fresh dill
4 Tb. (½ stick) butter	½ cup heavy cream
2 Tb. peanut or vegetable oil	Sprigs of fresh dill for garnish

Rinse chicken and cut into serving pieces. Combine one-half of the flour and salt and pepper to taste in a pie plate and dredge chicken lightly in the mixture.

Heat butter and oil in a large, heavy skillet, add chicken, and sauté over moderate heat on all sides till golden brown. Transfer chicken to a plate, add remaining flour to skillet, and cook, stirring, for 5 minutes. Add stock and wine, stir, bring to the boil, and reduce till slightly thickened. Return chicken to the skillet and sprinkle on the chopped dill. Reduce heat, cover, and simmer for 30 minutes or till chicken is tender but not overcooked, adding a little stock if sauce becomes too thick.

Transfer chicken to a heated serving platter. Stir cream into the sauce, heat sauce well, pour over chicken, and garnish with sprigs of dill.

Chicken Sauté with Wild Mushrooms

Serves 4

1½ oz. dried cèpe, chanterelle, or
    morel mushrooms
5 Tb. butter
3½-lb. chicken
Salt and freshly ground pepper
¼ cup flour

1 Tb. vegetable oil
12 small white onions
Pinch of dried thyme
1 bay leaf
½ cup dry red wine
½ cup heavy cream

Soak mushrooms in 1¼ cups of warm water for 30 minutes, pick for grit, rinse, chop coarsely, and pat dry with paper towels. Strain mushroom liquor through triple cheesecloth and set aside. Heat 2 tablespoons of the butter in a small skillet and sauté the mushrooms for 3 minutes over moderate heat.

Rinse chicken, cut into serving pieces, season with salt and pepper to taste, and dredge lightly in the flour. Heat remaining butter and the oil in a large, heavy skillet, add chicken, brown on all sides over moderate heat, and transfer to a plate. Add onions to the skillet and brown evenly over moderate heat. Return chicken to the skillet, add mushrooms, thyme, bay leaf, wine, and about ¼ cup of the mushroom liquor, cover, and simmer over low heat for about 45 minutes or till chicken is tender.

Transfer contents of the skillet to a hot serving platter. Skim fat from the cooking liquid, add cream, and boil, stirring, for about 3 minutes or till sauce thickens. Taste sauce for seasoning and pour over chicken.

Chicken Breasts with Orange in Chablis Sauce

Serves 6

This tangy chicken dish (which I've also prepared with sweetbreads) couldn't be more simple to prepare. It is important that you use a very good French chablis, and this just might be the right occasion to invest in a large attractive copper gratin dish.

½ cup flour
Salt and freshly ground pepper
6 large chicken breasts, skinned
4 Tb. (½ stick) butter
1 Tb. vegetable oil
1 cup chablis

¼ tsp. dried thyme
⅛ tsp. ground fennel
1 orange, peeled of all skin and
*   pith, sectioned, and seeded*
12 fresh mushrooms, cut in half
½ cup heavy cream

Preheat oven to 350°.
In a shallow pie plate, combine the flour with salt and pepper to taste and dredge chicken breasts lightly in the mixture.

Heat 2 tablespoons of the butter plus the oil in a large, oval, ovenproof baking or gratin dish, add the chicken, and brown over moderately high heat on both sides. Place dish in the oven and bake chicken for 30 minutes.

Remove dish from the oven and add the chablis, thyme, fennel, and orange segments. Bring liquid to the boil, reduce heat, cover, and simmer chicken for 20 minutes longer.

Meanwhile, heat remaining butter in a small skillet, add mushrooms, and sauté over low heat for 10 minutes, stirring.

Stir mushrooms and cream into chicken, increase heat slightly, and cook for 5 minutes longer. Taste for salt and pepper and serve immediately.

Singapore Chicken

If you're looking for a more exotic way to prepare fried chicken, this is it. Depending on how spicy you like your food, you could also add a little ground cumin, cardamom, and, if available, lemon grass. Serve the chicken with plenty of rice, sautéed pea pods, and either cold beer or a chilled bottle of Gewürztraminer.

2 cups peanut oil
6 large chicken breasts
10 scallions (trimmed of half the green tops), coarsely chopped
4 red chili peppers, seeded and chopped
¼ tsp. anise seeds

⅛ tsp. freshly ground cinnamon
¼ cup coconut milk
¼ cup soy sauce
2 Tb. fresh lime juice
¼ cup chopped fresh coriander (also called cilantro and Chinese parsley)

Heat the oil in a large skillet to moderately hot, add chicken breasts, and fry for 10 minutes on each side or till just cooked through. Drain chicken on paper towels.

Pour all but about ¼ cup grease from the skillet, reduce heat, add scallions, peppers, anise seeds, and cinnamon, and cook, stirring, for about 2 minutes or till scallions are softened. Add coconut milk, soy sauce, and lime juice, increase heat, and continue cooking, stirring, for 5–10 minutes.

Add chicken breasts to the sauce, spoon a little sauce over breasts, and continue cooking over moderate heat for 10 minutes.

Serve chicken sprinkled with chopped coriander.

Chicken Tajine

Serves 8

In Morocco, *tajine* is prepared with everything from chicken to lamb to seafood. This simple chicken version with olives is classic.

¼ cup olive oil
2 3-lb. chickens, cut into serving
  pieces
3 medium onions, minced
1 Tb. paprika
1½ tsp. ground ginger
½ tsp. turmeric

¼ tsp. ground cloves
Freshly ground pepper
1½ cups Chicken Stock (p. 521)
  or bouillon
3 lemons, quartered and seeded
7-oz. jar pimiento-stuffed green
  olives, drained

*H*eat the oil in a large, deep skillet, add chicken, brown on all sides over moderate heat, and transfer to a plate.

Add onions to the skillet and sauté for 2 minutes, stirring. Stir in the paprika, ginger, turmeric, cloves, and pepper to taste and continue to cook for 1 minute. Add the stock and chicken, stir well, then add the lemons. Bring liquid to the boil, reduce heat, cover, and simmer for 30 minutes or till chicken is tender.

Add the olives and simmer for 5 minutes longer. Transfer the chicken and lemons to a large, heated casserole, bring sauce to the boil, and reduce till thickened to desired consistency. Pour sauce over chicken and serve the *tajine* with Steamed Couscous (p. 406) or rice.

Mrs. Griswold's Chicken and Artichokes

Serves 6

There's nothing on earth I love more than a hearty breakfast (every morning!), a subject that led me to Essex, Connecticut, and the incredibly elaborate hunt breakfast buffet that is served at the historic Griswold Inn and that we featured in *Town & Country*. This simple but delicious chicken and artichoke sauté couldn't be any more American, and all you need as accompaniments are some brown rice and perhaps a few fried apples.

4 Tb. (½ stick) butter
1 Tb. vegetable oil
4 chicken breasts, boned but not
   skinned, cut into 1-inch pieces
16 canned artichoke hearts
   (2 cans)

2 cups sliced mushrooms (about
   ¼ lb.)
½ cup finely chopped shallots
½ garlic clove, minced
1 cup dry white wine
1 Tb. arrowroot

Heat one-half of the butter and the tablespoon of oil in a large heavy skillet, add chicken pieces, and sauté over moderate heat, turning, for about 5 minutes or till golden brown on all sides. Transfer to a heated platter.

Add another tablespoon of the butter to the skillet, add artichoke hearts, and sauté, turning, for about 5 minutes or till lightly browned. Transfer to platter with the chicken.

Add remaining butter to the skillet, add mushrooms, shallots, and garlic, stir well, reduce heat, and sauté, stirring, for 5 minutes. Return chicken and artichoke hearts to the skillet, add wine, increase heat to moderate, and simmer for 10 minutes or till chicken is tender.

Transfer chicken, mushrooms, and artichoke hearts back to the platter, stir arrowroot into the sauce, and let simmer for about 5 minutes or till thickened. Pour sauce over the chicken and serve immediately.

Murgh Ka Salan
(Chicken Curry)

I don't pretend to know much more about the subtle preparation of the various curries of India than what I'm exposed to in the Indian restaurants of New York and London. This particular curry, however, usually turns out rather well and makes a big hit with guests.

½ cup peanut or vegetable oil
3- to 3½-lb. chicken, cut into
serving pieces
1 large onion, thinly sliced
2 garlic cloves, minced
1 green chili pepper, seeded and
finely chopped

1½ Tb. ground coriander
2 tsp. ground turmeric
1 tsp. ground ginger
1 cup plain yogurt
1 cup water
Salt and freshly ground pepper

*H*eat oil in a large, heavy skillet, add chicken pieces, and sear on all sides over high heat. Remove chicken from skillet and drain on paper towels.

Reduce heat to low, add onion and garlic, and sauté for 2 minutes. Add chili pepper, coriander, turmeric, and ginger, stir, and sauté for 2 minutes longer. Return chicken to the skillet.

In a bowl, combine yogurt and water, stir till well blended, pour over chicken, and increase heat to moderate. Season with salt and pepper to taste, cover skillet, reduce heat, and simmer for 1½ hours or till chicken falls off the bone.

Serve with plenty of boiled dry rice and a very tart romaine or curly endive salad.

Smothered Chicken with Mushrooms and Onions

Craig Claiborne first told me about this old Mississippi recipe from his mother's kitchen when the two of us were serving as judges at a March of Dimes Gourmet Gala. It's comfort food at its very best, and I've prepared the dish on numerous occasions. It is indeed necessary to weight down the chicken while it is cooking for the best results.

3½-lb. chicken, split down
    backbone, breast left unsplit
Salt and freshly ground pepper
4 Tb. (½ stick) butter
½ lb. fresh mushrooms, sliced
16 very small white onions, peeled
1 bay leaf

¼ tsp. dried thyme
½ cup dry white wine
½ cup Chicken Stock (p. 521) or
    broth
2 Tb. finely chopped garlic
2 Tb. finely chopped parsley

Season chicken with salt and pepper to taste and fold wings under to hold them secure.

Heat one-half of the butter in a black cast-iron skillet, add chicken skin side down, cover firmly with a plate that fits inside the skillet, and add several weights to top of plate. Cook over low heat for 25 minutes, pour off most of the fat from the skillet, and add remaining butter. Turn chicken skin side up and scatter mushrooms and onions over and around chicken. Add bay leaf, thyme, wine, chicken broth, and garlic, replace the plate and weights, and continue cooking over low heat for 45 minutes longer.

Transfer chicken to a warm platter and spoon on mushrooms and onions. Reduce liquid in the skillet by half, pour over chicken, and sprinkle with parsley.

Fried Chicken

I don't suppose any article in my career ever created such commotion as the three-thousand-word treatise I devoted to the art of Southern fried chicken. Here is a tailored version of that highly intricate procedure guaranteed to yield the best fried chicken you ever sunk teeth into. Ideally, you should make every effort to obtain either a freshly killed or kosher chicken, but even those bland supermarket birds can be given character if you follow these directions to the letter. The recipe can be easily doubled or tripled to serve a larger crowd.

4-lb. chicken (preferably freshly killed)
3 tsp. salt
Freshly ground pepper
3 cups milk

½ lemon
3 cups (1½ lbs.) top-quality shortening
1½ cups flour
4 Tb. bacon grease

*C*ut chicken into serving pieces, rinse pieces under cold running water, dry with paper towels, and season with 1 teaspoon of the salt plus pepper to taste. Pour milk into a bowl and squeeze lemon into milk. Add chicken to the bowl to soak, cover with plastic wrap, and refrigerate for at least 2 hours.

Remove chicken from the refrigerator and allow to return to room temperature.

While melting the shortening over high heat to measure ½ inch in a black cast-iron skillet (add more shortening if necessary), combine the flour, remaining salt, and pepper to taste in a brown paper bag. Remove dark pieces of chicken from the milk, drain each momentarily over the bowl, drop in bag, and shake vigorously to coat. Add bacon grease to skillet, and when small bubbles appear on the surface, reduce heat slightly. Remove chicken pieces from the bag one by one, shake off excess flour, and, using tongs, lower the pieces gently into the fat, skin side down.

Quickly repeat all procedures with the white pieces of chicken. Arrange chicken in the skillet so it cooks evenly, reduce heat to moderate, cover, and cook for exactly 17 minutes. Reduce heat slightly, turn pieces with the tongs, and fry for 17 minutes longer, uncovered.

Drain chicken on a second brown paper bag for at least 5 minutes, transfer to a serving platter *without* reheating in the oven, and serve hot or at room temperature with potato salad, sliced ripe tomatoes, Jalapeño Cornbread (p. 436), and iced tea.

Frankenmuth Poached-Fried Chicken

Serves 6 – 8

Having once devoted no less than three thousand words in print to the step-by-step "correct" preparation of the Southern fried chicken on which I was raised, I thought I knew all there was to know about this great American specialty. Then, when I was exposed to the way they poach-fry chicken throughout the small town of Frankenmuth, Michigan, I quickly realized Southerners have stiff competition. Don't balk at the use of chicken bouillon cubes; it's the only way to produce the required highly concentrated stock unless you poach ninety chickens at a time the way they do at the family restaurants in Frankenmuth.

2 3-lb. chickens	½ tsp. dry mustard
4 cups Chicken Stock (p. 521)	⅛ tsp. cayenne
4 chicken bouillon cubes, crushed	2 eggs, beaten with ¼ cup milk
1 cup soda cracker crumbs	Vegetable oil for deep-frying
1 cup dry white bread crumbs	Parsley or watercress for garnish
1½ tsp. salt	

Place whole chickens in a large, deep kettle or casserole and add stock and crushed bouillon cubes. Bring stock to the boil, reduce heat, cover, and simmer chickens for 25 minutes. Remove chickens from stock, let cool slightly, cover with plastic wrap, and chill thoroughly to allow juices to set.

Combine cracker crumbs, bread crumbs, salt, dry mustard, and cayenne in a food processor and pulse till ingredients form a very fine mixture. Transfer mixture to a pie plate. Carve the chicken into serving pieces, dip each piece into the egg wash, and coat well with the crumb mixture.

Heat at least 2 inches of oil to 350° in a deep-fat fryer or large, deep cast-iron skillet, fry chicken pieces in batches for 2½ – 3 minutes, and drain on paper towels. Pile chicken on a heated serving platter and garnish with parsley or watercress.

Stuffed Chicken Legs

Serves 6

Since these boned chicken legs can be stuffed in advance, they are ideal for a busy-weekend supper or a casual lunch when the last thing you want to do is spend all morning in the kitchen. The legs could be stuffed with any number of other ingredients: a mixture of ground ham and olives, aromatic wild mushrooms, minced prosciutto and grated Romano, curried minced leftover turkey, or, for something fancy, *foie gras* and chopped truffles.

12 large chicken legs
1 onion, cut in half
1 celery rib, broken
1 carrot, quartered
Salt and freshly ground pepper
4 Tb. (½ stick) butter
½ lb. chicken livers, trimmed and
  cut in half

½ lb. fresh mushrooms, sliced
1 cup bread crumbs
1 tsp. minced shallots
¼ cup Madeira
1 egg, beaten with ¼ cup milk
Bread crumbs for coating

Combine chicken legs, onion, celery, carrot, and salt and pepper to taste in a large saucepan and add water to cover. Bring to the boil, reduce heat, cover, and simmer for 45 minutes. When cool enough to handle, slip bones out of legs without cutting meat and set meat aside.

Heat one-half of the butter in a medium skillet, add chicken livers and mushrooms, and sauté over low heat for 10 minutes, stirring. Transfer livers and mushrooms to a chopping board, chop very fine, and place in a large mixing bowl. Add bread crumbs, shallots, Madeira, and salt and pepper to taste, and mix thoroughly. Stuff equal amounts of the mixture into the legs, dip each leg into the egg wash, then roll each lightly in the bread crumbs.

Heat remaining butter in a large skillet, arrange chicken legs evenly in the skillet, and brown over moderate heat on all sides.

Jambonettes de Volaille à la Perigourdine
(Stuffed Chicken Thighs with Madeira Sauce)

Serves 4

This sumptuous classic, which I've eaten all over southwest France, is not really as fancy as it sounds and is basically quite simple to prepare. Traditionally, the stuffing has lots of truffles, but since these aromatic fungi are so prohibitively expensive, I usually make do with a few slivers under the skin of the chicken and substitute mushrooms in the stuffing.

8 chicken thighs
Salt and freshly ground pepper
1 medium black truffle
1 cup chopped mushrooms
1½ oz. foie gras
1½ qts. Chicken Stock (p. 521)

1 medium onion, chopped
1 celery rib, chopped
1 tsp. dried thyme
Minced parsley for garnish
Madeira Sauce (p. 529)

*B*one the chicken thighs with a sharp paring knife by scraping the meat from the bone, pulling it downward and turning it inside out like a glove. Cut the meat free at the bottom, season with salt and pepper to taste, and turn it skin side out.

Cut the truffle into 8 thin slices and slip 1 slice under the skin of each boned thigh.

Place mushrooms in a blender or food processor, reduce to a puree, and transfer to a mixing bowl. Add *foie gras* and salt and pepper to taste, and stir till mixture is well blended and smooth. Stuff the thighs with equal amounts of the mushroom mixture, re-form thighs as much as possible into the original shape, and tie with string or secure well with toothpicks.

Pour stock into a small baking pan or large, deep skillet, add onion, celery, and thyme, and set a rack in the pan, making sure rack does not touch liquid. Arrange stuffed thighs on the rack, bring liquid to the simmer, cover, and steam chicken for 30 minutes.

Sprinkle thighs with minced parsley and serve 2 per person, spooning a little Madeira sauce around each portion.

Chicken Saltimbocca

Serves 12

6 whole chicken breasts, split,
    skinned, and boned
6 oz. Emmenthaler (imported
    Swiss) cheese, cut into 3½×2-
    inch slices
12 thin slices prosciutto or smoked
    ham
3 Tb. flour
3 Tb. bread crumbs
3 Tb. freshly grated Parmesan
    cheese

¼ tsp. dried tarragon
1 garlic clove, minced
1 egg, beaten
6 Tb. (¾ stick) butter
12 fresh mushrooms, halved
¼ cup dry sherry
¼ cup dry white wine
½ cup Chicken Stock (p. 521)
1 Tb. cornstarch
1 Tb. water

Between pieces of wax paper, flatten each half of chicken breast with a mallet and place 1 slice of cheese and 1 slice of ham in the center of each. Roll up breasts lengthwise and secure with toothpicks.

In a shallow dish, combine flour, bread crumbs, Parmesan, tarragon, and garlic. Dip each chicken roll into the beaten egg, then coat lightly with some of the dry mixture.

Preheat oven to 350°.

Heat 4 tablespoons of the butter in a skillet, add chicken rolls, and brown on all sides over moderate heat. Transfer chicken to a 13×9×2-inch baking dish and set aside.

Heat remaining 2 tablespoons of butter in a small skillet, add the mushrooms, and sauté over moderate heat for 3 minutes, stirring. Spoon the mushrooms over the chicken.

Combine in a bowl the sherry, white wine, and chicken broth, stir, and pour over the chicken and mushrooms. Cover dish and bake for 30 minutes or till tender.

Transfer chicken and mushrooms to a heated serving dish, reserving the pan drippings. Combine cornstarch and water in a small saucepan, heat to moderate, and stir till smooth. Add reserved pan drippings, stir, and cook over moderate heat, stirring constantly, till thickened. Pour over chicken and mushrooms and serve immediately.

Chicken Hash à la Ritz

Serves 4–6

Louis Diat created both vichyssoise and this legendary chicken hash when he was chef at the old Ritz-Carlton Hotel in New York, and I never seem to tire of the hash. If you wish to present the dish exactly as Diat served it (I don't), pipe either duchesse potatoes or pureed peas around the edges.

6 chicken breasts
1 celery rib, broken
1 onion, cut in half
2 cups heavy cream
1½ tsp. salt

Freshly ground pepper
1¾ cups Mornay Sauce (p. 526)
3 Tb. freshly grated Parmesan
  cheese

Place chicken breasts, celery, and onion in a large saucepan or kettle and add water to cover. Bring to the boil, reduce heat, cover, and cook over moderate heat for 20 minutes or till chicken is just cooked through.

Lift chicken from the pan with a slotted spoon and let cool. When cool enough to handle, skin and bone chicken, cut meat into ½-inch cubes, and set aside.

Pour cream into a medium skillet, bring almost to the boil, reduce heat, and simmer, stirring often, for 30 minutes or till cream is reduced to about 1½ cups. Add salt and pepper to taste, stir, add chicken, and cook for 3 minutes or till chicken is heated through.

Preheat oven broiler.

Transfer chicken mixture to a 10½×7-inch gratin dish or large baking dish, cover with the Mornay sauce, sprinkle with the cheese, and broil for about 1 minute or till bubbly and lightly browned.

Low-Country Chicken Hash

Serves 6 – 8

I have no idea where this recipe came from, but I suspect my maternal grandmother or grandfather brought it inland from Savannah or Charleston, since my family has called it "Low-Country Hash" for as long as I can remember. My mother still serves it in a silver chafing dish on an elaborate Christmas breakfast buffet, but I like to serve it over crusty French bread as a cold-weather supper dish. Do not prepare this hash with anything but an old hen that has simmered for at least 3 hours.

4- to 5-lb. hen
4 medium carrots, sliced in thick rounds
1 bay leaf
2 tsp. salt
1 tsp. freshly ground pepper
6 Tb. (¾ stick) butter

6 Tb. flour
3 cups Chicken Stock (p. 521)
1 cup heavy cream
½ lb. fresh mushrooms, sliced
¼ tsp. paprika
Tabasco

Wash hen thoroughly and place in a large kettle or casserole with enough water to cover. Add the carrots, bay leaf, salt, and pepper, bring liquid to the boil, reduce heat, cover, and simmer for 3 – 4 hours or till chicken is tender.

Strain 3 cups of the stock into a bowl and reserve. When chicken is cool enough to handle, remove meat from the bones and cut into bite-size pieces.

Heat the butter in the top of a double boiler over simmering water, add flour, and stir steadily till well blended and smooth. Gradually add chicken stock and stir till thickened. Add cream, mushrooms, paprika, and Tabasco to taste, stir, then taste for seasoning. Fold chicken into sauce and continue cooking and stirring for about 10 minutes. (The hash may be prepared in advance and reheated for 5 – 10 minutes before serving.)

Serve hash over slices of French bread or on toast.

Bourbon Chicken with Chestnuts and Glazed Carrots

Serves 4

4 – 5 carrots, scraped and cut into
  rounds
8 Tb. (1 stick) butter
4 large chicken breasts, boned but
  not skinned
Salt and freshly ground pepper
½ cup flour
2 shallots, finely diced

1 celery rib, finely diced
2 oz. Bourbon
1 cup dry white wine
Pinch of dried tarragon
1 cup heavy cream
16 whole canned unsweetened
  chestnuts

*P*lace carrots in a large saucepan with water to cover by 1 inch, bring to the boil, reduce heat to moderate, cover, and cook for 10 minutes. Drain water from the saucepan, add 2 tablespoons of the butter, and shake pan vigorously to coat carrots with butter. Continue cooking over very low heat till carrots take on a nice glaze and set aside, covered.

Season chicken with salt and pepper to taste and dust each piece lightly in the flour. Heat 4 tablespoons of the butter in a large, heavy skillet, add chicken, and sauté over moderate heat for 7 minutes on each side or till golden brown. Transfer chicken to a platter and keep warm.

Pour fat from skillet, add remaining butter, shallots, and celery, and sauté over low heat for 5 minutes. Add Bourbon, increase heat, and cook for 1 minute. Add wine and tarragon, bring to the boil, and reduce liquid by two-thirds. Add heavy cream and continue reduction till sauce is slightly thickened. Return chicken to the skillet, baste with the sauce, add chestnuts, baste again, and heat thoroughly.

Reheat the carrots.

Arrange chicken and chestnuts on a heated serving platter, add the sauce, and garnish the edges with the carrot rounds.

Chicken and Onions in Zinfandel

Serves 4–6

3 Tb. butter
18 very small white onions
1½ cups Veal Stock (p. 523) or
   Chicken Stock (p. 521)
4½-lb. chicken
½ cup flour
4 strips of bacon, cut into 1-inch
   pieces

1 Tb. arrowroot
1 cup full-bodied Zinfandel wine
1 Tb. tomato paste
2 garlic cloves, crushed
Herb bouquet (½ tsp. dried
   thyme, 1 bay leaf, and 2 sprigs
   parsley wrapped in cheesecloth)
Salt and freshly ground pepper

*H*eat the butter in a medium skillet, add the onions, and brown them lightly over moderate heat, turning frequently. Add ½ cup of the veal or chicken stock, reduce heat, cover, and simmer onions for 30 minutes, adding a little water if necessary. Keep onions warm.

Rinse chicken, cut into serving pieces, and dredge lightly in the flour.

Fry the bacon over moderate heat in a large, deep skillet, drain on paper towels, and reserve. Add chicken to the skillet and sauté on all sides till golden. Transfer chicken to a plate and keep warm.

Add the arrowroot to the fat in the skillet and cook for 5 minutes, stirring. Add the wine, increase heat, and stir to collect the brown bits on the bottom and sides of skillet. Add the remaining stock plus the tomato paste and stir till well blended. Return chicken to the skillet, add reserved onions and bacon, the garlic, herb bouquet, and salt and pepper to taste, cover skillet, and simmer slowly for about 45 minutes or till chicken is tender, adding more stock if necessary.

Remove and discard the herb bouquet, arrange chicken and onions on a deep, heated serving platter, and pour sauce on top. Serve chicken with small boiled potatoes and green beans sautéed in butter.

Pollo en Pipían
(Mexican Chicken Stew)

Serves 4–6

Ever since I first went to Mexico to report on what authentic Mexican cooking is all about (and it's certainly not about what we find in most Mexican restaurants this side of the border), I've experimented with all types of those spicy stews known generally as *pipían*. This one, inspired by Elizabeth Lambert Ortiz, is just as good made with turkey, duck, or even pheasant and should be served either over rice or spread on tortillas.

4 ancho chili peppers
4- to 5-lb. hen, cut into serving
   pieces
2 medium onions, quartered
½ green bell pepper, seeded and
   cut into thin strips
2 carrots, scraped and cut into
   rounds

5 black peppercorns
Salt
2½ cups Chicken Stock (p. 521)
2 garlic cloves, crushed
½ cup shelled roasted peanuts
2 Tb. vegetable oil
¼ tsp. ground cinnamon
¼ tsp. ground cumin

Seed the chili peppers, tear the flesh into pieces, and soak for 1 hour in ½ cup hot water.

In a large casserole, combine the chicken, onions, bell pepper, carrots, peppercorns, salt to taste, and chicken stock, adding a little water, if necessary, to cover. Bring to the boil, reduce heat, cover, and simmer for 30 minutes.

Remove chicken and vegetables with a slotted spoon, strain stock into a bowl and reserve, rinse out casserole, and return chicken and vegetables to casserole.

Place soaked chili peppers and garlic in a blender, reduce to a paste, and scrape into a bowl. Place peanuts in the blender, pulverize, and mix into the chili paste.

Heat the oil in a medium skillet, add the paste, and cook over low heat for 4 minutes. Add 2 cups of the reserved stock plus the cinnamon and cumin, stir, and bring to the boil. Pour sauce over the chicken, cover casserole, and simmer for 30 minutes or till chicken is tender.

Home-Style Chicken Pie

Serves 6

3- to 3½-lb. chicken
1 medium onion, cut in half
1 celery rib (leaves included),
  broken
10 black peppercorns
A double recipe of Basic Pie
  Pastry (p. 411)

2 carrots, scraped and cut into
  thin rounds
Salt and freshly ground pepper
10 very small white onions, peeled
  and cut in half
1 tsp. dried tarragon
2 Tb. melted butter

Disjoint chicken and place in a large saucepan with the onion, celery, peppercorns, and enough water to cover. Bring to the boil, reduce heat, cover, and simmer for 30 minutes.

Transfer chicken to a plate with a slotted spoon, and when cool enough to handle, bone, cut meat into bite-size pieces, and set aside. Strain stock into a bowl and set aside.

Preheat oven to 350°.

On a lightly floured surface, roll out one-half of the dough ⅛ inch thick and line the bottom and sides of a greased 8×10-inch casserole or baking dish with the pastry. Roll out the other half of the dough very thin and cut one-half into long 1-inch-wide strips, reserving the other half for the top of the pie.

Arrange a layer of chicken over bottom of the casserole, scatter the carrots over the chicken, season with salt and pepper to taste, and arrange the strips of pastry over the carrots. Arrange the onion halves over the strips of pastry, add the tarragon and remaining chicken to make a final layer, and season again with salt and pepper to taste. Pour on enough of the reserved stock to almost cover the top layer of chicken.

Fit the remaining pastry snugly over top of pie, pressing down the edges and trimming off excess pastry. Brush top with the melted butter and bake for 30–40 minutes or till crust is nicely browned.

Boudins Blancs à la Flamande

(White Sausages with Onions and Apples)

Serves 6

I must have prepared these sausages a dozen times before finally coming up with a mixture and cooking technique that gave me the exact flavor and texture I was looking for. In Belgium, they're usually made with pork and veal; I find the chicken-veal combination much more subtle. If you can spare the time, remember that the sausages develop even better flavor if allowed to meld in the refrigerator overnight before frying.

4 feet large sausage casings
  (available in butcher shops)
3 Tb. butter
2 medium onions, minced
½ cup dry white wine
¼ cup milk
¼ cup heavy cream
1 cup bread crumbs
½ lb. skinned and boned chicken
  (preferably thigh meat), chilled
  and cut into cubes
½ lb. lean veal, chilled and cut
  into cubes
½ lb. pork fat, chilled and cut
  into cubes
¼ tsp. dried thyme
¼ tsp. ground allspice

¼ tsp. freshly grated nutmeg
⅛ tsp. ground fennel
1 Tb. salt
Plenty of freshly ground pepper
2 eggs
2 qts. Chicken Stock (p. 521)
1 leek, trimmed of one-half green
  tops, split, and rinsed well
  under running water
1 celery rib (leaves included),
  broken in half
1 carrot, cut into quarters
6 Tb. (¾ stick) butter
3 medium onions, sliced
3 Golden Delicious apples, peeled,
  cored, and cut into medium-
  thick wedges

POULTRY · 251

*R*inse casing under cold running water, soak for 1 hour in a bowl of cold water, rinse again, and drain.

Heat the 3 tablespoons of butter in a medium skillet, add onions, and sauté over low heat for 2 minutes. Add wine, bring to the boil, reduce heat to moderate, cook till liquid has evaporated, and set onions aside.

Combine milk, cream, and bread crumbs in a bowl, stir well, and let sit while preparing meats.

Grind chicken, veal, and pork fat twice through the fine blade of a meat grinder (not a food processor) and combine in a large mixing bowl. Add cooked onions, bread crumb mixture, thyme, allspice, nutmeg, fennel, salt, and pepper to taste, and mix well with a wooden spoon. Add eggs and beat mixture with an electric mixer till well blended and smooth.

To stuff sausage, gather all but 2 inches of the casing up over the mouth of a sausage funnel, tie a knot in the free end, and push meat mixture carefully through funnel into the casing. Tie a knot in the other end, twist sausage gently at 6-inch intervals, and tie the lengths with heavy thread.

Combine chicken stock, leek, celery, carrot, and salt and pepper to taste in a kettle, bring to the boil, and reduce heat to moderate. Lower sausage circle-wise into the liquid, poach gently for 25–30 minutes, and drain well on paper towels. Cut sausage into desired number of lengths. (If possible, let sausage cool in the cooking liquid overnight in the refrigerator before cutting into lengths.)

To serve, heat 2 tablespoons of the butter in a large skillet, fry sausages, turning, for 5–10 minutes (depending on whether they've been chilled) or till golden brown, and transfer to a heated platter. Add remaining butter to skillet, add the 3 sliced onions, reduce heat, and sauté for 2 minutes, stirring. Add the apples, stir, and continue sautéing till apples are just heated through and slightly soft. Spoon onions and apples into the center of the platter containing the sausages and serve immediately.

Creamed Turkey Scallops with Chestnuts

Serves 4–6

½ large uncooked turkey breast
Salt and freshly ground pepper
1 lb. chestnuts, shelled and peeled
1 celery rib (including leaves), cut
   in 3 pieces
8 Tb. (1 stick) butter

3 cups Chicken Stock (p. 521) or
   broth
1 onion, finely diced
2 Tb. finely diced carrots
½ cup white wine
¾ cup heavy cream

Skin turkey breast, slice on the diagonal against the grain into ¼-inch scallops, season lightly with salt and pepper, and set aside on wax paper.

In a large skillet, arrange chestnuts in a single layer, add celery and enough chicken stock to cover, and simmer for about 35 minutes or till chestnuts are tender.

Heat 2 tablespoons of the butter in another large skillet, add onion and carrots, cover, cook over low heat for 5 minutes, and transfer to a plate. Add 2 more tablespoons of the butter to the skillet, add half the turkey scallops, increase heat slightly, and sauté for 3 minutes on each side. Transfer scallops to a plate. Add 2 more tablespoons of the butter to the skillet and repeat with remaining scallops.

Pour off fat, deglaze skillet with the wine, and cook till reduced to a glaze. Add remaining stock, bring to the boil, and reduce by half. Add the cream plus the remaining butter, stir, and reduce slightly till sauce thickens. Reduce heat to moderate, add chestnuts, vegetables, and turkey scallops to sauce, and heat thoroughly, for about 2 minutes.

Divide scallops on heated serving plates, top with the vegetables and sauce, and arrange chestnuts around each portion.

Turkey and Ham Casserole with Water Chestnuts

This is the sort of satisfying dish I might put together when I just don't feel like cooking but would like to put something substantial on the table for close friends. Don't apologize for its lack of sophistication, for your guests will love the casserole.

2 Tb. butter
2 medium onions, finely chopped
3 Tb. flour
½ tsp. salt
Freshly ground pepper
1¼ cups milk
10 fresh mushrooms, sliced
2 cups cooked turkey, cut into
*   1-inch cubes*
1 cup cooked ham cut into 1-inch
*   cubes*

5-oz. can water chestnuts,
*   drained and sliced*
1 small hot red pepper, seeded
*   and chopped*
2 Tb. dry sherry
½ cup freshly grated Parmesan
*   cheese*
1 cup soft bread crumbs
3 Tb. melted butter

Preheat oven to 400°.
Heat the butter in a medium skillet, add onions, and sauté over low heat for 3 minutes, stirring. Sprinkle on the flour, add salt, and pepper to taste, mix well, and cook for 2 minutes longer.

Gradually stir in the milk, increase heat slightly, and cook for about 5 minutes, stirring, or till mixture is thickened and smooth. Add the mushrooms, turkey, ham, water chestnuts, red pepper, and sherry, increase heat to moderate, stir well, and cook for 5 minutes.

Transfer mixture to a 2-quart casserole or baking dish and sprinkle the top with the cheese. Combine the bread crumbs and melted butter in a small bowl, mix well, and spoon over the top of the casserole. Bake for 35 minutes or till top is lightly browned.

Curried Turkey Hash Cakes

2 medium boiling potatoes, peeled,
   boiled, and roughly chopped
8 Tb. (1 stick) butter, room
   temperature
3 cups chopped cooked turkey
½ cup chopped onions
¼ cup chopped celery
½ cup chopped green bell pepper

3 eggs, 2 beaten
½ cup heavy cream
1½ tsp. salt
Freshly ground pepper
1 tsp. curry powder
¾ cup flour
2 cups very fine bread crumbs
4–5 Tb. vegetable oil

In a mixing bowl, mash potatoes to a puree with a potato masher or fork, add half the butter in pieces, and beat with a wooden spoon or electric mixer till butter is completely absorbed.

In a blender or food processor, grind turkey, onions, celery, and bell pepper to a medium texture and transfer to the bowl with the potatoes. Add the whole egg and stir till well blended. Add the cream, salt, pepper to taste, and curry powder and beat well till mixture is smooth. Cover bowl with plastic wrap and chill for 30 minutes to firm up texture and allow the flavors to develop.

Shape hash into oval cakes, dust each evenly in the flour, dip in beaten eggs, roll in bread crumbs, and chill for 30 minutes.

Heat remaining butter with the oil in a large, heavy skillet, add the cakes, and sauté on both sides over moderate heat till golden brown.

Truffled Roast Turkey

For the French, truffled roast turkey ranks right up there with fresh *foie gras* and caviar when it comes to the ultimate in holiday entertaining, and even the least blessed will splurge once a year to serve this extravagantly delicious bird to family and guests. Friends in Paris think nothing of letting the stuffed turkey sit overnight in the refrigerator to intensify the flavors, oblivious to the American fear of food poisoning. I must say my French friends have yet to suffer any dire consequences from stuffing their fowl so long in advance, but I still feel less squeamish and get beautifully aromatic results by stuffing no more than 6 hours before roasting. The stuffing is more for flavor than bulk, and won't fill the cavity.

12- to 14-lb. turkey	*2 eggs, beaten*
¾ lb. fresh pork fat	*2 oz. Armagnac or Cognac*
5 shallots or 2 small onions	*Salt and freshly ground pepper*
2 sprigs parsley	*4 oz. preserved black truffles in*
2 slices of white bread, torn in	*truffle juice*
small pieces	*4 Tb. (½ stick) butter, softened*

Remove giblets and neck from the turkey. Clean meat from neck, chop giblets and neck meat finely, and place in a mixing bowl. Chop pork fat, shallots, and parsley finely and add to the giblets. Add the bread, eggs, Armagnac, and salt and pepper to taste, and mix till well blended. Open truffle container, pour juice over mixture, and mix. Chop coarsely all but one large truffle, add chopped truffles to mixture, and mix till truffles are well distributed.

Stuff mixture into the turkey cavity and truss the bird. Cut remaining truffle into thin slices, make random incisions in turkey skin with a sharp paring knife, and carefully insert slices between the skin and flesh. Wrap turkey snugly in plastic wrap, place in a large roasting pan, cover pan with lid, and place in refrigerator for 6 hours.

Preheat oven to 350°.

Remove plastic wrap from turkey and rub entire body of bird with the butter. Place turkey on a rack in the roasting pan and roast for 3 hours, basting frequently.

Roast Turkey with Orange, Prune, and Chestnut Stuffing

Serves at least 8

You may think it a waste of time having to soak the prunes and raisins overnight, but the maceration in the Port wine does make all the difference in the taste of the stuffing.

½ lb. pitted prunes
½ cup seedless raisins
1 cup Port
1 lemon, seeded and thinly sliced
1 medium onion, finely chopped
   and sautéed 1 minute in 1 Tb.
   butter
½ cup minced celery, tops included
1 large orange, peeled of all skin
   and pith, seeded, and coarsely
   chopped

1 cup coarsely chopped canned
   unsweetened chestnuts
½ tsp. mace
Salt and freshly ground pepper
2 Tb. lemon juice
2 cups bread crumbs
12- to 14-lb. turkey, giblets
   removed and reserved
1 Tb. dried sage
8 slices of thick bacon
1 Tb. flour

*C*ombine the prunes and raisins with the wine in a bowl and soak in refrigerator overnight.

Transfer contents of the bowl to a large saucepan and add the lemon slices. Bring to the boil, reduce heat, simmer for about 20 minutes or till fruit is tender, and drain. Transfer fruit to a chopping board, chop coarsely, and transfer to a large bowl. Add onion, celery, orange, chestnuts, mace, salt and pepper to taste, lemon juice, and bread crumbs, toss, and correct seasoning.

Preheat oven to 325°.

Season turkey with salt and pepper to taste inside and out, rub sage throughout the cavity, pack loosely with the stuffing, and truss. Bard the breast with the bacon slices, place turkey on a rack in a large roasting pan, cover, and roast for 2 – 2½ hours.

Meanwhile, place reserved giblets in a saucepan with at least 3½ cups of water, bring to the boil, reduce heat, cover, and simmer for 30 minutes. Transfer giblets to a chopping board and chop coarsely. Strain 3 cups of the stock into a bowl and set aside.

Remove bacon from turkey, baste the bird with pan juices, increase heat to 450°, and continue roasting, uncovered, for 30 minutes or till golden brown.

Transfer turkey to a heated platter, skim fat from the pan juices, add the flour, and stir for about 5 minutes or till well blended and smooth. Add reserved stock slowly over moderate heat, stirring constantly, then stir in the reserved giblets. Bring gravy to the boil and serve piping hot in a gravy boat.

Canard aux Olives Chez Allard
(Duck with Green Olives)

Serves 4

When people ask where I have my first meal after arriving in Paris, I tell them Allard, and when they ask what I order, I tell them *Canard aux Olives.* For decades Fernande Allard has been turning out her savory, *bourgeois,* inimitable dishes, but I find none so totally addictive, so consoling, so perfectly executed as the duck. Please don't tamper with this recipe.

2 lbs. green olives
2 Tb. chicken fat (or, if necessary, butter)
5 or 6 chicken wings
2 chicken gizzards
2 medium onions, sliced
3 Tb. flour
2 cups dry white wine
3 qts. Chicken Stock (p. 521)

Herb bouquet (¼ tsp. dried thyme, 1 bay leaf, 1 garlic clove, and 2 sprigs parsley wrapped in cheesecloth)
5 oz. tomato paste
Salt and freshly ground pepper
4½-lb. duck
2 Tb. butter

*P*lace olives in the large bowl, cover with cold water, and let soak for 6 hours.

Preheat oven to 300°.

Heat chicken fat in a large, heavy casserole, add chicken wings and gizzards, and brown lightly on all sides over moderate heat. Reduce heat, add onions, and sauté, stirring, till golden. Sprinkle on flour, stir, and cook for 5 minutes. Add wine, 2 quarts of the chicken stock, and the herb bouquet, and bring to the boil. Reduce heat, add tomato paste and salt and pepper to taste, and stir. Cover casserole, place in the oven, and cook for 4 hours. Remove casserole from oven, strain stock through a fine sieve into a bowl, and reserve.

Meanwhile, drain olives in a colander and place in a large saucepan with the remaining quart of chicken stock. Bring liquid to the boil, reduce heat, and simmer for 2 hours. Add reserved stock to the olives, continue cooking for 2 more hours, and adjust the seasoning.

One hour before cooking of olives is complete, place duck on a rack in a large roasting pan, prick skin with a fork, and roast for 1 hour in the 300° oven. Drain off fat from pan, add the 2 tablespoons of butter plus a little stock from the olives, and baste duck on all sides.

To serve, cut duck into serving pieces and place on a large hot serving platter. Drain olives and pour over and around duck. Serve immediately.

Caneton au Poivre
(Roast Duckling with Black Pepper Sauce)

Serves 4 – 6

It's no secret to anyone that La Caravelle has been my favorite French restaurant in New York for well over a decade, and friends know that when I attempt to duplicate Roger Fessaguet's inimitable *Caneton au Poivre,* I would never dream of tampering with perfection. Follow these directions to the letter, and you'll savor duck the likes of which practitioners of *nouvelle cuisine* are totally ignorant. Serve the dish with wild rice, lightly buttered asparagus, and a regal French red burgundy.

6 Tb. vegetable oil	*Pinch of dried thyme*
2 5- to 6-lb. ducklings	*1 tsp. cracked black peppercorns*
3 Tb. butter	*3 oz. Cognac*
2 shallots, chopped	*½ cup dry white wine*
1 small onion, chopped	*1 cup Chicken Stock (p. 521)*
1 small carrot, chopped	*Salt*
1 celery rib, chopped	*2 cups heavy cream*
4 fresh mushrooms, chopped	*4 Tb. (½ stick) butter*
2 garlic cloves, chopped	*Pinch of crushed black peppercorns*
2 bay leaves	

Preheat oven to 350°.

Heat one-half of the oil very hot in each of 2 large, heavy skillets or casseroles, add one duckling to each vessel, and brown quickly on all sides. Pour off and discard grease, place vessels in the oven, and roast ducklings for 1½ hours, pricking skin and degreasing vessels frequently. Transfer ducklings to a large platter and keep hot.

Heat the 3 tablespoons of butter in a large saucepan, add shallots, and sauté over low heat for 2 minutes. Increase heat to moderate, add onion, carrot, celery, mushrooms, garlic, bay leaves, thyme, and cracked peppercorns, and continue sautéing for 5 minutes longer, stirring. Add Cognac and cook for 2 minutes longer.

Add wine, increase heat, and reduce liquid by half. Add the stock plus salt to taste, increase heat, and reduce liquid by one-third. Add cream, reduce heat to moderate, and cook for 15 minutes, stirring from time to time. Strain sauce into another saucepan, add the 4 tablespoons butter in pieces plus the crushed peppercorns, and stir over low heat till well blended.

To serve, carve ducklings into serving pieces, spoon a film of sauce onto heated serving plates, and place duckling on top of sauce. Serve extra sauce on the side.

Foie de Canard à la Sainte Alliance
(Duck Liver with Madeira Sauce)

Serves 4

On the restored Venice–Simplon Orient Express, the luxury train that now travels round trip from London to Venice, this sumptuous dish is prepared with fresh goose *foie gras* and served with a truffle-enriched *périgueux* sauce. I've found that duck livers do just as well and that a Madeira sauce with black olives in not only much less expensive but considerably lighter and easier to prepare.

1 cup dry white wine
1 medium onion, thinly sliced
¼ tsp. dried basil
¼ tsp. dried marjoram
½ tsp. salt
Freshly ground pepper
1 – 1½ lbs. duck livers, trimmed
  of fat

¼ cup Madeira
¼ cup Beef Stock (p. 522)
3 Tb. finely chopped pitted black
  olives
3 Tb. sweet butter, cut into bits
2 Tb. finely chopped parsley

Combine wine, onion, basil, marjoram, salt, and pepper to taste in a medium saucepan. Bring liquid to the boil, reduce heat, add livers, cover, and simmer gently for 8–10 minutes or till livers are cooked but not too firm.

With a slotted spoon, transfer livers to a platter and keep warm. Strain cooking liquid into another saucepan, add Madeira and beef stock, bring liquid to the boil, and reduce to about 1 cup. Add olives, reduce heat, and simmer for 5 minutes, stirring. Taste sauce for seasoning, remove from heat, and stir in butter.

Spoon hot sauce over livers and sprinkle with chopped parsley.

Duck Paella with Olives and Almonds

Serves 6–8

Since I've always found classic *paella* made with chicken, seafood, and sausage a misconceived bore, I developed this moist, flavorful version prepared with duck. It does take somewhat longer to prepare since our fatty ducks must first be partially roasted to avoid a greasy finish, but I think the extra effort is fully justified. Once the rice is added, the *paella* should be stirred with a wooden spoon in small areas at frequent intervals.

2 4-lb ducklings (or 2 frozen
    ducklings, defrosted and patted
    completely dry)
Salt and freshly ground pepper
2 Tb. olive oil
2 medium onions, chopped
2 garlic cloves, finely chopped
2 medium ripe tomatoes, cored
    and coarsely chopped

⅛ tsp. oregano
3 cups rice
5 cups Chicken Stock (p. 521)
1 cup dry white wine
4 Tb. (½ stick) butter
1 lb. mushrooms, quartered
1 cup chopped stuffed green olives
½ cup salted almonds

Preheat oven to 350°.

Remove and discard the loose fat from the cavity and around the neck of the ducks and season the ducks all over with salt and pepper to taste. Truss ducks, place on a rack, back side down, in a large shallow roasting pan, and roast for 1 hour, pricking the skin all over with a fork every 20 minutes to release as much fat as possible. Pour fat from the pan, increase heat to 500°, and roast for 10–15 minutes longer.

Cut the ducks into serving pieces, remove and discard any excess fat from pieces, taking care to leave skin intact. Heat the oil in a large casserole, add the onions and garlic, and sauté over low heat for 2 minutes, stirring. Add the duck pieces, tomatoes, oregano, and rice, stir carefully with a wooden spoon, then add 3 cups of the chicken stock plus the wine. Bring liquid to the boil, reduce heat, cover, and simmer for about 1 hour or till the rice is tender, stirring from time to time.

In the meantime, heat the butter in a skillet, add the mushrooms, sauté over moderate heat for 3 minutes, stirring, and set aside.

Season casserole with salt and pepper to taste, add the olives and almonds, and stir well. Add enough of the remaining stock to keep the rice very moist, add the reserved mushrooms, stir, and cook over low heat for 15 – 20 minutes or till *paella* is moist but not soggy, watching constantly.

Serve the *paella* with a tossed green salad, Country Yeast Bread (p. 418), and a simple dry white wine.

Confit de Canard

(Preserved Duck)

Serves 10–12 in Cassoulet (p. 333)
or 4–6 when browned and served by itself

If *confit de canard* is still unfamiliar to you, all I can say is that you've so far missed out on one of the true marvels of French gastronomy. I can't imagine eating an authentic *cassoulet* that doesn't include *confit* (duck or goose), and when I'm traveling in southwest France I seek it out passionately in bean dishes, meat stews, and simply served by itself. Under refrigeration, *confit* will keep three to four months. Store any remaining fat in a covered jar in the refrigerator for making *cassoulet,* sautéing potatoes, browning meats for other stews, or enriching any number of vegetable dishes. *Confit* must be made *at least* two weeks in advance, so plan accordingly.

A fatty 4- to 5-lb. duck	1 bay leaf, crushed
4–5 Tb. coarse salt	2 cloves, crushed
Freshly ground pepper	1 garlic clove, minced
1 tsp. dried thyme	Lard
1 tsp. dried rosemary, crushed	

Remove wing tips of duck, then cut up duck into wings, drumsticks, thighs, and breasts (chopped crosswise into 3 pieces), reserving heart and gizzard. Remove all peripheral and cavity fat and fatty skin from pieces and remaining carcass and set aside.

Mix salt, pepper to taste, herbs, cloves, and garlic in a small bowl, rub mixture into duck pieces, including the heart and gizzard, and pack in a large bowl. Weight down with a plate and heavy canned goods, cover with plastic wrap, and refrigerate for 24 hours.

Meanwhile, cut reserved fat and skin into cubes, place in a saucepan with ¼ cup water, and render fat slowly over low heat for about 45 minutes. Strain fat into another bowl, continue frying cubes till crisp (cracklings), transfer to paper towels to drain, and reserve for use in *cassoulet.* When fat is cool, cover and refrigerate till ready to use.

Rinse duck pieces in warm water and dry thoroughly with paper towels. Heat duck fat in a large, deep saucepan or Dutch oven, add duck pieces, and cook over moderate heat for about 10 minutes to render more fat from skin. If necessary, add enough lard to assure pieces are covered completely by liquid fat, reduce heat, simmer duck gently and slowly for 1½ hours, and transfer pieces to a plate.

Strain 1 inch of fat into a large terrine, crock, or wide-mouthed canning jar and place in refrigerator for about 30 minutes or till fat congeals. Arrange duck pieces on top of fat, strain more fat over pieces to cover completely, shake container to distribute fat evenly, add more fat if necessary, and let cool. When fat has congealed, cover container with plastic wrap or lid and store in refrigerator for at least 2 weeks before using.

Goose Stew with Sausage and Chestnuts

Serves 6–8

Although chestnuts have not been harvested in America for over forty years because of a blight that began in 1904, close to twenty million pounds of succulent European varieties are imported each year and are available in larger cities from late October through January. Frozen chestnuts, stocked widely in supermarkets under the Napoli label, are of identical quality to fresh, much less perishable, cost about the same, and can be stored almost indefinitely without risk of rotting or drying up. Whichever you choose to use in this luscious stew, prepare them by cutting a deep *X* on the flat side of the nuts with a very sharp paring knife, tossing them into boiling water for about 15 minutes, and removing both shell and inner skin.

8- to 9-lb. goose
3 slices of bacon, diced
1 onion, sliced
1 carrot, sliced
1 garlic clove, crushed
1 cup dry red wine
3 cups Chicken Stock (p. 521) or broth
1 cup tomato sauce
½ tsp. thyme
⅛ tsp. ground fennel
1 bay leaf
Salt and freshly ground pepper
30 chestnuts, shelled and peeled
6 sweet Italian sausages
12 carrots, scraped
12 small white onions
2 Tb. softened butter kneaded with 2 Tb. flour

Rinse goose well under cold running water and remove as much fat as possible, reserving about 3 ounces. Cut goose into 8–10 serving pieces and pat dry with paper towels.

Heat reserved goose fat and the diced bacon in a large, heavy casserole till very hot, add goose pieces, and brown on all sides. Reduce heat, add onion, carrot, and garlic, stir, and cook for 5 minutes longer. Pour off all fat, increase heat, add wine, and boil till wine is almost a glaze. Add chicken stock, tomato sauce, thyme, fennel, bay leaf, and salt and pepper to taste, and stir, scraping bottom of the casserole. Bring liquid to the boil, reduce heat, cover, and simmer for 1½ hours.

Meanwhile, place chestnuts in a saucepan with water to cover, bring to a low boil, cook for 30 minutes, and drain. Arrange sausages in a medium skillet, prick all over with a fork, add enough water to come halfway up sides of sausages, bring water to a low boil, cook for 10 minutes, and drain. Quarter the carrots, place in a saucepan with enough water to cover, bring to a low boil, cook for 10 minutes, and drain. Place onions in a saucepan with enough water to cover, bring to a low boil, cook for 5 minutes, and drain.

Remove goose from casserole, strain cooking liquid into a bowl, and skim as much fat as possible. Return liquid to the casserole, add kneaded butter, and stir with a whisk till well blended. Return goose to casserole, add chestnuts, sausages, carrots, and onions, cover, and simmer for 20 minutes longer.

Faison à l'Ail
(Pheasant with Garlic Cloves)

Serves 4

Of all the dishes I've enjoyed over the years at the venerable Ernie's in San Francisco, this creation of chef Jacky Robert has got to be one of the most memorable. I've found this is also a great way to prepare chicken when pheasant is unavailable. Whether you use pheasant or chicken, it's a good idea to prepare the stock a day in advance, since it must be rich and full-flavored from long simmering.

2 young pheasants
1 onion, coarsely chopped
1 carrot, coarsely chopped
1 celery rib, coarsely chopped
Herb bouquet (¼ tsp. each dried thyme and fennel, 1 bay leaf, and 2 sprigs parsley wrapped in cheesecloth)

12 garlic cloves, peeled
4 Tb. olive oil
Salt and freshly ground pepper
3 cups heavy cream

Cut the pheasants into serving pieces as you would a chicken, splitting the breasts and reserving all other pieces for the stock. Wrap breasts in plastic wrap and place in the refrigerator.

Place reserved pheasant pieces, the onion, carrot, celery, and herb bouquet in a stockpot or large saucepan, add water to cover by 1 inch, bring to the boil, reduce heat, cover, and simmer slowly for about 3 hours. Strain stock into another saucepan and reduce over moderate heat to 2 cups. Add garlic cloves to the stock, reduce heat slightly, simmer for 15 minutes, remove garlic cloves, and reserve.

Preheat oven to 450°.

Heat oil in a large, heavy ovenproof skillet, season pheasant breasts with salt and pepper to taste, place skin side down in the skillet, and brown over moderate heat for about 5 minutes. Turn breasts, place skillet in the oven, and roast for 12 minutes or till cooked through but still moist. Remove breasts from skillet and keep warm.

Deglaze skillet with reserved stock and reduce over moderate heat by half. Add cream, simmer till slightly thickened, add garlic cloves and salt and pepper to taste, and continue simmering till garlic is heated through.

To serve, spoon sauce and 3 garlic cloves over each breast on heated serving plates.

English Pheasant Pie

Serves 4–6

The minute I hit the British Isles in late fall just to eat, the two items I seek out most diligently are thick mutton chops and pheasant pie as only the English know how to prepare them. If you can obtain wild pheasant during season for this dish, all the better; if not, try to find as mature a bird as possible so the pie will have a rich, slightly gamy flavor

4- to 5-lb. pheasant
1 large onion, studded with 2 cloves
1 celery rib, cracked in half
1 bay leaf
10 juniper berries
10 black peppercorns
1 Tb. salt
8 Tb. (1 stick) butter
6 Tb. flour
1 cup half-and-half
12 small white onions, parboiled
    15 minutes

12 fresh mushrooms, sliced and
    sautéed 5 minutes in 3 Tb.
    butter
10-oz. package frozen peas,
    defrosted
Salt and freshly ground pepper
1 recipe of Basic Pie Pastry
    (p. 411)
1 egg yolk
1 Tb. water

Cut pheasant into pieces as you would a chicken, rinse pieces, and place in a large kettle with enough water to cover. Add onion, celery, bay leaf, juniper berries, peppercorns, and salt, bring liquid to the boil, reduce heat, cover, and simmer for 2½ hours or till meat is tender.

When pheasant is cool enough to handle, remove the meat from the bones cut into ½-inch pieces, and set aside. Strain 2 cups of the cooking liquid into a bowl and reserve.

Heat the butter in a saucepan, add the flour, and stir steadily with a whisk over moderate heat till well blended. Gradually add the reserved cooking liquid, stirring constantly and maintaining the heat at moderate. Add the half-and-half and continue stirring over moderate heat till sauce has thickened. Set aside.

Place pheasant pieces in a 2-quart casserole, add onions, mushrooms, peas, and salt and pepper to taste, and stir gently to combine ingredients. Pour sauce over the top.

Preheat oven to 425°.

Roll out the pastry on a lightly floured surface into a circle slightly wider than the circumference of the casserole. Fit pastry over the top of the pie, press edges under with the fingers, and, with a small knife, cut a vent in the center to allow steam to escape. In a small bowl, blend the egg yolk with the water and brush the pastry all over with the glaze.

Bake the pie for 20 minutes or till crust is golden brown.

Quail Stuffed with Spicy Oysters

Serves 4

8 quail	*Tabasco*
½ lemon	*8 large fresh oysters, shucked*
¾ cup (1½ sticks) melted butter	*2½ cups cornmeal*
1½ Tb. dried tarragon	*8 strips of bacon*
Salt and freshly ground pepper	

*P*reheat oven to 450°

Rinse the quail well inside and out and pat dry with paper towels.

Squeeze the lemon into the butter, add the tarragon, salt and pepper to taste, and plenty of Tabasco, and stir. Dip oysters into the butter mixture, dredge lightly in the cornmeal, and stuff one into the cavity of each quail. Tie or skewer the birds with wings and legs close to body and bard each with a strip of bacon.

Place quail on a rack in a large shallow roasting pan and roast for 15 minutes. Remove bacon, baste the birds with the pan juices, and return to the oven for 10 minutes, basting once more.

Serve the quail with Wild Rice with Wild Mushrooms and Pine Nuts (p. 400) and Celery Root Puree (p. 340).

Sautéed Quail on White Corn Cakes

Serves 4

This dish was inspired by one served at The Mansion on Turtle Creek, one of the most distinguished hotels in Dallas, and illustrates how sophisticated the new style of American cookery can be when handled with a little common sense. If white corn is difficult to come by, use yellow. I see little need in having to bone the quail, as at the hotel, when they are just as delicious and delicate simply split and sautéed. You could also place 1 tablespoon of butter in each cavity, wrap bacon around the breasts, roast the birds for 20–25 minutes in a 450° oven, basting from time to time, and serve 2 whole birds per person.

8 quail
Salt and freshly ground pepper
1 cup cornmeal
1 cup half-and-half
4 egg whites
¼ cup white corn kernels

2 Tb. vegetable oil
2 large ripe tomatoes
½ tsp. dried thyme
3 Tb. olive oil
3 Tb. butter
Chopped parsley for garnish

Split the quail, salt and pepper each to taste, and set aside.
In a saucepan, combine the cornmeal and half-and-half, stir, and cook over moderate heat for 5 minutes, stirring. Remove pan from the heat and cool.

Beat egg whites in a large mixing bowl till stiff, add to cornmeal mixture, and fold in thoroughly. Add the corn kernels, salt and pepper to taste, and the vegetable oil, and mix well. Drop batter by the tablespoons onto a hot griddle or skillet, brown cakes on both sides, and keep warm.

Drop tomatoes momentarily into a pot of boiling water to loosen skins, discard skins, and place tomatoes in a blender. Add thyme, 2 tablespoons of the olive oil, and salt and pepper to taste, puree mixture, and transfer to a saucepan. Heat sauce and keep warm.

Heat remaining olive oil and the butter in a large skillet, add quail, and brown on all sides over moderate heat. Reduce heat and continue cooking for 15–20 minutes or till quail are tender.

Place equal numbers of corn cakes in the centers of 4 heated serving plates, arrange 4 quail halves on top, and spoon equal amounts of the tomato sauce around the cakes. Sprinkle chopped parsley on top and serve immediately with shoestring potatoes and a green vegetable.

Braised Squabs with Anchovies

Serves 4

4 squabs
8 anchovy fillets, drained and
    rinsed
¼ cup olive oil
2 Tb. butter
24 very small white onions
2½ cups Chicken Stock (p. 521)
2 cups dry white wine

24 cured small black olives
2 garlic cloves, minced
½ tsp. dried chervil
½ tsp. dried thyme
1 Tb. tomato paste
Salt and freshly ground pepper
1 Tb. flour

Rinse squabs, pat dry with paper towels, and truss wings and legs close to the bodies. Carefully insert 1 anchovy fillet lengthwise under the skin of each breast.

Heat the olive oil in a large, heavy casserole, add squabs, and brown on all sides over moderate heat. Heat butter in a medium skillet, add onions, brown lightly over low heat, turning, and add to the squabs. Add stock, wine, olives, garlic, chervil, thyme, tomato paste, and salt and pepper to taste, and stir gently but thoroughly. Bring liquid to the boil, reduce heat to low, cover, and braise squabs for 40–45 minutes or till tender.

Transfer birds to a large heated platter, surround with the onions, and keep warm. In a small bowl, stir a little of the hot liquid into the flour, add to the casserole, bring to the boil, and reduce till sauce is slightly thickened. Taste for salt and pepper, pour a little sauce over the squabs and onions, and serve the remaining sauce on the side.

Smoked Squab with Zinfandel Sauce

Serves 4

This creation of Jeremiah Tower, an expert at the art of grilling and one of the most impressive chefs specializing in California Cuisine, is done best in one of the Swedish smokers you can find now in any number of specialty appliance shops. The squabs can also be smoked on a lidded outdoor grill. Serve with a Gratin of Potatoes, Turnips, and Ham (p. 376) and Marinated Vegetable Salad (p. 167).

4 squabs, cleaned and trussed
8 Tb. olive oil
1 Tb. fresh chopped thyme (or
  1 tsp. dried thyme)
Salt and freshly ground pepper

2 qts. Veal Stock (p. 523) or
  Chicken Stock (p. 521)
1 cup Zinfandel
2 Tb. unsalted butter

Place squabs in a large glass or ceramic baking dish, drizzle on 4 tablespoons of the oil, and add thyme and salt and pepper to taste. Cover with plastic wrap and marinate at room temperature for at least 2 hours, turning once.

Meanwhile, light a low fire in a smoker or barbecue grill, using mesquite, hickory, or oak chips.

Heat 2 tablespoons of the oil in a large heavy skillet and brown squabs rapidly over high heat. (Leave skillet as is.) Place birds in the smoker or on the barbecue grill, close the lid, and smoke over a low fire for about 1 hour, dowsing coals with sprinklings of water if fire gets too hot.

Remove birds and let cool slightly. When cool enough to handle, remove meat as carefully as possible, keeping the breasts whole, and chop the carcasses well with a cleaver. Add remaining oil to the same skillet, add chopped carcasses, and brown well over moderate heat. Add stock, wine, and salt and pepper to taste, bring to the boil, reduce heat, cover, and simmer for 30 minutes, stirring from time to time.

Strain sauce into another large skillet, add squab meat and whole breasts, and heat slowly. Transfer squabs to a heated serving platter, whisk butter into sauce till well blended, and pour sauce over the squabs.

· PART EIGHT ·

Fish and Seafood

Halibut Steaks with Curried Tomato Sauce

Serves 4

6 Tb. (¾ stick) butter
1 large onion, chopped
5 large ripe tomatoes, peeled,
    seeded, and coarsely chopped
2 tsp. curry powder
Pinch of sugar

Salt and freshly ground pepper
4 halibut steaks, about 1 inch thick
¼ cup flour
1 Tb. vegetable oil
½ cup heavy cream
2 Tb. finely chopped parsley

*H*eat 2 tablespoons of the butter in a large saucepan, add the onion, and sauté for 2 minutes over low heat, stirring. Add the tomatoes, stir, and simmer for 40 minutes or till mixture is thick. Stir in the curry powder, sugar, and salt and pepper to taste, and cook for 2 minutes longer. Remove pan from the heat and cover.

Dust the halibut steaks lightly with flour. Heat remaining butter plus the oil in a large skillet, add steaks, and sauté over moderate heat for 5 minutes on each side. Transfer steaks to a heated platter and season with salt and pepper to taste.

Add the cream to the curried tomato mixture, stir, bring sauce to the boil, and pour over the steaks. Sprinkle parsley on top and serve immediately.

Poached Cod with Wild Mushrooms

Serves 4

The blandness of cod almost demands that the fish be prepared with a number of aromatic, flavorful ingredients. This dish, inspired by one Larry Forgione of An American Place in New York contributed to a lengthy article I did on wild mushrooms, is perfect for late spring or early fall entertaining on the terrace or deck. Fresh halibut or haddock work just as well for this recipe. Serve the fish with tiny boiled potatoes and, if in season, fresh asparagus.

½ oz. dried cèpe or porcini
   mushrooms
5 Tb. olive oil
1½ lbs. medium shrimp in shells,
   rinsed well
1 small onion, cut into large dice
1 small carrot, scraped and cut
   into large dice
1 celery rib, cut into large dice
2 garlic cloves, crushed
⅓ cup Bourbon
⅓ cup dry white wine

4 medium ripe tomatoes, cored,
   seeded, and coarsely chopped
4 cups (1 qt.) Chicken Stock
   (p. 521) or broth
6 black peppercorns
Pinch of thyme
4 6-oz. cod steaks, about 1 inch
   thick
Salt and freshly ground pepper
½ cup fresh, finely chopped spinach
1 ripe tomato, skinned, cored,
   seeded, and cut into small cubes

Soak mushrooms in ½ cup warm water for 30 minutes, pick for grit, rinse under running water, and set aside.

Heat the oil till very hot in a large, heavy skillet, add the shrimp, reduce heat to moderate, and sauté shrimp, turning, till shells turn pink. Add the onion, carrot, celery, and garlic, sauté for 3 minutes longer, stirring, pour off any excess oil, and transfer shrimp to a plate.

Add the Bourbon and wine to the skillet and stir. Add chopped tomatoes, increase heat slightly, and cook down almost to a paste. Add the broth, peppercorns, and thyme, bring to the boil, reduce heat, and simmer till mixture is reduced by one-third, skimming as foam arises. Strain broth through cheesecloth into a bowl and reserve.

Shell shrimp, devein, and keep warm.

Season fish steaks with salt and pepper to taste and arrange in a large, deep skillet. Ladle broth over the steaks, bring liquid to the boil, reduce heat to a simmer, and poach fish for 5 minutes or till just flaky but still moist inside. Transfer steaks to a large heated serving platter and top each with equal numbers of shelled shrimp. Strain broth into a saucepan, add the mushrooms, and simmer for 15 minutes. Add the spinach and cubed tomatoes, simmer for 2 minutes longer, and ladle hot sauce over the steaks and shrimp.

Striped Bass in Court Bouillon

Serves 4

I doubt there's a more refined fish preparation anywhere in the world than this light, aromatic miracle served at The Coach House in New York. "The dish illustrates better than any other the importance of chemistry in cooking," says owner Leon Lianides. "The ingredients must be the finest, the timing must be exact, and if the tomatoes are stirred after the stock is added to the vegetables, you end up with a cloudy broth." Serve with a Greek salad and fresh Corn Sticks (p. 438).

4-lb. striped bass
2½ qts. water
1 cup dry white wine
12 clams, scrubbed thoroughly and shucked
2 leeks, split lengthwise, washed under running water, and chopped
2 medium onions, chopped
2 celery ribs, chopped
2 bay leaves
4 parsley sprigs
4 garlic cloves, crushed
12 peppercorns
½ tsp. dried thyme
Juice of 1 lemon
Salt

¼ cup olive oil
Crushed pepper
2 medium yellow onions, sliced in thin julienne
2 leeks (whites only), split lengthwise, washed under running water, and sliced in thin julienne
2 carrots, scraped and sliced in thin julienne
2 celery hearts, sliced in thin julienne
3 medium ripe tomatoes, peeled, seeded, and coarsely chopped
2 oz. Pernod
2 Tb. chopped parsley

Clean, wash, and fillet the striped bass, reserving the head and bones, or have fishmonger fillet the bass, reserving head and bones.

Combine the water, wine, and reserved fish head and bones in a large kettle and bring liquid to the boil. Add the clams, chopped leeks, chopped onions, chopped celery, bay leaves, parsley, garlic, peppercorns, thyme, lemon juice, and salt, reduce heat, cover, and simmer for 20 minutes. Strain stock through cheesecloth and reserve clams for another use.

Rinse out kettle and dry with a towel. Heat the olive oil in the kettle, add salt and crushed pepper to taste, add the julienne vegetables, and sauté over low heat, stirring, for about 5 minutes or till vegetables are soft. Add the tomatoes, stir exactly 1 minute, then add the fish stock and Pernod. Bring liquid to the boil without stirring, reduce heat, and simmer for 30 minutes.

Add the fish fillets, cover kettle, poach fish for 10 minutes, and let rest off the heat for 3 minutes.

To serve, cut fillets in half, place halves in 4 wide, shallow soup bowls, and pour broth and vegetables around the sides. Sprinkle with chopped parsley and serve immediately.

Blackened Redfish

Serves 6 – 8

I've yet to understand all the excitement over Paul Prudhomme's blackened redfish since Southerners have been preparing catfish in this manner as long as I can remember. The dish, however, has been reproduced in restaurants all over the country, so I include the recipe for your appraisal. I first tasted Paul's redfish when he was head chef at Commander's Palace in New Orleans; it's now a must for anyone visiting his excellent K-Paul's restaurant in the French Quarter. Personally, I find the dish greatly enhanced when sprinkled with a few capers.

½ tsp. dried thyme
½ tsp. dried basil
½ tsp. oregano
3 tsp. paprika
1 Tb. salt
1 tsp. freshly ground pepper

½ tsp. cayenne
2 lbs. white fish fillets (redfish,
    red snapper, or striped bass),
    skinned
1 cup (2 sticks) melted butter

Combine the herbs, paprika, salt, pepper, and cayenne in a small bowl and mix thoroughly.

Heat a large cast-iron skillet over high heat for about 7 – 8 minutes or till extremely hot. In batches, dip the fish fillets in the melted butter, sprinkle both sides with some of the herb mixture, and place in the hot skillet. Drizzle a little butter on top of each fillet, cook for 2 minutes, turn, drizzle on more butter, and cook for 1 minute longer. Transfer fillets to a hot serving platter and serve as quickly as possible.

Catfish Caribbean en Papillote

Serves 6

I can't remember when or why a reader sent in this recipe, but apparently more than one person is aware of my lifelong devotion to a sweet, delicious fish that has yet to make it up the social ladder of success anywhere but in the South. Today catfish is available from time to time in better fish markets throughout the country, but if you're unable to obtain it, you might substitute fillets cut from large trout.

2 lbs. catfish fillets
Salt
2 Tb. vegetable oil
2 Tb. olive oil
1 cup chopped onions
1 cup chopped green bell pepper
1 Tb. chopped jalapeño pepper
2 garlic cloves, minced

1 bay leaf, crumbled fine
½ tsp. dried thyme
½ tsp. oregano
Freshly ground pepper
¼ cup minced parsley
3 Tb. toasted ground almonds
18 thin slices seeded lemon
Paprika

Cut catfish fillets into 12 equal portions and season with salt to taste. Fold each of 6 squares (12×12 inches) of aluminum foil in half and cut out the largest possible heart. Open hearts, brush insides with vegetable oil, and place one portion of catfish on right-hand side of each heart.

Heat olive oil in a large, heavy skillet, add onions, green pepper, jalapeño, garlic, bay leaf, thyme, oregano, and pepper to taste, and sauté over low heat for 5 minutes, stirring. Stir in the parsley and almonds, divide the mixture among the 6 fillets on the foil hearts, and spread evenly on the fillets. Top each fillet with another fillet, place three lemon slices on top of each portion, and sprinkle with paprika.

Preheat oven to 450°.

To close packages, fold left half of foil over fish and secure all edges tightly. Place packages on a baking sheet and bake for 15–20 minutes or till foil is puffed.

To serve, make a crosswise slit the length and width of each package and fold edges back.

Sautéed Tuna with Tarragon

Serves 4

Ever since the champions of California Cuisine rediscovered fresh tuna a few years ago, the fish has been subjected to every preparation imaginable, some sensible, some ridiculous (I mean, grilled tuna with chutney sauce, indeed!). This version comes from Richard Nelson, one of the more talented instructors on the West Coast.

⅔ cup dry white wine
1 Tb. chopped fresh tarragon (or
*   1 tsp. dried tarragon)*
4 Tb. (½ stick) butter

2-lb. fresh tuna steak at least 1
*   inch thick*
Freshly ground pepper

Combine wine and tarragon in a small bowl, stir well, and let sit for about 15 minutes.

Heat the butter in a large, heavy skillet, add the tuna, and brown lightly on both sides over high heat. Add the wine mixture and let it cook down rapidly, about 5 minutes, spooning it over the fish as it cooks (tuna is ready when it just flakes).

Transfer tuna to a heated serving platter, pour wine sauce over the top, and, to serve, cut tuna into 4 equal portions.

Sautéed Trout with Crabmeat in Red Wine Sauce

Serves 4

When Alex Brennan told me about this new dish being tested at Brennan's of Houston — for years one of my favorite restaurants in the country — my first reaction was "overkill!" I couldn't have been more wrong.

8 Tb. (1 stick) butter
4 medium trout fillets
1 Tb. finely chopped shallots
2 tsp. minced garlic
1 cup dry red wine
¼ cup half-and-half

Juice of 1 lemon
1 cup finely chopped scallions
1 lb. fresh lump crabmeat
Salt and freshly ground pepper
¼ cup finely chopped parsley

*H*eat one-half of the butter in a large, heavy skillet, add the trout fillets, and sauté over low heat for 5 minutes on each side or till fish flakes easily with a fork. Transfer fish to a heated serving platter and keep warm.

Add the shallots and garlic to the skillet and sauté, stirring, for 1 minute. Add the wine, increase heat to high, and reduce by half. Add the half-and-half and return to the boil. Remove skillet from the heat and whisk in 2 tablespoons of the butter plus the lemon juice.

Heat remaining butter in another skillet, add scallions, crabmeat, and salt and pepper to taste, and sauté for about 1 minute, stirring. Top each trout fillet with equal amounts of crabmeat mixture, coat each with wine sauce, and sprinkle chopped parsley on top.

Paupiettes of Salmon with Basil Sauce

Serves 4

Here is a good example of an elegant fish dish that can be prepared from scratch in no more than 30 minutes. Michel Blanchet serves the salmon at L'Ermitage in Los Angeles with only a julienne of zucchini sautéed in butter, but, because of all the butter in the sauce, I prefer steamed zucchini and a few simple boiled new potatoes.

1½-lb. boned fresh salmon steak
1-lb. flounder or sole fillet, cut
   into 1-inch chunks
2 egg whites
8 Tb. (1 stick) butter, softened
2½ cups heavy cream
Salt and freshly ground pepper

2 shallots, chopped
1 cup dry white wine
1 cup Fish Stock (p. 524)
1 large ripe tomato, peeled,
   seeded, and diced
10 fresh basil leaves, finely chopped

Carefully cut the salmon lengthwise into 8 thin slices and place slices on a sheet of wax paper.

Prepare a fish *mousseline* by combining in a food processor the chunks of flounder, egg whites, one-half of the butter, 1½ cups of the cream, and salt and pepper to taste, and reducing to a paste. Coat each salmon slice with a thick layer of *mousseline,* roll up the slices and secure the edges with toothpicks, and reserve the remaining *mousseline.*

Combine 2 tablespoons of the butter, the shallots, wine, and stock in a large skillet and bring to the simmer, stirring. Add the salmon *paupiettes,* return liquid to the simmer, and cook for 10 minutes. Remove *paupiettes* with a slotted spoon to drain momentarily on paper towels, remove toothpicks, and keep warm on a heated serving platter.

Scrape reserved *mousseline* into a saucepan, add remaining cream, the diced tomato, and the basil, and reduce liquid by half over moderately high heat. Add remaining butter, stir till well blended, and pour sauce over the *paupiettes.*

Serve 2 *paupiettes* per person.

Salmon Dumplings Stuffed with Caviar

Serves 4

This elegant dish, which was developed when I did a lengthy article on the new domestic caviar now being produced, is a bit complex but well worth the effort. Although they do not have the flavor of salmon, pike, sole, or flounder could also be used. Serve the dumplings with parsleyed boiled potatoes and perhaps a few Fried Asparagus (p. 326).

1 lb. fresh salmon, skinned, boned, and chilled	*Salt and freshly ground pepper*
2 egg whites	*4 Tb. sturgeon caviar*
4 cups dry vermouth	*1 cup (2 sticks) unsalted butter*
1½ cups heavy cream	*¾ cup finely chopped shallots*
	Sprigs of fresh dill for garnish

Cut the salmon into 1-inch pieces, place in a blender or food processor, and reduce to a puree. Add the egg whites, run machine for about 1 minute, add 2 tablespoons of the vermouth, and run machine till mixture is completely smooth. Transfer mixture to a bowl and chill for 30 minutes. Remove bowl from the refrigerator, fold one-half of the cream into the mixture, season with salt and pepper to taste, and chill for 30 minutes longer.

Grease a 12-inch skillet. Fill a wet soup spoon with salmon puree, make a lengthwise slit in the puree, and fill the slit with ¾ teaspoon of caviar. Cover openings with a little more puree and shape into smooth ovals with another wet spoon. As the dumplings are shaped (16 in all), transfer to the greased skillet. Place skillet in the refrigerator and chill dumplings for 30 minutes.

Meanwhile, heat 3 tablespoons of the butter in a saucepan, add the shallots, and sauté over low heat for 2 minutes. Add 2 cups of the vermouth, increase heat to high, and boil just till liquid evaporates. Add remaining cream and continue cooking till cream coats bottom of the pan. Gradually whisk in the remaining butter in pieces, remove pan from the heat, and strain sauce into the top of a double boiler over simmering water. Season with salt and pepper to taste and keep sauce warm.

In a large saucepan, combine 10 cups of water with the remaining vermouth, bring to the boil, and season the liquid with salt and pepper to taste. Place skillet with the chilled dumplings on top of the stove and carefully ladle the hot liquid around dumplings to barely cover. Bring liquid to a gentle simmer, cook for 5 minutes, and transfer dumplings with a slotted spoon to a clean towel to drain.

To serve, arrange 4 dumplings on each of 4 serving plates, spoon warm sauce around dumplings so it just covers the plate bottoms, and garnish plates with sprigs of dill.

Indian Salmon Poached in Mezcal

Serves 4

This unusual creation of Nancy Ames commanded first prize from me and other judges at a gourmet gala held in San Diego to help fund cancer research. Though less refined in flavor than tequila, mezcal lends itself beautifully to cooking and can be found in better liquor stores. Kumquats usually come on the market shortly before Christmas and add unique savor to whatever they're cooked with, but if these tiny, tart citrus fruits are unavailable, substitute one large orange in the sauce and garnish the dish with segments of tangerine.

*3-lb. center-cut fresh salmon
   fillet, cut into 4 equal portions
Mezcal
Chicken Stock (p. 521)
1 cup Fresh Mayonnaise
   (p. 541)
6 kumquats, peeled, seeded, and
   finely chopped
Juice of ½ orange*

*1 Tb. chopped fresh tarragon (or
   ½ tsp. dried tarragon)
Cayenne
1 small garlic clove, minced
1 tsp. chopped chives
1 Tb. cactus jelly (available in
   specialty food shops)
1 Tb. mezcal
Whole kumquats for garnish*

*P*lace salmon fillets in a large skillet, add equal parts of mezcal and chicken stock to just cover, bring liquid to the boil, lower heat, and poach gently for 10–15 minutes or till just flaky. Transfer salmon to a serving platter to cool and let the cooking liquid cool to room temperature.

In a mixing bowl, combine mayonnaise with the chopped kumquats, add the orange juice, and blend thoroughly. Add the tarragon, cayenne to taste, garlic, and chives, and mix well. In a small bowl, combine the jelly, tablespoon of mezcal, and ½ cup of the reserved cooking liquid, mix till slightly syrupy, add to the mayonnaise, and stir to blend well.

Spoon sauce over the cooled salmon and garnish edges of the platter with whole kumquats.

Swordfish Steaks in Apple Cider Sauce

Serves 4

Swordfish, like salmon and halibut, is a tricky fish to broil, grill, or sauté since it tends to dry out very quickly unless kept well lubricated. These steaks must be seared quickly, then sautéed in plenty of butter and oil and not cooked for more than 5 minutes on each side.

½ cup flour
Salt and freshly ground pepper
4 swordfish steaks, about 1 inch
  thick
8 Tb. (1 stick) butter
4 Tb. vegetable oil

½ cup apple cider
1 Tb. lemon juice
¼ cup heavy cream
1 Tb. butter, softened
1 Tb. chopped chives

Combine flour and salt and pepper to taste in a pie plate and dredge the steaks lightly on both sides.

Heat the 8 tablespoons of butter and the oil in a large skillet very hot, add the steaks, and sear quickly on both sides. Reduce heat to moderate, sauté steaks for 5 minutes on each side, and transfer to a heated serving platter.

Pour off all but 1 tablespoon of the grease from the skillet, increase heat, add cider and lemon juice, and reduce by half, stirring. Add the cream and continue to reduce till sauce is slightly thickened. Remove skillet from the heat, add the tablespoon of butter and the chives, and stir till well blended. Pour sauce over steaks and serve immediately.

Red Snapper with Garlic-Mayonnaise Sauce

Serves 4

Since the sturdy sauce for this Italian-style dish demands that the fish be firm and full-flavored, I would not recommend substituting sole, flounder, or even striped bass for the snapper. A nice accompaniment would be Broccoli Sautéed with Peanuts (p. 337).

1½ cups Fresh Mayonnaise
   (p. 541)
1 Tb. chopped fresh parsley
2 garlic cloves, crushed to a paste
   in a mortar
¼ cup flour
Salt and freshly ground pepper
4 red snapper fillets, about 7 oz.
   each

¼ cup vegetable oil
2 Tb. butter
1 medium onion, finely chopped
2 large ripe tomatoes, peeled,
   seeded, and coarsely chopped
¼ tsp. oregano
¼ cup freshly grated Parmesan
   cheese

In a small bowl, combine mayonnaise, parsley, and garlic paste, cover with plastic wrap, and refrigerate for 1 hour.

Combine flour and salt and pepper to taste in a pie plate and dust snapper fillets on both sides.

Heat the oil in a large skillet, add the fillets, and sauté over moderate heat for 2 minutes on each side or till golden. Transfer fillets to a large baking dish and keep warm.

Heat butter in a saucepan, add the onion, and sauté over low heat for 2 minutes. Add the tomatoes, oregano, and salt and pepper to taste, stir, increase heat slightly, and cook for 10 minutes.

Preheat oven broiler.

Spoon the tomato sauce over and around the fillets, then spread the garlic-mayonnaise on top. Sprinkle each fillet with cheese, place dish in the oven, and broil till sauce begins to bubble. Serve piping hot.

Stanley Demos' Stuffed Red Snapper

Serves 4

This is Stanley Demos' signature dish at his Coach House in Lexington, Kentucky, and one of the most popular recipes we've published in *Town & Country*. I've also stuffed a large striped bass in this manner.

4- to 5-lb. red snapper
Salt and freshly ground pepper
8 Tb. (1 stick) butter
½ cup finely chopped scallions (a little green part included)
⅓ cup finely chopped celery
1 cup bread crumbs
6 large shrimp, peeled, deveined, and diced

6 fresh oysters, chopped
3 Tb. lemon juice
½ cup dry white wine
1 tsp. salt
2 strips of bacon
2 lemons, quartered and seeded
Watercress for garnish

*B*one the snapper by first cutting open the belly all the way to the tail. Using a boning knife, carefully loosen the flesh from the ribs to the backbone, discard bones, spread the fish out in butterfly fashion, and season with salt and pepper to taste.

Heat one-half of the butter in a skillet, add the scallions and celery, and sauté over low heat for 2 minutes. Transfer vegetables to a mixing bowl, add the bread crumbs, shrimp, oysters, lemon juice, wine, salt, and pepper to taste, and mix thoroughly.

Preheat oven to 350°.

Place stuffing in the center of the spread snapper and fold sides up and over till the edges come together, removing excess stuffing, if any. Thread a large trussing needle with string and sew the edges securely, starting at the head of the fish. Place fish on a rack in a roasting pan, make 3 or 4 incisions in the flesh on top with a sharp knife, place bacon strips lengthwise on top, and bake for about 45 minutes or till flesh is flaky but still juicy.

Transfer fish to a heated serving platter and remove and discard bacon and string. Heat remaining butter in a small saucepan, pour over the fish, and garnish platter with the lemon wedges and watercress.

Sole Farcie au Foie Gras
(Sole Stuffed with Foie Gras)

Serves 8

Often when I lay hands on a much-cherished, valuable tin of pure *foie gras,* I will use it to stuff fish in the classic French manner. Garnished with mushroom caps sautéed in butter and a little chopped parsley, this simple but sinfully rich sole dish makes for an impressive presentation.

7-oz. tin of foie gras	*1 egg yolk*
8 large fillets of sole	*½ cup heavy cream*
1 cup chicken broth	*Pinch of dried tarragon*
½ cup dry white wine	*1 cup grated Gruyère cheese*
4 Tb. (½ stick) butter	*¼ cup finely chopped parsley*
Salt and freshly ground pepper	

Preheat oven to 350°.

With a sharp knife dipped in water, cut *foie gras* into 8 equal slices and place 1 slice in the center of each sole fillet. Fold ends of fillets securely over the *foie gras* and place packets fold side down in a shallow baking dish. Pour chicken broth and wine over packets, dot the top of each packet with equal amounts of the butter, and bake for 10–15 minutes or till fish just begins to flake.

Carefully spoon cooking liquid into a bowl, then strain liquid into a saucepan, keeping fish warm in the baking dish. Bring liquid to the boil, reduce to 1 cup, and remove pan from heat. In a small bowl, beat the egg yolk with the cream and tarragon, quickly whisk the mixture into the reduced liquid, and stir over low heat till sauce is slightly thickened.

Preheat oven broiler.

Spoon sauce over the fish, sprinkle cheese on top, and broil for 2–3 minutes or till top is golden. Sprinkle fish with chopped parsley and serve immediately.

Baby Flounder with Mushrooms and Pecans

Serves 4

Trout, small soles, and red snapper are also very good prepared in this manner. I happen to love flounder in any shape or form, but use whichever fish is freshest.

6 Tb. (¾ stick) butter	1 cup coarsely chopped pecans
1 cup coarsely chopped mushrooms	1 cup dry white wine
½ cup flour	Pinch of ground fennel
Salt and freshly ground pepper	¼ cup heavy cream
4 baby flounder fillets, skinned	

*H*eat 2 tablespoons of the butter in a small skillet, add mushrooms, and sauté over low heat for 5 minutes, stirring.

Combine flour and salt and pepper to taste in a pie plate and dredge the fillets lightly in the mixture. Heat remaining butter in a large skillet, add fillets, and sauté for 2 minutes on one side over moderate heat. Turn fillets over, scatter the mushrooms and pecans on top and around the sides, and continue sautéing fish for 2 minutes longer. Add the wine and fennel, cook for 1 minute, then pour on the cream, stirring gently but taking care not to break up the fish. Reduce heat to low, cover skillet, and let fish rest in the cooking liquid several minutes.

To serve, transfer fillets to a heated serving platter, reduce sauce over moderately high heat till slightly thickened, and pour mushrooms, pecans, and sauce over fish.

Fillet of Flounder with Shrimp-Tomato Sauce

Serves 4

8 Tb. (1 stick) butter
1 medium onion, diced
1 garlic clove, minced
½ lb. fresh shrimp, shelled,
    deveined, and diced
2 large ripe tomatoes, peeled,
    seeded, and chopped
1 Tb. finely chopped fresh basil

2 Tb. finely chopped parsley
Salt and freshly ground pepper
1 egg
½ cup milk
4 medium flounder fillets
¼ cup flour
Parsley sprigs for garnish

*H*eat one-half of the butter in a heavy saucepan, add the onion and garlic, and sauté over low heat for 2 minutes. Increase heat to moderate, add the diced shrimp, tomatoes, basil, chopped parsley, and salt and pepper to taste, stir well, and cook for 10 minutes, stirring occasionally. Keep sauce warm.

In a bowl, beat the egg with the milk, dip fish fillets in the mixture, then dust in the flour.

Heat the remaining butter in a large heavy skillet, add flounders (2 at a time if possible), and sauté on both sides over medium heat till golden. Transfer fish to a heated serving platter, spoon on the shrimp-tomato sauce, and garnish the platter with parsley sprigs.

Steamed Lobster

While nothing can be more tasty (and relatively economical) from time to time than a lobster prepared Newburg style or *à l'Américaine* (p. 298), the delicacy is never quite so luscious as when simply steamed, then dipped in hot melted butter spiked with lemon juice, or served cold with fresh mayonnaise. I find steaming lobsters much more preferable to boiling for the simple reason that almost any food submerged in boiling water seems to lose a certain amount of flavor. If boil you must, however, the most sensible rule of thumb to avoid overcooking is roughly 5 minutes for the first pound and 3 minutes for each additional pound. In any case, do try to buy female lobsters so you can have the added luxury of savoring the rich coral.

*T*o steam lobsters, place a rack in a very large pot or canning kettle, add 2 – 3 inches of sea water, or tap water with 1 tablespoon of salt per quart, and bring to a rapid boil. Place lobsters headfirst on the rack, cover, and when boil returns, begin timing according to the following: 1- to 1¼-pound lobsters, 10 – 12 minutes; 1½- to 2-pound lobsters, 15 – 18 minutes; 2½- to 5-pound lobsters, 20 – 25 minutes.

To serve, turn the lobster bottom side up, and with a heavy chef's knife slit down the middle of body and tail. Remove and discard both the dark intestinal vein running down the tail and the stomach sac in the head part. Place whole lobsters on individual platters and provide either individual bowls or one large communal bowl for shell scraps, bowls of hot drawn butter, nutcrackers, oyster forks, and plenty of napkins.

Lobster Stew with Leeks

Serves 4

4 medium leeks (whites only)   Salt and freshly ground pepper
2 2-lb. female lobsters   Dash of Worcestershire
8 Tb. (1 stick) butter   2 Tb. dry sherry
1 medium onion, minced   2 qts. milk

Split leeks lengthwise, wash thoroughly under running water, and place in a large skillet with ½ inch of water. Bring water to the boil, cover, and steam leeks for 18 minutes or till just tender. Drain, chop coarsely, and set aside.

Steam lobsters according to directions in Steamed Lobster (p. 296), split in half lengthwise with a large heavy knife, and drain, reserving the cooking liquid. Remove and discard both the dark intestinal vein running down the tail and the stomach sac in the head part. Remove meat, tomalley, coral, and all white substance from inside shells and cut meat into 1-inch chunks.

Heat 2 tablespoons of the butter in a large skillet, add onion, and sauté over low heat for 2 minutes. Add 2 more tablespoons of the butter, add tomalley, coral, and white substance, and sauté for 2 minutes longer. Increase heat, add remaining butter, the lobster chunks, reserved leeks, salt and pepper to taste, Worcestershire, and sherry, and cook, stirring, for 5 minutes.

Let mixture cool, add milk and reserved cooking liquid, and let stew sit in the refrigerator for 4–6 hours. When ready to serve, reheat thoroughly and taste for seasoning.

Lobster à l'Américaine

Food enthusiasts will go on and on about whether the correct name of this classic French lobster dish is *à l'Américaine* (referring to a Parisian chef who supposedly created it for an American client) or *à l'Armoricaine* (after the ancient province of Armorique in Brittany where lobsters are so plentiful). Personally, I couldn't care less about the origins of the name, content to dive, whenever possible, into a succulent stew that in many ways epitomizes the genius of the French kitchen. The coral does add a suave richness to the sauce, so shop for female lobsters.

3 1½-lb. live lobsters
¼ cup olive oil
1 medium onion, finely chopped
1 carrot, scraped and finely
  chopped
1 garlic clove, minced
½ cup dry white wine
½ cup water
4 Tb. Cognac

2 ripe tomatoes, peeled, seeded,
  and chopped
1 tsp. dried tarragon
Salt and freshly ground pepper
Cayenne
4 Tb. (½ stick) butter
Pinch of dried chervil
¼ cup chopped parsley

Plunge lobsters head-first into a large kettle of boiling water for about 5 seconds and place on a cutting board. Split each in half lengthwise with a heavy knife and remove and discard both the dark intestinal vein running down the tail and the stomach sac in the head part. Remove claws and crack, cut tail (still in shell) into 5 or 6 rings, and remove and reserve the tomalley and coral.

Heat the oil in a large, heavy skillet, add lobsters in batches, sauté over moderate heat for 2 minutes, turning, or till shells are red, and transfer to a large platter. Add to the skillet the onion, carrot, and garlic, sauté for 3 minutes over low heat, stirring, and drain off any excess oil. Increase heat to moderate, add wine, water, 2 tablespoons of the Cognac, tomatoes, tarragon, and salt, pepper, and cayenne to taste, and stir for 2 minutes. Place lobster pieces on top, reduce heat, cover, and simmer for 20 minutes.

Transfer lobster pieces to a heated serving platter and reduce liquid in the skillet by one-half. Force tomalley and coral through a fine sieve into the sauce, add 2 tablespoons of the butter plus the chervil, and stir well to blend. Increase heat, add remaining Cognac and butter, stir, pour sauce over the lobster, and top with chopped parsley.

Serve lobster, shells and all, with bowls for the shells, finger bowls, and plenty of steamed rice.

Indonesian Shrimp Curry with Coconut

Serves 6

3 Tb. peanut or vegetable oil
2 medium onions, finely chopped
1 garlic clove, minced
2 small red chili peppers, seeded
  and finely chopped
½ tsp. ground cinnamon
½ tsp. ground turmeric
½ tsp. ground cumin
½ tsp. ground cloves

½ tsp. chili powder
3 Tb. finely chopped fresh
  coriander (also called cilantro
  and Chinese parsley)
½ tsp. salt
1 cup grated fresh coconut
1¾ cups Fish Stock (p. 524)
2 lbs. medium shrimp, shelled,
  and deveined

Heat the oil in a large skillet, add the onions, garlic, and chili peppers, and sauté over low heat for 2 minutes, stirring. Add the cinnamon, turmeric, cumin, cloves, chili powder, 1 tablespoon of the coriander, and salt, stir well, and continue cooking for 1 – 2 minutes longer.

Add coconut and fish stock, bring liquid to the boil, reduce heat, and simmer for 3 minutes. Add the shrimp, stir, and cook for 5 – 8 minutes or till shrimp are just tender but not overcooked.

Serve the curry over steamed rice and sprinkle each portion with some of the remaining coriander.

Caraway Shrimp Stuffed in Cantaloupes

Serves 6

About twice a year I retire to the luxurious Brenner's Park Hotel in Baden-Baden, Germany, to take the restorative waters, participate in a life-saving antistress program, and knock off pounds painlessly. This is but one of the exquisite dishes included on my diet — minus, of course, the creamed mayonnaise. It might be a bit pretentious, but it serves a delicious purpose.

3 lbs. medium-size fresh shrimp
6 small cantaloupes
Juice of 1 orange
2 Tb. caraway seeds
1 Tb. finely chopped fresh dill
2 Tb. chili sauce
1 Tb. gin
¼ cup olive oil

Salt and freshly ground pepper
3 small ripe tomatoes, cut in half,
   seeded, and pulp removed
6 pitted black olives, sliced
¼ cup Fresh Mayonnaise
   (optional) (p. 541)
¼ cup whipped cream (optional)

Place the shrimp in a large saucepan with enough salted water to cover, cover, and bring to the boil. Immediately drain shrimp in a colander, and when cool enough to handle, shell and devein all but 6.

Cut lids out of melon tops in a serrated fashion, scoop out seeds and strings with a large spoon, and cut out the flesh with a melon ball scoop or a spoon. Reserve 6 melon balls.

Combine in a large mixing bowl all but the 6 reserved shrimp and 6 melon balls, the orange juice, caraway seeds, dill, chili sauce, gin, oil, and salt and pepper to taste, and toss to mix thoroughly. Fill each melon with equal amounts of the mixture and replace lids upside down, fixing each at an angle with a cocktail stick. Spear half a tomato on each stick open side up, arrange a reserved unshelled shrimp and a melon ball inside each tomato, and finish with a few slices of olive.

Serve melons on a bed of crushed ice, mix the optional mayonnaise and cream, and serve on the side.

Hong Kong Crystal Shrimp

Serves 4

I've consumed stuffed goose neck, sea slugs, and that hideous bivalve from Pacific Northwest waters known as geoduck, but when Ken Hom, a distinguished Chinese cooking teacher in San Francisco and Hong Kong, said I had to prepare this dish with live shrimp left to expire in a salt marinade, I drew the line on adventurous eating. My rendition, therefore, may not be totally authentic, but it's nevertheless delicious. Be sure to buy jumbo shrimp (prawns) about 3 inches long, and make every effort to get them as fresh as possible.

2 lbs. jumbo shrimp
½ cup coarse salt
3 Tb. peanut oil
4 garlic cloves, finely chopped
2 thin slices fresh ginger, finely chopped

6 scallions, trimmed partly of green tops and finely chopped
2 Tb. soy sauce
2 Tb. dry sherry

Place shrimp in a shallow glass container, sprinkle with the salt, cover with plastic wrap, and marinate for at least 2 hours. Rinse shrimp well in cold water and pat dry with paper towels.

Heat oil very hot in a wok or heavy skillet, add the shrimp, and stir-fry quickly, just to coat with the oil. Add the garlic, ginger, and scallions, and stir-fry for a few seconds longer. Add the soy sauce and sherry and continue stirring for about 2 minutes (the shells should become transparent and thus edible). Serve immediately with rice and blanched fresh vegetables.

Paul Prudhomme's Coconut Beer Shrimp

Serves 6

This is still another sensational dish the celebrated Cajun chef created when I first knew him in the kitchen of Commander's Palace in New Orleans. How well I recall popping so many of these shrimp in my mouth as we passed by the holding table in the kitchen that my appetite for lunch was totally destroyed. About four of the shrimp per person also make for a very nice appetizer.

1 Tb. cayenne
2¼ tsp. salt
1½ tsp. sweet paprika
1½ tsp. freshly ground pepper
1¼ tsp. garlic powder
¾ tsp. onion powder
¾ tsp. dried thyme
¾ tsp. oregano
2 eggs

1¾ cups all-purpose flour
¾ cup beer
1 Tb. baking powder
48 medium shrimp, shelled except
    for tails and deveined
3 cups grated fresh coconut
Vegetable oil for deep-frying
*Dipping Sauce

Combine cayenne, salt, paprika, black pepper, garlic powder, onion powder, thyme, and oregano in a small bowl, and mix thoroughly. In another bowl, combine 2 teaspoons of the seasoning mix with the eggs, 1¼ cups of the flour, the beer, and baking powder, and mix well till smooth. In another small bowl, combine remaining flour with 1½ teaspoons of the seasoning mix. And in a fourth bowl, place the coconut.

Sprinkle remaining seasoning mix over the shrimp, then, holding each shrimp by the tail, dredge each in the flour, dip in the beer batter, coat generously with coconut, and place on a baking sheet.

Heat oil in a deep fryer or small cast-iron skillet to 350°, drop the shrimp into oil in batches, fry for 1 minute, and drain on paper towels.

To serve, place about ⅓ cup of dipping sauce in each of 6 small bowls, place bowls on serving plates, and surround each bowl with 8 shrimp.

* *Dipping Sauce:* Combine in a bowl 1⅔ cups orange marmalade, 5 Tb. Creole mustard (available in specialty food shops), and 5 Tb. finely grated fresh or prepared horseradish, and mix well.

Shrimp Pilau

Serves 6

Seafood, poultry, and vegetable pilaus have been gastronomic staples in Savannah and Charleston since the towns were founded. No one really knows how the rice-based *pullao* of India made its way to the Southern Low Country, but today locals will still argue till sundown about what constitutes an authentic pilau — or purlow, or perlew!

6 slices of bacon, cut into 1/4-inch pieces
1 1/2 cups long-grain rice
1 1/2 cups finely chopped onions
2 1/4 cups Chicken Stock (p. 521)
1 1/2 cups (about 3 medium) peeled, seeded, and finely chopped ripe tomatoes
2 tsp. lemon juice

1 1/2 tsp. Worcestershire
1 1/2 tsp. salt
Freshly ground pepper
1/4 tsp. cayenne
3/4 tsp. nutmeg
2 lbs. medium shrimp, shelled and deveined
1/4 cup minced parsley

Preheat oven to 350°.
   Fry bacon in a large skillet till crisp, drain on paper towels, crumble, and reserve 3 tablespoons of the bacon grease.

Place rice in a fine sieve and wash under cold running water.

Heat the reserved bacon grease in a heavy casserole, add the onions, and sauté over low heat for 2 minutes, stirring. Add the rice and stir till well coated with the fat. Add the chicken broth, tomatoes, lemon juice, Worcestershire, salt, pepper to taste, cayenne, and nutmeg, stir, and bring liquid to the boil. Cover casserole, transfer to the oven, and bake for 20 minutes. Remove casserole from the oven, stir in the shrimp and reserved bacon, and bake, covered, for 15 minutes longer. Remove casserole from the oven and let stand for 10 minutes.

To serve, fluff pilau with a fork, season with salt and pepper if necessary, and sprinkle minced parsley on top.

Shrimp Pie

When members of the Junior League of Charleston prepared a dinner to illustrate for me and others at *Town & Country* what typical South Carolina coastal fare is all about, they were as proud of their humble shrimp pie as of any other item on the elaborate buffet. This makes for a nice, simple summertime casserole to be served outside on the deck or patio.

2½ cups fresh bread crumbs	*1 Tb. Dijon mustard*
(about 5 slices dry white bread)	*1 Tb. Worcestershire*
1 cup milk	*1 Tb. dry sherry*
6 Tb. (¾ stick) butter	*Tabasco*
1 small onion, minced	*Salt and freshly ground pepper*
½ green bell pepper, seeded and	*1½ lbs. medium shrimp, shelled*
minced	*and deveined*

Preheat oven to 350°.
Combine 2 cups of the bread crumbs and the milk in a large bowl and let soak.

Heat 2 tablespoons of the butter in a small skillet, add onion and bell pepper, sauté over low heat for 2 minutes, and add to the soaked bread. Melt remaining butter in a small saucepan, add one-half to the bread mixture, and stir. Add the mustard, Worcestershire, sherry, and Tabasco, salt, and pepper to taste, and stir to blend thoroughly.

Fold shrimp into the mixture and transfer mixture to a buttered casserole or baking dish. Distribute remaining bread crumbs over the mixture, drizzle remaining melted butter on top, and bake for 35–40 minutes or till top is golden brown.

Jean Anderson's Baked Stuffed Fresh Sardines

Serves 6

How often I've sat in waterfront restaurants along the French Riviera eating fresh fat sardines stuffed with everything from Swiss chard to cured black olives to a mixture of chopped herbs. Fresh sardines, which are totally different from the canned variety, can often be found in the better fish markets of our major cities and make for an interesting change in menu. Although large smelts can be stuffed in the same fashion (see Sautéed Smelts with Dill, p. 309), they're not nearly as delicate as fresh sardines. My friend Jean Anderson's stuffing is one of the most delicious I've tried.

5 Tb. olive oil
3 cups soft bread crumbs (about 6 slices of fresh white bread)
1/3 cup finely chopped pine nuts
1/4 cup minced golden seedless raisins
6 anchovy fillets, rinsed, patted dry, and minced

1/4 cup minced parsley
2 lbs. fresh sardines about 6 inches long, cleaned
16 bay leaves
2 Tb. sugar
1/4 cup lemon juice

Heat 3 tablespoons of the oil in a large, heavy skillet, add the bread crumbs, and brown over moderate heat, stirring. Place two-thirds of the crumbs in a mixing bowl, add the nuts, raisins, anchovies, and parsley, and mix thoroughly. Reserve remaining crumbs for topping.

Remove heads from sardines, loosen the backbones at the tail with your fingers, pull them out from the flesh, and discard them. Spread sardines open on a working surface, spoon about 1½ tablespoons of stuffing inside each, and fold flesh over stuffing, securing with toothpicks if necessary. Arrange sardines in one layer in a large baking dish, tuck bay leaves between the rows, and drizzle fish with remaining olive oil. Stir sugar into the lemon juice and sprinkle over fish, top with reserved crumbs and any extra stuffing, cover with plastic wrap, and refrigerate for 2 hours.

Remove sardines from the refrigerator and let stand while preheating oven to 375°. Bake, uncovered, for 35–40 minutes or till top is golden brown.

Sardines à la Basquaise

Serves 4–6

3 Tb. butter
3 Tb. olive oil
3 medium onions, finely chopped
2 carrots, scraped and finely
   chopped
1 celery rib, finely chopped
1 garlic clove, minced
½ cup chopped fresh mushrooms
¼ tsp. finely ground bay leaf

Salt and freshly ground pepper
5 medium ripe tomatoes, peeled,
   seeded, and coarsely chopped
2 small red bell peppers, seeded
   and chopped
5 4-oz. cans sardines, drained
¼ cup grated Parmesan cheese
Olive oil

*H*eat butter and oil in a large skillet, add onions, carrots, celery, and garlic, and sauté for 5 minutes over low heat, stirring. Add mushrooms, bay leaf, and salt and pepper to taste, and stir well. Increase heat slightly, cover, and cook for 10 minutes. Add the tomatoes and bell peppers, stir well, and cook for 10 minutes longer.

Preheat oven broiler.

Spoon tomato mixture evenly into a shallow baking dish, arrange the sardines across the top, sprinkle with the grated cheese, and drizzle a little oil over the cheese. Brown casserole under the broiler and serve very hot.

Gratin of Sardines and Tomatoes

Serves 4–6

3 Tb. olive oil
1 garlic clove, finely chopped
5 large ripe tomatoes, coarsely
   chopped
½ tsp. dried thyme
½ tsp. dried basil

Salt and freshly ground pepper
4 4-oz. cans sardines, drained
¼ cup grated Gruyère cheese
½ cup bread crumbs
Olive oil

Preheat oven to 400°.
    Heat the 3 tablespoons of olive oil in a large skillet, add garlic, and sauté over low heat for 2 minutes. Add tomatoes, thyme, basil, and salt and pepper to taste, stir, increase heat to moderate, cover, and cook for 5 minutes.

Arrange sardines on the bottom of a medium gratin dish or shallow ovenproof baking dish, sprinkle with cheese, and spoon tomato mixture on top. Sprinkle bread crumbs over the tomatoes, drizzle crumbs with remaining olive oil, and bake for 15 minutes or till top is nicely glazed.

Moroccan Sardine and Tuna Tart

Serves 8 – 10

Over the years we have run feature food articles in *Town & Country* on the most improbable of subjects, but never was the playback so gratifyingly positive as on the piece I did on the humble sardine. I even held an official sardine tasting with recognized food authorities, the results of which proved that certain American sardines (Port Clyde) can hold their own very well with the very finest French variety (Rödel). This was one of the more interesting recipes I developed.

A double recipe of Pâte Brisée
  (p. 412)
1 egg yolk, beaten
4 4-oz. cans sardines, drained
  and chopped
2 7-oz. cans tuna in oil, drained
  and flaked
3 anchovy fillets, drained and
  finely chopped
2 eggs, beaten
½ cup olive oil

3 hard-boiled eggs, chopped
1 medium onion, grated
1 cup chopped parsley
½ tsp. dried thyme
½ tsp. cumin
2 hot red peppers, minced
Pimiento strips for garnish
Pitted Greek olive halves for
  garnish
1 lemon, halved

Preheat oven to 400°.
Roll out dough ⅛ inch thick on a lightly floured surface, fit into a 12-inch tart pan with removable bottom, and trim excess dough. Line the shell with wax paper, cover paper with dried beans or rice, and bake shell for 10 minutes. Remove beans and paper, brush shell with the egg yolk, bake for 12 minutes more or till lightly browned, and let cool completely.
Reduce oven to 300°.
In a large mixing bowl, combine sardines, tuna, beaten eggs, and oil, and blend thoroughly. Add the chopped eggs, onion, parsley, thyme, cumin, and red peppers, and mix thoroughly. Spoon mixture into the tart shell, smooth top with a spatula, and decorate top with pimiento strips and olive halves. Bake tart for about 40 minutes or till slightly browned, squeeze the lemon halves over the top, and serve hot.

Sautéed Smelts with Dill

Serves 6

Served with potato salad, marinated green beans and red bell pepper, and a fine ale, sautéed smelts make for a delightful warm-weather meal. Since these smelts are stuffed, make sure to buy large ones.

12 large smelts, cleaned
1½ cups half-and-half
1 Tb. lemon juice
1 Tb. Worcestershire
Tabasco
1 garlic clove, crushed
2 shallots, chopped

12 sprigs fresh dill, chopped
1 cup flour
Salt and freshly ground pepper
8 Tb. (1 stick) butter
1 cup Horseradish Sauce
   (p. 530)

Remove heads from smelts, loosen the backbones at the tail end with your fingers, pull them out from the flesh, and discard them. Combine the half-and-half, lemon juice, Worcestershire, Tabasco to taste, garlic, and shallots in a large, shallow baking dish, add the smelts, and marinate for 2 hours in the refrigerator, turning once.

Lift smelts from the marinade, spread open on a working surface, and place equal amounts of chopped dill in the center of each. Fold flesh over stuffing and secure with toothpicks if necessary. Combine flour and salt and pepper to taste in a pie plate and dust the smelts lightly in the mixture.

Heat half the butter in a large skillet, add half the smelts, sauté over moderate heat for 2 minutes on each side or till nicely browned, and transfer to a heated platter. Repeat with remaining butter and smelts.

Serve the smelts with horseradish sauce on the side.

Hot Crabmeat Imperial with Coriander and Capers

Serves 4

2 Tb. butter
2 scallions (including 1 inch of
   green tops), finely chopped
½ celery rib, finely chopped
½ small green bell pepper, seeded
   and finely chopped
1 cup Mustard Mayonnaise
   (p. 542)

Tabasco
1 Tb. chopped fresh coriander
   (also called cilantro and
   Chinese parsley)
2 Tb. capers, rinsed and drained
1½ lbs. fresh lump crabmeat
Salt and freshly ground pepper

Preheat oven to 350°.
   Heat butter in a small skillet, add scallions, celery, and green pepper, and sauté over low heat for 2 minutes, stirring.

Transfer sautéed vegetables to a mixing bowl, add mustard mayonnaise, Tabasco to taste, coriander, and capers, and mix till well blended. Add crabmeat and salt and pepper to taste, and mix gently or just enough to coat crabmeat with the sauce.

Spoon the mixture into serving seafood shells and bake for about 15 minutes or till tops are lightly browned. Serve with Watercress, Apple, and Pecan Salad (p. 165) and Herbed Toast (p. 447).

Spicy Crab Cakes

Serves 6

Of all the dishes for which the American South is known, none is more abused (on home territory and elsewhere) than crab cakes. All too often what you find in homes and at restaurants are heavy, overbreaded, overcooked, greasy fried mounds with much too much onion, celery, and green pepper, when, all the time, it's so easy to produce a light, zesty cake that highlights the luscious crabmeat. Remember that one secret to great crab cakes is handling the mixed ingredients as little as possible. I love Tabasco with a passion, but never so much as in crab cakes.

6 Tb. (¾ stick) butter
1 small onion, minced
½ celery rib, minced
½ cup finely crushed cracker
  crumbs
2 eggs, beaten
1 tsp. dry mustard
1 Tb. lemon juice

2 Tb. Fresh Mayonnaise
  (p. 541)
Salt and freshly ground pepper
Tabasco
1½ lbs. lump crabmeat
2 Tb. vegetable oil
¼ cup finely chopped parsley

Heat 2 tablespoons of the butter in a small skillet, add the onion and celery, and sauté over low heat for exactly 1 minute.

Transfer onion and celery to a large mixing bowl, add the cracker crumbs, eggs, mustard, lemon juice, mayonnaise, salt and pepper to taste, and at least 4 shakes of Tabasco, and mix till well blended. Add the crabmeat, toss very lightly just to bind with mixture, and form gently into ½-inch cakes about 3 inches in diameter. Cover cakes with plastic wrap and refrigerate for 1 hour.

Heat the remaining butter and the oil to moderate in a large skillet, add the cakes, and sauté for about 2 minutes on each side or till golden brown. Drain briefly on paper towels and serve sprinkled with chopped parsley.

Pawleys Island Crab Cakes

Serves 3–6

This memorable version of crab cakes comes from Louis Osteen, owner of The Pawleys Island Restaurant on Pawleys Island, South Carolina, and one of the most gifted chefs in America. "Procuring the blue crab locally," says Louis, "varies from the efficient and easy trap method to the common method using net, string, and chicken necks, to the most basic and skillful method of 'bogging' whereby one simply wades through the marsh creeks and scoops up the tasty crustaceans." This dish is also terrific made with small crawfish. The recipe can be doubled easily.

1 cup Fresh Mayonnaise   *¼ tsp. lemon juice*
   (p. 541)   *1 egg white*
1½ Tb. extra-fine cracker crumbs   *1 lb. fresh lump crabmeat*
Large pinch of cayenne   *1¼ cups fine bread crumbs*
⅛ tsp. ground celery seed   *6 Tb. (¾ stick) clarified butter*
⅛ tsp. dry mustard   *Lemon wedges for garnish*

*I*n a large mixing bowl, combine the mayonnaise, cracker crumbs, cayenne, celery seed, mustard, lemon juice, and egg white, and mix till thoroughly blended. Carefully pick crabmeat free of shell and gently fold into mayonnaise mixture, taking care not to break up lumps.

Divide the mixture into 6 equal portions, form each portion into a patty, and gently roll the patties in one-half of the bread crumbs. Refrigerate patties for 1 hour and roll lightly in the remaining bread crumbs once more before cooking.

Heat the butter to moderate in a 10-inch skillet or sauté pan, add the crab cakes, and sauté for 2 minutes on each side. Drain cakes momentarily on paper towels, transfer to a heated platter, and serve immediately with lemon wedges.

Soft-Shell Crabs with Lemon-Peanut Sauce

Serves 4–6

Cleaned, ready-to-cook soft-shell crabs (i.e., blue crabs that have been caught just after they have molted) are readily available on the East Coast and at finer markets elsewhere from spring to midsummer and are a gastronomic delicacy. The smaller the crab, the better. Serve with Carolina Hush Puppies (p. 436) and Dilled Asparagus (p. 326).

12 soft-shell crabs, cleaned
3 cups milk
1 cup flour
Salt and freshly ground pepper
¾ cup vegetable oil
8 Tb. (1 stick) butter

1 cup peanuts coarsely chopped in
  a food processor
2 Tb. finely chopped parsley
Juice of 1 lemon
Tabasco

Arrange the crabs in a large, shallow baking dish, add the milk, and soak for 30 minutes.

Combine the flour and salt and pepper to taste in a pie plate and dust crabs lightly in the mixture. Heat the vegetable oil in a large skillet, add crabs (in 2 batches if necessary), and sauté over moderate heat for 3 minutes on each side or till golden brown. Drain crabs on paper towels and transfer to a hot serving platter.

Pour off excess oil from skillet, add the butter, and heat till butter foams. Add the peanuts and shake skillet over moderate heat for about 2 minutes. Add the parsley, lemon juice, and Tabasco to taste, stir well, and pour hot sauce over the crabs.

Shad Roe with Mushroom Cream Sauce

When the first buds of spring appear, the only delicacy I seek out more than fresh asparagus is shad roe. I bake it with a tomato sauce, grill it with bacon, and poach it for exotic salads, but never is it so delicious as when prepared according to this recipe inspired by my neighbor and colleague Pierre Franey.

4 pair of shad roe	*4 Tb. (¼ cup) flour*
1 cup milk	*1 cup heavy cream*
½ cup dry white wine	*Cayenne*
¼ tsp. dried thyme	*¼ lb. fresh mushrooms, thinly*
¼ tsp. dried tarragon	*sliced*
1 bay leaf	*Juice of 1 lemon*
Salt and freshly ground pepper	*1 Tb. chopped shallots*
4 Tb. (½ stick) butter	*Watercress for garnish*

Rinse the shad roe, place in a large skillet, and add one-half of the milk, the wine, enough water to just cover, the thyme, tarragon, bay leaf, and salt and pepper to taste. Bring liquid to the boil, reduce heat, cover, and simmer for 3 – 4 minutes. Transfer roe to a heated serving platter, keep warm, and reserve cooking liquid.

Heat 2 tablespoons of the butter in a saucepan, add the flour, and whisk over moderate heat for 2 minutes. Add remaining milk, 1 cup of the reserved cooking liquid, the cream, and cayenne, salt and pepper to taste, and stir well over moderate heat. Strain sauce through a sieve into another saucepan and keep warm.

Heat remaining butter in a skillet, add mushrooms and lemon juice, and cook over moderate heat, stirring, till mushrooms are golden. Add the shallots, stir well, and stir mixture into the cream sauce.

Pour mushroom cream sauce over the shad roe, garnish platter with watercress, and serve immediately.

Cioppino
(Shellfish Stew)

When I published this recipe in *American Taste* as an example of a foreign dish that has assumed such new identity over the years that it can now only be called American, I received numerous letters stating how no authentic *cioppino* should contain lobster, or shrimp, or green pepper. Exactly what the original Italian immigrants in California included in their stew I don't know, but I can assure you that this dish holds its own with any of the great fish stews of Europe. Do not simmer the stew longer than the time indicated.

1½- to 2-lb. lobster
1 lb. medium fresh shrimp, shelled and deveined
12 mussels, scrubbed thoroughly
12 cherrystone or littleneck clams, scrubbed thoroughly
½ cup olive oil
1 cup finely chopped onions
1 cup finely chopped green bell pepper
3 garlic cloves, finely chopped
6 medium ripe tomatoes, peeled, cored, and coarsely chopped

2 Tb. tomato paste
2 cups dry white wine
½ cup chopped parsley
Herb bouquet (1 bay leaf, 4 fresh basil leaves, and ¼ tsp. oregano wrapped in cheesecloth)
Salt and freshly ground pepper
3 lbs. thick striped bass or red snapper fillets, cut into serving pieces

FISH AND SEAFOOD · 315

*B*ring a large saucepan of water to the boil and plunge the lobster in head-first for 5 seconds. Split lobster down the middle, remove and discard both the intestinal vein running down the tail and the stomach sac in the head part, and hack the body into serving pieces, shell and all.

In a large kettle with 1 inch of water, place the lobster pieces, shrimp, mussels, and clams, bring liquid to the boil, cover, and steam shellfish for 10 minutes or till shells of mussels and clams open (discard any that remain closed). Transfer shellfish to a large platter, strain the broth into a bowl, and reserve.

Heat the oil in a large casserole, add onions, green pepper, and garlic, and sauté over low heat for 2 minutes, stirring. Add the tomatoes, tomato paste, wine, parsley, herb bouquet, salt and pepper to taste, and the reserved broth. Stir well, increase heat, cover, and simmer for 15 minutes. Add the fish pieces and simmer for 10 minutes longer. Add the shellfish, simmer for 15 minutes more, and taste broth for seasoning.

Serve stew in deep bowls with a tart salad, Italian bread, and a sturdy California Chardonnay.

New England Clam Pie

Serves 6 – 8

2 slices of bacon	*1 Tb. chopped parsley*
2 Tb. chopped shallots	*¼ tsp. finely chopped lemon rind*
1 garlic clove, minced	*⅛ tsp. dried tarragon*
1 cup diced mushrooms	*⅛ tsp. dried thyme*
3 Tb. flour	*Salt and freshly ground pepper*
1½ cups clam juice	*1 egg yolk, beaten*
2 Tb. dry sherry	*Basic Pie Pastry (p. 411)*
¼ cup heavy cream	*1 egg, beaten with 1 Tb. water*
3 cups chopped clams	

*F*ry bacon in a large skillet till crisp, drain on paper towels, and crumble.

Reduce heat to low, add shallots, garlic, and mushrooms, and sauté, stirring, for about 3 minutes or till mushrooms are just soft. Add the flour, stir, increase heat to moderate, and cook for 1 minute longer. Add the clam juice and sherry, bring to the boil, and cook for 1 minute. Add the cream, stir, and cook for 8–10 minutes or till liquid is slightly reduced. Add the clams, parsley, crumbled bacon, lemon rind, tarragon, thyme, and salt and pepper to taste, stir, return liquid to the boil, and cook for 1 minute longer.

Remove skillet from the heat, beat a little of the hot liquid into the egg yolk, then beat egg yolk into the clam mixture.

Preheat oven to 375°.

Pour clam mixture into a deep 9- or 10-inch baking dish. Roll out the pastry ¼ inch thick on a lightly floured surface, fit over top of the pie, trim the edges, and cut a small hole in center of the pastry to allow steam to escape while cooking. Brush pastry with the egg wash, place dish on a baking sheet in the oven, and bake for 20–25 minutes.

Yankee Clam Hash

Serves 6

6 slices of bacon	½ tsp. salt
4 Tb. (½ stick) butter	Freshly ground pepper
1 medium onion, finely chopped	Tabasco
2 cups diced boiled potatoes	4 egg yolks
3 cups minced fresh clams	1 cup heavy cream
2 Tb. chopped chives	1 Tb. softened butter

Fry the bacon in a large, heavy skillet till crisp, drain on paper towels, and crumble.

Pour off the grease from skillet, heat 4 tablespoons of butter in the same skillet, add the onion, and sauté over low heat for 2 minutes. Add the potatoes, stir, increase heat to moderate, and cook mixture for about 3 minutes or till underside is golden. Add the clams, chives, salt, and pepper and Tabasco to taste, cook for 2 minutes, then press down mixture with a spatula.

Preheat oven broiler.

Beat the egg yolks with the cream in a bowl, pour over the clam mixture, cover skillet, and cook for 2 minutes or till eggs are just set. Dot the surface with the softened butter, brown top under the broiler, loosen edges with the spatula, and slide hash onto a heated platter. Sprinkle crumbled bacon over hash and serve immediately.

Scalloped Oysters

Serves 6

2 cups coarsely crushed crackers
1 cup dry bread crumbs (2 slices of
  dry white bread)
¾ cup (1½ sticks) melted butter
1 qt. fresh shucked oysters, drained

1 cup heavy cream
⅛ tsp. nutmeg
Salt and freshly ground pepper
Tabasco

*P*reheat oven to 350°.
  Combine crackers and bread crumbs in a mixing bowl, add the melted butter, and mix thoroughly.

Spoon one-third of the cracker-crumb mixture on the bottom of a 2-quart casserole and arrange one-half the oysters in a layer on top. Pour half the cream on top of oysters, sprinkle with the nutmeg and salt and pepper to taste, and add a few shakes of Tabasco. Spoon on one-third more of the cracker-crumb mixture and arrange the remaining oysters in another layer. Pour on remaining cream, season again with salt and pepper to taste, and cover the top with remaining cracker-crumb mixture.

Bake casserole for 20–25 minutes and serve oysters directly from the casserole.

Oysters Poached in Vermouth on Croutons

Serves 4

1 cup (2 sticks) melted butter
Vegetable oil
8 slices day-old bread, trimmed of
  crusts and cut into 1½-inch
  discs (a total of 24)
2 Tb. chopped shallots

2 cups dry vermouth
2 cups heavy cream
24 fresh oysters, shucked and
  liquor reserved
Salt and freshly ground pepper
1 Tb. chopped fresh dill

*H*eat one-half of the butter and enough oil to measure 1 inch in a large heavy skillet till hot enough for a piece of bread to sizzle. Fry bread discs in batches for about 15 seconds or till golden brown, and drain on paper towels.

Heat 2 tablespoons of the butter in a large saucepan, add the shallots, and sauté over low heat for 2 minutes. Add 1 cup of the vermouth, increase heat to moderately high, and reduce liquid by half. Add the cream, stir, and reduce for about 5 minutes or till sauce coats the back of a spoon.

Strain sauce into another large saucepan, add remaining cup of vermouth plus reserved oyster liquor, bring to the boil, and reduce again for about 5 minutes or till sauce coats the back of a spoon.

Reduce heat to simmer, add oysters in batches, poach lightly for about 3 minutes or till oysters curl (adjusting heat to maintain a steady simmer), and transfer to a heated platter.

Whisk remaining butter into the sauce, increase heat slightly, add salt and pepper to taste and chopped dill, and stir well.

Arrange 6 croutons on each of 4 heated serving plates, top each crouton with an oyster, spoon sauce on top of oysters, and serve immediately.

Spicy Oyster Fritters

Serves 6

2 cups flour
1 Tb. baking powder
¼ tsp. salt
Freshly ground pepper
⅛ tsp. cayenne
⅛ tsp. allspice

2 eggs, beaten
1 cup milk
2 Tb. vegetable oil
1½ cups vegetable oil for frying
1 qt. fresh shucked oysters, drained
Mustard Sauce (p. 534)

Sift flour, baking powder, salt, pepper to taste, cayenne, and allspice into a mixing bowl. Add the eggs and milk and mix well. Add the 2 tablespoons of oil and mix till batter is smooth.

Heat the 1½ cups of oil in a heavy saucepan to moderately high (about 375°). While oil is heating, dip oysters in the batter to coat evenly. Drop battered oysters into the hot oil, taking care not to overcrowd the pan. Fry for 2 minutes or till golden brown, and drain on paper towels.

Serve with cole slaw, cornbread, and mustard sauce on the side.

Coquilles St.-Jacques Georges Blanc
(Scallops in Beaujolais Sauce)

Serves 4 – 6

Years before Chez la Mère Blanc in the tiny village of Vonnas, France, was showered with Michelin stars, I featured Georges Blanc in the magazine as one of the most promising young French chefs specializing in the *nouvelle cuisine*. Georges has come a long way since those days in terms of creativity, but this early dish is still one of my longtime favorites.

8 Tb. (1 stick) butter, softened	*½ cup flour*
¼ cup minced shallots	*Salt and freshly ground pepper*
2 medium ripe tomatoes, peeled,	*1 Tb. oil*
seeded, and chopped	*1½ cups fine Beaujolais*
⅔ cup heavy cream	*¼ cup minced parsley*
2½ lbs. sea scallops	

*H*eat 2 tablespoons of the butter in a skillet, add the shallots, and sauté over low heat for 2 minutes, stirring. Add the chopped tomatoes, increase heat to moderately high, and cook mixture for about 4 minutes or till most of the liquid has evaporated. Add the cream, increase heat, cook for 1 minute, and set skillet aside.

Rinse the scallops, pat dry with paper towels, and slice them in half. Combine the flour and salt and pepper to taste in a pie plate, and dust the scallops lightly in the mixture.

Heat 4 tablespoons of the butter plus the oil in a large skillet till very hot, add scallops, and sauté for 2 minutes, turning. Add the wine, reduce heat to moderate, and cook for 3 – 4 minutes or till sauce has thickened. Add the reserved tomato mixture plus salt and pepper to taste, stir gently, and simmer for 2 minutes. Remove skillet from the heat, add remaining butter, and stir till sauce is shiny.

Transfer scallops and sauce to a heated serving platter, sprinkle with the minced parsley, and serve immediately.

Mouclade le Soubise
(Curried Creamed Mussels)

Serves 4

While researching the cuisine of the coastal Charente-Maritime province of France, I must have sampled dozens of *mouclades* (not to be confused with *éclade* — mussels steamed in pine needles), but no version was as memorable as the sensuous one prepared by Madame Benoît at a remote country restaurant in the village of Soubise south of La Rochelle. Serve the mussels with a salad vinaigrette, plenty of French or Italian bread, and a chilled Muscadet.

4 qts. (about 8 lbs.) mussels	2 Tb. flour
1 cup dry white wine	3 tsp. curry powder
½ cup water	⅛ tsp. cayenne
3 Tb. butter	Salt and freshly ground pepper
1 medium onion, minced	½ cup heavy cream
1 garlic clove, minced	¼ cup minced parsley

Scrub mussels thoroughly with a stiff brush under running water and place in a kettle or large casserole. Add wine and water, bring liquid to the boil, cover, and steam mussels for 6–7 minutes or till they open (discard any that do not open).

Transfer the mussels to a large bowl with a slotted spoon and strain the cooking liquid through a fine sieve into a saucepan. Bring liquid to the boil, reduce to about 2 cups, and keep hot. Shell the mussels, remove and discard the black rims, and place mussels in a bowl. Discard tops of shells, arrange bottoms on a large, shallow serving platter, and set aside.

Heat the butter in a large saucepan, add the onion and garlic, and sauté for 2 minutes over low heat. Sprinkle on the flour, mix well with a whisk, and cook for 3 minutes, stirring constantly. Add the curry powder and cayenne, mix well, and continue cooking for 1 minute, stirring. Increase heat to moderate, gradually add the reserved cooking liquid, whisking constantly, and simmer for 5 minutes. Add the cream and salt and pepper to taste, and stir till well blended. Add the mussels, increase heat, and stir just till mussels are hot.

To serve, quickly transfer mussels back to the reserved shells, pour sauce over mussels, and sprinkle top with minced parsley.

PART NINE

Vegetables

Artichoke Hearts with Gruyère

Serves 6

2 9-oz. packages frozen artichoke
  hearts
2 Tb. butter
2 Tb. olive oil
¼ cup minced shallots

2 garlic cloves, minced
¼ cup dry white wine
Salt and freshly ground pepper
½ cup grated Gruyère cheese
Fresh chopped parsley

*C*ook artichoke hearts according to directions on package and drain. Heat butter and oil in a large, heavy skillet, add shallots and garlic, and sauté over low heat for 4–5 minutes. Add artichoke hearts, white wine, and salt and pepper to taste, and stir. Increase heat to moderate, cook till wine is reduced to about 1 tablespoon, and remove from heat.

Add Gruyère to the mixture, toss till cheese has melted, transfer to a heated serving platter, and garnish top with chopped parsley.

Fried Asparagus

Serves 6

Like strips of zucchini, thin asparagus that are battered and quickly fried make a delectable side dish to a simple meal. Since they really should be served as quickly as possible to avoid sogginess, I usually try to include them on a menu that involves mainly cold food. They also go very nicely with pasta and can be easily fried while the noodles are cooking.

2 lbs. thin fresh asparagus
1¾ cups peanut or vegetable oil
2 eggs, beaten with a few dashes
   of Tabasco

1½ cups fine bread crumbs
Salt

The entire stalk of the asparagus is edible, but, if necessary, scrape the lower parts with a small knife or vegetable peeler. Rinse the asparagus and dry with paper towels.

Heat the oil very hot in a large heavy skillet. One by one dip the asparagus into the beaten egg, roll lightly in bread crumbs, and fry 1 minute, making sure not to crowd the pan. As each spear finishes cooking, drain on paper towels, salt to taste, and serve hot.

Dilled Asparagus

Serves 4–6

Nothing distresses me more than the way amateur and professional chefs alike abuse asparagus by cutting or snapping off the white bases, which, when dealt with properly, are not only delicious but make for a much nicer presentation. The entire asparagus stalk is edible. All you have to do is carefully shave away a little of the woody exterior of the white base with either a vegetable peeler or sharp paring knife, exposing flesh that is just as succulent as the green tops. And how do I manage to keep fresh asparagus in perfect shape for days at a time? Easy. You simply slice off a bit of the bases, stand the bases in a container of water, and place in the refrigerator.

1 lb. fresh asparagus, bases peeled   1 cup white wine vinegar
1 garlic clove, minced   2 Tb. sugar
1 tsp. red pepper flakes   3 tsp. salt
10 sprigs fresh dill, chopped   1 cup water
¼ tsp. mustard seeds

*B*ring 1 inch of salted water to the boil in a large skillet or oval gratin dish, arrange asparagus in the water, maintain heat at moderate, cover, and cook asparagus for 6–8 minutes, depending on thickness. Drain water from the skillet, add cold water to refresh asparagus momentarily, then drain the asparagus on paper towels.

Arrange asparagus in a shallow, heatproof glass dish and add garlic, pepper flakes, dill, and mustard seeds.

Combine vinegar, sugar, salt, and water in a stainless-steel saucepan, bring mixture to the boil, stirring, and pour it over asparagus. Let cool, cover with plastic wrap, and refrigerate overnight.

Sautéed Green Beans and Pine Nuts

Serves 6

2 lbs. young green beans, trimmed   ½ cup finely chopped parsley
  and rinsed   2 garlic cloves, minced
8 Tb. (1 stick) butter   ½ cup pine nuts or chopped filberts

*D*rop the beans in a kettle of rapidly boiling salted water, return water to the boil, parboil beans till they are crunchy-tender (about 10 minutes), and drain.

Heat butter in a large skillet, add parsley and garlic, and stir over low heat for 1 minute. Add beans and nuts, toss well, and heat through for about 10 minutes, tossing occasionally.

Fasoulakia Giahne
(Greek Beans and Tomatoes)

Serves 4–6

Rarely in Greece will you find this dish anywhere but in the home, but I know of no more savory way to prepare green beans. They make the perfect accompaniment to roast lamb, and if you really want to follow the traditional Greek fashion, you will serve chunks of lamb literally smothered in the beans. Yes, the beans are overcooked (stewed, in fact) by present-day standards. So what? Here, the overall flavor is what matters.

2 lbs. green beans
4 Tb. olive oil
1 small onion, minced
3 garlic cloves, minced
2 cups coarsely chopped ripe
  tomatoes with their juices

¼ cup chopped pitted Greek olives
1 tsp. dried thyme
1 Tb. finely chopped fresh basil
Freshly ground pepper

*R*inse beans, remove ends, and snap in half. Place beans in a large saucepan or kettle with enough salted water to cover, bring to the boil, lower heat, cover, and simmer for 30–45 minutes or till very tender. Drain beans in a colander, pour off cooking water, and dry pan.

Heat the olive oil in the pan, add onion and garlic, and sauté over low heat for 2 minutes. Return beans to the pan and toss well with the onion and garlic. Add tomatoes with their juices, the olives, thyme, basil, and pepper to taste, and mix well with the beans. Increase heat to moderate-low, cover, and simmer beans and tomatoes for 30 minutes, adding a little water if necessary.

Lima Beans with Smoked Sausage

Serves 4–6

1 lb. chorizo, kielbasa, or other
   smoked pork sausage
1 Tb. butter
¼ lb. salt pork, finely diced
1 large onion, chopped
1 garlic clove, finely chopped
½ cup dry white wine

½ cup water
Pinches of dried thyme and chervil
1 bay leaf, crumbled
Freshly ground pepper
4 cups cooked fresh or frozen lima
   beans
Chopped parsley

*P*rick sausages, place in a large skillet with enough water to cover, bring liquid to the boil, reduce heat, and simmer for 10 minutes. Drain sausages on paper towels and slice into ¼-inch rounds.

Heat butter in a heavy 3- to 4-quart casserole, add salt pork, render over moderate heat till pieces are crisp, and drain on paper towels. Add onion and garlic to fat and sauté for 2 minutes. Pour the wine and water into casserole, add sausages, herbs, and pepper to taste, bring liquid to the boil, lower heat, cover, and simmer for 30 minutes. Uncover, add beans, increase heat to moderate, and cook for about 15–20 minutes.

Serve in a heated serving bowl topped with chopped parsley.

Red Beans and Rice

Serves 6–8

Aware of my penchant for red beans and rice, a longtime reader of *Town &
Country* and passionate food and wine lover, Ed Burks of Shreveport,
Louisiana, sent along this recipe with a note proclaiming it the state's best.
I agree. Like its foreign cousins, the French *cassoulet* and Brazilian *fejoida,*
this savory dish must be allowed to simmer slowly so the naturally form-
ing gravy is fully enriched with the bone marrow and spices. Chunks of
ham and pickled pork are often used down South, but take my word that
the smoked sausage makes this a truly extraordinary meal-in-itself.

1 – 1½ lbs. dried red kidney beans	*1 Tb. chopped garlic*
6 slices bacon	*½ tsp. dried thyme*
2 lbs. smoked Polish sausage (such	*½ tsp. ground cumin*
as kielbasa), sliced into ½-inch	*1 tsp. ground coriander*
rounds	*1 Tb. dried basil*
1 meaty ham bone (not smoked or	*½ tsp. cayenne*
cured country ham)	*½ tsp. freshly ground pepper*
2 cups chopped onions	*1½ Tb. Worcestershire*
1 cup chopped celery	*1 Tb. Angostura bitters*
½ cup chopped green bell pepper	*6 – 8 cups boiled rice*
¼ cup chopped parsley	

Place beans in a large, heavy casserole with enough water to cover and
soak overnight.

Drain beans in a colander, rinse out casserole, and wipe casserole dry.
Fry bacon in casserole till crisp, drain on paper towels, and crumble. Add
sausage and ham bone to fat in casserole, brown over moderate heat,
turning, for about 10 minutes, and transfer to a platter.

Add vegetables to casserole, lower heat slightly, and sauté for about 5
minutes, adding a little vegetable oil if necessary. Return sausage and ham
bone to casserole, add beans plus all remaining ingredients except rice,
and stir. Add enough water to cover by 2 inches (about 2 quarts), bring
water to the boil, reduce heat, cover, and simmer gently for 2½ – 3 hours,
stirring occasionally and scraping bottom and sides of casserole.

When beans are soft, mash some with the back of a large spoon and stir well to thicken gravy. Spoon beans and meat over rice in soup bowls and serve with Cornbread (p. 434), a green salad, and ice-cold beer.

Porotos Granados
(Chilean Beans with Corn and Squash)

Serves 6

Elizabeth Lambert Ortiz, my eternal source for the lusty Latin-American dishes I seem to enjoy more and more during the cold of winter, says this popular Chilean concoction is also very Indian. Don't worry when the squash disintegrates during the final simmering of the beans; it thickens the sauce.

2 cups dried navy beans, rinsed and soaked in cold water 3 – 4 hours
3 Tb. olive oil
2 Tb. sweet paprika
1 large onion, finely chopped
4 medium tomatoes, cored, peeled, and chopped

½ tsp. oregano
Salt and freshly ground pepper
1 lb. winter squash, peeled, seeded, and cut into 1-inch cubes (about 2 cups)
½ cup frozen kernel corn, defrosted

*D*rain beans and place in a large saucepan with enough fresh water to cover. Bring to the boil, lower heat, cover, and simmer for 1½ hours or till barely tender. Drain beans and reserve cooking liquid.

Meanwhile, heat the oil in a medium skillet, add the paprika, and stir very briefly over moderate heat. Add the onion and sauté for 2 minutes. Add the tomatoes, oregano, and salt and pepper to taste, and simmer mixture, stirring, till thick and well blended.

Add tomato mixture and squash to the saucepan with the beans, stir, and add enough of the reserved cooking liquid to cover. Cover pan, place over moderate heat, reduce heat, and simmer for 20 minutes. Stir in the corn and simmer for 5 – 10 minutes longer.

Serve beans in soup plates.

Sugarbush Baked Beans

Serves 8 – 10

If the only baked beans you've ever eaten are those tomatoey canned products more often than not seasoned with disgusting bits of processed frankfurters, try these authentic, unctuous beauties once served to me by fourth-generation Vermonters. By no means try to rush the cooking time, and by no means add either tomato sauce or catsup. Note that the beans must first be soaked overnight.

2 lbs. (4 cups) pea beans
1 tsp. baking soda
1 medium onion, studded with 2
  cloves
1 lb. salt pork, cut into ½-inch
  cubes

1½ cups dark molasses
2 tsp. dry mustard
1 Tb. salt
Freshly ground pepper
2 Tb. dark rum

Place beans in a kettle with enough water to cover by 3 inches and soak overnight.

Preheat oven to 300°.

Pour water off beans, add fresh water to cover by 1 inch, and add baking soda and onion. Bring beans to the boil, cook for 15 minutes, and transfer contents of the kettle to a 2-quart bean pot. Add salt pork to beans and combine thoroughly. Stir in molasses, mustard, salt, plenty of pepper, and the rum.

Place bean pot in oven and bake beans slowly for 5 – 6 hours. Add a little water if necessary, but allow top of beans to crust slightly during the final 30 minutes of baking.

Lean Cassoulet

My involvement in that unctuous marriage of bean and meat known throughout the civilized world as *cassoulet* approaches nothing less than a masochistic obsession. If it's true that once in southwestern France I drove a hundred miles out of the way when mere mention was made of a *cassoulet* reputed to be the best in the region, it's equally true that after consuming that voluptuous beauty I never yearned more for the modern miracle known as Alka-Seltzer. To produce, therefore, a *cassoulet* that is at once full-flavored and digestible, I've not only subjected the beans in this recipe to three changes of water but have also countered tradition by removing a good deal of fat once its essence has been incorporated in the stew. This version satisfies me; it will satisfy you. The dish requires time and love. Don't cheat.

2 lbs. boneless pork shoulder
2 ham hocks
Salt and freshly ground pepper
2 lbs. dry Great Northern beans
½ lb. salt pork, cut into ½-inch
   slices
1 onion, peeled and studded with
   3 cloves
Herb bouquet (½ tsp. dried
   thyme, 1 bay leaf, 1 sprig
   parsley, and 2 cloves tied in
   cheesecloth)
1 lb. Spanish cotechino *sausage*
   or other garlicky pork sausage
½ lb. slab bacon, cut into ½-inch
   dice

Pieces of 1 preserved duck (p. 264)
3 Tb. rendered duck fat from
   preserved duck (p. 264)
½ lb. fresh pork sausages
2 onions, peeled and sliced
2 carrots, cut into rounds
3 garlic cloves, minced
1 tomato, cored, peeled, and
   coarsely chopped
3 cups Beef Stock (p. 522) or
   bouillon
2 cups dry white wine
Duck cracklings (p. 264)

FIRST DAY:

Season pork shoulder and ham hocks with salt and pepper to taste, place in an earthenware or glass dish, cover, and let sit in refrigerator for 24 hours, turning once.

Pick over beans for debris and wash and drain them.

SECOND DAY:

Rinse beans and add fresh water to cover by at least 1 inch. Bring to the boil, let cook for 5 minutes, drain, and add more fresh water to cover by at least 1 inch. Place salt pork in another saucepan, add water to cover, bring to the boil, lower heat, simmer for 10 minutes to remove excess salt, and rinse in cold water. Add salt pork, studded onion, and herb bouquet to beans. Bring beans to the boil, lower heat, cover, and simmer for 1 hour or till beans are just tender. Cool and refrigerate.

While beans are cooking, prick garlic sausages, place in a skillet or saucepan, cover with water, bring to the boil, lower heat, and poach for 30 minutes. At the same time, blanch slab bacon in boiling water for about 3 minutes, drain, rinse under cold water, and pat dry with paper towels. Drain sausages, cool, and cut into chunks.

Heat duck fat in a large, deep, heavy skillet, add preserved duck pieces skin side down, cook for about 5 minutes or till lightly browned, and remove. Prick fresh sausages, place in the skillet, and fry till light brown. Cut seasoned pork shoulder into chunks, place in the skillet, and brown on all sides. Add onions and carrots, and sauté till onions are soft. Add ham hocks and slab bacon, raise heat, and cook till meats are slightly browned. Stir in the garlic and tomato, add stock and white wine, bring to the boil, reduce heat, and simmer, uncovered, for about 1 hour or till ham hocks are fully cooked. Add preserved duck and chunks of garlic sausage to the ragout, cover skillet, and place in refrigerator overnight.

THIRD DAY:

Preheat oven to 300°.

Lift off most of the congealed fat collected on top of the ragout and discard. Remove ham hocks from ragout, cut meat into chunks, discard bones, and return meat to the ragout. Remove beans from refrigerator, discard herb bouquet, and bring just to the simmer.

On the bottom of a 6-quart ovenproof casserole, arrange a layer of beans and salt pork, then a layer of ragout, dividing the meats as equally as possible and adding a few duck cracklings. Repeat with a layer of beans, then meat, ending with a layer of beans about 1 inch beneath the rim of the casserole. Add liquid from ragout plus enough bean liquid just to cover beans.

Place casserole in the oven and allow to heat through for 1 hour. Raise heat to 350° and bake for about 30 minutes or till *cassoulet* has crusted on top. Break the crust into the beans with a large spoon, reduce heat to 300°, and continue baking for about 20 minutes longer or till another crust forms. Break crust again, add a little more bean liquid if beans appear dry, and continue baking till a third crust forms. Remove *cassoulet* from the oven and serve within 30 minutes.

Beets in Orange Sauce

Serves 4–6

16–20 small beets
2 Tb. cornstarch
1¼ cups light brown sugar
6-oz. can frozen concentrated
    orange juice

¾ cup cider vinegar
1 Tb. butter

Remove and discard beet tops and root stems and scrub bulbs thoroughly. Place bulbs in a kettle or large saucepan with enough water to cover, bring to the boil, lower heat, cover, and cook for about 30 minutes or till tender. Transfer beets to a colander, reserving cooking liquid, and, when cool enough to handle, peel and set aside.

In a large saucepan, combine cornstarch, brown sugar, orange juice, vinegar, and 1 cup reserved beet liquid, and cook over moderate heat for about 8–10 minutes or till thick and clear, stirring constantly. Stir in the butter, add beets, and heat thoroughly, stirring.

Beet Soufflé

2½ cups milk
Salt and freshly ground pepper
Pinch of nutmeg
3 eggs, separated
4 Tb. cornstarch

2 Tb. butter, softened
¼ cup dry bread crumbs
1½ cups diced canned beets
1 small onion, minced

Combine 2 cups of the milk, salt and pepper to taste, and nutmeg in a saucepan, and scald the milk. Combine remaining milk, the egg yolks, and cornstarch in a bowl, mix well, and add to the scalded milk. Cook over moderate heat, stirring constantly, till mixture has thickened, remove pan from heat, and let cool.

Preheat oven to 400°.

Grease a 1-quart glass ovenproof soufflé dish with the butter, coat bottom and sides lightly with the bread crumbs, and discard excess crumbs by turning dish over and tapping with the fingers. Arrange beets on bottom of dish and scatter onion over beets.

Pour egg whites in a mixing bowl with a pinch of salt and beat with an electric mixer till almost stiff. Fold egg whites into cornstarch mixture and scrape mixture into soufflé dish with a rubber spatula, smoothing the top.

Place soufflé dish on a heavy baking sheet and bake for 25 – 30 minutes or till top is nicely browned. Serve as quickly as possible, as a side dish.

Steamed Broccoli with Foie Gras Sauce

Unorthodox as this dish may sound, take my word it's one of the most subtle, delicious ways of serving broccoli I know. You do not need to buy the most expensive *foie gras* on the market. I've even used a 6-ounce tin of *mousse de foie gras* with sensational results.

4 Tb. (½ stick) butter
¼ cup flour
2 cups Chicken Stock (p. 521)
3 egg yolks

½ cup heavy cream
½ cup mashed foie gras
Salt and freshly ground pepper
3 lbs. broccoli

*H*eat butter in a saucepan, add flour, and stir constantly with a whisk till flour browns slightly. Add chicken stock and stir over moderate heat till sauce thickens.

Combine egg yolks and cream in a small bowl, whisk till well blended, and gradually beat about one-half of the hot sauce into the mixture. Return mixture to the saucepan, add *foie gras* and salt and pepper to taste, and stir over low heat till sauce is velvety. Keep warm.

Wash broccoli well, trim and discard tough stems, and cut top parts into small bunches. Place broccoli in a vegetable steamer or large saucepan with 1 inch of boiling water, cover, and steam for 12–15 minutes or till just tender.

Serve broccoli piping hot with sauce on the side.

Broccoli Sautéed with Peanuts

Serves 4

2 lbs. fresh broccoli
4 Tb. (½ stick) butter

2 Tb. lemon juice
¼ cup crushed peanuts

*W*ash broccoli thoroughly, trim off and discard the lower tough stems, and cut the heads and remaining stalks lengthwise into slices.

Place stalks upright in a large deep saucepan half-filled with boiling salted water (the florets should be out of the water), cover, and steam for about 15 minutes or till barely tender. Drain thoroughly.

Heat butter in a large skillet, add lemon juice, and stir till butter just begins to sizzle over moderate heat. Add broccoli and crushed nuts and sauté, turning, for 5 minutes. Transfer broccoli and nuts to a heated vegetable dish and serve immediately.

Honey-Glazed Carrots

Serves 4–6

4 cups scraped carrots, cut into
   ½-inch rounds
½ cup orange juice

2 tsp. cornstarch
2 Tb. butter
2 Tb. honey

Place carrots in a saucepan with 1 cup of salted water, bring to the boil, lower heat, cover, and cook for 8–10 minutes or till just tender. Remove pan from heat.

Combine orange juice and cornstarch in a small saucepan and blend till smooth. Add butter and honey and stir constantly over moderate heat till thickened and clear.

Drain water from hot carrots, add the honey glaze, and mix well to coat carrots.

Baked Carrots with Horseradish

Serves 6

10–12 medium carrots
4 Tb. (½ stick) butter
1 medium onion, finely chopped
1 Tb. horseradish (freshly grated
   or prepared)

1 tsp. salt
Freshly ground pepper
⅛ tsp. ground fennel
2 Tb. water

Scrape the carrots, halve them lengthwise, and cut the halves into ¼-inch-thick slices. You should have about 3 cups.

Preheat oven to 350°.

Heat one-half of the butter in a large skillet, add onion, and sauté over low heat for 2 minutes. Add carrots, increase heat to moderate, add horseradish, salt, pepper to taste, and fennel, and stir till well blended.

Scrape all the contents of the skillet into a medium baking dish and add water. Dot top with remaining butter, cover very tightly with foil, and bake for 1 hour or till carrots are tender but not overcooked.

Baked Cauliflower with Feta Cheese

Serves 6

8 Tb. (1 stick) butter
1 large onion, chopped
1 large head (about 4 lbs.)
  cauliflower, separated into
  florets

¼ tsp. dried oregano
Salt and freshly ground pepper
1 cup Chicken Stock (p. 521)
½ lb. feta cheese, crumbled

Preheat oven to 350°.
  Heat 2 tablespoons of the butter in a large skillet, add the onion, sauté over low heat for 2 minutes, and scrape into a large baking dish. Heat remaining butter in the skillet, add the cauliflower florets, sauté over low heat for 5 minutes, tossing, and add to the onion.

Sprinkle the onion and cauliflower with the oregano, season with salt and pepper to taste, and toss lightly. Add the chicken stock, cover the dish with foil, and bake for 20 minutes. Sprinkle the cheese evenly over the top, return dish to the oven, uncovered, and bake for 10 minutes longer.

Celery Root Puree

Serves 4–6

This is one of the few vegetable purees that doesn't bore me to tears. Despite the popularity of celery root (or celeriac) in the form of mustardy *céleri rémoulade* at French bistros, this delicious root vegetable still hasn't caught on in most American kitchens. I love it pureed (especially with game birds), simply boiled and sprinkled with well-aged Colby or Vermont cheddar cheese, baked with potatoes *au gratin*, and stuffed with other finely chopped vegetables. When shopping for celery root, remember that generally the smaller the knob, the more flavorful.

4 small (or 3 medium) celery
roots, peeled and cut into cubes
¼ cup heavy cream

3 Tb. butter, softened
Salt and freshly ground pepper
Pinch of freshly grated nutmeg

Place celery root cubes in a large saucepan with enough water to cover, bring to the boil, lower heat, cover, and simmer for 10–15 minutes or till tender.

Drain cubes well, place in a food mill (not a food processor), and puree into a large mixing bowl. Add cream, butter, salt and pepper to taste, and nutmeg, and beat with an electric mixer till light and fluffy. Serve lukewarm. Keep warm till ready to serve by setting covered bowl in a large container of hot water.

Braised Celery Root and Endive

Serves 6–8

1 lb. celery root, peeled
1 lb. (about 6) Belgium endives,
discolored leaves discarded
½ cup Chicken Stock (p. 521) or
broth
¼ cup water
Juice of 1 lemon

1 Tb. sugar
Salt
4 Tb. (½ stick) butter
Freshly ground pepper
¼ cup freshly grated Parmesan
cheese

Preheat oven to 400°.

Place celery root and endives in a casserole and add chicken broth, water, lemon juice, sugar, and salt to taste. Bring to the boil, cover, place casserole in the oven, and bake for 30 – 40 minutes or till celery root is just tender. Drain.

Slice endives in half lengthwise and cut celery root into slices.

Heat butter in a large skillet, add endives and celery root, and brown lightly on both sides over moderate heat. Transfer vegetables to a heated serving platter, season with pepper to taste, and sprinkle cheese on top.

Chestnut Soufflé

Serves 4 – 6

1 lb. chestnuts, shelled and peeled	1 Tb. chopped onion
1½ cups Chicken Stock (p. 521)	½ tsp. sugar
or broth	⅓ cup heavy cream
1 cup water	3 eggs, separated
¼ cup chopped celery	Salt and freshly ground pepper

Place chestnuts in a large saucepan, add chicken stock, water, celery, onion, and sugar, bring liquid to the boil, lower heat, cover, and simmer for 35 minutes or till chestnuts are soft.

Preheat oven to 375°.

Transfer chestnut mixture to a blender or food processor and puree. Heat cream in another saucepan, but do not boil. Remove pan from heat, whisk in chestnut puree, two of the egg yolks (reserve the remaining yolk for another use), and salt and pepper to taste, and transfer mixture to a large bowl.

In another large bowl, beat the egg whites with a pinch of salt till stiff. Stir one-half of the whites into the chestnut mixture, add mixture to remaining whites, and fold gently but thoroughly.

Pour mixture into a large, well-buttered soufflé dish, place on a heavy baking sheet in the middle of the oven, and bake for 20 minutes or till puffed and golden.

Serve immediately with wild game.

Baked Eggplant Bon Ton

I don't think anybody knows how to handle eggplant any better than the Louisiana Cajuns, and no one prepares it with greater imagination than the old black cooks at the venerable Bon Ton restaurant in New Orleans.

1 large eggplant, stem removed
1 tsp. salt
Freshly ground pepper
2 Tb. vegetable oil
¼ cup chopped onion
¼ cup chopped green bell pepper

1 Tb. chopped celery
1 garlic clove, chopped
½ cup coarsely cut-up chicken livers
7½ oz. fresh lump crabmeat
⅓ cup dry bread crumbs
1 Tb. butter

Cut eggplant in half lengthwise, place in a large saucepan with 1 inch of boiling water, cover, and steam for about 12–15 minutes or till tender. Drain, remove skin when cool enough to handle, and chop the flesh coarsely. Transfer eggplant to a large mixing bowl, mash with a potato masher or heavy fork, stir in salt and pepper to taste, and set aside.

Heat oil in a large skillet, add onion, pepper, celery, and garlic, cover, and cook over low heat for 10 minutes. Uncover, add chicken livers, and cook for 10 minutes, stirring.

Preheat oven to 375°.

Remove skillet from heat, stir in crabmeat, add mixture to the eggplant, and stir till well blended. Spoon mixture into a 1-quart shallow baking dish, sprinkle crumbs on top, and dot with butter. Bake uncovered for 20 minutes or till golden brown.

Iranian Eggplant and Pumpkin Casserole

Serves 6–8

Once, while lunching in Houston with Carolina Hunt Schoellkopf, I learned that this fascinating lady has such a passion for pumpkin that she not only named the family's air charter service Pumpkin Air but also produced and published a fat cookbook devoted to nothing but pumpkin dishes. And that's what I call true gastronomic dedication! This is one of her best recipes.

1-lb. pumpkin
2 large eggplants, washed and
  stemmed
1 tsp. salt
4 Tb. lemon juice
Freshly ground pepper

Imported paprika
3 Tb. butter
1 medium onion, finely chopped
5 eggs
½ cup plain yogurt

Preheat oven to 300°.
   Peel pumpkin, remove and discard seeds, cut flesh into dice, and place in a large mixing bowl. Cut eggplants lengthwise into quarters, slice 2 inches thick, and add to the pumpkin. Add salt and let the vegetables stand for 15 minutes. Place in a colander and rinse well under cold water. Place in a large saucepan with 1 inch of water, bring water to the boil, lower heat, cover, and steam for 10 minutes or till vegetables are tender. Transfer to a large baking dish and sprinkle with one-half of the lemon juice and pepper and paprika to taste.
   Heat the butter in a small skillet, add onion, sauté over low heat for 2 minutes, and stir in the remaining lemon juice.
   In a small bowl, beat eggs, add sautéed onion, and stir. Pour the egg mixture over the vegetables and bake 20 minutes.
   Serve each portion topped with a dollop of yogurt.

Steamed Escarole with Mushrooms and Almonds

Serves 6

2 lbs. (2 large heads) escarole	½ lb. mushrooms, sliced
4 Tb. (½ stick) butter	Pinch of nutmeg
2 shallots, finely chopped	3 Tb. heavy cream
1 garlic clove, minced	¼ cup toasted sliced almonds
1 Tb. finely chopped anchovy	

Separate leaves of escarole, snap off and discard tough stems, and wash leaves thoroughly under cold running water. Place wet leaves in a large saucepan or kettle with 1 inch of water, cover, and cook over moderate heat for 20 minutes. Drain and chop leaves coarsely.

Heat 2 tablespoons of the butter in a large skillet, add shallots, garlic, and anchovy, and sauté over low heat for 1 minute. Add remaining butter, the mushrooms, and nutmeg, stir, increase heat to moderate, and cook for 4–5 minutes, stirring.

Add the chopped escarole and cream, stir well, and cook over moderate heat for about 3 minutes. Add sliced almonds, stir well, and serve immediately.

Baked Fennel with Ham

Serves 6

3 large fennel bulbs	⅓ cup flour
1 cup Chicken Stock (p. 521)	1½ cups half-and-half
1 cup water	Salt and freshly ground pepper
8 Tb. (1 stick) butter	Pinch of mace
1 small onion, minced	½ cup grated Gruyère cheese
1 cup ham, cut into ¼-inch cubes	

Trim and discard fennel stalks and cut bulbs into ⅛-inch-thick slices. Place slices in a large saucepan and add chicken stock and water. Bring to the boil, lower heat, cover, and simmer for 15 minutes or till tender. Lift fennel out of liquid with a slotted spoon and drain on paper towels. Bring cooking liquid to the boil, reduce to about 1 cup, and set aside.

Heat 3 tablespoons of the butter in a medium skillet, add onion, and sauté over low heat for 1 minute. Add ham, increase heat slightly, and cook mixture, stirring, for 2 minutes.

Preheat oven to 350°.

Heat remaining butter in another saucepan, add flour, and whisk over moderate heat for 2 minutes. Gradually stir in the reduced cooking liquid and the half-and-half and continue cooking over moderate heat till sauce thickens. Add salt and pepper to taste and mace, stir, and cook for 1 minute longer.

Add fennel to the sauce, stir well, and spoon mixture into a large gratin dish. Sprinkle grated cheese on top and bake for 15–20 minutes or till golden.

Glazed Fennel and Zucchini

Serves 4–6

2 large fennel bulbs
2 zucchini, scrubbed and cut into
    ½-inch slices
¼ cup (½ stick) melted unsalted
    butter

Salt and freshly ground pepper
5 Tb. freshly grated Parmesan
    cheese

*T*rim and discard fennel stalks and cut bulbs into ½-inch-thick slices. Bring a large saucepan or kettle of salted water to the boil, add fennel and zucchini, and cook over moderate heat for about 8 minutes or till tender but still crisp. Drain on paper towels.

Preheat oven to 400°.

Brush a large baking dish with a little of the melted butter and layer half the fennel and zucchini on the bottom of dish. Salt and pepper to taste, sprinkle with one-half of the cheese, and drizzle with one-half of the remaining butter. Make another layer of fennel and zucchini, grind on a little more pepper, sprinkle with remaining cheese, and drizzle with remaining butter. Bake for 15–20 minutes, then run briefly under the broiler till top is golden brown.

Sautéed Fiddlehead Ferns and Mushrooms

Serves 4–6

Come spring, among the delicacies I seek out most are the pencil-thin asparagus and fiddlehead ferns, which grow in great abundance in the fields and along the roadsides in New England and Nova Scotia. Occasionally you can find fresh fiddleheads in the finest (and most expensive) big-city vegetable markets during the season, and they should be very tight and unopened. The best specialty food shops also carry frozen ferns during the months of April, May, and June. Somewhat between asparagus and mushrooms in flavor, fiddleheads make for a very unusual and elegant side-dish vegetable.

4 Tb. (½ stick) butter	1 lb. fresh or frozen (and
¼ lb. small mushrooms, thinly	defrosted) fiddlehead ferns
sliced	Salt
1 Tb. dry sherry	Freshly grated Parmesan cheese

Heat 2 tablespoons of the butter in a large skillet, add the mushrooms, and sauté over moderate heat for 1 minute, stirring. Add sherry, cook for 1 minute longer, and remove from heat.

Add fiddleheads to a large saucepan of boiling water, blanch for 1 minute, drain, squeeze dry in a towel, and reshape heads.

Return skillet containing mushrooms to the heat, and add remaining 2 tablespoons of butter. Add fiddleheads plus salt to taste, and sauté with mushrooms over moderate heat for 1 minute, stirring. Transfer mixture to a hot serving dish and sprinkle top with Parmesan cheese.

Creamed Leeks with Italian Sausage

Serves 6

One morning, as I joined my celebrated East Hampton neighbors Craig Claiborne and Pierre Franey testing a leek and sausage pie prepared with simple link breakfast sausages, I commented on how much more interesting the concept might be if Italian sweet sausages were used. "But we've already used *cotechino* in our creamed leeks," Craig replied. Suffice it to say that I rushed home to the kitchen, grabbed a package of regular supermarket Italian sausages I'd just bought on sale, and have yet to get my fill of this luscious dish. If you love leeks as much as I do, you could easily serve this to three as a main course with nothing more than bread, salad, and a good wine.

½ lb. Italian sweet sausages
10 leeks (about 3 lbs.)
2 Tb. butter
2 garlic cloves, minced
1½ cups heavy cream

Salt and freshly ground pepper
Pinch of nutmeg
¼ cup bread crumbs
3 Tb. melted butter

Prick sausages on all sides with a fork and place in a skillet with just enough water to cover. Bring to the boil, lower heat to moderate, and poach for about 3 minutes. Pour off water from skillet, fry sausages for 15–20 minutes, turning, drain on paper towels, and cut into thin round slices.

While sausages are frying, trim leeks of all but about 2 inches of the green tops, slice whites down the middle almost to the root end, and rinse leaves thoroughly under cold running water to remove all grit. Chop whites crosswise at 2-inch intervals.

Preheat oven to 425°.

Heat the 2 tablespoons of butter in a large saucepan, add garlic, and sauté over low heat for 1 minute. Add the chopped leeks, increase heat to moderate, and cook, stirring, till leeks are wilted. Add cream, salt and pepper to taste, and nutmeg, return heat to moderate, and cook for 10–15 minutes or till leeks are tender.

Pour leeks into a large shallow baking dish and arrange sausage rounds on top. Sprinkle on bread crumbs, drizzle crumbs with the melted butter, and bake for 20 minutes or till top is golden brown.

Pan-Fried Leeks

I'm crazy about leeks in any form — steamed, braised in bouillon, sautéed in butter, dropped in a *pot au feu,* marinated in vinaigrette, added to a savory pie, and, now, battered and fried. Since cut leeks fall apart easily if not tied, they must be handled very carefully in this preparation. It's essential that they be as dry as possible before battering and that they be allowed to firm up for at least 1 hour in the refrigerator before frying.

12 small leeks, green leaves removed
2 cups Basic Vinaigrette (p. 542)
2 cups flour seasoned with salt, freshly ground pepper, and dried thyme to taste

3 eggs, beaten
Bread crumbs
Vegetable oil for frying

Carefully slit leeks down one side (taking care not to cut through stem) and rinse thoroughly of all grit under running water. Place leeks in a large saucepan or deep skillet with 1 inch of water, bring water to the boil, lower heat, cover, and steam for 10 – 15 minutes or till tender. Transfer to one or more clean towels and squeeze gently but thoroughly to extract as much liquid as possible.

Place leeks in a shallow baking dish, pour on the vinaigrette, and let marinate for about 30 minutes, turning once.

One by one, dredge the leeks lightly in seasoned flour, dip into egg, then coat with bread crumbs. Place battered leeks in a dish or on a plate, cover with plastic wrap, and let chill in refrigerator for at least 1 hour.

When ready to fry, heat 1 inch of oil to moderate in a large, heavy skillet, add leeks (in 2 batches if necessary), fry for about 5 minutes or till golden, and drain on paper towels. Serve immediately.

Lentils with Lamb and Tomatoes

Serves 6

This is one of the best ways I know to utilize the leftovers of a roasted leg of lamb. The lamb bone adds good flavor to the lentils, but if you don't have a saw to cut the bone so it will fit the pot, or a few bones from thick lamb chops, it's all right to cook the lentils with just the seasoning.

2 cups dried lentils
1 lamb bone (sawed from leg of
  lamb)
1 onion, studded with 2 cloves
1 bay leaf
3 Tb. olive oil
2 onions, finely chopped
2 garlic cloves, minced

1 tsp. crushed dried rosemary
2 ripe tomatoes, cored, seeded, and
  coarsely chopped
½ lb. lean cooked lamb, cut into
  ¼-inch dice (about 1½ cups)
1½ tsp. salt
Freshly ground pepper

Combine lentils, lamb bone, studded onion, and bay leaf in a heavy casserole or kettle. Add water to cover by 2 inches, bring to the boil, reduce heat, and simmer, uncovered, for 45 minutes or till lentils are tender. Drain lentils in a colander and remove and discard the bone, onion, and bay leaf.

Heat the oil in a large skillet, add chopped onions, and sauté over low heat, stirring, for about 5 minutes. Add garlic, rosemary, and tomatoes, stir, and cook for 3 minutes. Add lentils, lamb, salt, and pepper to taste, stir, raise heat slightly, and simmer for about 10 minutes.

Lentils with Chipolatas

Serves 4–6

While on assignment at Jerez de la Frontera in western Spain to do a feature on sherry, I was first exposed to those small, spicy Spanish sausages known as *chipolatas* (available in the U.S. at specialty food shops) at a bar where I went each evening to sip *fino* and munch on *tapas* with the locals. I love all sausages, but I have a veritable passion for *chipolatas* — simply grilled, broiled on a skewer with shrimp (as at The Four Seasons in New York) or ocean scallops, or used to add special flavor to something like lentils.

8 – 10 chipolata *sausages*
2 cups lentils
8 cups water
3 Tb. olive oil
2 onions, chopped

2 celery ribs, chopped
2 carrots, chopped
2 garlic cloves, chopped
1 Tb. chopped parsley

Place *chipolatas* in a saucepan with water to cover, bring to the boil, reduce heat, and poach for about 10 minutes. Remove sausages and reserve cooking liquid.

In another large saucepan, bring lentils and 8 cups of water to the boil, reduce heat, cover, cook for about 20 minutes or till lentils begin to soften, and drain.

Heat olive oil in a large, heavy skillet, add onions, celery, carrots, and garlic, and sauté over moderate heat, stirring, for 10 minutes. Add lentils to skillet with about 1 cup of the reserved cooking liquid, increase heat, cover, and cook for 15 minutes or till lentils are tender. Slice *chipolatas*, add to lentils, and continue cooking for about 10 minutes.

Serve sprinkled with parsley.

Mushrooms Stuffed with Spinach-Pecan Puree

Serves 6

Almost any seasonal fresh vegetable could be used in the stuffing for these mushrooms, and I've also prepared them with a spicy sausage and red bell pepper filling. The mushrooms make a beautiful accompaniment to any roasted meat.

24 large mushrooms
8 Tb. (1 stick) butter, softened
½ lb. fresh spinach
2 shallots, chopped
1 garlic clove, chopped

¼ cup chopped pecans
2 Tb. heavy cream
Salt and freshly ground pepper
Tabasco

*W*ipe mushrooms lightly with a damp cloth. Remove stems from mushrooms, chop stems, and set aside.

Heat one-half of the butter in a large skillet, add mushroom caps, and sauté over medium heat, turning, for about 3 minutes or till golden. Transfer mushroom caps to a large baking dish, arranging them close together stem side up, and set dish aside.

Rinse spinach thoroughly, place wet spinach in a saucepan, cover, and steam over moderate heat for 3 – 5 minutes or till wilted. Drain spinach and chop.

Preheat oven to 400°.

Combine reserved mushroom stems, spinach, shallots, garlic, pecans, cream, and salt, pepper, and Tabasco to taste in a food processor and process till well blended. Spoon equal amounts of mixture into the mushroom caps and bake for 15 minutes.

Woodland Mushrooms with Port and Cream Sauce

Serves 4–6

This velvety creation of Michael Quinn, head chef at the Ritz in London, is as good an excuse as any to linger over lunch in the Edwardian splendor of the hotel's majestic dining room. I do not recommend substituting dried mushrooms in this dish.

4 Tb. (½ stick) butter	1 cup heavy cream
2 Tb. finely chopped shallots	4 Tb. Chicken Stock (p. 521) or
½ lb. fresh chanterelles, rinsed	broth
thoroughly	¼ cup Port
½ lb. fresh shiitake mushrooms,	½ lemon
rinsed thoroughly	2 Tb. unsalted butter, softened
Salt and freshly ground pepper	1½ tsp. finely chopped chives

*H*eat the 4 tablespoons butter in a medium skillet, add shallots, and sauté over low heat for 1 minute, stirring with a wooden spoon. Add mushrooms and salt and pepper to taste, increase heat to moderate, and cook for 1 minute, tossing. Keep mushrooms warm.

Combine cream and chicken stock in a saucepan, bring to the boil, lower heat slightly, and reduce by one-third. Add Port and reduce slightly more. Squeeze the half lemon into the sauce, whisk in the 2 tablespoons butter slowly, and taste for salt and pepper.

To serve, divide mushrooms among individual salad plates, spoon equal amounts of sauce on each portion, and sprinkle each with chopped chives.

Okra with Tomatoes and Chilies

Serves 4 – 6

5 slices of bacon
1½ lbs. small fresh okra, washed
   and cut crosswise into ¼-inch
   rounds
2 small onions, chopped

2 tsp. salt
Pinch of oregano
4 ripe tomatoes, peeled and chopped
1 dried hot red chili pepper,
   seeded and chopped

*F*ry bacon in a heavy skillet till crisp, drain on paper towels, and crumble.

Add okra, onions, salt, and oregano to the skillet and sauté over moderate heat for about 10 minutes, stirring a couple of times. Add tomatoes and chili pepper, increase heat, stir well, reduce heat, and simmer for about 20 minutes or till okra and tomatoes are soft.

Transfer to a serving bowl, sprinkle on crumbled bacon, and serve immediately.

Honey-Glazed Onions with Coriander

Serves 6

36 small white onions
4 Tb. (½ stick) butter
¼ cup honey

2 Tb. finely chopped fresh
   coriander (also called cilantro
   and Chinese parsley) or fresh
   dill

*P*eel onions. Trim root ends but do not slice them off as they will keep the onion whole. Place whole onions in a large saucepan with enough salted water to cover, bring to the boil, lower heat to moderate, cover, and cook for 20 minutes or till tender. Drain well.

Heat the butter in another large saucepan and blend in the honey. Add the onions and cook over low heat, turning frequently, till they are well glazed.

Transfer onions to a heated vegetable dish and sprinkle with chopped coriander.

Moroccan Onion Kammama

Serves 6

The important thing to remember about this dish is that the onions should be highlighted (I often add even one more than indicated during the last 20–25 minutes of simmering) and the meat or poultry considered only a seasoning. Frankly, the *kammama* is better if a little strong chicken stock and dry white wine are added to the initial simmer, but since stocks and wine are never used in Moroccan cooking, I've decided to remain as authentic as possible. Serve the stew over rice, accompanied by a spinach and fresh mushroom salad and plenty of Pita Bread (p. 424).

3 Tb. olive oil
2 lbs. lamb shoulder or boned chicken thighs cut into 1-inch cubes
1 large onion, chopped
1 tsp. imported paprika
½ tsp. cumin
¼ tsp. powdered ginger
Pinch of saffron

2 garlic cloves, finely chopped
1 bunch (about 8 sprigs) fresh coriander (also called cilantro and Chinese parsley)
Salt and freshly ground pepper
3 lemons
6 large yellow onions (about 4 lbs.), cut lengthwise into half moons

*H*eat the olive oil in a large casserole, add the lamb or chicken and the chopped onion, and sauté for 5 minutes over moderate heat, stirring. Add the paprika, cumin, ginger, saffron, garlic, coriander, salt and pepper to taste, the juice of 1 lemon, and enough water to just cover ingredients, cover casserole, and simmer very slowly for 2 hours.

Add the remaining onions, stir, cover, and continue simmering for 20–25 minutes or till onions are just tender.

Preheat oven to 450°.

Transfer ingredients from the casserole to a large bowl with a slotted spoon, reduce cooking liquid by half over high heat, and return ingredients to the casserole. Add juice of the remaining 2 lemons, stir well, and place casserole in the oven for about 10 minutes or till top of the *kammama* is slightly glazed.

Spiced Baked Onions with Pine Nuts

Serves 8

4 large Spanish onions (about 3
  lbs.)
½ cup Chicken Stock (p. 521)
½ cup dry white wine
3 Tb. butter
2 tsp. sugar

1 tsp. grated lemon rind
⅛ tsp. ground cinnamon
⅛ tsp. ground cloves
Salt and freshly ground pepper
¼ cup crushed pine nuts

*R*emove skins from the onions, cut onions in half crosswise, and arrange halves cut side up in a baking dish just large enough to hold them.

Preheat oven to 350°.

In a medium saucepan, combine the stock, wine, 1 tablespoon of the butter, the sugar, lemon rind, cinnamon, cloves, and salt and pepper to taste, and bring liquid to the simmer. Pour mixture over the onions, cover the dish tightly with foil, and bake for 45 minutes or till onions are tender.

Melt remaining butter in a butter pot or small saucepan. Remove the foil from the baking dish, sprinkle onions with the nuts, drizzle melted butter over nuts, and continue baking onions, uncovered, for 15 minutes or till nuts are golden brown.

Transfer onions to a heated platter with a slotted spoon and serve as a side dish.

Daube d'Oignons
(Onions Braised in Red Wine)

Serves 4–6

These silky onions from southwest France were perfected by my friend Paula Wolfert. They can be served hot, lukewarm, or cold with grilled squab or chicken, calf's liver, braised duck, or on toast rounds with cocktails. The onions keep 2–3 days in the refrigerator and can be frozen.

4 Tb. (½ stick) unsalted butter
5 medium Spanish onions (about
   3 lbs.), halved lengthwise and
   thinly sliced

1 Tb. sugar
1½ cups full-bodied dry red wine
Salt and freshly ground pepper
1 tsp. or more red wine vinegar

Heat the butter in a large stainless-steel or enameled saucepan, add the onions, cover, and cook over low heat for 45 minutes, stirring occasionally.

Uncover the pan, increase heat to moderately high, and cook the onions for 20 minutes, stirring frequently, or till they are glazed and golden brown. Sprinkle with the sugar, increase heat, and boil down for 2–3 minutes to glaze, stirring. Reduce heat to low, add the wine, and continue cooking for 1½ hours, stirring frequently, or till onions are very soft and deep mahogany in color. Season with salt and pepper to taste, stir in the vinegar, and taste to determine if a little more vinegar is desired.

White Onion and Scallion Custard

Serves 6

This unusual and delicious dish was developed when I ran a feature trying to upgrade the social status of the onion and its relatives, the leek, scallion, shallot, chive, and garlic. The custard should be served as a side dish to roast prime ribs of beef, chicken, or lamb.

4 Tb. (½ stick) butter
4 or 5 medium white onions (1½
lbs.), thinly sliced
2 bunches medium scallions
(whites only), thinly sliced

1 garlic clove, minced
2 eggs
1 cup half-and-half
¼ tsp. ground nutmeg
Salt and freshly ground pepper

*H*eat the butter in a large skillet, add the sliced onions and scallions, and sauté over moderate heat, stirring, for about 8 minutes or till golden and very soft. Remove skillet from the heat and let the onions cool.

Preheat oven to 300°.

Combine the eggs, half-and-half, nutmeg, and salt and pepper to taste in a large mixing bowl and whisk till well blended. Add the onion mixture, stir well, and scrape mixture into a well-greased 1-quart baking dish. Bake for 45 minutes or till custard is golden.

Puree of Parsnips, Apples, and Potatoes

Serves 6

This spicy dish comes from my fellow North Carolinian colleague, Jean Anderson. Initially I tried the recipe without the potatoes but realized quickly that the starch is absolutely essential for a smooth, silky texture. Also, I do not recommend using a food processor for this dish. The puree is out of this world with baked ham or roast pork.

1 lb. parsnips, peeled and sliced thin

1 large tart apple, peeled, cored, and sliced thin

2 small all-purpose potatoes, peeled and diced

1 cup Chicken Stock (p. 521) or broth

⅛ tsp. dried thyme

Pinch of ground mace

Pinch of ground cinnamon

2 Tb. heavy cream

Combine parsnips, apple, potatoes, chicken broth, thyme, mace, and cinnamon in a medium-size, heavy saucepan and bring to the boil. Reduce heat, cover tightly, and simmer for 10–12 minutes or till all the vegetables and fruit are tender. Uncover pan and cook for 15 minutes longer, stirring periodically to make sure vegetables don't scorch.

Transfer vegetables to a large mixing bowl, add cream, and mash with a potato masher till very smooth. For real fluffiness, beat momentarily with an electric mixer. Serve immediately.

Moroccan Spinach

Serves 4–6

2 lbs. fresh spinach

¼ cup olive oil

½ cup raisins

¼ cup chopped almonds

⅛ tsp. ground cardamom

⅛ tsp. ground cumin

Pinch of ground cinnamon

1 garlic clove, minced

Rind of 1 lemon, cut into thin strips

1 tsp. fresh lemon juice

Salt and freshly ground pepper

Remove stems from spinach and wash leaves thoroughly under cold running water. Place wet spinach in a large saucepan or kettle, cover, and steam over moderate heat for 3–5 minutes or till wilted. Drain spinach in a colander, rinse under cold water, and squeeze between paper towels.

Heat oil in a large skillet, add raisins, almonds, spices, and garlic, and sauté over moderate heat for about 2 minutes or till nuts are golden. Add lemon rind and sauté for 1 minute longer, stirring. Add spinach, sprinkle with lemon juice, season with salt and pepper to taste, toss well to distribute ingredients, and continue cooking for 2 minutes longer, tossing.

Spiced Acorn Squash

Serves 4

2 acorn squash (about 3 lbs.)
2 Tb. butter, melted
2 tsp. brown sugar
1 tsp. ground cinnamon

¼ tsp. ground mace
3 cloves, ground
Salt and freshly ground pepper

Cut squash in half, scoop out seeds, then scoop out most of the flesh, reserving shells. Place flesh in a saucepan with enough lightly salted water to just cover, bring to the boil, lower heat, cover, and simmer for 15 minutes. Drain, transfer to a large mixing bowl, and mash well with a heavy fork.

Preheat oven to 350°.

Add all remaining ingredients to squash, blend well, and pack mixture into the reserved shells. Place shells in a baking dish with 2 inches of water, cover with foil, and bake for 30 minutes.

Baked Butternut Squash with
Macadamia Nuts

Serves 4 – 6

3 small butternut squash (about
    1½ lbs.), washed but not peeled
4 Tb. (½ stick) butter
1 medium onion, finely chopped
Salt and freshly ground pepper
⅛ tsp. ground nutmeg

⅛ tsp. ground cloves
1¼ cups heavy cream
½ cup bread crumbs
½ cup coarsely chopped
    macadamia nuts

Cut squash in half, remove and discard the seeds and filaments, and cut into ½-inch slices.

Heat one-half of the butter in a small skillet, add onion, and sauté over low heat for 2 minutes.

Preheat oven to 350°.

Grease the bottom and sides of a 1-quart baking dish and add one-half of the squash slices. Distribute the onion over the squash, season with salt and pepper to taste, add the nutmeg and cloves, then add remaining squash. Pour cream over and around the squash.

In a small bowl, combine the bread crumbs and nuts, sprinkle over the top of squash, and dot top with remaining butter cut into small pieces. Bake for 40 minutes or till squash is tender but not dried out.

Squash Soufflé

Serves 4

6 medium yellow squash (about 2
   lbs.), scrubbed and cut into
   1-inch rounds
2 large onions, coarsely chopped
1 jumbo egg, beaten
⅛ tsp. finely minced garlic
Pinch of thyme

Pinch of nutmeg
¼ tsp. salt
Freshly ground pepper
¼ cup bread crumbs
¼ cup freshly grated Parmesan
   cheese

Combine squash and onions in a large saucepan with enough water to cover by 1 inch, bring to the boil, lower heat, cover, and simmer for 20–30 minutes or till squash is tender. Drain in a colander and let cool for at least 10 minutes.

Preheat oven to 350°.

Place cooled vegetables in a food processor and process for 5 seconds. Transfer to a mixing bowl, add all remaining ingredients but 1 tablespoon of the cheese, and mix thoroughly with a spoon.

Spoon mixture into a well-buttered, medium gratin dish, sprinkle with remaining tablespoon of cheese, and bake for 35 minutes or till golden on top, making sure not to overcook.

Vegetable Ragout

Serves 4 – 6

When my triglyceride count soars over four hundred and I face the cruel fact that last year's custom-made suit might prove to have been a waste of good money, this healthy, delicious array of fresh vegetables is what I nourish myself on for an entire week — changing the variety, of course, according to the season. It's also a superb ragout to serve as a side dish to almost any meal.

6 Tb. (¾ stick) butter
1 medium onion, chopped
2 garlic cloves, finely chopped
1 medium yellow squash, scrubbed
  and cut into 1-inch cubes
1 cup fresh broccoli florets (cut in
  half if desired)
1 cup fresh cauliflower florets (cut
  in half if desired)

1 carrot, scraped and cut into
  ½-inch rounds
1 small fennel bulb, trimmed of
  feathery leaves and sliced
1 small red bell pepper, seeded
  and thinly sliced
2 Tb. chopped fresh basil
Salt and freshly ground pepper
½ cup Chicken Stock (p. 521)

Heat 2 tablespoons of the butter in a large deep skillet, add onion and garlic, and sauté over low heat for 2 minutes. Add remaining butter, increase heat to moderate, add squash, broccoli, and cauliflower, and toss to coat with butter. Add sliced fennel, carrot, bell pepper, basil, and salt and pepper to taste, and toss again.

Add stock to skillet, bring liquid to the boil, lower heat to moderate, and cook vegetables, tossing, till stock has reduced to a glaze.

Serve hot.

Glazed Vegetable Hash

Serves 4–6

3 slices of bacon
⅓ cup diced onions
1 garlic clove, minced
⅓ cup sliced red bell peppers
2 Tb. butter
⅓ cup sliced zucchini
⅓ cup fresh sliced mushrooms
⅓ cup broccoli florets
½ cup diced boiled potatoes

1 cup cooked beef, chicken, or
   turkey cut into small cubes
1 cup beef, chicken, or turkey gravy
⅓ cup tomato puree
Pinch each of dried thyme and basil
Dry bread crumbs
Butter
Freshly grated Parmesan cheese

*F*ry bacon in a large, heavy skillet till crisp, drain on paper towels, crumble, and pour off all but 2 tablespoons of fat from skillet.

Add onions, garlic, and red peppers to skillet and sauté over low heat for 4 minutes, stirring. Add 2 tablespoons butter and remaining vegetables, stir well, cover, and cook for about 5 minutes, stirring once. Mix in cubed meat and crumbled bacon, add gravy, tomato puree, and herbs, stir, and heat thoroughly.

Preheat oven broiler.

Spoon hash into 4–6 individual baking dishes and sprinkle top of each with bread crumbs. Dot tops with butter, add generous sprinklings of Parmesan, and brown under broiler to a golden crust.

Timbales of Zucchini and Mushrooms

Serves 6

1½ cups shredded zucchini
4 Tb. (½ stick) butter
1½ cups chopped mushrooms
4 eggs, beaten
½ cup heavy cream
1 Tb. vegetable oil

½ tsp. dry mustard
Pinch of nutmeg
Salt and freshly ground pepper
3 Tb. freshly grated Parmesan
  cheese

Drop zucchini in a saucepan of boiling water, blanch for 2 minutes, drain, and pat dry with paper towels.

Heat butter in a medium skillet, add mushrooms, sauté for 3 minutes over moderate heat, turning, and drain on paper towels.

Preheat oven to 350°.

In the top of a double boiler over simmering water, combine eggs, cream, oil, mustard, nutmeg, and salt and pepper to taste. Stir well for 3 minutes, add cheese, and continue stirring till mixture begins to thicken. Remove pan from heat and fold in vegetables evenly before mixture starts to set.

Pour equal amounts of the mixture into 6 individual custard cups, place cups in a roasting pan, and pour in enough boiling water to come halfway up the cups. Bake for 15–20 minutes or till custard is set and turn out carefully onto small salad plates.

Zucchini Moussaka

Serves 12 as a vegetable dish
or 6 – 8 as a main course

4 – 5 zucchini (about 3 lbs.)
¼ cup olive oil
6 Tb. (¾ stick) butter
1 medium onion, finely chopped
1 garlic clove, minced
1 lb. ground lean lamb
½ tsp. ground cinnamon

⅛ tsp. ground nutmeg
2 Tb. finely chopped parsley
Salt and freshly ground pepper
4 Tb. flour
2½ cups milk
1 egg, beaten
½ lb. feta cheese, crumbled

Scrub zucchini under running water, cut in half lengthwise, and cut halves crosswise into ¼-inch slices.

Heat oil in a large heavy skillet to very hot, add zucchini, fry very quickly on all sides till slightly browned (in batches if necessary), and drain on paper towels.

Add 2 tablespoons of the butter to the skillet, lower heat to moderate, add onion and garlic, and sauté for 1 minute. Add the lamb, cinnamon, nutmeg, parsley, and salt and pepper to taste, stir well, and cook till lamb is nicely browned. Remove skillet from heat.

Heat remaining butter in a saucepan, add flour, and stir rapidly with a whisk over moderate heat for 2 minutes. Gradually add the milk, stirring, then the egg, stirring constantly till the sauce thickens.

Preheat oven to 350°.

In a greased 9×13×2-inch baking pan, arrange a layer of zucchini, top with lamb mixture, sprinkle with one-half of the crumbled cheese, cover with remaining zucchini, sprinkle on remaining cheese, and pour on the sauce. Bake for 45 minutes or till golden brown.

PART TEN

Potatoes, Pasta, and Grains

Mashed Potatoes with Horseradish

Serves 6–8

Being one who has never lost his childhood love of fluffy mashed potatoes, I'm forever trying to give them new flair without destroying their wonderful natural flavor. Whether you prepare the potatoes with green olives, pureed celery root, caraway seeds, a little ground ham, or the horseradish featured here, do not use a food processor unless you want a heavy, gloppy result.

3 lbs. (about 6) medium baking potatoes, scrubbed thoroughly
1 cup hot milk
6 Tb. (¾ stick) butter, softened

1 Tb. freshly grated or prepared horseradish
Pinch of freshly grated nutmeg
Salt and freshly ground pepper

Place potatoes in a large saucepan or kettle with enough salted water to cover, bring to the boil, lower heat to moderate, cover, and cook for about 30 minutes or till potatoes are tender. Transfer potatoes to a colander and let cool slightly, reserving cooking liquid.

When just cool enough to handle, peel potatoes, cut into chunks, place in a large mixing bowl, and mash with a potato masher. Add 1 cup of the hot cooking liquid plus the hot milk and beat potatoes with an electric mixer till smooth. Add butter, horseradish, nutmeg, and salt and pepper to taste, and continue beating till potatoes are light and fluffy.

Serve immediately or place bowl in a larger container of hot water to keep potatoes warm (but not more than 15 minutes).

Alice Waters' Gratin of Potatoes and Wild Mushrooms

Serves 6

1½ lbs. new red potatoes
1½ oz. dried Boletus mushrooms, chanterelles, or morels
4 Tb. (½ stick) unsalted butter

2 – 3 Tb. heavy cream
½ tsp. minced garlic
Salt and freshly ground pepper

Peel potatoes, slice ¼ inch thick, place in cold water, and soak, changing water three times at 10-minute intervals.

Soak mushrooms in 1¼ cups of hot water for about 20 minutes, pick for grit, rinse, and chop coarsely. Strain mushroom liquor through triple cheesecloth and set aside.

Preheat oven to 425°.

Pat mushrooms dry, heat 2 tablespoons of the butter in a small skillet, and sauté mushrooms over moderate heat for 3 minutes. Add cream, garlic, ½ cup of the mushroom liquor, and salt and pepper to taste, and cook for 3 minutes.

Dry potatoes well and arrange a layer of them in a lightly buttered 9×9-inch baking dish. Salt potatoes lightly, spoon on some of the mushroom mixture, and continue layering, ending with a layer of potatoes. Dot with remaining butter and bake for 15 – 20 minutes or till potatoes are a deep golden brown.

Pommes à l'Huile

(Warm Potato Salad Vinaigrette)

Serves 4–6

2 lbs. small boiling potatoes,
    scrubbed
¾ cup olive oil
3 Tb. white vinegar
3 Tb. dry white wine

1 onion, minced
2 sprigs parsley, minced
1 Tb. minced chives
Salt and freshly ground pepper

Place potatoes in a large saucepan with enough salted water to cover, bring to the boil, lower heat, cover, and cook for 15–20 minutes or till just tender. Drain, cut into ½-inch slices, and place in a large mixing bowl.

In another bowl, whisk together the oil, vinegar, and white wine, add all remaining ingredients, and whisk again lightly.

Pour dressing over potatoes, toss gently but thoroughly to coat, let stand for 20 minutes to allow potatoes to absorb dressing, and serve while still warm.

Potatoes in Puff Pastry

Serves 4–6

There are two very important reasons for allowing the potatoes in this dish to marinate, so by no means skip the initial step thinking the results will be the same. First, the potatoes need the seasoning of the fresh chervil and onions for full flavor, and second, unless you allow the salt to withdraw excess liquid from the spuds, the pie will be soggy.

4 or 5 all-purpose potatoes, peeled
   and cut into ¼-inch slices
1 large shallot, minced
1 tsp. salt
Freshly ground pepper

1 Tb. finely chopped fresh chervil
1 Tb. finely chopped scallions
1 lb. Quick Puff Pastry (p. 413)
1 egg, beaten with pinch of salt
¼ cup half-and-half, heated

Combine potatoes and shallot in a large mixing bowl, add salt, pepper to taste, chervil, and scallions, toss well, and let sit for 20 minutes.

Divide pastry dough into 2 pieces, and on a floured surface roll one-half of the dough ⅛ inch thick. Place a 10-inch pot or casserole lid in the center of the dough and, following the edge of the lid with a small knife, cut out a circle of dough. Place circle on a baking sheet and arrange potatoes in 3 or 4 layers on top, leaving a 1-inch border of dough.

Preheat over to 450°.

Roll other half of the dough ¼ inch thick and carefully cut out another circle about ½ inch wider than the lid. Brush outer edges of dough on baking sheet with a little egg glaze, and place second circle of dough across potatoes. Secure edges of pie by pressing down all around with fingers, turn glued edges up snugly, and crimp edges with fingers.

With a sharp knife, carefully trace an oval across the top, and make a few decorative lines or patterns on the oval. Brush top of pie with egg glaze, place in oven, and bake for 20 minutes.

Remove pie from oven, lift off oval cutout, and spoon cream over potatoes, carefully lifting potatoes to allow cream to seep down. Replace oval cutout, reduce oven to 375°, and continue baking for 30 minutes.

Ocopa Arequipeña
(Peruvian Potatoes with Cheese, Walnuts, and Hot Pepper Sauce)

Serves 4

While researching the potato's pre-Columbian origins in the Peruvian Andes, I came across this fascinating dish in Elizabeth Lambert Ortiz's *The Book of Latin American Cooking,* possibly one of the first ways this lowly but wonderful root vegetable was prepared by the Incas. In my adaptation, I've substituted our splendid dry Monterey Jack cheese for the more traditional Spanish *queso blanco* and think the change is for the better. This dish is really a full meal in itself and should be served with no more than plenty of ice-cold beer and a light dessert.

4 large baking potatoes
½ cup peanut or vegetable oil
2 onions, sliced
2 garlic cloves, finely chopped
1 medium jalapeño chili pepper, seeded and coarsely chopped
1 cup walnut meats, ground
¼ lb. crumbled dry Monterey Jack cheese

1¼ cups milk
Salt
Romaine lettuce
4 hard-boiled eggs, shelled and halved
12 black olives, pitted
Strips of pimiento

Preheat over to 425°.
Wash, scrub, and dry the potatoes, prick each with a fork, bake for about 1 hour or till soft, and keep warm.

Heat oil in a small skillet, add onion and garlic, sauté for 2 minutes over low heat, and transfer to a blender or food processor, oil included. Add chili pepper, walnut meats, cheese, milk, and salt to taste, and blend to a smooth, thick sauce.

Arrange a bed of lettuce on 4 serving plates, cut potatoes in half lengthwise, and arrange 2 halves, cut side down, on top of each bed of lettuce. Pour sauce over potatoes and garnish each plate with eggs, olives, and pimiento strips.

Oyster-Stuffed Potatoes with Horseradish

Serves 4 as a main course

4 large Idaho potatoes
6 Tb. (¾ stick) butter
1 small onion, minced
½ pint shucked oysters plus their
   liquor

¼ cup dry sherry
Salt
Pinch of allspice
⅓ cup heavy cream
⅓ cup freshly grated horseradish

Preheat oven to 425°.

Wash, scrub, and dry the potatoes, prick each with a fork, and bake for about 1 hour or till soft.

In the meantime, melt one-half of the butter in a saucepan, add onion, and sauté over low heat for 2 minutes. Add oysters (reserving liquor) and cook for about 1 minute or till oysters curl. Add sherry, bring to the boil, transfer oysters to a bowl, and reserve cooking liquid.

Slice tops off potatoes lengthwise, scoop out pulp and place half in a mixing bowl, and reserve remaining pulp for another use. Add remaining butter, salt to taste, and allspice to pulp in bowl, mash with a fork till smooth, and spoon equal parts of the mixture on the bottom and up the sides of the potato jackets.

In a saucepan, bring oyster liquor and reserved cooking liquid to the boil, reduce to about 3 tablespoons, add cream, and cook for 1 minute. Remove saucepan from heat, add oysters and one-half of the horseradish, and stir.

Spoon oysters and sauce into prepared potatoes and sprinkle top of each with remaining horseradish.

Potato and Feta Cheese Soufflé

Serves 6 as a sidedish or 4 as a main luncheon course

4 medium boiling potatoes
4 eggs, separated
¾ cup half-and-half
5 Tb. butter

1 small onion, minced
1 celery rib, minced
1 cup finely crumbled feta cheese
Salt and freshly ground pepper

Place potatoes in a large saucepan with enough salted water to cover and boil for about 30 minutes or till tender.

When cool enough to handle, peel potatoes, transfer to a large mixing bowl, and mash with a fork. Add egg yolks and half-and-half, and beat to a smooth puree with an electric mixer.

Preheat oven to 400°.

Heat 3 tablespoons of the butter in a small skillet, add onion and celery, sauté over low heat for 3 minutes, and stir into potato mixture with the cheese and salt and pepper to taste.

Grease the bottom and sides of a 7-inch soufflé dish with remaining butter. In another large bowl, beat egg whites with a pinch of salt till stiff, fold one-third of the whites into the potato mixture, then fold mixture into remaining whites. Pour mixture into prepared dish, place dish on a baking sheet, and bake for 40–45 minutes or till puffed and golden brown.

Gratin of Potatoes, Turnips, and Ham

Serves 6 as a sidedish

3 Tb. unsalted butter

6 or 7 medium all-purpose
  potatoes, washed, scrubbed,
  and cut into very thin slices

Salt and freshly ground pepper

Nutmeg

1 bay leaf

1 large turnip, peeled and cut
  into very thin slices

1 garlic clove, minced

1 cup diced cooked ham

2 cups half-and-half

Preheat oven to 350°.

Grease the bottom and sides of an 11- or 12-inch gratin dish with 1 tablespoon of the butter. Layer one-half of the potato slices in dish in overlapping fashion, season with salt and pepper to taste and very lightly with nutmeg, add 1 tablespoon butter in pieces, and place bay leaf in center. Layer all the turnip slices on top of the potatoes, sprinkle on garlic and ham evenly, season again with pepper, and dot with remaining butter in pieces. Layer remaining potatoes on top of the turnips, season once again with pepper, and pour half-and-half into the dish to come about two-thirds of the way up the potatoes.

Bake for about 1 hour or till potatoes and turnips are tender and the top is golden brown.

Potato and Salmon Torte

Serves 6 as a main course

4½ cups all-purpose flour
4 tsp. baking powder
2 tsp. salt
2 cups lard, diced
4 tsp. lemon juice
1 egg, beaten
6 slices of bacon, cut into 1-inch
  pieces

1 medium onion, chopped
2 cups peeled all-purpose potatoes
  cut into ½-inch cubes
1-lb. salmon steak, boned,
  skinned, and cut into ½-inch
  pieces

Combine flour, baking powder, salt, and one-half of the diced lard in a large mixing bowl and mix till ingredients are well blended. Place remaining lard in a small bowl, add ¾ cup boiling water, and stir well till lard is melted. Add lemon juice and egg, blend well, pour mixture over flour mixture, and stir thoroughly to form a smooth dough. Turn dough onto a lightly floured surface, knead lightly, wrap in plastic wrap, and chill for 1 hour.

Preheat oven to 400°.

In a large, heavy skillet, fry bacon till almost crisp, pour all but 2 tablespoons of fat from the pan, add chopped onion, and sauté over low heat for 2 minutes. Add potatoes, sauté for 1 minute, add enough boiling water to cover, cover skillet, and simmer for 15 minutes or till potatoes are tender. Remove skillet from heat, add salmon, stir, and let mixture cool.

Roll out half the dough ¼ inch thick, line a 9×2-inch baking dish with the dough, and fill shell with the salmon mixture. Roll out remaining dough, lay it over filling, seal edges by pressing them down with a fork, and cut several slits on top.

Bake torte for 15 minutes, reduce heat to 350°, and continue baking for 30 minutes longer or till crust is golden.

Twice-Baked Potato Skins with Cheese and Bacon

Serves 4 as a light luncheon course
or 6 as a side vegetable

6 strips of bacon
4 very large Idaho potatoes
⅓ cup (¾ stick) melted butter

Freshly ground pepper
¾ cup grated Swiss or Parmesan
cheese

*F*ry bacon in a skillet till crisp, drain on paper towels, and crumble. Preheat oven to 425°.

Wash, scrub, and dry the potatoes, prick each with a fork, and bake for 1 hour or till soft.

Cut potatoes in thirds lengthwise, scoop out all but about ¼ inch of pulp from each piece, and reserve pulp for another use. Place shells skin side down in a large baking dish, brush liberally with melted butter, and season with plenty of fresh pepper. Sprinkle bacon and cheese on top of each piece, place potatoes in the oven, and continue baking for about 15 minutes or till tops are golden brown and skins are crisp.

Potato-Spinach Dumplings with Stilton Sauce

Serves 4–6 as a main course

The one thing to remember when preparing this dish is not to crowd the dumplings while they are boiling. These make a very nice main course accompanied by a very tart salad, perhaps some broiled herbed mushroom caps, and a slightly chilled Chardonnay.

6 or 7 medium boiling potatoes
3/4 cup (1½ sticks) butter
Salt and freshly ground pepper
Nutmeg
1 cup flour

3 eggs
1/3 cup spinach
1 cup heavy cream
1/4 lb. Stilton cheese, crumbled

Puree spinach in a blender or food processor.
Place potatoes in a large saucepan with enough salted water to cover and boil for about 30 minutes or till tender. When cool enough to handle, peel potatoes, transfer to a large mixing bowl, and mash with a fork.

Heat 1 cup of water in a saucepan, add 4 tablespoons of the butter plus salt, pepper, and nutmeg to taste, bring to the boil, and remove from heat. Beat in flour gradually, then beat in eggs one at a time.

Combine mixture with the mashed potatoes, blend in spinach puree, and form dough with lightly floured hands into 2-inch balls. Drop balls in batches into a large saucepan or kettle of boiling salted water, cook them for exactly 15 seconds after they rise to the surface, and with a slotted spoon transfer dumplings to paper towels.

Preheat broiler.

Heat remaining butter in a large skillet over low heat, add the cream and crumbled cheese, and cook mixture till cheese has melted and the sauce is smooth.

Place dumplings in a large baking dish, run momentarily under the broiler to brown slightly, and cover with the sauce.

Potatoes and Squash Anna with Pimiento

It seems I'm forever trying to come up with different ways to add dignity to the spud and illustrate this denigrated vegetable's incredible versatility. Adding slices of yellow squash to that classic potato cake known as *pommes Anna* gives the dish not only more flavor but also that extra degree of moistness it always seems to need. Sliced zucchini, eggplant, or turnips might also be used with excellent results, but this is one potato dish in which I feel the addition of cheese would defeat the whole purpose — much like in authentic *pommes dauphinoise*.

4 medium yellow squash, washed and cut into very thin rounds
8 medium boiling potatoes, peeled and cut into very thin rounds
8 Tb. (1 stick) butter, melted and clarified

Salt and freshly ground pepper
Long strips of pimiento
Chopped parsley

Preheat oven to 425°.
Pour 3 tablespoons of the butter into a large skillet, add squash, sauté lightly on both sides over moderate heat till golden, and transfer to paper towels.

Grease the bottom and sides of a 9-inch heavy, ovenproof skillet with 2 tablespoons of the butter and arrange a ring of potato and squash slices around edge of the skillet bottom, overlapping alternate layers of potato and squash. Continue to arrange potato and squash slices in overlapping circles till bottom of the pan is covered. Drizzle butter over top and salt and pepper to taste. Repeat with a second layer. Arrange 2 overlapping layers of potatoes around edges of skillet and continue layering potatoes and squash in center, drizzling with butter and seasoning with salt and pepper. Press top layer down firmly with a spatula, cover skillet, place in oven, and bake for 30 minutes.

Remove from oven, press down firmly again in center, and continue baking, uncovered, for 30 minutes more or till top is slightly browned. Loosen potatoes from the sides of skillet with spatula, invert cake onto a heated platter, arrange pimiento strips across top, and sprinkle with chopped parsley.

Maple Sweet Potatoes and Apples

Serves 6–8

2 Tb. butter
3 lbs. sweet potatoes (about 6),
    peeled and cut into ¼-inch slices
2 medium apples, cored and cut
    into ¼-inch slices

Nutmeg
Salt and freshly ground pepper
3 Tb. maple syrup
¾ cup sherry

Preheat oven to 350°.
    Grease a large baking dish with the butter and layer one-half of the potato slices in the dish. Layer all the apple slices over the potatoes, then layer remaining potato slices over the apples.

Sprinkle nutmeg lightly over potatoes and season with salt and pepper to taste. Drizzle the maple syrup evenly over top, and pour sherry gently around the edges.

Cover the dish with foil and bake for 1 hour. Remove foil and continue baking for about 20 minutes or till top of casserole is well glazed.

Sweet Potato and Walnut Pudding

Serves 6 – 8

6 sweet potatoes
2 eggs, beaten
1 tsp. vanilla
½ cup half-and-half
⅛ tsp. cinnamon

1 cup light brown sugar
⅓ cup flour
6 Tb. (¾ stick) butter
1 cup chopped walnuts

P lace potatoes in a large kettle with enough salted water to cover, bring to the boil, lower heat, cover, and cook for 25 minutes or till very tender. Drain potatoes, and, when cool enough to handle, peel, place in a large mixing bowl and mash with a potato masher.

Preheat oven to 350°.

Add eggs, vanilla, half-and-half, and cinnamon to mashed potatoes, blend well, and transfer mixture to a large baking dish or casserole.

Combine sugar and flour in a bowl, cut in butter with a pastry cutter, add walnuts, and stir till well blended. Distribute walnut mixture evenly over the top of the pudding and bake for 30 minutes or till golden brown. Serve pudding with baked ham, roast turkey, or game dishes.

Baked Yams with Coconut

Serves 6

Among my fondest memories of Chapel Hill, North Carolina, are the genuine Southern meals served at the two-hundred-year-old Colonial Inn in neighboring Hillsborough. There is salty country ham with red-eye gravy, homemade biscuits, and spicy apple cobbler, but I'd make a special return trip if for no other reason than to savor once again what the restaurant refers to as "Cornwallis Yams."

3 medium yams (or sweet potatoes)
¾ cup milk
½ cup sugar
¼ cup crushed canned pineapple
4 Tb. (½ stick) butter

2 eggs, beaten
¼ tsp. salt
¼ tsp. ground cinnamon
¼ cup flaked packaged coconut

*W*ash yams and place in a large saucepan with water to cover. Bring to the boil, lower heat, cover, and simmer yams for about 30 minutes or till tender. Drain and place in a large mixing bowl.

Preheat oven to 350°.

When cool enough to handle, peel yams, return to the mixing bowl, and mash with a fork. Add all remaining ingredients except the coconut and mix well. Pour mixture into a greased medium-sized baking dish and bake for 45 minutes.

To serve, sprinkle top with the flaked coconut.

Rigatoni with Olives and Cold Tomato Sauce

Serves 4–6

½ cup virgin Italian olive oil
4 Tb. sherry wine vinegar
4 garlic cloves, minced
2 sprigs fresh parsley, minced
1 cup shredded fresh basil leaves
½ tsp. salt
Freshly ground pepper

10 ripe tomatoes
1 lb. rigatoni or penne pasta
¼ cup small cured black olives, pitted
1 cup freshly grated Parmesan cheese

*C*ombine olive oil and vinegar in a large glass or stainless-steel mixing bowl and whisk till well blended. Add garlic, parsley, basil, salt, and pepper to taste, and stir.

Slice tomatoes in half, squeeze slightly to extract as many seeds and as much juice as possible, and dice. Add tomatoes to oil and vinegar mixture, stir, cover with plastic wrap, and let marinate for at least 2 hours.

Bring 4 quarts of salted water to the boil in a large kettle, add pasta, return to the boil, and cook for 7–8 minutes or till *al dente*. Drain pasta in a colander, let cool slightly, and transfer to a deep serving platter. Add olives, spoon tomato mixture on top, sprinkle with the cheese, and toss lightly with two forks.

Linguine with Chicken Livers

Serves 4–6

4 Tb. (½ stick) butter
2 medium onions, finely chopped
1 garlic clove, minced
½ green bell pepper, finely chopped
1 lb. chicken livers, trimmed and
  cut in half

1 Tb. chopped fresh basil
1½ cups Hot Tomato Sauce
  (p. 539)
Salt and freshly ground pepper
¼ cup heavy cream
1 lb. linguine pasta

*H*eat butter in a medium saucepan, add onions, garlic, and green pepper, and sauté over low heat for about 3 minutes or till peppers are soft. Add chicken livers, raise heat to moderate, and sauté, tossing, till livers are golden but slightly pink on the inside. Add basil, tomato sauce, and salt and pepper to taste, stir, return heat to moderate, and simmer till sauce is heated through. Remove pan from heat and stir in the cream.

Bring 4 quarts of salted water to the boil in a large kettle, add pasta, return to the boil, cook for 7–8 minutes or till *al dente,* and drain in a colander.

Heat sauce again.

Transfer pasta to a large serving bowl, pour on sauce with chicken livers, and toss with two forks.

Pasta con le Sarde
(Pasta with Sardine Sauce)

Serves 4–6

This is probably the most popular pasta dish in Sicily and, without doubt, one of the more memorable I've ever tasted. Ideally, wild fennel (found occasionally in California markets) should be used, but I've found the feathery leaves of our bulb fennel work very nicely. And, although no housewife in Palermo would dream of substituting canned sardines for the fresh, top-grade tinned sardines combined with anchovies yield a marvelous sauce.

3 Tb. raisins
1 cup bulb fennel leaves
¼ cup olive oil
1 small onion, chopped
2 4-oz. cans boneless sardines

3 anchovy fillets, chopped
2 Tb. red wine vinegar
Freshly ground pepper
1 lb. penne or bucatini pasta
¼ cup pine nuts

Place raisins in a small bowl of warm water to soak while preparing sauce and pasta.

Bring 4 quarts of salted water to the boil in a large kettle, add fennel leaves, lower heat, and simmer for 15 minutes.

Meanwhile, heat oil in a medium enameled or stainless-steel skillet, add onion, and sauté for 2 minutes over low heat. Add sardines and anchovies and mash well with a fork or the back of a spoon. Add red wine vinegar and pepper to taste, stir, raise heat to moderate, cook for 2–3 minutes, and remove pan from heat.

Transfer fennel leaves from boiling water to a chopping board and chop coarsely. Bring water in kettle back to the boil, add pasta, return to the boil, and cook for 8–10 minutes or till *al dente*.

Meanwhile, drain raisins, chop, and add to the sardine sauce. Add chopped fennel leaves and the pine nuts, stir, return skillet to moderate heat, and cook sauce for 2 minutes longer, stirring.

Drain pasta, transfer to a large serving bowl or dish, pour on sauce, and toss well with two forks.

Fettucine with Snails and Peas

Serves 4–6

4 Tb. (½ stick) butter
7½-oz. can snails, drained
2 garlic cloves, minced
1½ cups heavy cream
¾ cup freshly grated Parmesan
   cheese

9-oz. package frozen peas,
   defrosted
Salt and freshly ground pepper
1 lb. fettucine

*H*eat butter in a heavy saucepan, add snails and garlic, and sauté over low heat for 3 minutes. Add cream, stir, increase heat to moderate, and simmer till mixture thickens slightly. Add cheese, peas, and salt and pepper to taste, stir, and cook for 6–8 minutes longer or till peas are just tender. Keep warm.

Bring 4 quarts of salted water to the boil in a large kettle, add fettucine, return to the boil, and cook for 7–8 minutes or till *al dente*. Drain pasta, transfer to a large serving bowl, add snail and pea mixture, and toss well with two forks. Serve immediately.

Fettucine with Bulb Fennel and Avocado

Serves 4 – 6

Readers of *Town & Country* never seem to tire of new ways to deal with *fettucine Alfredo* and must sense (rightly so) that I could eat a portion of this classic creamy pasta every night of the week. I prepare the dish with wild mushrooms, broccoli, zucchini, white truffles, bits of chicken, water chestnuts, and who knows what else, but one of my truly favorite versions features crisp, anise-flavored fresh fennel pitted against smooth avocado. Remember not to add the avocado till you're ready for the final tossing at table.

2 firm avocados	1 cup freshly grated Parmesan
½ lemon	cheese
1 bulb fennel	1 lb. dried fettucine
4 Tb. (½ stick) butter	Salt and freshly ground pepper
1 cup heavy cream	Pinch of nutmeg

Peel avocados, cut in half, remove pits, and rub all exposed surfaces with the lemon.

Cut off and discard the stalks and feathery leaves of the fennel, as well as any ribs that are blemished or wilted. Remove remaining ribs, cut vertically into ½-inch slices, then cut slices into 1-inch pieces. Place pieces in a colander and rinse thoroughly under cold water.

Heat the butter in a very large enameled skillet, add two-thirds of the cream and one-third of the cheese, and simmer over moderate heat for about 1 minute or till sauce has thickened. Turn off heat.

Bring 4 quarts of salted water to the boil in a kettle, add fettucine, return to the boil, and cook for 3 – 4 minutes. Drain pasta and transfer to the skillet with the sauce.

Cut avocados into ½-inch cubes.

Return heat under skillet to low and toss pasta in the sauce with two forks. Add remaining cream and cheese, salt and pepper to taste, the nutmeg, and the fennel, and toss till the pasta is well coated.

Transfer pasta to a heated serving bowl, distribute avocado cubes evenly over the top, toss lightly, and serve immediately.

Cold Pasta with Chicken and Vegetables

Serves 4

½ lb. vermicelli or spaghetti
1 cup Basic Vinaigrette with
  garlic (p. 542)
10 mushrooms, sliced
1 cup broccoli florets, blanched 2
  minutes
1 cup fresh (or frozen and
  defrosted) green peas, blanched
  2 minutes

12 – 14 cherry tomatoes
1 large cooked chicken breast,
  boned, skinned, and cut into
  1-inch cubes
⅓ cup pine nuts
⅓ cup chopped fresh basil

*B*ring 3 quarts of salted water to the boil in a kettle, add pasta, return to the boil, and cook for 4–7 minutes or till *al dente*. Drain pasta in a colander, transfer to a large serving bowl, add ⅓ cup of the dressing, toss, let cool, and chill for at least 3 hours.

Pour remaining dressing into another bowl, add vegetables, and toss to coat thoroughly.

When ready to serve, add chicken to the pasta and toss lightly with two forks. Add vegetables plus nuts and chopped basil, and toss once more.

David K's Imperial Noodles with Peanut Butter-Garlic Sauce

Serves 2

This dish illustrates as well as any why David K is considered to be one of the finest restaurateurs in New York. What I find so remarkable about this recipe is the way so many assertive seasonings blend to produce such subtle results. Some Chinese produce a more intense sauce by using twice the amount of peanut butter and water.

1 tsp. granulated sugar
2 Tb. soy sauce
1½ Tb. wine vinegar
1 Tb. sesame oil
1 tsp. chili oil
1½ tsp. smooth peanut butter plus
    2 Tb. water

Pinch each of minced garlic clove,
    minced scallion, and grated
    fresh ginger
½ lb. egg noodles

Blend all ingredients except the noodles in a large mixing bowl, stir vigorously, and set aside. (If sauce separates, it can be reintegrated by adding 1 or 2 drops of boiling water and stirring lightly.)

Bring 3 quarts of salted water to the boil in a kettle, add noodles, and cook till desired tenderness is achieved. Place noodles in a colander, run under cold running water, drain thoroughly, and transfer to a large serving bowl.

Pour sauce over noodles and serve lukewarm or cold.

Spaghetti Primavera Le Cirque

Serves 4

Perhaps the finest tribute to the *spaghetti primavera* at New York's Le Cirque restaurant was made a few years back when France's two celebrated three-star chefs, Paul Bocuse and Michel Guérard, asked to taste it as an appetizer, then ordered it as a main course, then returned for the recipe so they could reproduce it back home. Created by the restaurant's suave owner, Sirio Maccione, while experimenting with pasta one weekend at his country retreat, the dish is relatively simple to turn out and best accompanied by no more than a tart green salad, Italian bread sticks, and a good bottle of white wine. Appropriately enough, this now-famous recipe was published first in the pages of *Town & Country.*

3 Tb. olive oil
2 tomatoes, cored, seeded, and
    coarsely chopped
1 tsp. chopped garlic
¼ cup chopped parsley
Pinch of salt
Freshly ground pepper
1 lb. spaghetti
10 mushrooms, sliced
1 cup sliced zucchini, blanched 2
    minutes
1½ cups sliced broccoli, blanched
    2 minutes

1½ cups snow peas
6 sliced asparagus, blanched 2
    minutes
1 cup fresh (or frozen and
    defrosted) green peas, blanched
    2 minutes
½ cup freshly grated Parmesan
    cheese
6 Tb. (¾ stick) butter
1 cup warm heavy cream
⅓ cup chopped fresh basil
⅓ cup pine nuts
12 whole cherry tomatoes

Heat 1 tablespoon of the oil in a medium skillet, add tomatoes, half the garlic, the parsley, salt, and pepper to taste, and sauté over moderate heat for 2 minutes. Set aside.

Bring 4 quarts of salted water to the boil in a large kettle, add spaghetti, return to the boil, cook about 7–8 minutes or till *al dente,* and drain.

Meanwhile, heat remaining oil in another skillet, add the mushrooms, the remaining garlic, zucchini, broccoli, snow peas, asparagus, and green peas, and sauté for about 2 minutes, stirring, or just long enough to heat vegetables.

Place spaghetti in a large serving bowl, add the cheese, butter, heavy cream, basil, and more pepper to taste, and toss lightly but thoroughly with 2 forks. Top pasta with the vegetables, add pine nuts and sautéed tomatoes, and garnish with whole cherry tomatoes.

Spätzle with Cabbage and Sausage

Serves 4

In Germany the small pasta known as *spätzle* is generally served as a side dish with no more than melted butter, salt, and plenty of freshly ground pepper. It can, however, be combined with any number of other ingredients to make a satisfying main course. This particular example is purely German in nature, but you could also try smoked fish, lots of fresh wild mushrooms, and all sorts of blanched vegetables. Serve this dish with a tart green salad and Russian Black Bread (p. 422).

2 Tb. butter
1 lb. spicy lean German sausage, casings removed
¾ cup full-bodied imported beer
1 medium head red cabbage, shredded

1 tsp. caraway seeds
Salt and freshly ground pepper
3 cups all-purpose flour
¼ tsp. ground nutmeg
4 eggs, slightly beaten
1 cup milk

*H*eat butter in a large saucepan, crumble sausage into pan, and fry over moderate heat till cooked through. Add beer, cabbage, caraway seeds, and salt and pepper to taste, and stir well. Bring liquid to the boil, lower heat, cover, and cook for about 20 minutes or till cabbage is tender. Keep warm.

Meanwhile, combine flour, ½ teaspoon salt, and the nutmeg in a mixing bowl, add eggs, and beat till well blended. Add milk in a thin stream, stirring constantly with a wooden spoon, and stir till dough is smooth.

Bring 2 quarts of salted water to the boil in a large, heavy saucepan, set a large-holed metal colander over the pan, and, little by little, press the dough through the colander directly into the boiling water. Stir the *spätzle* gently to prevent sticking, boil them for 6–8 minutes or till tender, and drain.

Transfer *spätzle* to a large serving bowl. Drain off any excess liquid from the cabbage, add cabbage and sausage mixture to the *spätzle,* and toss to combine ingredients well.

Potato Gnocchi and Sausage Casserole

Serves 4

Potato *gnocchi* can be one of the most delicate forms of pasta in the Italian repertory so long as you don't follow the misconceived practices of adding egg yolks (which toughen the dough) and allowing the small pieces of dough to cook for more than 8 – 10 seconds after they've risen to the top of the boiling water. *Gnocchi* are also delicious topped with meat sauce or Pesto Sauce (p. 532), baked in a light cream sauce, or simply buttered, sprinkled with a little strong cheese, and run under the broiler.

1 Tb. olive oil
4 sweet Italian sausages, casings removed
3 lbs. large boiling potatoes (about 6 or 7)
3 cups flour, sifted
½ cup (1 stick) melted butter

Freshly ground pepper
1 cup Hot Tomato Sauce (p. 539)
2 Tb. chopped fresh basil
½ cup freshly grated Parmesan or finely crumbled Gorgonzola cheese

*H*eat olive oil in a medium skillet, crumble sausage into oil, fry for 10 minutes or till well cooked, stirring, and drain on paper towels. Set aside.

Place potatoes in a large saucepan or kettle with enough salted water to cover, bring to the boil, lower heat, cover, and cook for about 30 minutes or till tender. Drain potatoes, and when cool enough to handle, peel, cut into quarters, mash in a food mill, and let cool completely.

Place mashed potatoes in a large mixing bowl and gradually mix in the flour with your hands to form a smooth, delicate dough. Shape dough into thumb-size rolls, then cut rolls into 1-inch lengths, pinch the center of each with your thumb, and place on a lightly floured towel.

Bring 5 quarts of salted water to the boil in a kettle and drop the *gnocchi,* one by one, into the water. As they float to the top, let them cook for about 8 seconds more, then transfer them with a slotted spoon to paper towels.

Preheat oven to 425°.

Grease a medium ovenproof casserole or baking dish and layer half the *gnocchi* in the dish. Drizzle half the melted butter over the top, then distribute the sausage evenly over the *gnocchi.* Layer remaining *gnocchi* over the sausage, drizzle with remaining butter, and season with pepper to taste. Pour tomato sauce over top and around the sides, sprinkle top with basil and cheese, and bake for 15 minutes or till top is golden.

Serve as a main course with a large arugula and endive salad.

Coconut-Orange Rice

Serves 6 – 8

3 Tb. butter
1 small onion, minced
1½ cups orange juice
4 Tb. slivered orange rind

½ cup cream of coconut
2 cups water
1¼ tsp. salt
1½ cups rice

*H*eat butter in a large saucepan, add onion, and sauté over low heat for 2 minutes. Add orange juice, orange rind, cream of coconut, water, and salt, and bring to the boil. Add rice gradually, cover, and cook over low heat for 25 – 30 minutes or till all liquid is absorbed. Fluff rice with a fork and let stand 5 minutes to dry thoroughly.

Serve with Assyrian Rack of Lamb (p. 199), Lamb Steaks with Dilled Cream Sauce (p. 200), or any lamb curry.

Curried Pilaf with Pine Nuts

Serves 4

4 Tb. (½ stick) butter
1 medium onion, minced
2 tsp. curry powder
1 cup long-grain rice

2 cups Chicken Stock (p. 521)
Salt and freshly ground pepper
¼ cup pine nuts

*H*eat butter in a large saucepan, add onion and curry powder, and sauté over low heat for 2 minutes, stirring. Raise heat slightly, add rice, stir, and cook for 5 minutes, stirring.

Add chicken stock and salt and pepper to taste, stir, bring liquid to the boil, lower heat, cover, and simmer rice for 20 minutes or till liquid is absorbed.

Add pine nuts to pilaf, fluff with a fork, and let stand for 5 minutes uncovered over very low heat to dry thoroughly.

Artichoke Pilaf

2 Tb. butter
1 onion, minced
½ tsp. cumin
½ tsp. dried coriander
10-oz. package frozen artichoke
   hearts, defrosted

1 cup rice
3 cups Chicken Stock (p. 521) or
   broth
2 Tb. tomato paste
4 Tb. (½ stick) butter
Salt and freshly ground pepper

Heat the 2 tablespoons of butter in a large saucepan, add onion, cumin, coriander, and artichokes, and cook over moderate heat for about 4 minutes or till onion and artichokes are slightly browned. Add rice, stir, and cook for 2 minutes longer.

In another saucepan, bring chicken stock to the boil, add tomato paste, stir well, and add mixture to the rice and artichokes. Cover and simmer for 20–30 minutes or till all the liquid is absorbed.

Brown the 4 tablespoons of butter in a small skillet, pour over rice mixture, add salt and pepper to taste, and stir well. Let stand for 5 minutes before serving.

Vegetable Paella

Serves 6

Who says *paella* must always be prepared with chicken and seafood? The saffroned rice in this classic Spanish specialty serves as a perfect foil for all sorts of garlicky vegetables, and if you choose your vegetables carefully, there's really no more colorful dish you can put on the table or buffet. Serve the *paella* with plenty of crusty bread and butter and a crisp white wine.

9-oz. package of frozen peas, defrosted
1 large zucchini, cut crosswise into quarters
2 carrots, scraped
1 cup cauliflower florets
½ red bell pepper, seeded
5 Tb. olive oil
1 medium onion, minced
2 garlic cloves, minced

¼ lb. chorizo *sausage (or Hungarian sausage), cut into ¼-inch slices*
1½ cups short-grain rice
2½ cups Beef Stock (p. 522)
1 Tb. tomato paste
Pinch of saffron
Salt and freshly ground pepper to taste

Place peas in a saucepan with salted water to cover, bring to the boil, lower heat to moderate, cook for 5–7 minutes, and drain.

Place zucchini, carrots, cauliflower, and bell pepper in a steamer or on a rack in a large skillet with 1 inch of water, bring water to the boil, cover, and steam till individual vegetables are tender but still slightly crisp. Cut zucchini and bell pepper into thin strips, cut carrots into ¼-inch rounds, and either cut cauliflower florets in half or leave whole.

Preheat oven to 375°.

Heat the oil in a metal *paella* pan or a large, deep skillet, add onion and garlic, and sauté over moderate heat for 2 minutes. Add the sausage and cook with the onion and garlic for 2 minutes. Remove sausage, add rice to pan, stir well, and cook for 2 minutes. Add stock, tomato paste, saffron, and salt and pepper to taste, stir, and bring liquid to the boil. Place pan in the oven and bake for about 20 minutes or till rice has absorbed most of the liquid but is still soft. Remove pan from oven, add vegetables to rice, stir, and bake for 10 minutes longer.

Savannah Red Rice

Serves 6 – 8

While on assignment in Savannah to produce a feature on Low Country cookery, I was treated to a feast of regional specialties prepared by members of the city's Junior League that would have made health fanatics stagger. I must have gone back to the groaning buffet table three or four times for more of this spicy rice, testimony to the fact that still nobody understands rice like those whose ancestors cultivated field after field of the grain on the great plantations. Although in Savannah and Charleston they cook rice in special steamers, it can be prepared with almost as fluffy results in a saucepan. If you're squeamish about ingesting bacon grease, you might as well forget about preparing this dish.

½ lb. bacon
2 medium onions, finely chopped
6 oz. (1 small can) tomato paste
2 cups water

3 tsp. salt
2 – 3 tsp. sugar
Tabasco and freshly ground pepper
2 cups rice

Fry bacon till crisp in a large skillet, drain on paper towels, and crumble. Pour off half the grease and reserve.

Add onions to bacon grease in skillet and sauté over moderate heat for 2 minutes, stirring. Add tomato paste, water, salt, sugar, and Tabasco and pepper to taste, stir well, and cook for 10 minutes.

Transfer contents of the skillet to a large saucepan, add reserved bacon grease, and bring to the boil. Add rice, lower heat to moderate, stir, cover, and cook for about 30 minutes or till rice has absorbed most of the liquid. Remove pan from heat, add crumbled bacon, stir well, and let rice stand for 5 minutes to dry slightly.

Chawal Dhania Podina
(Lemon Rice with Mint and Coriander)

Serves 4–6

If you still think rice must always be the bland, sticky, disgusting variety found in all Chinese and most American restaurants, try this zesty Indian version the next time you're trying to think of something different and delicious to serve with roasted chicken or lamb stew. For fluffy results, you must use long-grain rice and wash the rice well.

1½ cups long-grain rice
½ tsp. salt
½ tsp. turmeric powder
2 Tb. butter
2 Tb. finely chopped cashew nuts
1 tsp. ground cinnamon
2 green chili peppers, seeded and
  finely chopped

2 Tb. lemon juice
1 Tb. finely chopped fresh mint
1 Tb. finely chopped fresh
  coriander (also called cilantro
  and Chinese parsley)
½ cup plain yogurt

Place rice in a saucepan with cold water to cover and let soak for 1 hour. Drain, add fresh water to cover, wash rice well with your hands, and drain once again.

Bring 3 cups of water to the boil in another saucepan, add salt, turmeric powder, and the rice, return water to the boil, and cook rice for 15 minutes. Drain rice.

Heat the butter in another large saucepan, add nuts, cinnamon, and chilies, and sauté over moderate heat for 2 minutes, stirring. Add rice, stir, and sauté for 2 minutes longer. Add the lemon juice, mint, coriander, and yogurt, increase heat to moderate, cover, and cook till all the liquid is absorbed, shaking the pan constantly. Remove pan from heat, stir rice, and let stand for 5 minutes.

Wild Rice with Wild Mushrooms and Pine Nuts

Serves 4

Now that more and more varieties of exotic native wild mushrooms are being marketed in America, I never miss the chance to utilize these delicious, aromatic fungi in any number of dishes. Combining them with earthy wild rice and pine nuts produces an ideal accompaniment to lamb and game.

½ lb. fresh shiitake or oyster mushrooms (or 1 oz. dried Boletus mushrooms, chanterelles, or morels)	*1 cup wild rice*
	2 cups Chicken Stock (p. 521) or broth
	½ tsp. salt
5 Tb. butter	*¼ cut pine nuts*
1 onion, finely chopped	*Freshly ground pepper*

*I*f using fresh mushrooms, wash, pat dry, and cut into thin slices. If using dried, soak mushrooms in 1 cup of warm water for 30 minutes, pick for grit, rinse, and chop coarsely.

Preheat oven to 350°.

Heat 2 tablespoons of the butter in a heavy casserole, add onion, and sauté over low heat for 2 minutes. Add wild rice, stir well, add chicken stock and salt, and bring mixture to a boil, stirring. Cover casserole tightly, place in the oven, and bake for 1 hour. Remove from oven and let rest for 15 minutes.

Meanwhile, heat remaining butter in a skillet, add mushrooms, and sauté over low heat, stirring, for about 15 minutes.

Combine mushrooms with the rice, add pine nuts and pepper to taste, toss well, and transfer to a warm bowl.

Riz à la Bayonnaise

(Baked Rice, Country Ham, and Eggs)

Serves 4

3 Tb. goose or duck fat (or bacon
 grease)
1 onion, finely chopped
2 Tb. finely chopped green pepper
1 cup rice
2 oz. country ham, diced

1½ cups canned beef bouillon
1 bay leaf
Freshly ground pepper
½ cup grated Gruyère cheese
2 eggs

*H*eat fat in a large skillet, add onions and chopped pepper, and sauté over low heat for 3 minutes. Add rice and ham and continue to sauté, stirring, till rice is softened. Add bouillon, bay leaf, and pepper to taste, bring liquid to the boil, lower heat, cover, and simmer for 30–35 minutes or till liquid has been absorbed. Discard bay leaf, add three-quarters of the cheese, and stir well.

Preheat oven to 400°.

Grease well a medium soufflé dish and spoon rice mixture into dish. With the back of a spoon make two indentions on top of mixture, break an egg into each indention, sprinkle top with remaining cheese, and bake for 15 minutes or till eggs are just set.

Pumpkin Risotto with Nutmeg

Serves 6

Because of its extraordinarily subtle flavor, pumpkin is one of the trickiest ingredients to work with in the kitchen but one which constantly fascinates me. This dish developed one Sunday evening when some friends and I decided to whip up a little *risotto* with wild mushrooms for dinner and discovered at the last minute that the mushrooms were simply too far over the hill. Spotting a small pumpkin that somebody had brought into town from the country, I suggested we give it a try in the *risotto* along with a little nutmeg. Served with rolls of cured ham, a green salad, and an elegant Barolo, the dish made a big hit.

*3 cups Chicken Stock
    (p. 521) or broth
2-lb. pumpkin
6 Tb. (¾ stick) butter
6 Tb. olive oil
1 large onion, chopped*

*1 rib celery, minced
Big pinch of ground nutmeg
Salt
2 cups Arborio Italian rice
1 cup freshly grated Parmesan
    cheese*

Bring the chicken stock to the boil. Have ready about 3 cups of boiling water.

Cut pumpkin in half, remove seeds and stringy filaments, and chop flesh coarsely.

Heat one-half of the butter plus the olive oil in a large casserole, add onion, celery, and nutmeg, and sauté over low heat for about 3 minutes or till vegetables are just soft. Add chopped pumpkin, stir, and continue sautéing for 5 minutes. Add 1 cup chicken stock, salt to taste, cover, and cook for 15 minutes or till pumpkin is tender.

Add rice to casserole, stir, and cook over moderate heat till liquid is absorbed, stirring constantly. Add another cup of stock and continue cooking as before, always stirring. Add remaining stock plus the water and continue cooking for about 20 minutes or till *risotto* is moist but not watery.

Remove from heat, add remaining butter plus half the cheese, stir, cover, and let *risotto* stand 3 minutes. When ready to serve, sprinkle with remaining cheese.

Baked Cheese Grits

4 cups water
1 cup quick grits
2 tsp. salt
3 cups milk
4 eggs, beaten
½ cup grated extra-sharp cheddar
  cheese

1 tsp. Worcestershire
8 Tb. (1 stick) butter, cut into
  pieces
Freshly ground pepper

*P*reheat oven to 350°.
    Bring the water to a roaring boil in a large saucepan, add grits and salt, and stir. Lower heat slightly and cook grits for 5 minutes or till thick, stirring often.

Add 2 cups of the milk, return mixture to the boil, stir, lower heat, and continue cooking grits for 5 minutes or till thickened.

Add remaining ingredients plus remaining 1 cup milk, mix thoroughly with a wooden spoon till cheese and butter have melted, pour mixture into a buttered 2-quart baking dish, and bake for 1 hour.

Serve grits as a breakfast dish or with a baked ham dinner.

Jalapeño Corn Pudding

Serves 6

Why use frozen corn in this recipe? For the simple reason that unless I happen to have access to freshly harvested corn, I'm sadly convinced that frozen and even canned whole corn kernels are better today than the tough, starchy, so-called fresh ones you find on ears sold in even the most reputable markets. If you do use fresh corn that is more than a day old, you might be wise to add about a tablespoon of sugar to the dry ingredients.

3 eggs
3 cups frozen corn kernels, defrosted
2 tsp. minced onion
3 Tb. flour
1 tsp. salt
Cayenne

Freshly grated nutmeg
4 Tb. (½ stick) melted butter, cooled
1½ cups half-and-half
1 small jalapeño pepper, seeded and chopped

Preheat oven to 350°.

Beat eggs in a large mixing bowl with an electric mixer till frothy, then stir in the corn and onion with a wooden spoon. Mix flour, salt, cayenne and nutmeg to taste in a small bowl and add to corn mixture, stirring constantly. Add butter, cream, and jalapeño, and stir well.

Pour mixture into a well-greased 1½-quart baking dish, place dish in a large roasting pan, place pan in the oven, and pour enough boiling water into pan to come one-quarter up the sides of the baking dish. Bake pudding for 15 minutes, stir gently with a fork to distribute corn and pepper as evenly as possible, and bake for 45 minutes longer or till top is golden brown.

Bourbon Spoonbread

Serves 4

Spoonbread, so called because this delicious cornmeal pudding has traditionally always been eaten with a large spoon, is served in the American South either with breakfast or as a side dish to meals featuring roasted meats — much like Yorkshire pudding in England. This version, which takes on new character with the addition of Bourbon and extra eggs, is much lighter and fluffier than standard spoonbread and is particularly good with roast pork or lamb. I like to top each portion with a dab of butter.

2 cups milk
1 cup white cornmeal
1 cup (2 sticks) butter, softened
½ tsp. salt

1 Tb. sugar
5 eggs, separated
1½ Tb. Bourbon

Preheat oven to 350°.

Scald the milk in a saucepan, stir in the cornmeal, beat thoroughly, and cook over low heat till thick. Remove from heat, add butter, salt, and sugar, beat well till butter has melted completely, and set aside to cool.

Beat egg yolks in a small bowl and stir into cooled cornmeal mixture. Beat egg whites till stiff, fold into mixture, and add Bourbon, mixing lightly.

Pour mixture into a buttered casserole and bake for about 40 minutes or till a straw inserted in center comes out clean.

Steamed Couscous

Serves 6 with a stew

Couscous, the national dish of Morocco, has two meanings: the tiny semo-lina grain itself and a complete dish involving the grain that is steamed (and flavored) over a bubbling meat, poultry, or vegetable stew and served with that stew. Traditionally, *couscous* is prepared in a special cooker *(une couscousière)* equipped with a deep bottom for the stew and a perforated top in which the semolina is steamed uncovered. I've found that a large saucepan filled with a cheesecloth-lined colander works fine for simply steaming the grains over boiling water, and, though it makes my friend Paula Wolfert (author of *Couscous and Other Good Food from Morocco!*) cringe, I do cover the top for the first 15 minutes to speed up steaming. Try *couscous* with Chickan Tajine (p. 234), Picadillo (p. 180), Badami Josh (p. 202), or Vegetable Ragout (p. 362).

2 cups (¾ lb.) couscous
(available in specialty food
shops)

4–5 cups water
2 Tb. vegetable oil
½ tsp. salt

Line a metal colander with a double thickness of cheesecloth and pour the *couscous* in the colander. Place the colander on top of a large saucepan filled with the water, wrap foil snugly over the colander, bring the water to a steady boil, and steam the *couscous* for 15 minutes. Remove foil, stir the grains with a fork, and continue steaming, uncovered, for about 40 minutes.

Remove the colander, run the *couscous* under cold water while separat-ing the grains with your fingers, and drain. Transfer *couscous* to a mixing bowl, add the oil and salt, and fluff with a fork.

When ready to serve, return *couscous* to the colander and steam for about 15 minutes longer. To serve, mound *couscous* on a large platter, make a well in the center, and fill the well with whichever stew you are serving.

Kasha with Onions and Mushrooms

Serves 6

Kasha, or buckwheat groats, is a crunchy staple of Eastern Europe and an interesting accompaniment to creamed meat and poultry dishes that would normally call for rice or noodles on the side. The grains should be soft but fluffy.

8 Tb. (1 stick) butter
1 cup buckwheat groats
1 egg, beaten
½ tsp. salt
1½ cups boiling Chicken Stock
  (p. 521)

Freshly ground pepper
1 large onion, finely chopped
½ lb. mushrooms, chopped

*H*eat one-half of the butter in a large saucepan, add the groats, beaten egg, and salt, and stir vigorously till grains are separated and well coated. Stir in the hot stock, cover pan, and simmer for about 20 minutes or just till the stock is absorbed. Add pepper to taste, fluff the grains with a fork, cover again, and let rest off the heat a couple of minutes.

While the groats are cooking, heat the remaining butter in a medium skillet, add the onion and mushrooms, and sauté over low heat for 5 minutes, stirring.

When ready to serve, add the sautéed onion and mushrooms to the *kasha* and toss with a fork.

Polenta with Sausages and Mushrooms

Serves 6 as a side dish
and 4 as a main course

Polenta, which is very popular throughout northern Italy, is a fancy name for what is basically cornmeal mush. Baked with meat, fish, or vegetable sauces, the dish takes on fascinating dimensions. I also love *polenta* mixed with Parmesan, fried in butter, cut into small squares, and served topped with well-seasoned sautéed mushrooms, tomatoes, spinach, or chicken livers as an appetizer.

4 cups Chicken Stock (p. 521)
1 tsp. salt
1½ cups cornmeal
6 Tb. (¾ stick) butter
3 Tb. vegetable oil
1 lb. hot Italian sausages, casings removed

1 lb. mushrooms, coarsely chopped
2 cups Hot Tomato Sauce (p. 539)
Salt and freshly ground pepper
1 cup freshly grated Parmesan cheese

Combine one-half of the stock and the teaspoon of salt in a large saucepan and bring to the boil. In a bowl, combine the remaining stock and the cornmeal, stir well, and gradually add the mixture to the saucepan, stirring constantly. Maintaining the heat at a very low simmer, cook the cornmeal for 40–45 minutes or till a crust begins to form on top. Add the butter and stir till well incorporated.

While *polenta* is cooking, heat the oil in another large saucepan, crumble the sausages in the oil, and cook over moderate heat for 10 minutes, stirring. Add the mushrooms, reduce heat, stir, and cook for 5 minutes. Add the tomato sauce and salt and pepper to taste, stir well, cover, and simmer for about 20 minutes.

Preheat oven to 350°.

Pour the *polenta* into a greased baking dish, spoon the sauce over the top, sprinkle with the grated cheese, and bake for 15–20 minutes or till the top is slightly browned.

PART ELEVEN

Breads, Doughs, and Cookies

Basic Pie Pastry

Yield: Enough dough for a 9- or 10-inch pie plate

2 cups all-purpose flour
1/4 tsp. salt

2/3 cup vegetable shortening
1/4 cup ice water

Combine the flour and salt in a mixing bowl and cut in the shortening with a pastry cutter till the texture is like a coarse meal. Stirring with a wooden spoon, gradually add the water till a firm ball of dough is formed. Wrap the dough in plastic and chill for at least 30 minutes before using.

TO BAKE PIE SHELL:

Preheat oven to 425°.

Place the dough on a lightly floured surface and roll it out from the center (not to and fro) with a lightly floured rolling pin to a ⅛-inch thickness. Carefully fold pastry in half, lay the fold across center of the pie plate, unfold it, and press it loosely on bottom and sides of the pan.

Line the plate with a sheet of wax paper and add enough dried beans to cover the bottom. Place the plate on a baking sheet, bake for 12–15 minutes or till shell browns evenly, and remove beans and wax paper before allowing to cool.

Pâte Brisée

(Short Pastry Dough)

Yield: Enough dough for an 8- or 9-inch pie shell

1¼ cups all-purpose flour, sifted
6 Tb. (¾ stick) cold unsalted
   butter, cut into bits

2 Tb. cold vegetable shortening
¼ tsp. salt
3 Tb. ice water

Combine the flour, butter, shortening, and salt in a large mixing bowl and blend with fingers till mixture is mealy. Add the water, mix, and form dough into a ball. Place dough on a lightly floured surface and knead for 20–30 seconds to distribute fat evenly. Re-form into a ball, dust with flour, wrap in plastic wrap, and refrigerate for 1 hour.

TO BAKE PIE SHELL:

Preheat oven to 425°.

Place the dough on a lightly floured surface and roll it out from the center (not to and fro) with a lightly floured rolling pin to a ⅛-inch thickness. Carefully fold pastry in half, lay the fold across center of the pie shell, unfold it, and press it loosely on bottom and sides of the pan.

Line pan with a sheet of wax paper and add enough dried beans to cover the bottom. Place pan on a baking sheet and bake for 10 minutes. Remove beans and wax paper and bake for 2 minutes longer.

Pâte Brisée Sucrée

(Sweet Short Pastry Dough)

Yield: Enough dough for an 8- or 9-inch pie shell

1¼ cups all-purpose flour
¼ cup sugar
8 Tb. (1 stick) cold unsalted
   butter, cut into bits

1 egg, beaten
1 Tb. ice water

Sift the flour and sugar together into a large mixing bowl, add the butter, and cut with a pastry cutter or work with the fingers till the mixture is mealy. Add the egg and blend well. Add the water, mix, and form dough into a ball.

Place the dough on a lightly floured surface and knead for 20–30 seconds to distribute the fat evenly. Re-form dough into a ball, dust lightly with flour, wrap in plastic wrap, and refrigerate for 1 hour.

TO BAKE PIE SHELL:

Follow directions for preceding recipe for *pâte brisée*.

Quick Puff Pastry

Yield: 3 lbs. pastry

3 cups unbleached all-purpose flour
1 cup cake flour
1 tsp. salt

1 lb. (4 sticks) unsalted butter,
    cut into ½-inch pieces
1 tsp. lemon juice
1 cup ice water

Combine the flours and salt in a food processor fitted with the metal blade, add the butter, and pulse 2 or 3 times or till butter pieces are just chunky. Add the lemon juice and water and pulse till dough begins to collect along sides of the bowl but before it becomes a solid mass. Collect dough in hands and form into a solid mass. (If weather is warm or if work must be delayed, chill dough for 30 minutes.)

Place dough on a lightly floured surface, press into a rectangle with hands, and flour lightly. Roll into a 12×6-inch rectangle ½ inch thick and fold in thirds as with a letter. Roll folded dough into another 12×6-inch, ½-inch-thick rectangle and fold again in thirds. Roll out dough in similar fashion a third time and fold in thirds a final time.

Wrap dough in plastic wrap, chill for 4–6 hours, and either roll out (after allowing to rest for 15 minutes) for any recipe calling for puff pastry or freeze for future use.

Almond Pastry

Yield: Enough dough for a 10- or 11-inch tart

This delectable pastry is ideal for almost any open-face fruit tart with a cream base.

2 cups all-purpose flour
1 cup ground toasted almonds
½ cup sugar
2 tsp. grated lemon rind

¼ tsp. salt
¾ cup (1½ sticks) unsalted
   butter, room temperature
1 egg plus 1 egg yolk, beaten

Combine the flour, almonds, sugar, lemon rind, and salt in a large mixing bowl, add the butter, and cut with a pastry cutter till mixture is mealy. Add the eggs and stir thoroughly.

Form the dough into a ball, wrap in plastic wrap, and refrigerate for at least 1 hour.

Basic Food Processor Brioche Dough

Yield: About 1½ lbs. dough

1 envelope active dry yeast
¼ cup warm water
2 Tb. sugar
2½ cups all-purpose flour
1 tsp. salt

8 Tb. (1 stick) unsalted butter,
   cut into pieces
2 eggs plus 2 egg yolks, room
   temperature

Combine the yeast and water in a small bowl, stir, and let proof for 10 minutes.

Combine the sugar, flour, salt, and butter in a food processor fitted with the metal blade and process for about 30 seconds or till butter is incorporated into the flour. Add the yeast mixture, pulse the machine 2 or 3 times, add the eggs, and process till liquid is incorporated. Stop the machine, scrape sides of the bowl, and process for 1 minute more to knead.

Scrape dough into a well-greased bowl, shape into a ball, cover with a towel, and let rise in a warm area for about 2 hours or till dough has doubled in bulk.

Punch dough down, cover with plastic wrap, and refrigerate overnight.

Basic Pizza Dough

Yield: Dough for 2 12-inch pizzas

1 envelope active dry yeast
1 cup lukewarm water
4 cups all-purpose flour

1 tsp. salt
2 Tb. olive oil

Combine the yeast and water in a small bowl, stir, and let proof for 10 minutes or till bubbly.

In a large bowl, combine 3¾ cups of the flour and the salt, add the yeast mixture plus the olive oil, and mix till a firm ball of dough can be formed. Sprinkle remaining flour on a working surface, place ball of dough on the surface, and knead for about 10 minutes or till dough is elastic. Place dough in a greased bowl, turn to coat the sides evenly, cover with a towel, and let rise in a warm area for at least 1 hour or till doubled in bulk.

Punch dough down, wrap in plastic wrap, and either refrigerate overnight or freeze for future use.

Quiche Pastry

Yield: Enough pastry for a 9- or 10-inch quiche

2 cups all-purpose flour
½ tsp. salt
8 Tb. vegetable shortening

4 Tb. (½ stick) butter
3–4 Tb. ice water

Combine flour and salt in a large mixing bowl, add the shortening, butter, and 1 tablespoon of the water, and begin mixing with a wooden spoon. Mixing constantly, continue to add water till the dough easily clears the sides of the bowl and can be handled.

Pat dough out into a rectangle, wrap in plastic wrap, and chill for at least 1 hour before using.

Basic Crêpes

Yield: About 16 crêpes

¾ cup all-purpose flour, sifted
¾ cup water
⅔ cup milk
3 eggs

2 Tb. melted butter
¾ tsp. salt
1 cup vegetable oil

Combine flour, water, milk, eggs, butter, and salt in a blender and blend for 5 seconds. Stop machine, scrape sides with a spatula, and blend for 20 seconds longer. Transfer batter to a mixing bowl, cover with plastic wrap, and let stand for 1 hour.

Heat a 7- or 8-inch iron crêpe pan till moderately hot, brush pan lightly with oil, heat till oil is very hot, and remove pan from the heat. Stir batter, half-fill a ¼-cup measure with batter, and pour into the pan. Rotate the pan quickly so batter covers bottom in a thin layer, return pan to heat, loosen crêpe with a spatula, and cook till underside is golden. Turn the crêpe, brown other side, and transfer to a plate. Continue in like manner till batter is used up, stacking crêpes. Wrapped in plastic wrap, the crêpes can be stored in the refrigerator for up to 2 days or frozen.

Wheat Tortillas

Yield: About 24 tortillas

Once you've sampled wheat tortillas, you'll most likely never touch one made with corn again. These light, flavorful discs are, of course, ideal for rolling all sorts of Mexican fillings, but, as I learned in Mexico, purists love nothing more than serving wheat tortillas stacked under a cloth and eating them just as you would bread with the meal.

3 cups all-purpose flour	*½ cup shortening*
½ tsp. baking powder	*1 cup warm water*
½ tsp. salt	

Combine the flour, baking powder, and salt in a large mixing bowl, add the shortening, and work the mixture with the fingers till crumbly. Add the water and continue to work mixture with the fingers till a soft ball is formed, adding a little more water if necessary. Place the dough on a lightly floured surface and knead for 5 minutes.

Divide the dough in half, roll each half into a 12-inch log, and cut each log into 12 pieces. Shape one piece into a 2-inch ball and roll out on a lightly floured surface to a 5- to 6-inch disc. Repeat with remaining pieces, stacking discs on top of one another as they are made.

Heat a griddle or large, heavy skillet to moderate, place a disc on top, and cook for about 30 seconds or till underside is slightly browned. Flip disc over with a spatula, cook for 30 seconds, and flip again. Press down momentarily with the spatula, flip again, press again, and transfer disc to a plate. Repeat process with remaining discs, stacking tortillas on top of one another as they come off the griddle.

Serve tortillas immediately wrapped in a cloth or reheat in foil for 5 minutes in the oven.

Country Yeast Bread

Yield: 1 oval loaf

This is the sort of basic crusty bread I like to have in the house at all times. I like it hot from the oven with meals, smeared with pâté as an emergency midafternoon snack, or sliced, toasted, and heavily buttered for breakfast.

1 envelope active dry yeast
1 cup lukewarm water
2 tsp. salt
1 tsp. sugar

3 cups all-purpose flour
Cornmeal
1 egg yolk beaten with 1 Tb. water

Combine the yeast and one-half of the water in a small bowl, stir, and let proof for about 10 minutes or till mixture becomes bubbly. Pour mixture into a large mixing bowl, add remaining water, salt, and sugar, and mix well. Add the flour 1 cup at a time and mix with a wooden spoon for about 2 minutes or till dough is smooth. Place dough in a well-greased bowl and turn to coat all sides evenly. Cover dough with a slightly damp towel, place in a warm area, and let rise for about 2 hours or till doubled in bulk.

Preheat oven to 400°.

Punch dough down, turn onto a lightly floured surface, knead for about 1 minute, and shape into an oval loaf. Place loaf on a baking sheet sprinkled with cornmeal, make slashes on the top with a razor, and brush the top with the egg wash.

Place a shallow pan of boiling water on the lower rack of the oven, place loaf on the middle rack, and bake for 30 – 40 minutes or till bread is crusty and sounds hollow when thumped.

Bâtards Parisiens
(French Bread)

I've insisted for as long as I can remember — and contrary to what *anybody* tells you — that it is humanly impossible to reproduce perfect French bread in the United States due to the differences in our flour, water, yeast, and (I'm convinced) even the air we breathe. Still, I love to make these traditional yeasty *bâtards* by hand (not with a food processor) and think they are about as close as you can come to the real item. Do note that this bread turns stale after only a few hours since it contains no fat, so don't double the recipe unless you plan to serve many people or have room to freeze the long loaves (which can be served by merely reheating for about 15 minutes in a 400° oven).

1 package active dry yeast	*2 tsp. salt*
1½ cups warm water	*3½ cups unbleached flour*

Sprinkle yeast over the water in a large mixing bowl, stir, and let stand for 5–7 minutes or till yeast starts bubbling. Add the salt, then gradually add the flour, stirring, till dough is very stiff.

Transfer the dough to a lightly floured working surface and knead for about 15 minutes or till smooth and springy in texture. Place dough in a large bowl (ungreased), cover with a towel, and let rise in a warm area for about 1 hour or till doubled in bulk.

Punch dough down, re-cover, and let rise again for about 1 hour or till doubled in bulk.

Transfer dough to a lightly floured working surface, divide into 3 equal parts, and, with your hands, form each part into a long 16×3-inch loaf. Flatten each loaf slightly, fold the long edges into the middle, and re-form loaves into original size. Place loaves on a baking sheet, mist with a plant mister, cover with the towel, and let rise for 1 hour.

Preheat oven to 450° and place a shallow pan with 1 inch of boiling water on the bottom of the oven.

BREADS, DOUGHS, AND COOKIES · 419

Slash the top of each loaf three times lengthwise with a razor blade, mist again, and bake for 25 minutes, misting again at 3-minute intervals during the first 6 minutes of baking to help produce crusty tops.

Cool loaves on a rack to room temperature or stand straight up in a basket till ready to use.

Sourdough Bread

Yield: 4 loaves

*1½ cups Sourdough Starter
3 cups lukewarm water
10 cups unbleached all-purpose
  flour

2 envelopes active dry yeast
5 tsp. salt

Combine sourdough starter, 1½ cups of the water, and 1½ cups of the flour in a large mixing bowl, stir well, cover with plastic wrap, and set aside in a draft-free area for 1 hour.

Add the remaining water and the yeast, stir, and let sit for 10 minutes. Add 4 cups of the flour plus the salt, mix thoroughly, and gradually stir in remaining flour 1 cup at a time till the dough is soft and pliable.

Turn dough out onto a lightly floured surface and knead for 5 minutes. Place dough in a greased bowl, turn to coat the sides evenly, cover with a towel, and let rise in a warm area for 1½ hours or till doubled in bulk.

Punch dough down, transfer back to the floured surface, and divide into 4 portions. Cover with the towel and let sit for 10 minutes.

Grease 4 long, narrow bread pans. With hands, form the 4 portions of dough into long rolls, fit into the pans, cover with towels, and let rise for 1 hour.

Preheat oven to 425°.

Slash tops of the loaves lengthwise with a razor, mist the loaves with a plant mister, and bake for 30 minutes or till golden brown and crusty. Cool loaves on racks.

* *Sourdough Starter:* Combine 1 envelope active dry yeast, 1 tablespoon sugar, 2 cups unbleached all-purpose flour, and 2 cups lukewarm water in a mixing bowl, whisk till smooth, and let stand at room temperature for at least 48 hours.

Cover with plastic wrap and refrigerate. When ready to use, return the starter back to room temperature. Yield: 2½ cups starter. (To keep starter going indefinitely, add 1½ cups flour and 1½ cups water for every 1½ cups removed, stir, cover with plastic wrap, and let stand in a warm area for 1 hour or till bubbling action is renewed.) Store in refrigerator.

Russian Black Bread

Yield: 1 large round loaf

Most Russian black breads require a very time-consuming starter, but Judith and Evan Jones, authors of *The Book of Bread,* came up with this chocolate-enriched version that is not only simple to make but satisfies the craving I've always had for rugged black bread with plenty of rye and fennel flavor. For my taste, however, I have discovered that the bread needs a full hour of baking for a really dark, crusty top. It takes the most part of a day to make this bread, but it's worth every minute.

1 envelope active dry yeast
1 cup strong black coffee, lukewarm
4–5 Tb. dark molasses
4 Tb. vinegar
4 Tb. (½ stick) butter
1 square (1 oz.) unsweetened
*   dark chocolate, cut up*

3 cups rye flour
2 tsp. salt
2 Tb. caraway seeds
½ tsp. fennel seeds
1 cup white unbleached flour

Combine the yeast and coffee in a large mixing bowl, stir, and let yeast dissolve completely.

Combine the molasses and vinegar in a saucepan and bring to the boil. Remove pan from the heat, stir in the butter and chocolate and allow to melt, and set aside to cool.

Add butter-chocolate mixture to the yeast and stir in the rye flour, salt, caraway, fennel, and as much of the cup of flour as can be readily absorbed. Turn dough out on a lightly floured surface, then wash, dry, and grease the bowl.

Knead the dough for about 10 minutes or till smooth, adding more white flour when necessary. Place dough in the greased bowl, cover with plastic wrap, and let rise for 5 hours in a warm area or a cold closed oven till doubled in bulk.

Punch dough down, knead for 5 minutes more, and shape into a round loaf. Place loaf on a greased baking sheet, cover with a towel, and let rise for 2 hours.

Preheat oven to 375° about 15 minutes before loaf has doubled in size and bake for 45 minutes to 1 hour or till dark and crusty on top. Cool bread on a rack.

Irish Soda Bread

Yield: 4 or 5 small loaves

In Ireland, they seem to eat this bread round the clock — at breakfast, with tea, even while slugging down single malts. I particularly enjoy nibbling on a spicy loaf with early-morning coffee while preparing breakfast. The loaves freeze beautifully.

5 cups all-purpose flour	1 cup sugar
1 Tb. ground nutmeg	¾ cup white raisins
1 Tb. ground cinnamon	3 eggs
1¼ Tb. baking powder	1 cup milk

Sift the flour, nutmeg, cinnamon, baking powder, and sugar together into a large mixing bowl and blend thoroughly. Add the raisins and mix.

In another bowl, beat the eggs and milk together till well blended, add to the dry mixture, and stir well with a wooden spoon till dough is smooth. Cover bowl with plastic wrap and let rest for 30 minutes.

Preheat oven to 325°.

On a lightly floured surface, form dough into 4 or 5 small round loaves, place on a baking sheet, and bake for 25 – 30 minutes.

Pita Bread

Yield: 12 6-inch pitas

2 envelopes active dry yeast
3 cups warm water
1 tsp. sugar

2 tsp. salt
2 Tb. olive oil
5 cups unbleached all-purpose flour

Combine the yeast and 1 cup of the water in a small bowl, add the sugar, stir, and let proof for 10 minutes or till bubbly.

Add the remaining water, salt, and olive oil, and stir. Add the flour 1 cup at a time, mixing constantly till dough is soft. Place the dough on a lightly floured surface and knead for about 5 minutes, adding a little more flour if necessary. Place dough in a greased bowl, turn to coat the sides evenly, and let rise in a warm area for about 1½ hours or till doubled in bulk.

Punch dough down and divide into 12 equal pieces. Shape each piece into a smooth, unbroken cake, cover with a towel, and let rest for 20 minutes.

Preheat oven to 500°.

Place each cake on a well-floured surface, roll into flat 6-inch rounds, and prick each with a fork. Place the rounds 1 inch apart on floured baking sheets, let rest for about 20 minutes, and bake for 8 minutes or till slightly browned on top. Cool on racks.

Buttermilk Bread

Yield: 1 large loaf

It seems the more I bake breads, biscuits, scones, and the like on weekends in my East Hampton kitchen, the more I at least partially substitute buttermilk for whole milk in order to have richer flavor. Do remember, however, that when baking with buttermilk, you must counteract the additional acidity with an alkali such as baking soda. Here's a good yeasty loaf that's perfect for making *croques monsieur* and almost any other type of sandwich. And once you've toasted this bread for breakfast, you'll never again be satisfied with commercial sliced bread.

½ cup warm water
1 envelope active dry yeast
1 tsp. sugar
1 cup buttermilk
½ cup whole milk

3 tsp. salt
4 cups all-purpose flour
½ tsp. baking soda
1 egg white beaten with 1 Tb.
* cold water*

Pour the water into a small bowl, sprinkle the yeast and sugar on top, stir, and let proof for about 10 minutes or till mixture becomes bubbly.

Combine the buttermilk and whole milk in a mixing bowl and add the yeast mixture and salt. Add 1 cup of the flour plus the baking soda and mix well. Continue adding the flour 1 cup at a time, mixing steadily with a wooden spoon and, if necessary, adding a little more flour till the dough is smooth and not sticky. Turn dough out onto a lightly floured surface and knead for about 5 minutes. Place dough in a well-greased bowl, turn to coat all sides, cover bowl with a towel, and let rise in a draft-free area for 2½ hours or till fully doubled in bulk.

Transfer dough back to the working surface, punch down, and knead for about 5 minutes. Place dough in a large greased loaf pan, cover, and let rise for 2 hours longer or till doubled in bulk.

Preheat oven to 400°.

Slash three lines along top of the dough with a razor blade, brush top with the egg wash, and bake for 45 minutes or till bread sounds hollow when thumped. Transfer bread to a rack and let cool.

Swedish Limpa Bread

Yield: 2 loaves

6½ cups all-purpose flour
2 cups rye flour
2 envelopes active dry yeast
2 tsp. salt

2 tsp. caraway seeds
2 tsp. grated orange peel
2 Tb. butter, softened
2⅔ cups hot water

*I*n a large mixing bowl, combine all but 1 cup of the all-purpose flour, the rye flour, yeast, salt, caraway seeds, and orange peel, and mix thoroughly.

Add the butter and water to the dry ingredients and mix till well blended. Add just enough of the reserved 1 cup all-purpose flour to make a soft dough.

Turn out dough on a lightly floured surface and knead for 8–10 minutes. Transfer dough to a well-greased bowl, turn to coat all surfaces, cover with plastic wrap, and let rise in a warm area for 30–40 minutes or till doubled in bulk.

Punch dough down, transfer to the floured surface, and shape into 2 equal balls. Transfer balls to a greased baking sheet, cover with plastic wrap, and let rise for 30–40 minutes more.

Preheat oven to 400°.

Make two slashes across tops of balls with a razor blade, bake loaves for 30 minutes or till hollow sounding when thumped, and cool on a rack.

Whole Wheat Caraway Bread

Yield: 1 round loaf

1 envelope active dry yeast
1½ cups lukewarm water
4 Tb. honey
2 Tb. vegetable oil

1 Tb. caraway seeds
1½ tsp. salt
1½ cups unbleached flour
2 cups whole wheat flour

Combine the yeast and one-half of the water in a small bowl, stir, and let proof for 10 minutes or till bubbly. Pour mixture into a large bowl, add remaining water, honey, oil, caraway seeds, and salt, and stir to blend well. Add the flours 1 cup at a time and mix well.

Turn dough out onto a floured surface and knead for 5 minutes. Transfer dough to a well-greased bowl, turn to coat all sides evenly, cover with a towel, and let rise in a warm area for 1½ – 2 hours or till doubled in bulk.

Preheat oven to 400°.

Punch dough down, shape into a round loaf, place loaf on a greased baking sheet, and bake for 10 minutes. Reduce heat to 375° and continue to bake for 30 minutes or till bread is browned and sounds hollow when thumped. Cool on a rack.

Pecan Whole Wheat Bread

Yield: 2 loaves

3 cups all-purpose flour
3 cups whole wheat flour
1 cup finely chopped pecans
⅓ cup sugar
4 tsp. salt

2 envelopes active dry yeast
4 Tb. (½ stick) butter
1½ cups water
¾ cup milk

Combine flours, nuts, sugar, salt, and yeast in a large mixing bowl and blend well.

In a saucepan, heat the butter, water, and milk till hot, stir into the dry mixture, and mix well to form a smooth ball of dough. Turn out dough onto a lightly floured surface and knead for 8–10 minutes. Place the dough in a well-greased bowl, turn to coat all exposed surfaces, cover with plastic wrap, and let rise in a warm area for 30–40 minutes or till doubled in bulk.

Preheat oven to 400°.

Punch dough down, transfer back to the working surface, and shape into 2 loaves. Fit loaves snugly into 2 greased 8½×4½×2½-inch loaf pans, cover with plastic wrap, and let rise for 30–40 minutes more or till doubled in bulk.

Bake the loaves for 30 minutes or till hollow sounding when thumped. Remove from pans, and cool on a rack.

Farmhouse Poppy Seed Bread

Yield: About 12 rolls or 6 small loaves

Tremendous efforts have been made to turn The Stone Farmhouse at the luxurious Mahogany Run resort on the island of St. Thomas into the finest restaurant in the Caribbean. Ask anybody who's dined there about the cuisine, and the first thing they'll exclaim about is this remarkable bread.

1½ envelopes active dry yeast
1 cup warm water
1½ Tb. sugar
2 Tb. vegetable oil

1½ tsp. salt
¼ cup poppy seeds
3½ cups all-purpose flour

Sprinkle the yeast over the water in a small bowl, add the sugar, mix, and let proof for 10 minutes.

Pour the yeast mixture into a large mixing bowl and mix in the oil, salt, and poppy seeds. Gradually add the flour 1 cup at a time, mixing steadily with a wooden spoon till dough comes away from the sides of the bowl.

Transfer the dough to a lightly floured surface and knead for about 10 minutes. Place dough in a greased bowl, turn to coat all sides evenly, cover with a clean towel, and let rise in a warm area for about 1½ hours or till doubled in bulk.

Punch dough down, knead for 1 minute, and shape into about 12 round rolls or 6 small loaves. Place on a large greased baking sheet, cover with the towel, and let rise for 1 hour longer.

Preheat oven to 400°.

Bake bread for 25–35 minutes (depending on size) or till golden brown.

Butter Rolls

Yield: About 40 rolls

As far as I'm concerned, ninety-nine percent of the dinner rolls found in America would serve a much better purpose if thrown to the porkies. These luscious beauties are one of the few exceptions. What's particularly nice is that the roll mixture will keep up to one week covered in the refrigerator.

2 envelopes active dry yeast	*2 eggs, well beaten*
1 cup warm water	*6 cups unsifted all-purpose flour*
1 cup sugar	*1 Tb. salt*
1 cup vegetable shortening, room temperature	*8 Tb. (1 stick) butter*
	4 Tb. (½ stick) melted butter
1 cup boiling water	

*I*n a small bowl, sprinkle yeast over the warm water, stir, and set aside. In a large mixing bowl, cream the sugar and shortening with an electric mixer, add the boiling water, and beat till all the sugar and shortening have dissolved. When mixture is lukewarm, add the eggs and stir in the yeast. Add the flour and salt gradually and mix till blended thoroughly and dough is smooth. Cover bowl tightly with plastic wrap and store in refrigerator till ready to use, punching down if necessary.

Three hours before baking, transfer the dough to a floured surface, roll out ½ inch thick, and cut out rounds with a biscuit cutter or small juice glass. Make a small indention with a table knife in the center of each round, place a small piece of butter in each indention, and fold edges carefully over butter, pinching the tops together. Place rolls on one or more lightly greased baking sheets, brush each with melted butter, place in a warm area, and let rise for 2–3 hours or till doubled in bulk.

Preheat oven to 400°.

Bake rolls for 5 minutes or till lightly browned on top.

Potato Yeast Rolls

Yield: About 30 rolls

Knowing that my enthusiasm for American dinner rolls has never been exactly overwhelming, my mother was all the more insistent that I try this recipe she developed. Yes, they are very good, and, yes, they do freeze beautifully.

2 medium boiling potatoes, peeled and quartered	¼ cup melted shortening
2 envelopes active dry yeast	½ cup honey
1 tsp. sugar	2 eggs, beaten
8 Tb. (1 stick) melted butter	2 tsp. salt
	6½ cups all-purpose flour

Place potatoes in a saucepan, cover with water, bring to a low boil, cover, and cook for 15–20 minutes or till tender. Drain potatoes, reserving 1 cup of the potato water.

Cool potato water to about 110°, combine with the yeast and sugar in a small bowl, and set aside.

Mash potatoes to measure 1 cup and place in a mixing bowl. Add the butter, shortening, honey, eggs, salt, yeast mixture, and 2½ cups of the flour, and beat with an electric mixer for 2 minutes. Gradually stir in enough of the remaining flour to make a soft dough, turn dough out onto a lightly floured surface, and knead for 8–10 minutes or till smooth and elastic. Place dough in a well-greased bowl, turn to coat all surfaces, cover with a towel, and let rise in a warm area for 1–1½ hours or till doubled in bulk.

Punch dough down, shape into 1½-inch balls, and place balls in three 9-inch cake pans. Cover with towels and let rise in a warm area for about 1 hour or till doubled in bulk.

Preheat oven to 400°.

Bake rolls for 25 minutes or till golden brown on top.

Orange Oatmeal Bread

Yield: 1 loaf

1 medium orange
3/4 cup sugar
1 1/2 cups flour
4 1/2 tsp. baking powder
1/2 tsp. salt

1/4 tsp. baking soda
1 cup rolled oats
2 eggs, beaten
2 Tb. melted butter

Grate the rind of the orange into a small bowl and reserve. Remove and discard the white membrane from the orange. Slice the orange thinly and cut each slice into small dice, discarding seeds. Mix the pieces with 2 tablespoons of the sugar in a bowl, and reserve.

Preheat oven to 350°.

Sift the flour, remaining sugar, baking powder, salt, and baking soda into a large mixing bowl, and stir in the oats. In another bowl, combine the eggs, butter, grated orange rind, orange mixture, and 2/3 cup of water and stir till well blended. Add the liquid mixture to the dry ingredients and mix till well blended.

Pour the batter into a greased 9×5×3-inch loaf pan and bake for 1 hour or till a straw inserted in center of the bread comes out clean.

Walnut Bread

Yield: 2 5×9-inch loaves

The Rancho Bernardo Inn in San Diego is one of the most luxurious hostels in America, and their walnut bread kept me haunting the chef for days till he finally agreed to part with the recipe. I think this particular bread loses a great deal by freezing.

1 cup (2 sticks) butter, softened
2 cups sugar
4 eggs
4 cups flour
1/2 tsp. salt

2 tsp. baking soda
2 tsp. vanilla
2 cups sour cream
1 1/2 cups finely chopped walnuts

Cream the butter and sugar with an electric mixer in a large mixing bowl till frothy, then add eggs one by one, mixing constantly.

Sift the flour, salt, and baking soda together into a bowl, add to the butter mixture, and stir till well blended. Add the vanilla, sour cream, and nuts, and stir thoroughly.

Preheat oven to 350°.

Grease and lightly flour two 5×9-inch loaf pans, fill each pan two-thirds full of batter, and bake for 45 minutes to 1 hour. Cool bread in the pans for 10 minutes, then invert onto a rack.

Walnut Pumpkin Bread

Yield: 2 loaves

3-lb. pumpkin, stem removed	1½ tsp. salt
½ cup vegetable oil	1½ cups brown sugar
½ cup water	1 tsp. ground cinnamon
3 eggs, beaten	½ tsp. mace
3 cups flour	Pinch of ground cloves
1 Tb. baking soda	1 cup coarsely chopped walnuts

Preheat oven to 350°.

Cut pumpkin in half, remove and discard the seeds and stringy pulp, cut pumpkin into large wedges, and place in a baking pan. Bake for about 1 hour or till pumpkin is soft and tender.

When cool enough to handle, remove flesh from the rind with a heavy spoon, place in a food processor, puree till very smooth, and transfer puree to a large mixing bowl.

Add the oil, water, and eggs to the pumpkin puree and beat with an electric mixer. Combine the flour, baking soda, salt, sugar, and spices in a bowl and gradually stir into the pumpkin mixture. Stir in the chopped walnuts.

Turn batter into two greased 9-inch loaf pans, bake for 1 hour or till a straw inserted into loaves comes out clean, and cool on a rack.

Brioches

*1 recipe Basic Food Processor   1 egg, beaten with 2 Tb. water
Brioche Dough (p. 414)*

*B*utter the sides and bottoms of 10 small brioche molds.
Divide the dough into 10 pieces, pinch off a third of each piece, and shape both large and small pieces into balls. Set a large ball in the base of each mold, press center down to form a hollow, and set a smaller ball inside each hollow. Let rise in a warm area for 15 minutes.

Preheat oven to 425°.

Brush brioches with the egg wash and bake for 15–20 minutes or till well browned and hollow-sounding when thumped. Cool on racks.

Southern Cornbread

Serves 6–8

This is the simple cornbread on which I was raised and the one my mother still whips up a couple of times a week. Sliced in half and drenched with butter, the cornbread squares go especially well with broiled or fried fish, Brunswick Stew (p. 78), and Carolina Gumbo (p. 64).

*1½ cups cornmeal   1¾ cups buttermilk
3 Tb. all-purpose flour   1 egg
1 tsp. salt   2 Tb. vegetable shortening
1 tsp. baking soda*

*C*ombine the cornmeal, flour, salt, and baking soda in a mixing bowl, and set aside. In a small bowl, beat the buttermilk and egg till well blended, add the mixture to the dry ingredients, and stir till batter is well blended.

Preheat oven to 475°.

Heat the shortening till it melts in a 9-inch cast-iron skillet. Pour the melted shortening into the batter, stir till well blended, and pour batter into the hot skillet. Bake for 20 minutes or till cornbread is golden brown.

Mrs. Wilkes' Crackling Cornbread

Serves 6

On assignment in Savannah, Georgia, to do a feature on Low Country cookery, I was told by every native that for the best Southern food in the city, I'd have to join the long line that forms every day at lunch outside Mrs. Wilkes' Boarding House. Suffice it to say that the experience is unique and that this lady's cornbread is addictive.

1 cup diced fresh pork fat
1¼ cups cornmeal
¾ cup all-purpose flour, sifted
1 tsp. salt

1 tsp. baking powder
⅔ cup milk
⅓ cup vegetable oil
1 egg, beaten

*P*lace pork fat in a heavy skillet, fry over moderate heat for about 45 minutes or till fully rendered and crisp, and drain cracklings on paper towels.

Preheat oven to 425°.

Combine cornmeal, flour, salt, and baking powder in a mixing bowl and blend well. Add the milk, oil, and egg, and mix thoroughly with a wooden spoon. Add the cracklings and blend so they are well distributed throughout the mixture. Transfer the mixture to an 8×8×2-inch baking pan and bake for 25 minutes or till golden.

To serve, cut cornbread into 2-inch squares.

Jalapeño Cornbread

Serves 6

1½ cups cornmeal
1 tsp. baking powder
1 tsp. salt
1 cup cream-style corn
1 cup (¼ lb.) grated sharp
  cheddar cheese

1 Tb. finely chopped jalapeño chili
  pepper
2 eggs, beaten
8 Tb. (½ stick) melted butter
1 cup milk
1½ Tb. corn oil

Preheat oven to 400°.
    Combine the cornmeal, baking powder, and salt in a mixing bowl, and mix to blend well. Add the corn, cheese, and pepper, and stir well. Add the eggs, melted butter, and milk, and mix thoroughly.

Heat the oil in an 8- or 9-inch cast-iron skillet, pour batter into skillet, smooth with a spatula, and bake for 30–35 minutes or till golden brown on top.

Carolina Hush Puppies

Yield: At least 40 hush puppies

It seems that I spend at least two weeks each summer on the Carolina coasts seeking out the ultimate hush puppies, those round or oblong little fried corn balls that go so perfectly with pit-cooked pork barbecue or fried fish or, for that fact, almost anything. Once I was convinced that the perfect example was served at the Center Pier restaurant at Carolina Beach, North Carolina; then it was the fat dodgers made with buttermilk, scallions, and bacon bits at the legendary Henry's in Charleston; and now it's this sublime rendition served at The Sea Captain in Murrell's Inlet, South Carolina. Since people tend to devour great hush puppies as if they were peanuts, there's no way I can indicate a serving portion. This recipe should, however, satisfy the craving of about six hungry souls.

2 cups flour
1½ cups cornmeal
3 Tb. sugar
1 tsp. baking powder
1 tsp. salt
½ cup finely minced onion

2⅓ cups milk
⅓ cup vegetable oil
1 egg, beaten
*Corn or vegetable oil for deep-
frying*

Sift together the flour, cornmeal, sugar, baking powder, and salt into a large mixing bowl and combine thoroughly. Add the onions, milk, oil, and egg, and stir only long enough to blend ingredients.

In a deep-fat fryer or deep cast-iron skillet, heat about 2½ inches of oil to 375°, drop the batter in batches by spoonfuls into the fat, and fry the hush puppies till golden brown. Drain briefly on paper towels and serve immediately.

Corn Sticks

Yield: About 20 5-inch corn sticks

These are the legendary corn sticks passed to all tables at The Coach House in New York. I've reduced the amount of sugar since, as an incurable Southerner, I like very little sugar if any in my cornbread, corn sticks, and hush puppies. If, however, you want to reproduce the sticks exactly as owner Leon Lianides prefers them, use 5 tablespoons of sugar. Do not attempt these marvels without the correct corn stick molds, available in most hardware and kitchen equipment stores.

4 cups cornmeal	4 eggs
3 cups all-purpose flour	3 cups milk
2 Tb. sugar	1 cup vegetable shortening, heated
2 Tb. baking powder	but not fully melted
1¼ tsp. salt	

Combine the cornmeal, flour, sugar, baking powder, and salt in a large mixing bowl and blend well. Add eggs one at a time, mixing well after each is added. Blend milk in thoroughly, add shortening, and mix well. Cover the bowl with plastic wrap and refrigerate for 1 hour.

Preheat oven to 500°.

Grease 2 or 3 heavy cast-iron corn stick molds and set in the oven till molds are very hot. Spoon batter into the hot molds, bake for 10–12 minutes or till tops are golden and crisp, and serve immediately.

Rhode Island Johnnycakes

Yield: 4 6-inch cakes or 8 3-inch cakes

This recipe for johnnycakes (which differs considerably from the one for Johnnycakes with Creamed Shrimp and Oysters, p. 118) came from a very serious-minded reader in Rhode Island who couldn't emphasize enough how the white cornmeal must have a very fine texture. If you can't find packaged johnnycake meal, buy regular white cornmeal and refine it in a food processor. In addition to serving these cakes simply with butter and maple syrup for breakfast, I also find they work beautifully as a foundation for all sorts of creamed dishes. The recipe can be easily doubled.

2 cups johnnycake meal (or white cornmeal)
2 Tb. flour
2 Tb. sugar
1½ tsp. salt
1½ cups half-and-half
½ cup milk

Combine the meal, flour, sugar, and salt in a mixing bowl and blend well. Add the half-and-half, mix, then add the milk plus a little more if necessary to make the batter thin enough to pour.

Grease a griddle or large, heavy skillet, heat to moderate, pour on small cakes of batter, and cook on both sides till nicely browned. Repeat process till batter is used up.

Baking Powder Biscuits

Yield: 12–15 biscuits

These are the biscuits on which I was weaned and the ones my mother still serves religiously with her short ribs of beef and squash casserole. Remember that if you want the biscuits to be light and flaky, handle the dough as little as possible.

2 cups all-purpose flour
1 tsp. salt
1 Tb. baking powder
4 Tb. vegetable shortening
¾ cup milk

Preheat oven to 450°.

Sift flour, salt, and baking powder together into a large mixing bowl, add the shortening, and work quickly into the flour with fingertips till particles of shortening are about the size of oatmeal flakes. Add the milk and stir quickly with a fork or just long enough to dampen the flour.

Transfer the dough to a lightly floured surface, knead for about 10 seconds, and roll out to ½-inch thickness. Cut into rounds with a biscuit cutter or small juice glass, place rounds on a baking sheet, and bake for 12 minutes or till golden on top.

Southern Buttermilk Biscuits

Yield: About 16 biscuits

If you want to know what real biscuits are all about, forget the other recipes included in this chapter and bake up a batch of these beauties. I fix these biscuits every Saturday morning for breakfast, and the following Sunday morning I love them even more cut in half, buttered, and run under the broiler till well browned on top. If you must use sweet milk, omit the baking soda.

2 cups all-purpose flour
4 tsp. baking powder
½ tsp. salt

½ tsp. baking soda
4 Tb. vegetable shortening
1 cup buttermilk

*P*reheat oven to 450°.
Sift the flour, baking powder, salt, and baking soda together into a large mixing bowl, add the shortening, and mix with a pastry cutter till well blended. Add the buttermilk and mix with a large spoon till dough is soft, adding a little more buttermilk if necessary.

Turn dough out onto a lightly floured surface and toss lightly with hands till outside looks smooth. Pat dough out with hands to a ½-inch thickness, cut into rounds with a biscuit cutter or small juice glass, place on a baking sheet, and bake for 12 minutes or till lightly browned on top.

Cheese Biscuits

Yield: About 75 biscuits

I don't recall just how long I've been making these zesty little cheese biscuits, but every time I serve them, people beg for the recipe. I always keep them on hand to nibble throughout the day, but they are also very nice added to a cookie plate after dinner. It's very important that both the butter and cheese be at room temperature, and I can't emphasize enough the importance of using nothing but *extra strong* New York State cheddar cheese (I will walk blocks or drive miles to find A&P's version).

*1 cup (2 sticks) butter, room
  temperature*
*½ lb. extra strong New York
  State cheddar cheese, finely
  grated and brought to room
  temperature*

¼ tsp. salt
Big dash of cayenne
2 cups all-purpose flour
Pecan halves

Preheat oven to 375°.
   Combine the butter, cheese, salt, and cayenne in a large mixing bowl and mix with a wooden spoon till very well blended. Add the flour gradually and stir till the mixture is firm and smooth, adding a little more flour if necessary. Roll pieces of dough in palms of hands into balls the size of large marbles, place on baking sheets about 1½ inches apart, and bake for 10 minutes.

Remove biscuits from oven, press a pecan half into the center of each, return to oven, and continue baking for 20 minutes or till slightly brown.

Buttermilk Scones

Yield: About 8 scones

While in Devon, England, researching the regional cookery in that shire's charming country inns, I came to love these scones often served at breakfast (smeared with country butter and strawberry preserves) and with afternoon tea (loaded with clotted cream). Cut in several horizontal slices, these "savoury" scones also make great toast.

1 cup all-purpose flour
2 Tb. sugar
¼ tsp. salt
½ tsp. baking soda

½ tsp. cream of tartar
3 Tb. softened lard or butter
½ cup buttermilk

*P*reheat oven to 400°.
 Sift flour, sugar, baking soda, and cream of tartar together into a mixing bowl, add the lard, and work the mixture with the fingers till mealy. Add the buttermilk and stir till mixture forms a soft, moist dough.

 Turn dough out onto a lightly floured surface, roll out into a circle about ½ inch thick, and cut dough into 2-inch rounds with a cookie cutter or juice glass, gathering up scraps, rerolling, and cutting into rounds.

 Place rounds about 1½ inches apart on a greased baking sheet and bake for 15 minutes or till golden brown. Wrap scones in a clean cloth and serve warm — sliced in half and buttered.

Orange Muffins

Yield: About 25 medium-size muffins

In the fine American tradition, these muffins are delicious served at breakfast with a little additional marmalade on the side, but I find they are also perfect with a light cold lunch — minus the powdered sugar.

¾ cup (1½ sticks) butter, softened   *1 tsp. vanilla*
1½ cups sugar   *2½ cups flour*
3 eggs   *2 tsp. baking powder*
½ cup orange juice   *½ tsp. salt*
Grated rind of 2 medium oranges   *Powdered sugar*

Cream the butter and sugar with an electric mixer in a large bowl till frothy, then add the eggs one at a time, beating constantly. Add the orange juice, orange rind, and vanilla, and mix till well blended.

Sift the flour, baking powder, and salt together into a mixing bowl, add to the orange mixture, and stir lightly till batter is only slightly moist but still lumpy.

Preheat oven to 350°.

Grease and lightly flour small muffin pans, fill each mold about one-half full, and bake for 20 minutes or till a straw inserted in the center of muffins comes out clean. Remove muffins from pans and dust the tops lightly with powdered sugar.

Blueberry Muffins with Streusel Topping

Yield: 12 muffins

TOPPING:

2 Tb. butter

2 Tb. brown sugar

¼ tsp. ground cinnamon

¼ cup finely chopped nuts

MUFFINS:

1½ cups all-purpose flour

2 tsp. baking powder

½ tsp. salt

4 Tb. (½ stick) butter, room temperature

½ cup sugar

1 egg

1 tsp. vanilla

½ cup milk

1½ cups blueberries, picked over and rinsed

*T*o prepare topping, heat the butter in a small saucepan, add the sugar, and stir over low heat till sugar is dissolved. Add the cinnamon and nuts, stir well, and set aside.

Sift the flour, baking powder, and salt together into a bowl and preheat oven to 400°.

Combine the butter and sugar in a large mixing bowl and cream with an electric mixer till fluffy. Add the egg and vanilla, and continue beating till well blended. Stir in the flour mixture and milk alternately, mix well and fold in the blueberries.

Grease a muffin tin well with butter or oil, fill containers two-thirds full with batter, spoon a little streusel topping on each, and bake for 20 minutes.

Spicy Parmesan Muffins

Yield: 12 muffins

I include very little sugar and salt in these muffins for the simple reason that the beer and Parmesan contribute enough sweetness and saltiness to satisfy most palates. And it's remarkable how you don't miss the salt when a zesty chili pepper is used. Since fermented beer adds lightness to any number of baked breads, you might try it in other recipes

2 cups all-purpose flour
1 Tb. sugar
1 Tb. baking powder
½ tsp. salt
1 cup beer
1 egg
4 Tb. (½ stick) butter, melted
  and cooled

1 small jalapeño or serrano chili
  pepper, scraped of seeds and
  membranes and minced
1 cup freshly grated Parmesan
  cheese

Sift the flour, sugar, baking powder, and salt together into a large mixing bowl. In another bowl, combine the beer, egg, and butter, and beat lightly with a whisk.

Preheat oven to 400°.

Pour beer mixture over the dry mixture and stir with a wooden spoon till batter is lumpy. Add the minced chili pepper and cheese, and stir to distribute as evenly as possible.

Lightly grease 12 muffin cups, fill each three-quarters full with batter, and for bake 25 minutes or till tops are golden. Transfer muffins to a rack to cool.

Cheddar Shortbread

Yield: 42 shortbreads

1¼ cups all-purpose flour
½ tsp. paprika
¼ tsp. nutmeg
8 Tb. (1 stick) butter, softened

2 cups grated sharp cheddar
  cheese, room temperature
½ cup finely chopped walnuts

Preheat oven to 400°.
   Combine flour, paprika, and nutmeg in a small bowl and blend well.

In a large mixing bowl, cream the butter with an electric mixer, add the cheese gradually, and beat till well blended. Add the dry ingredients gradually, beating steadily.

Transfer the dough to a greased baking sheet, roll into a 12×7-inch rectangle, cut into 1×2-inch pieces, and sprinkle walnuts over top. Bake for 12–15 minutes or till golden, separate pieces carefully, and cool on wire racks.

Serve with fresh fruit or ice cream.

Stilton Popovers

Yield: 6 popovers

2 Tb. butter
¼ cup very finely crumbled
  Stilton cheese
1¼ cups flour

1¼ cups milk
4 Tb. (½ stick) melted butter
¼ tsp. salt
6 eggs, beaten

Preheat oven to 450°.
   Grease the molds of a 6-cup popover pan with the 2 tablespoons of butter and place pan in the oven for 2 minutes. Remove pan from oven and sprinkle with the crumbled cheese.

Combine the flour, milk, melted butter, salt, and eggs in a large mixing bowl and blend thoroughly till batter is smooth. Spoon equal amounts of batter into each mold and bake for 15 minutes. Reduce heat to 350°, continue baking for 20 minutes longer or till popovers are golden brown, and serve immediately.

Herbed Toast

Yield: 40 pieces

There's virtually no bland dish that a little herbed toast can't manage to enhance, and I never prepare these small diagonals that I don't think of all the soups, pâtés, and vegetable mousses with which Pearl Byrd Foster served the toast when she was producing her culinary masterpieces at Mr. & Mrs. Foster's Place in New York. While you can feel free to use any combination of fresh herbs that might be available (don't bother with this toast if you must use dried herbs), I love nothing more than a mixture of parsley, chives, basil, and tarragon.

8 Tb. (1 stick) unsalted butter　　*10 slices white bread*
1 Tb. finely chopped mixed fresh
* herbs*

*P*reheat oven broiler.
　　Heat the butter in a saucepan till melted, add the herbs, stir, and set pan aside.
　Toast the bread lightly on both sides under the broiler, trim off the crusts, and, cutting on the diagonal, divide each slice into 4 pieces. Dip each piece into the herbed butter and return momentarily to the oven to crisp.

Nutty Fingers

Yield: About 75 fingers

2 cups (4 sticks) butter, softened
½ cup plus 2 Tb. sifted powdered
  sugar
5 cups all-purpose flour

2 cups finely chopped pecans
2 tsp. vanilla
Dash of salt
Sifted powdered sugar for rolling

Preheat oven to 350°.

In a large mixing bowl, cream the butter and sugar with an electric mixer and gradually blend in the flour with a wooden spoon. Add the nuts, vanilla, and salt, and mix thoroughly.

Take small pieces of dough and form into finger shapes, place fingers on a cookie sheet about 1½ inches apart, and bake for about 30 minutes or till lightly brown. Let fingers cool, then roll in powdered sugar.

Peanut Butter – Chocolate Chip Cookies

Yield: About 50 cookies

8 Tb. (1 stick) butter, softened
½ cup chunky peanut butter
½ cup sugar
½ cup light brown sugar
2 eggs
1 tsp. vanilla

1¼ cups flour
½ tsp. baking soda
½ tsp. salt
6 oz. chocolate chips
½ cup peanuts, coarsely chopped
  in a food processor

Preheat oven to 350°.

In a large mixing bowl, cream the butter and peanut butter with an electric mixer till soft. Add the two sugars and continue creaming till well blended. Add the eggs and vanilla and beat till light and fluffy.

Combine the flour, baking soda, and salt in a small bowl, add to the butter mixture, and mix well. Add the chocolate chips and peanuts and stir well with a wooden spoon.

Drop the batter by teaspoons 2 inches apart onto an ungreased baking sheet and bake for 12 minutes or till browned.

Fruitcake Cookies

Yield: About 85 cookies

1½ cups flour
¼ tsp. baking soda
½ tsp. salt
½ tsp. ground cinnamon
4 Tb. (½ stick) butter, softened
½ cup brown sugar
2 eggs
1 cup sherry

1 tsp. sherry extract
3½ cups chopped nuts
3 slices candied pineapple, chopped
1 cup candied cherries, chopped
1 cup dates, chopped
¼ lb. white raisins
¼ cup crystallized orange and
  lemon peel, chopped

*P*reheat oven to 300°.
In a small mixing bowl, combine the flour, baking soda, salt, and cinnamon and set aside.

In a large mixing bowl, cream the butter and sugar with an electric mixer, add the eggs, and beat well.

Combine the dry ingredients and sherry alternately with the butter mixture, add the sherry extract, stir in the nuts and fruit, and mix well. Drop the mixture by heaping teaspoons onto a greased baking sheet about 1½ inches apart and bake for 20 minutes.

Benne Cookies

Yield: About 85 cookies

1 cup benne (sesame) seeds
¾ cup (1½ sticks) butter, melted
1½ cups light brown sugar
1¼ cups all-purpose flour

¼ tsp. baking powder
¼ tsp. salt
1 tsp. vanilla
1 egg

Heat oven to 300° and toast benne seeds on a baking sheet for 10 – 15 minutes, stirring. Remove from oven and increase heat to 325°.

In a large mixing bowl, combine the butter, sugar, flour, baking powder, salt, vanilla, egg, and cooled seeds, and mix thoroughly with a wooden spoon. Drop batter by ½ teaspoons onto a greased, foil-lined baking sheet about 1½ inches apart and bake for 15 – 20 minutes or till evenly browned (if pale in center and puffed, the cookies are not ready), watching constantly to avoid burning. Carefully peel cookies from foil and cool on paper towels.

Jelly Cookies

Yield: About 100 cookies

1½ cups (3 sticks) butter, softened
1 cup sugar
4 egg yolks

4 cups all-purpose flour
Currant or mint jelly or orange
  marmalade

Preheat oven to 325°.

In a large mixing bowl, cream the butter and sugar with an electric mixer, add egg yolks, and mix thoroughly. Gradually add the flour and mix till well blended and batter is firm.

Roll pieces of batter into small balls in the palm of the hand, place balls on cookie sheets about 1½ inches apart, press a thimble or fingertip in the center of each, and bake for 10 minutes. Remove cookies from the oven, place a dot of jelly in the holes, and continue baking for about 10 minutes or till cookies are slightly brown. Let cool till jelly is hard.

Kourambiethes
(Greek Sugar Cookies)

Yield: About 100 cookies

Coming from a part-Greek background, I can't imagine Christmas without these traditional little cookies rolled over and over in powdered sugar. The clove stuck in the top of each recalls the spices brought by the Wise Men to the Christ Child. In a tightly closed tin, the cookies seem to keep forever.

2 cups (4 sticks) butter, room
   temperature
4 Tb. confectioners' sugar, sifted
1 egg yolk
1 Tb. Grand Marnier or
   Cointreau

4 cups cake flour, sifted
1 cup lightly toasted almonds,
   ground
100 whole cloves
1 cup confectioners' sugar, sifted,
   for coating

In a large mixing bowl, cream the butter with an electric mixer till thick and gradually beat in the 4 tablespoons of sugar. Add the egg and liqueur and continue creaming till smooth.

With a wooden spoon, gradually work in the flour and ground almonds to make a soft dough that rolls easily in the palm of the hand without sticking. If sticky, refrigerate the dough for 1 hour.

Preheat oven to 350°.

Pat and shape the dough into 1½-inch rounds and stud each cookie with a clove. Place on ungreased baking sheets about 1½ inches apart and bake for 15 minutes or till sandy colored but not brown. Cool cookies and roll them generously in the cup of confectioners' sugar.

Pecan Diamonds

Yield: About 200 diamonds

Don't ask me why this luscious confection from the Culinary Institute of America at Hyde Park, New York never once turned out right when I cut the recipe in half. Don't try. Two hundred is a lot of cookies, but they make great gifts during the Christmas holidays.

COOKIE DOUGH:

10 Tb. (1¼ sticks) butter, softened *½ tsp. vanilla*
9 Tb. granulated sugar *3 cups all-purpose flour*
6 Tb. vegetable shortening *1 tsp. baking powder*
1 egg *½ tsp. salt*

FILLING:

2 cups (4 sticks) butter *2½ cups light brown sugar*
1⅛ cups honey *8 cups chopped pecans or walnuts*
½ cup sugar *½ cup heavy cream*

To make cookie dough, combine the butter, sugar, shortening, egg, and vanilla in a large mixing bowl and cream with an electric mixer. Sift the flour, baking powder, and salt together in a bowl and add to the creamed ingredients. Mix well to form a smooth dough and refrigerate overnight.

Preheat oven to 350°.

Divide the cold dough into 3 equal parts, place each part between 2 sheets of plastic wrap, and roll into a 5×12-inch rectangle ⅛ inch thick. Remove top piece of plastic from one piece of dough, invert the dough onto a 12×16-inch baking sheet, and remove other piece of plastic. Repeat procedure with the other two pieces of rolled-out dough, stack on first piece of dough, then prick top layer with a fork. Bake for 10 minutes and let crust cool while preparing filling.

Combine the 2 cups of butter, honey, and sugars in a large saucepan over moderate heat, bring mixture to the boil, and boil for exactly 3 minutes. Remove from heat and let cool. Fold in the nuts and heavy cream, mix well, and spread mixture over the baked crust.

Bake for 35 minutes, cool completely, and cut into small diamonds.

Macadamia Wafers

Yield: About 48 wafers

When my friend Richard Sax (author of *Cooking Great Meals Every Day*), came up with this highly original recipe, I baked up a batch of the wafers and managed to eat each and every one in a matter of days. I also took Richard's suggestion, quickly draped some of the wafers over a rolling pin as they came out of the oven, and produced delicately Americanized *tuiles* (French tile cookies).

1 cup (2 sticks) unsalted butter, room temperature
½ cup sugar
2 egg whites
½ tsp. vanilla
½ cup ground toasted macadamia nuts
½ cup all-purpose flour
½ cup coarsely chopped macadamia nuts

Preheat oven to 350°.

In a large mixing bowl, cream the butter and sugar with an electric mixer, add egg whites and vanilla, and continue beating till very smooth. Add the ground nuts and flour and stir with a wooden spoon to blend gently but thoroughly into butter mixture.

In batches, drop the batter by teaspoons 2 inches apart onto two lightly buttered and floured baking sheets and flatten mounds slightly with the back of a spoon dipped in cold water. Sprinkle each mound generously with chopped nuts and bake for 8–10 minutes or till edges of wafers are golden. Carefully lift cookies onto a wire rack to cool.

BREADS, DOUGHS, AND COOKIES · 453

PART TWELVE

Fruits, Preserves, and Pickles

Sautéed Apples and Walnuts

Serves 4–6

This incredibly simple dish can be served either with breakfast or an elaborate pork dinner.

2 Tb. butter

½ cup coarsely chopped walnuts

4 cooking apples, peeled, cored, and cut into thick slices

Juice of 1 orange

½ cup brown sugar

*H*eat butter in a large skillet, add the walnuts, and sauté over moderate heat, stirring for 5 minutes or till nuts and butter are brown but not black. Add the apple slices, orange juice, and brown sugar, stir, and cook over moderate heat till apples are just heated through.

Baked Apples Stuffed with Beets, Pine Nuts, and Currants

Serves 8

Gaston Lenôtre may be France's most famous pastry chef, but he's also an expert at concocting sensational accompaniments such as this to the various game dishes he loves to prepare.

8 Granny Smith apples	*Salt and freshly ground pepper*
Juice of 1 lemon	*1 tsp. red wine vinegar*
5 Tb. butter, softened	*½ cup pine nuts*
½ cup cooked beets (fresh or	*½ cup dried currants*
canned), cut into small cubes	*1 Tb. brown sugar*

Peel the apples and drop into a kettle of cold water to which has been added the lemon juice.

Preheat oven to 400°.

When all the apples have been peeled, remove them from the water one by one, cut a thin slice off the bottom of each so they will stand on a heavy baking sheet or large, shallow baking dish, and slice off the top quarters of the apples to serve as lids. Carefully core the apples, rub the insides with 3 tablespoons of the butter, replace the lids, and bake for 15 minutes.

Meanwhile, salt and pepper the beets to taste, heat remaining butter in a small skillet, and sauté the beets over low heat for 2 minutes, turning. Add vinegar, increase heat, stir for 1 minute, then stir in pine nuts and currants.

Increase oven to broil.

Stuff apples with the beet mixture, replace lids, sprinkle with a little brown sugar, and run under the broiler for 3 minutes to caramelize the tops.

Prunes Frederick

Serves 8

I still don't know at what point over the past twenty years I first tasted Louis Szathmáry's Prunes Frederick at The Bakery in Chicago, and I still have no idea who the Frederick was who inspired the dish. I do know that Chef Louis' prunes make an ideal side dish to any form of pork chops and serve to illustrate why this fruit should not always automatically be relegated to the dessert section of cookbooks.

1 Tb. butter
1 lb. pitted prunes
1 cup pecan halves
1 cup brown sugar

1 cup water
1 lemon, seeded and thinly sliced
⅓ cup Bourbon

Preheat oven to 350°.

Grease an 8- or 9-inch pie plate with butter. Stuff each prune with a pecan half and arrange them in the dish. Chop the remaining pecans and sprinkle them over the prunes.

Combine the brown sugar, water, and sliced lemon in a saucepan, bring to the boil, cook for 2 minutes, and strain the syrup over the prunes. Bake prunes for 20 minutes, cover with the strained lemon slices, and bake for 10 minutes longer.

Warm Bourbon in a small saucepan, ignite it, pour over the prunes, and let burn till flames die.

Remove and discard lemon slices and serve prunes immediately.

To Sterilize and Seal Jars for Canning

Unscrew ring bands from canning jars, remove lids, arrange jars in a large pot, and cover with water. Bring water to the boil, cover, and sterilize jars for 10 minutes.

Remove jars from the water with tongs and pack with food to be canned, taking care not to touch the insides of the jars once they have been sterilized. Wipe rims clean with paper towels, use tongs to dip sealing lids into the water used for sterilizing jars, fit lids on top of jars, and screw ring bands on tightly.

Place filled jars in a draft-free area till lids ping and remain down when pushed with the finger (signs they are sterile). Store any jars whose lids remain convex in the refrigerator and use first.

Watermelon Rind Pickle

Yield: About 7 1-pint jars

These are probably the most elegant and delectable pickle you'll ever serve. They are time-consuming to prepare, but once you taste them, you'll never again go near the watermelon rind pickle you purchase on the commercial market. Do remember that every ounce of pink flesh must be removed from the rind. The calcium hydroxide is available at all drugstores.

6 lbs. watermelon rind
11.5-gram bottle of lime (calcium hydroxide)
1 Tb. alum (available in spice section of supermarket)
½ lb. fresh ginger root
6 lbs. sugar

6 cups white vinegar
3 cups water
1 Tb. whole allspice
1 Tb. whole cloves
2 sticks cinnamon, about 3 inches long

Remove all dark green outer rind and all pink flesh from the watermelon rind and cut rind into 2-inch fingers. Place fingers in a large glass or enameled container. Dissolve the lime in 1 gallon of water, pour over the melon, cover with plastic wrap, and let stand overnight.

Combine the alum with 1 gallon of water in a large container, transfer drained melon fingers to the solution, and let soak for 5 minutes. Drain melon.

Combine the ginger root with 1 gallon of water in a large enameled pot, add the melon, bring to the boil, reduce heat, and simmer for 30 minutes. Drain water from the pot, remove the ginger root, and rinse melon thoroughly under cold running water for exactly 5 minutes. Rinse out pot.

Combine the sugar, vinegar, water, allspice, cloves, and cinnamon in the pot. Bring liquid to the boil and add melon. Return liquid to the boil, reduce heat, and simmer for 3 hours.

Pack hot sterilized jars with the watermelon fingers, fill each jar with hot liquid to ¼ inch from the top, seal, and store in a cool area for at least two months before serving.

Bread and Butter Pickle

Yield: 8 1-pint jars

4 qts. (about 6 lbs.) cucumbers,
  scrubbed and sliced into
  ¼-inch rounds
6 medium onions, thinly sliced
⅓ cup salt

4½ cups sugar
1½ tsp. turmeric
1½ tsp. celery seed
2 Tb. mustard seed
3 cups cider vinegar

*I*n a large mixing bowl, arrange alternate layers of cucumber rounds and sliced onions, sprinkling each layer with salt. Cover top of the mixture with ice cubes or crushed ice, mix ice thoroughly with cucumbers and onions, and let stand for 3 hours. Drain thoroughly.

Combine the sugar, turmeric, celery seed, mustard seed, and vinegar in a large enameled pot and bring liquid to the boil. Add the cucumbers and onions and return just to the boil.

Pack cucumbers and onions into hot sterilized jars, fill jars with hot liquid to ¼ inch from tops, seal, and store in a cool area.

Pickled Squash

Yield: 6 1-pint jars

4 qts. (about 6 lbs.) yellow
   summer squash
6 medium white onions, thinly
   sliced
¼ cup salt

5 cups sugar
1½ tsp. celery seed
1½ Tb. mustard seed
1 tsp. turmeric
3 cups cider vinegar

Scrub the squash under cold running water and slice into ¼-inch rounds.

Combine the squash rounds, onions, and salt in a large glass or enameled container, cover with ice cubes or cracked ice, and let stand for 3 hours. Drain thoroughly.

Combine the sugar, celery seed, mustard seed, turmeric, and vinegar in a large enameled pot, add the squash and onions, and bring just to the boil.

Pack the mixture into hot sterilized jars, fill jars with hot liquid to ¼ inch from the top, seal, and store in a cool area.

Pickled Peaches

Yield: 5 1-pint jars

I'd find it difficult getting through the winter without these pickled peaches to serve with briskets of beef and almost any pork dish. Put up the peaches as soon as the crop begins to arrive in July, for they're much better if allowed to mellow a few months before serving.

1½ pts. white vinegar
2 lbs. sugar
5 sticks cinnamon, about 3 inches
   long

4 qts. (about 6 lbs.) small firm
   peaches
Cloves

Combine the vinegar, sugar, and cinnamon in a large saucepan and bring liquid to the boil. Stir well, reduce heat slightly, and cook for 20 minutes or till a medium thick syrup forms.

Meanwhile, bring a large kettle of water to the boil, dip peaches in the water in batches, and remove skins as the peaches are withdrawn from the water. Stud each peeled peach with 2 cloves.

Add the peaches in batches to the hot syrup, increase slightly, and cook peaches for 5–10 minutes or till tender. Pack peaches in hot sterilized jars, add syrup to within ¼ inch of tops, seal, and store in a cool area for at least two months before serving.

Pickled Okra

Yield: 4 1-pint jars

4 tsp. dill seeds
3½ lbs. small fresh okra, rinsed
    thoroughly
4 small hot red peppers
4 small green hot peppers

8 garlic cloves
1 qt. white vinegar
1 cup water
6 Tb. salt

Sterilize 4 1-pint jars and place ½ teaspoon of dill seeds in the bottom of each jar. Pack okra in jars, taking care not to bruise, add another ½ teaspoon of dill seeds to each jar, and add 1 of each hot pepper and 2 garlic cloves to each jar.

Combine the vinegar, water, and salt in a large saucepan, bring to the boil, and pour equal amounts of liquid over the okra to ¼ inch from top of jars. Seal and store in a cool area for at least one month before serving.

Squash Relish

Yield: 6 1-pint jars

6 large yellow squash, cut into
   chunks
4 medium onions, chopped
1 medium green bell pepper,
   chopped
1 medium red bell pepper, chopped

¼ cup salt
3 cups sugar
2 cups vinegar
2 tsp. celery seed
2 tsp. turmeric

Combine the vegetables in a food processor and process coarsely. Transfer to a large mixing bowl, add the salt plus water to cover, and let stand for 1 hour. Place vegetables in a colander, rinse quickly under cold running water, and drain well.

Combine the sugar, vinegar, celery seed, and turmeric in a large saucepan, bring to the boil, and cook for 3 minutes. Add the vegetable mixture, stir, return to the boil, reduce heat, and simmer for 3–5 minutes.

Pour mixture into hot sterilized jars, seal, and store in a cool area.

Mustard Chow Chow

Yield: 15 1-pint jars

6 cups chopped cabbage
6 cups chopped green tomatoes
¾ cup salt
6 cups chopped red bell peppers
6 cups chopped green bell peppers
6 cups chopped onions
1½ chopped celery ribs

½ head cauliflower, chopped
3 pts. white vinegar
2 lbs. brown sugar
½ cup all-purpose flour
3 Tb. dry mustard
1 Tb. turmeric
3 Tb. water

Combine the chopped cabbage, tomatoes, and salt in a large bowl, cover with water, and soak overnight.

Drain mixture thoroughly and transfer to a large kettle. Add the two peppers, onions, celery, cauliflower, vinegar, and brown sugar, and bring mixture almost to the boil. Combine the flour, mustard, turmeric, and water in a small bowl, mix to make a paste, and add the paste to the kettle. Gradually bring liquid to a roaring boil, stirring constantly. Remove kettle from the heat, spoon equal amounts of the chow chow into hot sterilized jars, seal, and store in a cool area.

Green Tomato and Apple Chutney

Yield: 4 1-pint jars

The time to put up chutney is late summer and early fall when fruits and vegetables are in such abundance and offer limitless possibilities for imagination and experiment. Here is a good, honest, not-too-sweet, not-too-sharp chutney that goes well with all curries and any number of cold meat dishes.

2 cups cider vinegar
3 lbs. green tomatoes, cut into
    ½-inch cubes
1 lb. green tart apples, peeled,
    cored, and cut into ½-inch cubes
3 medium onions, coarsely chopped
½ cup seedless raisins

1 cup dark brown sugar
1 Tb. grated fresh ginger
1 Tb. ground cloves
1 Tb. crushed mustard seeds
3 garlic cloves, minced
1½ tsp. red pepper flakes
2 Tb. salt

Combine all the ingredients in a large saucepan and bring to the boil. Reduce heat, cover, and simmer mixture for 1 hour or till soft, thick, and well blended, adding a little more vinegar if chutney becomes too stiff and dry.

Spoon chutney into hot sterilized jars, seal, and allow to mellow for at least two months in a cool area before serving.

Cantaloupe Chutney

Yield: 4 ½-pint jars

Here is but one way I like to make use of all those fragrant, inexpensive cantaloupes that fill the markets in July and August. Try serving this chutney with roast lamb.

2 medium cantaloupes, not too ripe
¼ cup salt
2 cups cider vinegar
2 cups light brown sugar
½ tsp. ground ginger
½ tsp. ground cinnamon
½ tsp. dry mustard
¼ tsp. cayenne

¼ tsp. grated lemon rind
6 cloves, crushed
1 cup chopped scallions
½ cup chopped green bell pepper
1 garlic clove, minced
½ cup dried currants
½ cup seedless raisins
½ cup brandy

Slice cantaloupes in half, cut flesh from the rind, and cut flesh into 1-inch pieces. Place pieces in a large mixing bowl and add water to cover plus the salt. Stir, cover with plastic wrap, and chill overnight. Drain melon and rinse in cold water.

In a large stainless-steel saucepan, combine the vinegar, sugar, ginger, cinnamon, mustard, and cayenne, and stir. Add the lemon rind, cloves, scallions, green pepper, and garlic, and bring to a low boil. Add the cantaloupe, currants, raisins, and brandy, stir well, and simmer chutney over low heat for about 2 hours or till reduced by half.

Spoon chutney into hot sterilized jars, seal, and store in a cool area.

Cranberry Conserve

Yield: About 5 ½-pint jars

1 lb. fresh cranberries
1½ cups water
1 cup sugar
½ cup seedless raisins

2 oranges, cleanly peeled, seeded,
    and cut into small chunks
¾ cup chopped pecans

*P*lace the cranberries in a large saucepan, add the water, and bring to the boil. Reduce heat and simmer for 3 – 5 minutes or till berries just pop open. Add the sugar, raisins, and orange chunks, stir, and simmer for about 15 minutes longer. Stir in the nuts, simmer for 2 minutes longer, remove pan from the heat, and let cool slightly.

Spoon the conserve into hot sterilized jars, seal, and store in a cool area. Or spoon mixture into the jars, cover lightly with lids, and refrigerate till ready to serve with roasted poultry or pork (keeps about two weeks under refrigeration).

Peach Preserves

Yield: 7 1-pint jars

2 qts. (about 3 lbs.) hard fresh
    peaches, peeled and sliced ¼
    inch thick

6 cups sugar

*C*ombine the peaches and sugar in a kettle and let stand overnight to allow peaches to leech out and moisten the sugar.

Bring mixture slowly to the boil, stirring frequently, reduce heat slightly, and cook for about 40 minutes or till fruit is clear and syrup thick. Spoon mixture into hot sterilized jars, seal, and store in a cool area.

Strawberry Preserves

Yield: 4 ½-pint jars

1 qt. strawberries, washed   *2 tsp. lemon juice*
4 cups sugar   *2 Tb. pectin (Certo)*

Combine the strawberries and 2 cups of the sugar in a large saucepan, bring slowly to the boil, and cook rapidly for 5 minutes, stirring. Add the remaining sugar, return to the boil, and cook for 10 minutes longer, stirring in the lemon juice 2 minutes before removing pan from the heat. Add the pectin, stir well, pour mixture into a large mixing bowl, and let stand for 30 minutes.

Spoon strawberries into hot sterilized jars, seal, and store in a cool area.

Fig Preserves

Yield: 10 ½-pint jars

7 cups sugar   *2 qts. fresh figs (about 4¼ lbs.),*
¼ cup lemon juice   *stems removed*
1½ cups hot water   *2 lemons, thinly sliced*

In a large kettle, combine the sugar, lemon juice, and hot water, bring to the boil, reduce heat, and cook for about 5 minutes, stirring, or till sugar has dissolved.

Add the figs, increase heat, and cook rapidly for 10 minutes, stirring occasionally. Add the sliced lemons and continue to cook rapidly for 10–15 minutes or till figs clear. (If the syrup thickens too much before figs clear, add boiling water ¼ cup at a time.)

Pack figs into hot sterilized jars, add syrup to ¼ inch from the top of jars, seal, and store in a cool area.

Pear Preserves

Yield: 5 ½-pint jars

3 cups sugar
3 cups water
9 medium hard pears (about 3 lbs.), cored, peeled, and cut into eighths

1 lemon, thinly sliced
5 pieces preserved ginger

Combine one-half of the sugar and the water in a large saucepan, bring to the boil, and cook for 2 minutes, stirring. Add the pears, reduce heat slightly, and boil gently for 15 minutes. Add remaining sugar and the lemon slices, stir till sugar has dissolved, and cook rapidly for about 25 minutes or till fruit is clear. Cover and let stand overnight.

Pack the fruit into hot sterilized jars and add a piece of ginger to each jar. Cook syrup for about 5 minutes and pour over the fruit, leaving ¼ inch at top of jars. Seal jars and store in a cool area.

Orange Marmalade

Yield: 7 ½-pint jars

I'm resolutely convinced that it's impossible to make genuine English marmalade unless you can manage to lay hands on bitter, thick-skinned Seville oranges. The temple oranges that appear on the market will do, however, and if, like myself, you hate to spend a fortune on imported jars of marmalade, you'll learn to make your own. Also, if you like a really hearty marmalade, add about a teaspoon of extra coarse-cut orange rind to each ½-pint jar. I think this marmalade should be stored at least 2 months before using.

4 medium temple oranges, washed
  thoroughly
1 lemon, washed thoroughly
1½ cups water

¼ tsp. baking soda
6 cups sugar
3 oz. pectin (Certo)

Remove the rind from oranges and lemons and scrape off and discard the white membranes. Place one-half of the rind and half the water in a blender or food processor, chop rinds coarsely, and transfer to a large saucepan. Repeat process with remaining rind and water and add to saucepan.

Add baking soda to the pan, bring to the boil, reduce heat, cover, and cook for 10 minutes.

Meanwhile, quarter the fruit and remove all seeds. Place fruit in the blender or processor, cover, and reduce to a puree. Add the puree to the saucepan, cover, and simmer over low heat for 20 minutes.

Transfer mixture to a large kettle or Dutch oven (not cast iron) and add the sugar. Bring to a full rolling boil and boil hard for 4 minutes, stirring occasionally.

Remove kettle from heat, add the pectin, skim the surface if necessary, and stir for 5 minutes. Pour marmalade into hot sterilized jars, seal, and store in a cool area.

Three-Fruit Marmalade

Yield: 12 ½-pint jars

Here is a stunning recipe that has been in my English friend Mary Homi's family for at least three generations. In many respects it is the ultimate marmalade.

2 grapefruits
2 temple oranges
4 lemons

6 pts. water
6 lbs. sugar

Wash fruit thoroughly, remove the rind, and cut into shreds. Remove all pithy white membrane from the fruit, cut up fruit into chunks, and tie all membrane and seeds in a cheesecloth.

Combine the shredded rind, cut-up fruit, and cheesecloth package in a large pot, add the water, and let soak overnight.

Bring liquid to the boil, reduce heat, cover, and simmer mixture for 1½ hours or till peel is just soft. Remove cheesecloth package and, when cool enough to handle, squeeze its juices back into the pot. Add sugar to the pot, stir till well dissolved, bring mixture to the boil, and boil rapidly for 5–10 minutes or till desired consistency, tested on a chilled plate.

Pour marmalade into hot sterilized jars, seal, and store in a cool area.

Hot Pepper Jelly

Yield: 6 ½-pint jars

Spread this tangy jelly on crackers with cream cheese or serve it with cold ham or pork.

2 medium red bell peppers, seeded
  and chopped (about 1 cup)
3 hot green peppers, seeded and
  finely chopped

2 cups cider vinegar
6½ cups sugar
6-oz. bottle pectin (Certo)

Combine the two types of peppers with 1 cup of the vinegar in a blender or food processor and blend till peppers are finely minced.

Transfer mixture to a stainless-steel saucepan, add the sugar and remaining vinegar, and bring to the boil. Stir, remove pan from the heat, and skim the surface. Stir in the pectin, return pan to the heat, and boil hard for 1 minute. Remove pan from the heat and skim again.

Pour the jelly into hot sterilized jars, seal, and store in a cool area.

Lemon Curd

My close English friend Mary Homi introduced me to this luscious con-
diment years ago, and now I'm rarely without a jar in the refrigerator. It's
delicious spread on toast, biscuits, and, indeed, Scones (p. 442), and Mary
even spoons it over ice cream.

2 lemons
8 Tb. (1 stick) butter, softened

1¼ cups superfine sugar
2 eggs, beaten

Grate the rind of both lemons and set aside. Cut the lemons in half,
squeeze the juice from both through a sieve into a small bowl, and set
aside.

In a saucepan, cream the butter and sugar with an electric mixer and
cook over low heat for 10 minutes or till the consistency of honey, stirring. Add the grated lemon rind and juice, stir well, remove pan from the
heat, and let cool for 10 minutes. Add the eggs, stir well, and cook over
low heat for about 10 minutes or till mixture is custardlike.

Pour mixture into lidded jars and store in the refrigerator at least 2
weeks before serving.

PART THIRTEEN

Desserts

Red Wine Pear Tart with Hazelnut Ice Cream

Serves 6

One of the most original and gifted chefs in San Francisco is Jeremiah Tower, owner of the Santa Fe Bar & Grill and the new Stars restaurant. While he is best known for his succulent grilled fish and meats and his highly creative pastas, this striking pear tart must now be considered one of his signature dishes.

6 bosc pears	4 Tb. (½ stick) butter
1 bottle fine Zinfandel	1 recipe of Pâte Brisée Sucrée
2 cups sugar	(p. 412)
Rind of 1 small lemon	1 pt. hazelnut ice cream

Peel, halve lengthwise, and core the pears. Place pear halves in a large stainless-steel saucepan, add the wine, sugar, and lemon rind, bring liquid to the simmer, and cook gently for about 5 minutes or till pears are barely tender. Transfer pears to a plate, increase heat to high, and reduce cooking liquid by half.

Preheat oven to 400°.

Grease a 10-inch nonstick skillet or deep tart pan with the butter and lay the pears coreside up in a neat pattern.

On a lightly floured surface, roll out the pastry about ⅛ inch thick in a circle just smaller than the diameter of the skillet, fit the pastry over the pears, and bake for about 25 minutes or till crust is golden.

Cool the tart for 5 minutes, turn it onto a platter pastry side down, and serve each portion with a scoop of the ice cream.

Papaya Tart with Macadamia Nuts

Serves 6 – 8

Acting as a judge at a gourmet gala held to raise funds for the University of San Diego Cancer Center, I was particularly impressed by a papaya and kiwi tart with macadamia nuts. When I later tested the recipe, however, I found the tart much better without the overworked kiwi fruit.

1 cup (2 sticks) unsalted butter,
cut into cubes
½ cup sugar
1 cup ground roasted macadamia
nuts
2 cups all-purpose flour
2 large papayas

1 Tb. cornstarch
1½ cups orange juice
2 Tb. Grand Marnier
2 Tb. finely chopped orange rind
Ground macadamia nuts for
garnish

*P*reheat oven to 350°.
Combine the butter and sugar in a food processor and process for 15 seconds or till smooth. Add the ground nuts and the flour, and process for 45 seconds or till the dough forms a ball. Roll dough out slightly, press into a 9-inch tart pan, and bake for about 12 minutes or till pastry is light brown.

Cut the papayas in half lengthwise, scoop out the seeds, peel, cut flesh into ¼-inch slices, and layer slices in the pie shell in circles, beginning in the center.

In a saucepan, mix the cornstarch with a small amount of the orange juice till cornstarch is thoroughly dissolved, add remaining orange juice, the Grand Marnier, and orange rind, bring to the boil, and cook over moderate heat, stirring, till mixture thickens. Pour the glaze over the papaya slices, let cool, then chill well in the refrigerator.

To serve, sprinkle top of the tart with ground macadamia nuts.

Tarte au Citron Girardet
(Lemon Tart with Orange)

Unlike most others, I do not champion many of Fredy Girardet's dishes at his famous restaurant in Crissier, Switzerland, but I must admit that when I traveled there shortly after the restaurant opened to see what all the commotion was about, I fell in love with this extraordinary tart.

2 cups all-purpose flour
1 cup sugar
1 cup (2 sticks) cold butter
5 eggs
⅔ cup lemon juice

½ cup orange juice
Grated rind of 2 lemons
¼ cup heavy cream
Confectioners' sugar

Sift the flour and ¼ cup of the sugar together into a large mixing bowl, add ¾ cup (1½ sticks) of the butter plus 1 lightly beaten egg, and blend the mixture till ingredients are well combined. Transfer dough to a lightly floured surface, knead just long enough to distribute the butter evenly, and form dough into a ball. Wrap dough in plastic wrap and chill for 1 hour.

Preheat oven to 400°.

Return dough to the floured working surface and roll it into a ⅛-inch-thick round. Press it firmly into a 10-inch flan pan with a removable fluted ring, and trim off the excess, allowing ¼ inch of dough to hang over the edges. Fold the overhang to inside, press it onto the sides of the shell, and crimp the edges. Prick the shell with a fork and line with wax paper. Sprinkle small raw beans over the paper and bake the shell for 10 minutes. Remove beans and paper and bake shell for 15 minutes longer. Remove shell carefully from pan and let cool on a rack.

In a bowl, whisk together the remaining eggs and sugar, the lemon juice, orange juice, and grated lemon rind. Heat the remaining butter in a saucepan, add the cream, and stir. Add the egg mixture and cook over low heat, stirring, till mixture thickens, making sure it never boils. Let custard cool.

Reduce oven heat to 375°.

Pour the custard into the prepared shell and bake for 20 minutes. Remove from the oven and increase heat to broil.

Sift confectioners' sugar over the top of the tart, return to the oven, and glaze the top for about 1 minute.

Tarte aux Fraises
(Fresh Strawberry Tart)

Serves 6

I don't think there's a dessert on earth I love more than a French-style tart with plenty of fresh fruit nestled in vanilla-flavored cream custard. Sliced pears, apricots, figs, apples, and whole raspberries or blueberries work just as well as the strawberries. If you want the pastry to be light, be sure to use the shortening.

THE PASTRY:

2 cups flour

¼ cup sugar

1 tsp. salt

8 Tb. (1 stick) unsalted butter, cold

2 Tb. vegetable shortening, cold

Ice-cold water

THE FILLING:

⅓ cup heavy cream

1 large egg

¼ cup sugar

2 tsp. vanilla

2 Tb. orange liqueur

1 qt. large ripe fresh strawberries, hulled and rinsed

THE GLAZE:

½ cup red currant jelly

1 Tb. sugar

½ Tb. orange liqueur

*T*o make the pastry, sift together the flour, sugar, and salt into a large mixing bowl. Add the butter and shortening in small pieces and work the mixture with fingertips till it becomes crumbly. Tossing the mixture with a fork, gradually sprinkle on enough cold water till the pastry can be gathered into a ball. Knead the pastry very briefly in palms of the hands, gather into a ball, wrap in plastic wrap, and chill for 1 hour.

Preheat oven to 325°.

To prepare the custard, combine the cream, egg, sugar, vanilla, and liqueur in a bowl, mix till well blended, and set aside.

Roll out the chilled pastry about ⅛ inch thick, press into the bottom and sides of a well-buttered 10-inch tart pan, trim pastry till just a little hangs over the edges of the pan, and press down along edges. Bake for 10 minutes. Remove the shell from the oven and pour custard into the shell. Arrange the strawberries closely together and evenly over the custard and bake the tart for 30 minutes or till a straw inserted in the custard comes out clean and the pastry is slightly browned. Let tart cool on a rack.

To make the glaze, boil the jelly, sugar, and liqueur in a small saucepan till just sticky and quickly brush tops of the strawberries with a thin coating of the glaze. Chill tart for about 1 hour and serve wedges topped with freshly whipped cream or vanilla ice cream.

Glazed Prune Tart

Serves 4 – 6

One of the most delightful havens in the south of England is Chewton Glen, a luxurious country house – hotel where the quality of the accommodations is matched by the precision of the cooking. Believe it or not, I first tasted this creamy tart one morning at breakfast and immediately asked owner Martin Skan for the recipe. Since, I have also made the tart with both plums and large grapes.

1 recipe of Pâte Brisée Sucrée
(p. 412)
1 lb. pitted prunes
2 cups heavy cream

3 eggs, beaten
⅓ cup sugar
½ cup apricot jam

On a lightly floured surface, roll the dough into a ⅛-inch-thick round. Using a 9- or 10-inch pie pan with a removable rim, line the bottom and sides with the pastry and trim the edges. Prick the shell with a fork and chill for 30 minutes.

Place the prunes in a saucepan, cover with water, and simmer for 10 minutes. Drain prunes, arrange them evenly in the pie shell, and place pan on a baking sheet.

Preheat oven to 350°.

Combine the cream, eggs, and sugar in a large mixing bowl, whisk lightly, and pour mixture over the prunes. Bake for 30 minutes, let tart cool to room temperature, remove rim, and transfer tart to a round serving platter. Heat the jam in a small saucepan, strain, and brush over the tart.

Apricot Tourte

Serves 10–12

1 cup dried apricots
½ cup sugar
1 egg, beaten
1 tsp. lemon juice
¼ tsp. grated lemon rind

½ recipe of Quick Puff Pastry
(p. 413)
½ cup chopped toasted almonds
1 beaten egg for glaze

Place the apricots in a medium saucepan and add water to cover. Bring to the boil, lower heat, cover, and simmer for about 30 minutes or till apricots are soft. Drain apricots, place in a food processor, reduce to a puree, and transfer to a mixing bowl. Add the sugar, egg, lemon juice, and grated lemon rind, blend thoroughly, and cool.

Divide the puff pastry in half, roll out one-half of the dough ⅛ inch thick on a lightly floured surface, cut out a circle 10 inches in diameter, and place circle on a well-buttered baking sheet. Roll out the other half ⅛ inch thick and cut out a circle 11 inches in diameter.

Sprinkle the nuts over the 10-inch circle and mound the apricot filling in the center, leaving a 1½-inch border. Moisten outer edge of the base with water, cover with the 11-inch circle of pastry, press down edges all around, and crimp pastry at 2-inch intervals. With a paring knife, cut a small circle in the center of the pastry cover, then cut 10 curving lines from the circle to outer edges. Chill for 1 hour.

Preheat oven to 425°.

Brush tourte all over with the egg glaze and bake for 30 minutes. Reduce heat to 375° and continue baking for 20 minutes longer or till tourte is golden brown.

Serve hot or at room temperature with vanilla ice cream.

Huguenot Torte

This interesting confection reflects the strong Huguenot heritage of Charleston, South Carolina, and is still one of the most respected desserts in that historic town's finest homes.

¼ cup all-purpose flour
2½ tsp. baking powder
¼ tsp. salt
2 eggs
1½ cups sugar
½ tsp. vanilla

1 cup finely chopped pecans
1 cup peeled and finely chopped
   apples
1 cup heavy cream
1 Tb. sherry

Grease the bottom and sides of an 8×12-inch baking dish and set aside. Preheat oven to 350°.

Sift the flour, baking powder, and salt together into a large mixing bowl. In another bowl, whisk the eggs, sugar, and vanilla till frothy, add to the dry mixture, and blend thoroughly.

Gently fold the pecans and apples into the mixture with a rubber spatula, scrape mixture into the prepared baking dish, and bake for 35 minutes. Let cool.

In a bowl, beat the cream and sherry till stiff, spread cream mixture evenly over top of the torte, and serve cut into squares.

Southern Pecan Pie

Serves 6

This is the recipe I sent when a reader in Devon, England, wrote that he was in possession of two pounds of American pecans, had never tasted what friends had told him was Southern pecan pie, and could not find a single recipe in the British Isles. If he has indeed mastered this classic, I wonder whether or not he ever substituted treacle for the corn syrup — which I should think would make a splendid pie!

1 baked shell of Basic Pie Pastry
(p. 411)
1½ cups shelled pecans
3 eggs
1½ cups dark corn syrup or light
molasses

1 tsp. vanilla
3 Tb. melted butter
¼ tsp. salt

*P*reheat oven to 425°.
Sprinkle the pecans evenly over the bottom of the prepared pie shell.

In a large mixing bowl, beat the eggs well with a whisk. Gradually pour in the syrup, beating constantly till the eggs and syrup are blended thoroughly. Add the vanilla, melted butter, and salt, and continue beating till mixture is smooth and silky.

Pour mixture over the pecans, place pie in the oven, and bake for 10 minutes. Reduce heat to 325° and continue baking for about 30 minutes or till filling is just firm.

Serve the pie warm or at room temperature topped with freshly whipped cream or vanilla ice cream.

Sweet Potato Pecan Pie

We at *Town & Country* were among the first to "discover" the Cajun chef Paul Prudhomme when he was heading the kitchen at Commander's Palace in New Orleans, and the second I tasted this remarkable variation of pecan pie, I knew this man had a very special talent.

3 medium sweet potatoes, cooked
    and mashed
¼ cup brown sugar
2 Tb. sugar
1 Tb. butter
1 Tb. vanilla
1 egg, beaten
1 Tb. heavy cream
¼ tsp. cinnamon
Pinch each of nutmeg and allspice
1 recipe of Basic Pie Pastry
    (p. 411)

½ cup chopped pecans
¾ cup sugar
2 eggs
¾ cup dark corn syrup
1 Tb. butter, melted
Salt
Cinnamon
2 tsp. vanilla
Whipped cream

Preheat oven to 300°.

In a large mixing bowl, combine the potatoes, brown sugar, 2 tablespoons sugar, butter, 1 tablespoon vanilla, 1 egg, cream, ¼ teaspoon cinnamon, and nutmeg and allspice, and blend with an electric mixer till smooth.

On a lightly floured surface, roll pastry out ⅛ inch thick, fit into a 9-inch pie pan, trim the edges, and crimp edges with fingers. Spoon the sweet potato mixture into the pie shell and sprinkle on the chopped pecans.

In another large mixing bowl, combine the ¾ cup sugar, 2 eggs, corn syrup, melted butter, salt and cinnamon to taste, and 2 teaspoons vanilla, blend well, and pour mixture over the pecans. Bake for 1½ hours, cool pie, and serve topped with fresh whipped cream.

Greek Walnut Pie

I learned this simple, updated rendition of *baklava* from a talented Greek cook in Kansas City, Susanne Vantzos, and have found it always to be a big hit on any buffet table.

10 frozen phyllo *leaves, defrosted and kept covered with a damp towel*
½ cup honey
¼ cup sugar
1 Tb. flour
1 Tb. melted butter

2 eggs, beaten
1 tsp. vanilla
½ tsp. ground cinnamon
¼ tsp. salt
1½ cups chopped walnuts
8 Tb. (1 stick) melted butter
2 Tb. honey

*L*ine a 9-inch pie plate with 4 of the *phyllo* leaves, trimming or tucking under the overhanging edges.

In a large mixing bowl, combine all remaining ingredients except the ½ cup melted butter and the 2 tablespoons honey, mix till blended thoroughly, and pour mixture into the lined pie plate.

Preheat oven to 300°.

Lay 1 of the remaining *phyllo* leaves on a working surface, brush with melted butter, roll lengthwise into a rope. Roll rope into a spiral and place in the center of the pie filling. Repeat with remaining leaves, arranging ropes in concentric circles around the first spiral up to the edge of the pie. Bake for 1 hour.

Increase oven heat to broil.

Remove pie from the oven, brush the top with butter and the 2 tablespoons of honey, and broil 4 inches from the heat for 1 minute. Let cool and, to serve, cut into wedges.

Tarte Froide au Chocolat
(Chilled French Chocolate Pie)

Serves 6

Most people like rich, heavy chocolate cakes and pies. I don't, so I satisfy my occasional craving for chocolate with this light, fluffy confection prepared in the French manner.

2 egg whites
Pinch of salt
Pinch of cream of tartar
½ cup sugar
½ cup finely chopped walnuts or
   hazelnuts

½ tsp. vanilla
¼ lb. sweet baking chocolate
3 Tb. water
1 Tb. Cognac
1 cup heavy cream
¼ cup shaved chocolate for garnish

Preheat oven to 300°.
   Combine the egg whites, salt, and cream of tartar in a large mixing bowl and beat with a whisk or electric mixer till foamy. Add the sugar 2 tablespoons at a time, beating after each addition, and continue beating till whites form stiff peaks.

Fold nuts and vanilla into egg whites, then spoon mixture into a lightly greased 8- or 9-inch pie plate. Form a nestlike indention in the mixture, building sides of nest up ½ inch above edges of the plate but not over the rim. Bake for 50 minutes and cool the shell.

Combine the chocolate and water in a saucepan over low heat, stir till chocolate melts, and cool. Add the Cognac and stir.

Pour the cream into a mixing bowl, whip to a soft consistency, and fold chocolate mixture into whipped cream. Pile into the meringue shell, chill for 2 hours, and serve garnished with shaved chocolate on top.

Yogurt Pie

Serves 8–10

Long before most Americans even knew what yogurt was, my friend and mentor Pearl Byrd Foster had already created numerous dishes using the cultured milk (she even made her own yogurt!). This light velvety pie was one of the first recipes she gave me and remains one of my favorite desserts.

2 cups finely crumbled graham crackers	½ lb. Neufchâtel cheese
4 Tb. (½ stick) butter, softened	½ lb. cream cheese
¼ cup sugar	1 tsp. vanilla
¾ Tb. unflavored gelatin	1 tsp. molasses
2 egg yolks, beaten into ¼ cup milk	1 Tb. honey
	2 cups plain yogurt

*P*reheat oven to 375°.

Combine the cracker crumbs, butter, and sugar in a mixing bowl, blend well, and reserve ½ cup of the mixture. Press the remaining mixture firmly against the bottom and sides of a 10-inch pie pan, bake for 10 minutes, and let cool.

Let gelatin soften momentarily in ¼ cup of cold water, then dissolve, stirring, in the top of a double boiler over slowly boiling water. Add the egg yolk mixture and continue cooking over the boiling water, stirring, till mixture coats a spoon. Remove from the heat and let cool.

Combine the two cheeses, vanilla, molasses, and honey in a large mixing bowl and cream with an electric mixer. Add 1 cup of the yogurt and continue to cream till smooth.

Pour the cooled gelatin mixture over the cheese mixture, stirring steadily. Add the second cup of yogurt, mix well, and pour mixture into the prepared pie shell. Sprinkle the top with the reserved crumb mixture and chill pie for 1 hour before serving.

Praline Ice Cream Pie

Serves 6 – 8

½ cup brown sugar
½ cup whipping cream
2 Tb. butter
1 cup chopped pecans
1½ tsp. vanilla
1½ qts. vanilla ice cream

1 baked 9-inch Basic Pie Pastry
  shell (p. 411)
3 egg whites
¼ tsp. cream of tartar
⅓ cup sugar
Rum Sauce (p. 552)

*H*eat and stir the brown sugar in a medium skillet till sugar just begins to melt (10 – 12 minutes). Gradually blend in the cream, cook for 2 – 3 minutes or till smooth, and remove from heat. Stir in the butter, pecans, and 1 teaspoon of the vanilla, and let cool.

Place ice cream in a large mixing bowl, stir just to soften, and quickly fold in the praline mixture. Turn mixture into the baked pastry shell and freeze.

Preheat oven to 475°.

Just before serving, place egg whites, the remaining vanilla, and the cream of tartar in a mixing bowl and beat till whites form stiff peaks. Gradually add the sugar, beating into the stiff whites. Spread the meringue on top of the ice cream, sealing to the edges. Place pie in the oven, bake for 4 minutes or till lightly browned, and serve with the rum sauce.

Strawberry-Rhubarb Pie

Fresh sweet strawberries combined with tart rhubarb makes for an exciting culinary marriage when warm weather arrives, and this example, served at Texarkana in New York, is especially luscious when it is cooled and served with freshly whipped cream.

1 pt. fresh strawberries	1 recipe of Basic Pie Pastry
8 stalks (about 1 lb.) fresh rhubarb	(p. 411)
1¼ cups sugar	1 Tb. bread crumbs
Pinch of salt	4 Tb. heavy cream
3 Tb. instant tapioca	2 Tb. butter
1 tsp. grated orange rind	½ cup whipped cream

Wash and drain the strawberries and rhubarb. Stem the strawberries, slice them in half, and place in a mixing bowl. Remove and discard the bottoms and leaves of the rhubarb, slice rhubarb ¼ inch thick, and add to the strawberries. Add ¼ cup of the sugar and the salt, mix lightly, let mixture stand for 10 minutes, and drain.

In another bowl, combine the remaining sugar, the tapioca, and orange rind, and toss lightly.

Roll out enough dough to fit a 9-inch pie plate, line plate with dough, and chill for 10 minutes. Cut remaining dough into strips for lattice top. When pie shell is chilled, dust the bottom with the bread crumbs, flute the edges of the shell, and brush edges with one-half of the cream.

Preheat oven to 400°.

Toss the drained strawberry-rhubarb mixture with the tapioca mixture, spoon into the prepared pie shell, and dot the top with the butter. Brush the pastry strips with remaining cream, weave strips over the top of pie, and cover the rim of crust with aluminum foil to prevent scorching. Bake the pie for 50 minutes, remove foil, and bake for 10–15 minutes longer or till pastry is golden brown.

Cool pie and serve each portion topped with a spoonful of whipped cream.

Strawberry-Peach Cobbler

Serves 6–8

2 lbs. fresh peaches, peeled, pitted,
    and cut into ½-inch slices
    (about 4 cups)
4 cups fresh strawberries, sliced in
    half
1 cup sugar
2 cups all-purpose flour

1 Tb. baking powder
2 tsp. sugar
1 tsp. salt
¼ cup vegetable shortening
1 cup heavy cream
2 Tb. butter
Vanilla ice cream

Combine the peaches, strawberries, and 1 cup of sugar in a mixing bowl, toss, and set aside.

Sift the flour, baking powder, 2 tsp. sugar, and salt together into another mixing bowl, add the shortening, and mix with a pastry cutter till well blended. Gradually add the cream, stirring with a wooden spoon till dough forms a ball.

Preheat oven to 400°.

Place the dough on a lightly floured surface, roll out ¼ inch thick, and trim edges to form a 12-inch circle. Crimp edges of the shell.

Spoon the fruit mixture into a 10-cup shallow baking dish 12 inches in diameter, dot filling with the butter, fit circle of dough over the filling so that the edges of the dough come just to the edge of the dish, and bake for 30 minutes or till pastry is golden brown.

Let the cobbler cool for about 15 minutes and serve in deep bowls topped with a spoonful of vanilla ice cream.

Cranberry-Apple Cobbler

Serves 4 – 6

This is a different approach to the traditional American cobbler (see Strawberry-Peach Cobbler, p. 492) in that the filling is topped with a loose batter instead of firm, rolled-out pastry. You might try the dish also made with a combination of blackberries and apples or raspberries and sliced papaya.

3½ cups fresh cranberries, stems carefully removed
1 cup cranberry juice
2 small apples
1 Tb. finely chopped orange rind
1 cup all-purpose flour
2 tsp. baking powder

1 cup sugar
2 eggs, beaten
1 cup milk
1 tsp. vanilla
1 tsp. grated lemon rind
Thick whipped cream or vanilla ice cream

Combine the cranberries and cranberry juice in a saucepan, bring to the boil, lower heat, and simmer for 15 minutes. Meanwhile, peel, core, and cut apples into ½-inch-thick slices (about 2 cups). Add the apples and orange rind, return heat to the simmer, and continue cooking for about 10 minutes.

Meanwhile, sift the flour and baking powder together into a mixing bowl, add the sugar, eggs, milk, vanilla, and lemon rind, and mix with a wooden spoon till well blended, adding a little more flour if necessary to produce a loose but not wet batter.

Pour cranberry and apple mixture into a 2-quart baking dish, scrape the batter evenly over the top, and bake for 1 hour or till top is golden brown.

Serve hot or at room temperature with vanilla ice cream or thick whipped cream.

Lemon Buttermilk Cake

Serves 8 – 10

THE CAKE:

4 eggs

2 cups sugar

1 cup vegetable shortening, room
   temperature

1 cup buttermilk

3 cups all-purpose flour, sifted

2 Tb. lemon extract

½ tsp. baking powder

½ tsp. baking soda

½ tsp. salt

THE ICING:

5 Tb. orange juice

5 Tb. lemon juice

2½ cups confectioners' sugar

½ tsp. salt

Preheat oven to 325°.
   In a large mixing bowl, combine the eggs, sugar, shortening, and buttermilk, and beat with an electric mixer till frothy. Add the flour 1 cup at a time, beating constantly. Add the lemon extract, baking powder, baking soda, and salt, and continue beating till well blended.

Scrape the mixture into a 10×5-inch lightly greased and floured tube pan and bake for 1 hour or till golden brown.

Meanwhile, combine the ingredients for the icing in another mixing bowl and beat with the electric mixer till well blended and smooth.

Loosen the edges of the hot cake, spread icing over the top, and return to the oven for 3 minutes. Let cool and invert on a large plate to serve.

Dutch Honey Cake

Serves 8 – 10

This cake should be made at least two days in advance to allow flavors to mellow.

1 envelope active dry yeast	2 cups all-purpose flour
2½ tsp. lukewarm milk	1 tsp. ground cinnamon
Pinch of sugar	½ tsp. mace
6 eggs, separated	¼ tsp. ground ginger
1⅓ cups honey	¼ tsp. salt
⅓ cup cool strong-brewed coffee	¾ cup ground almonds
½ tsp. vanilla	Confectioners' sugar

Combine yeast, milk, and sugar in a small bowl and proof for 10 minutes.

In a large mixing bowl, combine the egg yolks, honey, coffee, and vanilla, mix well, and gradually add the flour sifted with the cinnamon, mace, ginger, and salt. Add the yeast mixture and ground almonds, and mix to blend well.

In another bowl, beat the egg whites till stiff, fold one-quarter into the batter, then pour mixture onto the remaining whites. Fold mixture thoroughly but gently till there are no traces of white.

Turn batter out into a lightly buttered and floured 9×9-inch cake pan and let rise in a warm area for about 30 minutes.

Preheat oven to 350°.

Bake cake for 30 – 35 minutes, let cool in pan for 10 minutes, and turn out onto a rack to cool completely. Wrap cake in plastic wrap and store in a cool area for at least 2 days before serving. When ready to serve, sprinkle the top with confectioners' sugar.

Peanut Butter Pound Cake

Serves 12

My shameless love of fresh caviar is equaled only by my shameless love of peanut butter, and I make no bones about it. When, therefore, we ran a rather unorthodox piece in *Town & Country* on peanut butter as "The Pâté of the People," I couldn't have been more enthusiastic that Abby Rand obtained Rosalynn Carter's recipe for this very serious pound cake.

1¼ cups (2½ sticks) butter,
   softened
2 cups sugar
6 eggs

½ cup smooth peanut butter
2 cups all-purpose flour
½ cup crushed roasted peanuts

Preheat oven to 350°.
   In a large mixing bowl, cream the butter with an electric mixer, add the sugar gradually, and beat till fluffy. Add the eggs one at a time, beating after each addition. Blend in the peanut butter, add the flour 1 cup at a time, and mix till well blended.
   Pour the batter into a lightly greased 10×5-inch loaf pan and bake for 15 minutes. Remove pan from the oven, sprinkle the crushed peanuts over the batter, and continue baking for 1 hour longer.
   Let cake cool and invert onto a platter to serve.

Coconut Pound Cake

Serves 10–12

1 cup (2 sticks) butter, softened
3 cups sugar
4 eggs
1 Tb. lemon extract
3 cups flour

½ tsp. baking powder
⅛ tsp. salt
1 cup milk
1 cup grated fresh coconut

Preheat oven to 325°.

In a large mixing bowl, cream the butter and sugar with an electric mixer, add eggs and lemon extract, and continue beating till well blended.

Sift the flour, baking powder, and salt together into a bowl and add alternately with the milk to the sugar-butter mixture, beating constantly with mixer.

Stir in the coconut, pour mixture into a 10-inch tube pan, and bake for about 1 hour or till a straw inserted in the center comes out clean.

Chocolate Mousse Cake with Rum

Serves 8 – 10

This is a delicately rich, unbaked cake that is simple to prepare but must be refrigerated for at least 24 hours before serving. Presented in a thin pool of *crème anglaise,* it makes a very elegant dessert.

5 oz. sweet chocolate, broken up	*¾ cup confectioners' sugar*
5 oz. bittersweet chocolate, broken up	*6 eggs, separated*
	3 Tb. dark rum
1 cup (2 sticks) butter, softened	*Crème Anglaise (p. 551)*

Melt the two kinds of chocolate in the top of a double boiler over simmering water, add the butter, and stir till completely blended. Add ½ cup of the sugar and mix well. Add the egg yolks and rum, stir till well blended, and remove pan from the heat.

In a mixing bowl, beat the egg whites with an electric mixer till almost stiff, add the remaining sugar, and continue beating till whites are stiff. Add half the egg whites to the chocolate mixture and fold in thoroughly but gently. Add remaining whites and fold in just to the point where the whites are well incorporated, taking care not to overmix.

Spoon the mixture into a medium springform loaf pan, smooth the top with a rubber spatula, cover with plastic wrap, and refrigerate for at least 24 hours.

To serve, spoon 2 tablespoons of *crème anglaise* on each small plate, unmold cake, and place thin slices of cake in the center of each plate.

Marjolaine Cake

Serves 8

Although I have modified the recipe a little, this is basically the same cake served in Fournou's Ovens at my beloved Stanford Court Hotel in San Francisco. The cake is not easy to make (just whisking the egg whites requires plenty of energy and courage!), but the results justify the effort.

1 lb. shelled almonds, blanched
   and skinned
10 oz. shelled hazelnuts
6 cups sugar
2 oz. cornstarch
20 egg whites
1 lb. semisweet chocolate

8 Tb. (1 stick) unsalted butter
2 cups heavy cream
2 cups whipped cream
1 Tb. confectioners' sugar
2 oz. finely grated semisweet
   chocolate

Preheat oven to 350°.
   Place the almonds and hazelnuts on separate baking sheets. Toast the almonds till browned, stirring frequently, then toast the hazelnuts till skins begin to loosen.
   Reduce oven to 200°.
   Rub hazelnuts in a cloth till skins come off. Mix nuts together, grind finely in a food processor, and set one-half of the mixture aside. Sift the other half with 1 cup of the sugar and cornstarch.
   Combine the egg whites and remaining sugar in a large copper or stainless-steel bowl, place over medium heat, and stir with a whisk till whites are warm. Whisk till egg whites form stiff peaks and gently fold in the sugar and cornstarch mixture.
   Using a pastry bag with a 1-inch open tip, tube out 4 strips, each 20 by 3 inches, on a greased baking sheet, place in oven and bake for 2 hours.
   Break the pound of chocolate into small bits, place in the top of a double boiler over boiling water, and melt. Add the butter in small pieces, stirring constantly, remove from heat, and cool slightly. Whip the heavy cream till stiff, fold into the chocolate, stir till smooth, and chill.
   Cover one of the four meringue strips with a layer of chocolate cream, place a second layer of meringue on top, and spread with reserved nuts and the whipped cream. Cover with a third layer of meringue, another layer of chocolate cream, then the last strip of meringue. Sprinkle the top

of the cake with confectioners' sugar and grated chocolate, smooth the remaining chocolate cream over the sides, and decorate with the remaining chocolate flakes.

Slice cake very carefully with a thin-bladed knife dipped in warm water.

Chocolate-Chestnut Log

Serves at least 12

1 Tb. butter softened
9 eggs
½ cup sugar
2 Tb. unsweetened cocoa
6 Tb. flour
½ Tb. unflavored gelatin

1 cup canned chestnut puree
1 cup heavy cream
2 Tb. rum
4 oz. bittersweet chocolate in block
   or bar form

Preheat oven to 325°.
Line an 11½×15½-inch baking pan with foil and grease foil with the softened butter.

Separate 6 of the eggs, beat the yolks with 4 tablespoons of the sugar, and set aside. Place the whites in a large bowl with a pinch of salt and beat till stiff. Add 2 tablespoons of the sugar, beat till stiff and glossy, add the egg yolks, and mix gently. Fold in the cocoa, then the flour, transfer the mixture to the prepared pan, and bake for 25 minutes.

Lift foil and cake out of the pan, transfer to a lightly floured clean towel, roll up cake and foil from the long side, and set aside.

Break the remaining eggs into a double boiler, add remaining sugar, and stir over hot water till mixture is thick. Soften the gelatin in 2 table-spoons of warm water, add to the egg mixture, stir, remove from heat, and stir in the chestnut puree. Whip the cream and, when chestnut mixture is cool, fold in the whipped cream.

Unroll the cake, remove foil, and spread on the filling, reserving about one-third. Carefully reroll the cake, place on a long serving platter, sprinkle with the rum, and spread remaining filling on top and sides.

Prepare chocolate curls by carefully drawing a vegetable peeler across the broad flat surface of the chocolate. Sprinkle the curls generously over the top of the log.

To serve, slice log into equal rounds.

Sicilian Cassata

Here is one of the rare times I find a commercial sponge cake or pound cake perfectly acceptable to use in a dessert recipe.

1 sponge cake or pound cake, about 9×3 inches
1 lb. ricotta cheese
3 Tb. heavy cream
¼ cup sugar
3 Tb. Amaretto liqueur
2 oz. baking chocolate, coarsely chopped
¼ lb. glazed mixed fruit, coarsely chopped
12 oz. sweet chocolate, cut into pieces
¾ cup brewed black coffee
1 cup (2 sticks) unsalted butter, cut into small pieces
½ cup chopped nuts

Trim the cake of all crusts till surfaces are perfectly even, and cut lengthwise into ¾-inch layers.

Rub ricotta through a sieve into a small bowl and beat with an electric mixer till smooth. Still beating, add the cream, sugar, and Amaretto, then fold in the baking chocolate and all but 1 tablespoon of the glazed fruit.

Spread part of the mixture evenly on the bottom cake layer, place another layer on top, and continue mounting layers spread with mixture till cake is reassembled. Refrigerate for 2 hours or till cake is firm.

Combine the sweet chocolate and coffee in a saucepan and stir over moderate heat till mixture is smooth. Remove from the heat and gradually beat in butter piece by piece till frosting is smooth. Chill to spreading consistency and frost cake all over, making decorative swirls on the top and sides. Decorate the top with remaining glazed fruit and the chopped nuts.

Lindy's Original Cheesecake

No matter what you might have read in newspapers, food magazines, and other cookbooks about the quintessential cheesecake created at the old Lindy's in New York, I say with no modesty that I am one of the few enthusiasts anywhere who possesses the original, genuine, inalterable recipe, obtained decades ago at the restaurant when my father palmed our trustworthy waiter, Sammy, a crisp ten-spot. It is smooth, silky, rich, and sinful.

THE PASTRY:

1 cup all-purpose flour	Dash of vanilla
¼ cup sugar	1 egg yolk
1 tsp. grated lemon rind	8 Tb. (1 stick) butter, softened

THE FILLING:

2½ lbs. cream cheese, room temperature	1½ tsp. grated orange rind
1¾ cups sugar	¼ tsp. vanilla
3 Tb. all-purpose flour	5 eggs plus 2 egg yolks
1½ tsp. grated lemon rind	¼ cup heavy cream

To make the pastry, combine the flour, sugar, lemon rind, and vanilla in a large mixing bowl. Make a well in the center, add the egg yolk and butter, and mix with your hands till well blended, adding a little cold water if necessary to make a workable dough. Wrap the dough in plastic wrap and chill for 1 hour.

For the filling, cream the cheese in another large mixing bowl with an electric mixer, add the sugar, flour, lemon and orange rinds, and vanilla, and beat well. Add the eggs and egg yolks one at a time, beating lightly after each addition. Add the heavy cream, beat lightly, and set mixture aside.

Preheat oven to 400°.

Butter the base and sides of a 9-inch springform pan and remove the top from the pan. Roll out about one-third of the dough ⅛ inch thick, fit it over the bottom of the pan, and trim by running a rolling pin over the edges. Bake for 15 minutes or till golden, and let cool.

Increase oven heat to 550°.

Place the top of the pan over the base. Roll the remaining dough ⅛ inch thick, cut in strips to fit almost to the top of the sides of the pan, and press so that the strips line the sides completely. Fill the pan with the cheese mixture, bake for 10 minutes, reduce heat to 200°, and continue baking for 1 hour.

To serve, remove the top of the pan very carefully and cut the cake into 12 wedges.

Dresden Stollen

Yield: 2 loaves

When I published this recipe in the magazine, readers responded about how much they loved the loaves but wondered if there were not an easier way to produce them. Sorry, but if there is a quick, easy method, I don't know about it. Not, that is, if you're looking for authentic *stollen* like the ones found in German pastry shops.

1 cup mixed glazed fruit, cut into
   small dice
½ cup seedless raisins
½ cup dried currants
½ cup candied cherries, halved
½ cup candied citrus peel
½ cup rum
¼ cup lukewarm water
2 envelopes active dry yeast
Pinch of sugar
1 cup milk
5½ cups all-purpose flour

2 eggs, lightly beaten
¾ cup (1½ sticks) unsalted
   butter, cut into pieces and
   softened
¾ cup sugar
½ tsp. salt
½ tsp. almond extract
1 cup toasted slivered almonds
4 Tb. (½ stick) melted unsalted
   butter
Confectioners' sugar

*I*n a large bowl, combine the glazed fruit, raisins, currants, cherries, and citrus peel, add the rum, toss well, and let soak for at least 1 hour. Drain fruit, set aside, and reserve the rum.

Combine the water, yeast, and sugar in a small bowl and let proof for 10 minutes.

Scald the milk in a saucepan, allow to cool, and stir into yeast mixture. In a large mixing bowl, combine the yeast mixture with 2 cups of the flour, place in a warm area, and let dough rise for about 1½ hours or till doubled in bulk.

Punch dough down, add the eggs, butter, one-half of the sugar, salt, almond extract, reserved rum, and 2 more cups of the flour, and mix with a wooden spoon till well blended. Turn dough out onto a lightly floured surface and gradually knead in 1 more cup flour till dough is smooth and elastic.

Dust macerated fruit with remaining flour, work both the fruit and slivered almonds into the dough, place dough in a lightly buttered bowl, turn to coat the sides evenly, and let rise for another 1½ hours.

Punch dough down and divide into 2 equal portions. Roll out each portion into a rectangle about 12 inches long, 8 inches wide, and ½ inch thick and brush each with melted butter. Sprinkle each rectangle with remaining sugar and fold each over on itself lengthwise, pressing edges together. Place loaves on a buttered baking sheet and let rise in a warm area for about 1 hour.

Preheat oven to 375°.

Brush loaves again with melted butter and bake for about 45 minutes or till golden brown. Let cool on a rack, brush once more with melted butter, and dust lightly with confectioners' sugar.

Missy's White Fruit Cake

Yield: 1 large 5- to 6-lb. cake
and 2 2½-lb. loaf cakes

I've eaten fruit cakes the world over but have yet to find one that equals the boozy beauties my mother still bakes every Christmas and generously passes out to friends. I like to use Bourbon in place of rum in my cake, but whichever spirit you choose, remember to let the cake "cure" for at least 3 weeks before serving. I have one of these fruit cakes that's been in the refrigerator for well over a year, and every month it just gets better.

2 cups (4 sticks) butter, room temperature	2 tsp. vanilla
3 cups sugar	2 tsp. almond extract
14 eggs	2 tsp. lemon extract
5 cups flour	2½ lbs. crystallized pineapple
2 tsp. baking powder	2½ lbs. crystallized cherries
1½ cups rum or Bourbon	2¼ lbs. chopped nuts

In a large mixing bowl, cream the butter and sugar with an electric mixer and add the eggs one at a time, mixing constantly. Sift 3 cups of the flour and the baking powder into the mixture and blend thoroughly with the mixer. Add 1 cup of the rum, the vanilla, and almond and lemon extracts, and blend thoroughly.

Coarsely chop the pineapple and all but about 8 of the cherries, mix the chopped fruit and the nuts with the remaining flour, and fold well into the butter mixture.

Preheat oven to 250° and place a small pan of water in the bottom of the oven.

Spoon the batter into 1 large 10×4-inch tube cake pan and 2 small 8×4½×2½-inch loaf pans, arrange the reserved cherries on tops, and bake for 3 hours or till a straw inserted in centers comes out clean.

Pour remaining rum over top of cakes and let cakes cool in the pans. Wrap cakes securely in cheesecloth soaked in rum and store in tightly closed tins for at least 3 weeks before serving.

Maple Mousse with Rum Sauce

Serves 10

I've always taken pride in the fact that *Town & Country* was championing the cause of American cookery long before the "New American Cuisine" became so fashionable. This recipe appeared in an article I did in 1976 entitled "American Cuisine Comes of Age" where we illustrated Julia Child holding a chicken drumstick and Colonel Sanders.

1 envelope plus 2 tsp. unflavored gelatin	*½ cup brown sugar*
½ cup warm water	*2 cups heavy cream, chilled*
1 cup maple syrup	*Double recipe of Rum Sauce*
4 eggs, separated	*(p. 552)*

Sprinkle the gelatin into the water and stir till dissolved and clear. Combine the gelatin mixture and the maple syrup in a bowl and stir till well blended.

In a saucepan, beat the egg yolks thoroughly, add the maple syrup mixture, and cook over moderate heat, stirring constantly, till mixture coats a spoon heavily, taking care never to let boil. Remove from heat, stir in the brown sugar, transfer mixture to a large bowl, and let cool to room temperature.

In one bowl, beat the egg whites till they form stiff peaks. In another bowl, beat the cream till it holds its shape softly. With a rubber spatula, fold the cream gently but thoroughly into the maple mixture, then fold in the egg whites till white no longer shows.

Rinse a 1½-quart mold in cold water, pour the mousse mixture into the mold, and chill in the refrigerator for at least 4 hours or till firm.

To serve, spoon mousse into the middle of chilled dessert plates and spoon rum sauce around the sides of each portion.

Caramelized Chestnut Flan

¾ lb. chestnuts	4 eggs
1 cup sugar	2 cups milk
¼ cup water	1 Tb. rum

Shell and peel the chestnuts, place in a saucepan with enough water to cover, and boil for 35 minutes. Drain chestnuts and let cool.

In a heavy saucepan, beat one-half of the sugar in the water till sugar dissolves, bring to the boil, and cook down to a dark caramel. Immediately pour caramel into a 5-cup cake pan, tilt pan to coat the bottom and sides evenly with a thin layer of caramel, and set aside to cool.

Preheat oven to 350°.

Chop the chestnuts finely.

Break the eggs into a large mixing bowl, add the remaining sugar, and beat well with an electric mixer. Add the milk and rum, beat well, pour mixture into the prepared pan, and place pan in a shallow baking pan with enough water to come halfway up the sides of the cake pan. On top of the stove, bring water to the boil, transfer both vessels to the oven, and bake for 10 minutes or till mixture is just thickened.

Carefully remove baking pan from oven, distribute chopped chestnuts evenly over the mixture, and continue baking for 25 minutes or till set. Remove pan from water bath.

To serve flan, unmold on a serving platter.

QE 2 Plum Pudding

Yield: 4 puddings

This sinfully rich, elegant, traditional plum pudding, which head chef John Bainbridge taught me how to prepare during one of my many crossings aboard the *QE 2,* is, without doubt, the best I've ever put in my mouth. The puddings just get better and better if stored several months in the refrigerator and may be frozen indefinitely. And if you really want these puddings to taste authentic, be sure to flame them with nothing less than the 151-proof rum.

4 cups white bread crumbs
2 tsp. salt
2 tsp. ground allspice
2 tsp. ground ginger
2 tsp. ground nutmeg
2 cups all-purpose flour
3 cups brown sugar
¾ lb. suet, finely chopped
3 cups seedless raisins
2 cups currants
½ cup mixed candied peel,
  roughly chopped

1 cup blanched slivered almonds
1 cooking apple, peeled, cored, and
  coarsely chopped
¾ cup grated carrots
2 Tb. grated orange rind
6 eggs, beaten
1 cup dark rum
¼ cup milk
¼ cup lemon juice
½ cup 151-proof rum for flaming
Hard Sauce (p. 550)

*I*n a large mixing bowl, combine the bread crumbs, salt, allspice, ginger, nutmeg, flour, brown sugar, and suet, and mix with your hands to blend thoroughly. Add the raisins, currants, candied peel, almonds, apple, carrots, and orange rind, tossing all ingredients about with your hands till well blended.

In another bowl, add the dark rum, milk, and lemon juice to the beaten eggs, pour over the fruit mixture, and knead vigorously till ingredients are thoroughly blended. Cover with a damp towel and let stand overnight.

When ready to cook, divide the mixture into 4 buttered 1-quart pudding molds and secure foil tightly on top of each. Place the molds in a large, heavy pot, add enough water to come about halfway up the sides, and bring water to the boil. Lower heat to a light simmer, cover, and steam the puddings for 8 hours, adding more water when necessary.

Allow puddings to cool at room temperature overnight, wrap tightly in fresh foil, and age for at least one month in the refrigerator.

To serve one pudding, turn out on a pewter or silver plate, warm the 151-proof rum in a saucepan, pour on the plate around pudding, ignite, and ladle flaming rum over the pudding. Decorate the plate with red-berried holly and serve pudding with hard sauce on the side.

Lemon Soufflé

Serves 4

3 lemons
1 cup sugar
4 eggs, separated

1½ oz. all-purpose flour, sifted
2 cups milk
1 tsp. vanilla

Squeeze juice from the lemons into a small bowl and remove seeds. Scrape the lemon rinds of all leftover flesh, discard flesh, and mince rind very finely. Combine the lemon juice, minced peels, and 2 tablespoons of the sugar in a saucepan and bring to the boil. Reduce heat to moderate, stir, cook till reduced to a syrup, and set aside.

Preheat oven to 400°.

In a bowl, beat the egg yolks with the remaining sugar and stir in the flour. Heat the milk and vanilla in a saucepan, add the yolk mixture just before milk comes to the boil, and cook for 1 minute, stirring constantly. When mixture thickens, remove pan from the heat and stir in the syrup.

Beat the egg whites till stiff and fold into the base mixture. Pour the mixture into a buttered medium soufflé dish and bake for 15 minutes.

Serve the soufflé immediately.

Soufflé Glacé aux Framboises

(Frozen Raspberry Soufflé)

Serves 4–6

This is one of the first of André Soltner's desserts I tasted years ago at Lutèce in New York and one of the most popular recipes I ever published in *Town & Country*. "Normally I'm altering recipes constantly," says Soltner, "but this one has remained the same for close to twenty years."

ALMOND PASTE:

5 egg whites
1 cup sugar

1½ cups almond flour (available
   in specialty food shops)

FILLING:

1 lb. sugar
1 cup water
10 egg whites
1½ pts. fresh or defrosted frozen
   raspberries

Juice of 2 lemons
1 pt. whipped cream

*L*ine the bottom and sides of an 8-inch soufflé dish with wax paper. Preheat oven to 200°.

To make the paste, beat the 5 egg whites till stiff and blend in the sugar and almond flour with a rubber spatula. Spread the paste ¼ inch thick on a piece of wax paper on a baking sheet, bake for about 1½ hours, transfer paste to a rack, and let cool.

To make the filling, combine the sugar and water in a saucepan, bring to a low boil, and cook till temperature reaches 260° on a candy thermometer. Beat the 10 egg whites till stiff and slowly pour the cooked syrup over them while continuing to beat till cold.

Puree the raspberries in a blender or food processor and gradually add about 1 pint of puree to the syrup mixture along with the lemon juice, reserving remaining puree for serving. Fold in the whipped cream.

Cut almond paste into 8-inch circles and fit a circle on bottom of prepared soufflé dish. Alternate layers of almond paste and raspberry mixture in the dish, ending up with paste on top, and place in the freezer for at least 3 hours. To serve, unmold on a plate, remove wax paper, cut the soufflé into wedges, and serve each portion surrounded by a little of the remaining raspberry puree.

Prune and Banana Soufflé

Serves 6

When my friend and colleague Marina Polvay in Miami told me about this "healthy" dessert soufflé she had created as a pick-me-up for sports enthusiasts, I must say my eyebrow raised. Then I tested, tasted, and raved with delight.

1 cup fine bread crumbs	*5 egg whites*
12-oz. package of pitted prunes	*Pinch of cream of tartar*
1 cup Port	*⅔ cup light brown sugar*
2 Tb. light rum	*2 large bananas, mashed*

Butter well a 2-quart soufflé dish, sprinkle the bottom and sides with the bread crumbs, and set aside.

Chop the prunes well, place in a saucepan, add the Port, and simmer till the wine has cooked down and has been absorbed by the prunes. Remove pan from the heat, mash prunes with a wooden spoon, stir in the rum, and set aside.

Preheat oven to 350°.

In a large mixing bowl, beat the egg whites and cream of tartar with an electric mixer till soft peaks form, add the sugar, and continue beating till very stiff. Fold the mashed prunes and bananas into the egg whites, transfer the mixture to the prepared soufflé dish, and bake for 35 minutes.

Serve the soufflé hot or at room temperature.

Cognac Peach Fritters

Serves 4–6

You might also want to try these fritters with Bourbon or Scotch whisky. By no means substitute canned peaches for the fresh, and make sure the peaches are not fully ripe.

½ cup milk
¼ cup half-and-half
2 eggs, separated
1 Tb. melted butter
1 tsp. vanilla
2 oz. Cognac
½ cup all-purpose flour, sifted

¼ tsp. salt
1 Tb. sugar
1 Tb. sifted brown sugar
½ tsp. ground cinnamon
5 or 6 large firm fresh peaches
Vegetable oil for frying
Powdered sugar

*I*n a large mixing bowl, combine the milk, cream, egg yolks, butter, vanilla, and Cognac, and whisk till well blended. Add the flour, salt, and sugar, and blend well. Cover batter and chill for 2–3 hours.

In a small bowl, combine the brown sugar and cinnamon. Peel peaches, remove the stones very carefully, and cut each peach into quarters. Place in a bowl, add the brown sugar and cinnamon mixture, and toss.

Heat about 2 inches of oil to 360° in a deep-fat fryer or heavy saucepan. Meanwhile, beat the chilled batter, whisk the egg whites till stiff, and fold gently into the batter. Roll peach quarters in the batter and fry for 3–4 minutes in the oil, making sure not to crowd the pan with too many slices at a time. Drain on paper towels and sprinkle with powdered sugar.

Serve fritters hot or cold with ice cream or sherbet.

Chestnut Fritters

Serves 4

Ever since a blight devastated our great chestnut trees during the first part of this century, we've had to depend on some twenty million pounds of succulent European *Castanea sativa* to satisfy the demand during the holidays. Since the chestnut is unique as both a savory and a sweet, there's really no reason why Americans shouldn't exploit the nut's many possibilities as they continue to move full force in the development of a new national style of cooking. This delectable dish, for example, can be served with fruit preserves for breakfast or as a dessert.

1 cup flour	*1 egg yolk, beaten*
¼ tsp. salt	*2 Tb. heavy cream*
1 cup beer	*1 tsp. sugar*
2 tsp. vegetable oil	*¼ tsp. vanilla*
2 egg whites	*Vegetable oil for frying*
1 cup canned chestnut puree	*Confectioners' sugar*

Sift the flour into a bowl and add the salt. Stirring constantly, add the beer and oil in a slow stream. Strain batter into another bowl, cover with plastic wrap, and let stand for 3 hours (batter can stand overnight).

Stir the batter, beat the egg whites till stiff, and fold egg whites into the batter. In another bowl, combine the chestnut puree with one beaten egg yolk, the heavy cream, sugar, and vanilla, mix well, and shape into small ovals. Dip ovals into the batter and stack on a plate.

Heat about 2 cups of the oil in a deep-fryer or heavy saucepan to 375°, fry the ovals in batches till golden brown, and drain on a paper bag.

Sift confectioners' sugar over the fritters and serve as quickly as possible.

Mango Sorbet

Yield: About 1½ quarts

This simple sorbet can be made with almost any soft fruit—banana, papaya, cantaloupe, pear, etc. The sorbet can be finished in an ice-cream machine, but I much prefer the French method of allowing it to intensify in flavor by slowly hardening in the refrigerator freezer.

2 large mangoes, peeled and pitted
1 cup orange juice
1 Tb. lime juice
2 Tb. dark rum

⅛ tsp. ground cinnamon
1 cup sugar
1 cup water

Place the mangoes in a food processor, reduce to a puree, and scrape into a mixing bowl. Add the orange juice, lime juice, rum, and cinnamon, and stir till well blended.

Combine the sugar and water in a saucepan over high heat, stir constantly till sugar dissolves, and remove from heat just before syrup comes to the boil.

Add the syrup to the mango mixture and stir till well blended. Transfer mixture to a metal container, cover with plastic wrap, and place in the refrigerator freezer for 1 hour. Remove sorbet from the freezer, stir well again, and freeze for 2 hours longer or till firm.

Mexican Corn Custard Ice Cream

Yield: 1 quart

When my friend Marion Gorman was unable to find a recipe for this unusual ice cream she had tasted both in great Mexican homes and on the streets of Mexico City, she set about to re-create the dish according to her gustatory memories. The result is extraordinary, although I personally prefer even less nutmeg than the teaspoon included here.

4 cups fresh or defrosted frozen
  corn kernels
1 cup half-and-half
⅓ cup light honey
3 egg yolks

1 tsp. fresh lemon juice
1 tsp. vanilla
1 cup heavy cream
1 tsp. freshly grated nutmeg
⅛ tsp. ground cardamom

*B*ring 1 cup of water to the boil in a heavy saucepan, add the corn kernels, cover, and steam for 3–4 minutes or till just cooked. Drain corn at once and cool. Combine the corn and half-and-half in a food processor and puree till very smooth. Rub mixture through a fine wire sieve and set aside.

Heat the honey with 2 tablespoons of water in a small saucepan till mixture comes to the boil. In a mixing bowl, beat egg yolks with an electric mixer till thick and creamy and, while beating, very slowly add the hot honey. Continue to beat till mixture is cool. Still beating, add the lemon juice, vanilla, heavy cream, reserved corn mixture, nutmeg, and cardamom.

Pour the mixture into an ice-cream machine and process till firm. Transfer to refrigerator freezer and freeze till hard.

Espresso Ice Cream

Yield: About 1 quart

When I sampled this sublime concoction served at Bruce's restaurant in Wainscott, Long Island, I wasted no time asking if I could publish the recipe.

1 cup half-and-half	*4 egg yolks*
1 cup heavy cream	*1 cup superfine sugar*
¾ cup very finely ground espresso	*1 Tb. vanilla extract*
coffee	*Fresh mint leaves*

Combine the half-and-half, heavy cream, and espresso in a heavy saucepan, heat over moderate heat, set pan aside, and allow mixture to steep.

Meanwhile, combine the egg yolks and sugar in a mixing bowl and whisk till light and ribbony. Pour the espresso mixture through a fine strainer into the egg mixture and whisk till smooth. Transfer the mixture to the top of a double boiler over boiling water and stir till custard coats a spoon. Stir in the vanilla, transfer mixture to a bowl, cover with plastic wrap, and chill for at least 6 hours and preferably overnight.

Transfer mixture to an ice-cream freezer and freeze according to machine directions. Store in freezer of the refrigerator till ready to serve, and serve garnished with mint leaves.

Glace au Miel
(French Wild Honey Ice Cream)

Yield: 1½ quarts

If you've never prepared ice cream in the French manner (i.e., without an ice-cream machine), let this elegant example from the luxurious Château du Domaine St.-Martin in Vence serve as a starting point.

10 egg yolks	*4 cups milk, scalded*
1 cup wild honey	

*I*n a large mixing bowl, combine the egg yolks and honey, and beat with an electric mixer till mixture is thick and ribbons when the mixer is lifted up.

Add the milk in a stream, stirring with a wooden spoon. Transfer the custard to a heavy saucepan and cook over moderate heat, stirring constantly and never allowing to boil, till it coats the spoon.

Transfer custard to a metal bowl set in a larger bowl filled with cracked ice, let cool, then place in freezer of the refrigerator till it is just firm.

Chocolate Truffles

Yield: About 36 truffles

I have no idea where I found this recipe, but I do know it was in my files years before chocolate truffles became the rage of the *nouvelle cuisine*. I've been exposed to these delightful little conceits the world over during the last decade, but I've yet to sample any that equal these classics. Remember that the truffles are only as good as the chocolate used.

1¾ cups (10 oz.) semisweet   *⅓ cup heavy cream*
   chocolate, broken into pieces   *2 Tb. golden rum*
1 cup confectioners' sugar   *2 Tb. unsweetened cocoa*

*C*ombine the chocolate pieces with 2 tablespoons of water in the top of a double boiler and stir over boiling water till chocolate is melted.

Scrape chocolate into a mixing bowl, add the sugar, cream, and rum, stir till well blended, and beat with an electric mixer till smooth and light. Place a sheet of wax paper directly on the surface of the chocolate and refrigerate for about 1 hour.

Spread the cocoa on another sheet of wax paper, drop rounded teaspoons of chocolate mixture onto the cocoa, and roll with the palm of the hand into balls, covering completely with cocoa. Cover and store truffles in the refrigerator.

Basic Stocks, Sauces, and Dressings

Chicken Stock

Yield: About 2 quarts

Good chicken stock, which is indispensable to all forms of fine cookery, requires a flavorful old fowl that is simmered for at least 3 hours with the right vegetables and seasonings. Since so many dishes call for a strong stock, I simmer mine till the liquid is reduced by half and simply dilute it when a recipe calls for a lighter base. If you have room to freeze plenty of this stock, double or triple the recipe.

4- to 5-lb. fowl, neck and giblets
   included
4 qts. cold water
2 medium onions, cut in half
2 carrots, cut in half
2 celery ribs, broken in half
2 leeks, rinsed of all grit and
   chopped

2 tsp. salt
Herb bouquet (1 tsp. dried thyme,
   1 garlic clove, 4 cloves, 8
   peppercorns, 1 bay leaf, and 6
   sprigs parsley tied in cheesecloth)

Place the fowl, neck, and giblets in an 8- to 10-quart stockpot or large kettle and add the water. Bring liquid to the boil, reduce heat, simmer for 30 minutes, and skim off any scum.

Add the onions, carrots, celery, leeks, salt, and herb bouquet, and continue simmering stock for 3–3½ hours, adding more water if necessary to keep contents barely covered.

Strain stock through cheesecloth into a large bowl, let cool, chill (preferably overnight), and remove all fat from the top. (Remove meat from the fowl and reserve for chicken salad or hash.)

TO CLARIFY STOCK AND PRODUCE A DELICATE CONSOMMÉ:

After stock has been chilled and the fat removed, pour stock into a large saucepan or pot. Add 2 egg whites plus the shells, beat lightly, bring to the boil, and simmer for 15 minutes. Strain the broth through a double thickness of cheesecloth.

Beef Stock

Yield: About 2 quarts

4 lbs. beef bones, cut into 3-inch
  pieces
¼ cup all-purpose flour
3 carrots, sliced
3 medium onions, sliced
1 pig's foot or veal knuckle
2 tomatoes, chopped
2 leeks, rinsed of all grit and
  chopped
3 garlic cloves, chopped

2 celery ribs, chopped
1 turnip, chopped
1 tsp. dried thyme
8 sprigs parsley
1 bay leaf
4 cloves
8 peppercorns
4 qts. cold water
1 Tb. salt

*P*reheat oven to 450°.
    Place the beef bones and half the carrots and onions in a roasting pan, sprinkle with the flour, and brown in the oven for 30 minutes.

Transfer bones and vegetables to a 8- to 10-quart stockpot. Drain fat from roasting pan, deglaze pan with a little water, and pour juices into the stockpot. Add the pig's foot or veal knuckle, the remaining carrots and onions, and all other ingredients except the salt to stockpot. If necessary, add more water to cover by 3 inches and bring mixture to the boil. Reduce heat to simmer, skim off scum, cover partly, and simmer for 2 hours. Add the salt and simmer for 3 hours longer, adding more water if necessary.

Strain broth into a large bowl, cool, chill thoroughly (preferably over-night), and remove fat from the top.

To clarify stock and produce a delicate consommé, see recipe for Chicken Stock (p. 521).

Veal Stock

Yield: About 2 quarts

2 lbs. veal knuckles
4 qts. cold water
2 medium onions, cut in half
2 carrots, cut in half
2 celery ribs, broken in half
2 leeks, rinsed of all grit and
   chopped

2 tsp. salt
Herb bouquet (1 tsp. dried thyme,
   1 bay leaf, 8 peppercorns, and
   6 sprigs parsley wrapped in
   cheesecloth)
1 lb. chicken wings and/or giblets

Place knuckles in an 8- to 10-quart stockpot or large kettle and add the water. Bring liquid to the boil, reduce heat, simmer for 30 minutes, and skim off any scum.

Add the onions, carrots, celery, leeks, salt, and herb bouquet and continue simmering stock for 3 hours, adding more water if necessary to keep contents barely covered.

Add the chicken wings and continue to simmer for 1 hour longer, skimming any scum and adding water if necessary.

Strain stock through cheesecloth into a large bowl, let cool, chill (preferably overnight), and remove all fat from the top. (Reserve chicken wings for chicken salad.)

To clarify stock, see recipe for Chicken Stock (p. 521).

Fish Stock

Yield: 1 quart

2 Tb. butter
1 medium onion, sliced
1 carrot, sliced
2 celery ribs, chopped
Salt
2 cups dry white wine
3 cups water
2 tsp. lemon juice
2 lbs. washed lean fish bones
   (bass, scrod, cod, or flounder),
   tails, and heads

Celery leaves
8 sprigs parsley
1 tsp. dried chervil
1 bay leaf
3 cloves
6 peppercorns

Heat the butter in a large skillet, add the onion, carrot, and chopped celery, and sauté over moderate heat for 2 minutes. Add salt to taste.

Add the wine, water, and all other ingredients, bring liquid to the boil, reduce heat immediately, and simmer gently for no more than 30 minutes. Skim off scum and strain through a double thickness of cheesecloth.

Court Bouillon

Yield: About 1 quart

1 celery rib with leaves, cracked
6 sprigs parsley
1/4 tsp. dried thyme
1/4 tsp. fennel seeds
12 peppercorns

1 qt. water
1 cup dry white wine
1 medium onion, sliced
1 carrot, sliced
1 tsp. salt

Tie the celery, parsley, thyme, fennel seeds, and peppercorns in cheesecloth to make an herb bouquet.

Pour the water and wine into a large enameled or stainless-steel saucepan and add the herb bouquet plus remaining ingredients. Bring liquid to the boil, reduce heat, cover, and simmer for 30 minutes.

Strain broth through a fine sieve.

Marchand de Vin Sauce

Yield: About 2 cups

This classic French sauce can transform an ordinary steak into a culinary masterpiece. Use also with any form of sliced beef.

6 Tb. (¾ stick) butter
1 medium onion, minced
1 cup dry red wine

1½ cups Beef Stock (p. 522)
2 Tb. lemon juice
Salt

Heat one-half of the butter in a medium skillet over moderate heat, add the onion, and sauté for 2 minutes or till golden. Add the wine, stir, and cook till liquid is reduced to ¼ cup. Add the stock, lemon juice, and salt to taste, and return heat to moderate. Add remaining butter in pieces and stir till well blended.

Béchamel Sauce

Yield: About 2¼ cups

3 Tb. butter
1 Tb. minced onion
¼ cup flour

3 cups hot milk
¼ tsp. salt
White pepper

Heat the butter in a saucepan, add the onion, and sauté over low heat for 2 minutes. Stir in the flour and cook the roux over low heat for 3 minutes, stirring constantly with a whisk.

Remove pan from the heat, add the milk, and whisk rapidly till mixture is thick and smooth. Add salt and the pepper to taste, stir, and simmer for 15 minutes. Strain sauce through a fine sieve.

Mornay Sauce

Yield: About 1¾ cups

1½ cups Béchamel Sauce (p. 525)
2 egg yolks

2 Tb. freshly grated Parmesan
    cheese
Dijon mustard

*I*n a saucepan, bring the béchamel just to the simmer. In a bowl, whisk the egg yolks, slowly add 2 tablespoons of the hot béchamel to the egg yolks, whisking briskly, then whisk egg yolks into the béchamel. Continue whisking over low heat for about 2 minutes or till sauce is thickened and smooth, remove pan from the heat, and stir in the cheese. Add 1 tablespoon of mustard or to taste and stir till well blended.

Blender Hollandaise Sauce

Yield: About 1 cup

8 Tb. (1 stick) butter
3 egg yolks
2 tsp. lemon juice

¼ tsp. salt
Cayenne

*H*eat the butter in a saucepan till it begins to foam, then remove from heat.

In a blender, combine the egg yolks, lemon juice, salt, and cayenne to taste, cover the container, and blend for 1 second. Turn blender on high, remove the cover, and pour the hot butter slowly into the mixture. When butter is used up, turn off the blender.

Keep the sauce warm in a shallow pan of hot water till ready to use.

Blender Béarnaise Sauce

Yield: About 1 cup

3 Tb. dry white wine
1½ Tb. tarragon vinegar
3 tsp. finely chopped shallots
3 tsp. minced fresh tarragon (or 1
   tsp. dried tarragon)

½ tsp. freshly ground pepper
1 cup Blender Hollandaise Sauce
   (p. 526)

*I*n a saucepan, combine the wine, vinegar, shallots, tarragon, and pepper, and cook over high heat till most of the liquid has evaporated.

Transfer the mixture to a blender, add the hollandaise, cover the container, and blend at high speed for 5 seconds.

Mousseline Sauce

Yield: About 1½ cups

This is the perfect sauce for steamed vegetables and poached or grilled fish.

1 cup Blender Hollandaise Sauce
   (p. 526)

3 Tb. whipped cream

*F*old the whipped cream into the hollandaise and serve the sauce hot or at room temperature.

Choron Sauce

Yield: About 1¼ cups

A delightful, elegant sauce for grilled meats and fish.

1 cup Blender Béarnaise Sauce   ¼ cup pureed fresh tomatoes
   (p. 526)   (cored, skinned, and seeded)

Add the pureed tomatoes to the béarnaise, stir gently but thoroughly, and serve the sauce hot or at room temperature.

Cumberland Sauce

Yield: About 1 cup

A classic sauce that goes with not only all game dishes but also cold ham and duck.

Juice of 2 oranges   2 tsp. brown sugar
Juice of 1 lemon   1 tsp. dry mustard
Grated rind of 1 orange   ¼ tsp. powdered ginger
Grated rind of ½ lemon   Cayenne
¼ tsp. ground cloves   ¼ cup Port
½ cup red currant jelly

In a heavy saucepan, combine the orange juice, lemon juice, grated orange rind, grated lemon rind, cloves, and jelly. Bring mixture to the simmer, stirring, and simmer for about 10 minutes or till liquid is reduced by half.

In a bowl, combine the brown sugar, mustard, ginger, cayenne to taste, and wine, stir till dry ingredients are dissolved, and add to the hot jelly mixture. Bring sauce to the boil, stirring constantly, remove from the heat, and let cool to room temperature.

Serve sauce reheated or at room temperature.

Spicy Peanut Sauce

Yield: About 2½ cups

This is an excellent sauce for main-course noodle dishes and, believe it or not, lamb and pork chops.

2 Tb. peanut oil
1 small onion, finely chopped
1 garlic clove, minced
½ tsp. red pepper flakes
½ tsp. ground ginger
¼ tsp. ground cloves

¼ tsp. turmeric
1 cup smooth peanut butter
1 Tb. lime juice
1 Tb. sugar
½ tsp. salt
1½ cups boiling water

Heat the oil in a large saucepan, add the onion and garlic, and sauté over low heat for 2 minutes. Add all remaining ingredients except the water, increase heat to moderate, and blend well with a spoon.

Add 1¼ cups of the boiling water and stir briskly with a whisk. If sauce begins to curdle, add a little more water and stir.

Serve sauce immediately.

Madeira Sauce

Yield: About 1½ cups

This sauce is sublime with roasted beef tenderloin, sautéed beef steaks, and even sautéed medallions of *foie gras*.

2 cups Beef Stock (p. 522)
2 tsp. arrowroot dissolved in 3 Tb.
  cold water

½ cup Madeira

Bring stock to the boil in a saucepan, reduce heat slightly, and simmer for 15 minutes. Stir in the arrowroot solution and continue cooking over moderate heat, stirring, till thickened.

Return stock to the boil and reduce to about 1 cup. Add the Madeira, return to the boil, and remove pan from the heat before stirring.

Serve sauce piping hot.

Black Pepper Sauce

Yield: About 2 cups

Traditionally this *sauce poivrade* is served with venison and other forms of game, but I like it also with steaks and even thick hamburgers.

4 Tb. (½ stick) butter
1 medium onion, chopped
1 carrot, scraped and chopped
3 sprigs parsley, chopped
1 bay leaf
¼ cup red wine vinegar

2 cups Beef Stock (p. 522) or
   bouillon
2 tsp. tomato paste
10 peppercorns
½ cup red wine

*H*eat the butter in a large skillet, add the onion and carrot, and sauté for 5 minutes over low heat, stirring. Add the parsley, bay leaf, and wine vinegar, increase heat to moderate, and simmer till liquid is reduced by half. Add the stock and tomato paste and stir well. Bring liquid to the boil, lower heat, cover, and simmer for 1 hour.

Add the peppercorns, simmer for 5 minutes longer, and strain the sauce into a large saucepan. Add the wine, return to the simmer, and cook for 20 minutes longer.

Horseradish Sauce

Yield: About 2 cups

Dreamed up by interior designer Lee Bailey, this onion-enriched horse-radish sauce is delicious with boiled brisket, roast prime ribs of beef, and fried or sautéed fish

4 Tb. (½ stick) unsalted butter
½ cup finely chopped onion
2 Tb. flour
2 cups hot Chicken Stock (p. 521)

1 Tb. lemon juice
Freshly ground pepper
¼ cup freshly grated or prepared
  horseradish

Heat the butter in a large saucepan, add the onion, and brown lightly over moderate heat. Add the flour, stir for 1 minute, add the stock, stir, and simmer for 4–5 minutes or till the mixture begins to thicken. Add the lemon juice and pepper to taste, stir, reduce heat, and simmer for 10 minutes.

Shortly before serving, stir in the horseradish.

Dill Sauce

Yield: About 1½ cups

Serve this sauce with grilled fish, sautéed scallops, and other seafood.

1 Tb. butter
1 Tb. minced shallots
1 Tb. all-purpose flour
⅔ cup Fish Stock (p. 524)

1 cup heavy cream
Salt and freshly ground pepper
2 Tb. finely chopped fresh dill

Heat the butter in a saucepan, add the shallots and flour, and stir briskly with a whisk over moderate heat for 1 minute. Add the fish stock and whisk briskly for 3 minutes.

Add the cream, and salt and pepper to taste, bring to the boil, and cook, stirring, for about 10 minutes. Stir in the dill.

Watercress Sauce

Yield: About 2 cups

This sauce is delicious with hot seafood pâtés and grilled fish.

4 Tb. (½ stick) butter
2 Tb. finely chopped shallots
1 cup Chicken Stock (p. 521) or
   Fish Stock (p. 524), depending
   on dish to be sauced

2 large bunches of watercress,
   rinsed and stems removed
½ cup heavy cream
Salt and freshly ground pepper
⅛ tsp. freshly grated nutmeg

Heat half the butter in a large saucepan, add the shallots, and sauté over low heat for 2 minutes, stirring. Add the stock, increase heat to moderate, and reduce liquid to about ⅓ cup.

Add the watercress and stir till it wilts. Add the cream, stir, and cook over high heat for 1 minute.

Transfer mixture to a blender or food processor and reduce to a puree. Return sauce to the saucepan and cook over moderate heat for 3 minutes. Add salt and pepper to taste and the nutmeg, stir, then swirl in the remaining butter in pieces.

Pesto Sauce

Yield: About 2 cups

Some cooks say they turn out great *pesto* in either a blender or food processor, but I've yet to taste one that can touch the paste made the old-fashioned way in a mortar. *Pesto* is wonderful not only over pasta but also served with roast hot or cold veal and pork.

2 cups loosely packed fresh basil
   leaves
2 garlic cloves, crushed
½ tsp. salt
1 Tb. toasted pine nuts

3 Tb. freshly grated Parmesan
   cheese
3 Tb. freshly grated Pecorino or
   Romano cheese
1 cup virgin olive oil

ombine the basil leaves, garlic, salt, and pine nuts in a large mortar and pound to a paste. Add the cheeses gradually, pounding all the time. When paste is smooth, gradually blend in the olive oil with a wooden spoon.

Commander's Creole Sauce

Yield: About 3 cups

This sauce from Commander's Palace in New Orleans should be spooned over fancy egg dishes and such sturdy vegetables as broccoli, cauliflower, and eggplant.

4 Tb. (½ stick) butter
¼ cup flour
2 cups Chicken Stock (p. 521)
2 Tb. minced onion
1 Tb. dry white wine
1 tsp. Worcestershire
½ garlic clove, minced

½ tsp. salt
½ tsp. freshly ground pepper
8 Tb. (1 stick) butter
¾ cup (about 6 oz.) smoked ham,
*   finely chopped*
3 Tb. minced onion
½ cup heavy cream

eat the 4 tablespoons of butter in a small cast-iron skillet, add the flour, and cook roux, stirring constantly, till mixture forms a smooth paste. Remove from heat.

Bring stock to the boil in a medium saucepan, reduce heat, and simmer till reduced to about 1 cup. Add the 2 tablespoons of onion, the wine, Worcestershire, garlic, salt, and pepper, and blend well. Stir in the reserved paste, increase heat, and continue simmering for about 20 minutes or till sauce is the consistency of slightly whipped cream.

In the meantime, heat 2 of the 8 tablespoons of butter in a small skillet, add the chopped ham and 3 tablespoons onion, sauté over low heat for 2 minutes, stirring, and set aside.

Remove the sauce from heat and add remaining butter gradually in chunks, whipping constantly with a whisk. Gently stir in the cream, add the ham and onion mixture, and blend well.

Rouille à la Sardine
(Garlicky Sardine Sauce)

Yield: About 1½ cups

This unusual sauce found along Mediterranean shores is delicious over pasta, added in small quantities to fish soups and stews, and spread lightly on grilled fish. For even more flavor, I often add a good pinch of ground fennel seeds.

2 tsp. finely minced garlic
½ tsp. imported paprika
2 small canned sardines, drained
1 anchovy fillet, drained

1 large egg yolk
Juice of ½ lemon
Freshly ground pepper
1¼ cups olive oil

Place the garlic and paprika in a mortar, crush to a paste, and transfer mixture to a mixing bowl.

Place the sardines and anchovy on a small plate, mash well with a fork to make a paste, and blend well with the garlic mixture.

Add the egg yolk, lemon juice, and pepper to taste, and beat briskly with a whisk. Beating rapidly, add the oil gradually till sauce is thickened and smooth.

Mustard Sauce

Yield: About 1 cup

8 Tb. (1 stick) butter, cut into
* pieces*
3 Tb. lemon juice
3 large egg yolks

Freshly ground pepper
2 Tb. water
2 Tb. Dijon mustard

Combine the butter, lemon juice, egg yolks, and pepper to taste in the top of a double boiler over boiling water and whisk rapidly till mixture thickens. Whisk in the water, remove sauce from the heat, and let cool slightly.

Add the mustard and whisk till well blended and the sauce is smooth. Serve sauce hot or at room temperature.

Foie Gras Sauce

Yield: About 2 cups

An excellent way to utilize a tin of *foie gras* that does not look fine enough to serve by itself. The sauce can add a new dimension to steamed broccoli or asparagus, poached chicken breasts or fish, and even Eggs Benedict.

4 Tb. (½ stick) butter	*3 egg yolks*
¼ cup all-purpose flour	*½ cup heavy cream*
2 cups Chicken Stock (p. 521) or	*½ cup mashed foie gras*
broth	*Salt and freshly ground pepper*

*H*eat the butter in a saucepan, add the flour, and cook over low heat, whisking constantly, till flour begins to brown. Add the chicken stock and stir over low heat till liquid begins to thicken.

In a bowl, beat the egg yolks with the cream, then gradually beat about one-half of the hot sauce into the mixture. Return mixture to the saucepan, add the *foie gras,* and stir over low heat till sauce thickens. Season to taste with salt and pepper.

Beurre Blanc
(White Butter Sauce)

Yield: About ¾ cup

Although miserably abused by practitioners of the French *nouvelle cuisine* and neophyte exploiters of the new style of American cookery, this simple, age-old French peasant sauce, originally used only to dress grilled fish, is delicious with the right seafood — and in small quantities.

8 Tb. (1 stick) butter
¼ cup finely chopped shallots
½ cup dry white wine

¼ cup heavy cream
Salt and freshly ground pepper

*H*eat 2 tablespoons of the butter in a saucepan, add the shallots, and sauté over low heat for 2 minutes, stirring. Add the wine, increase heat to moderate, and continue cooking till liquid is almost evaporated.

Add the cream, increase heat slightly, and cook till cream is reduced by half. Cut the remaining butter into pieces and add to the cream, stirring briskly with a whisk. Pour sauce into a blender or food processor and blend till very smooth. Return sauce to the saucepan, season with salt and pepper to taste, and reheat slightly.

Shallot Sauce

Yield: About 1¼ cups

This classic French sauce is traditionally served with steak, but it is also delicious with roasted or grilled meats and poultry.

3 Tb. butter
½ cup finely chopped shallots
1 Tb. Port
1 Tb. all-purpose flour

½ cup Chicken Stock (p. 521)
½ cup half-and-half
¼ tsp. salt
Freshly ground pepper

Heat the butter in a medium saucepan, add the shallots and wine, and sauté over moderate heat for 5 minutes, stirring. Sprinkle on the flour, stir, then gradually add the stock and half-and-half, stirring. Add the salt, and pepper to taste and continue to cook over moderate heat, stirring constantly, till sauce has thickened.

Mushroom Sauce

Yield: About 2 cups

4 Tb. (½ stick) butter
3 Tb. finely chopped shallots
½ lb. mushrooms, thinly sliced
1 Tb. lemon juice

Salt and freshly ground pepper
1 cup Chicken Stock (p. 521) or
   Veal Stock (p. 523)
½ cup heavy cream

Heat one-half of the butter in a large, heavy saucepan, add the shallots, and sauté over low heat for 2 minutes, stirring. Add the mushrooms, stir, and increase heat to moderate. Add the lemon juice, and salt and pepper to taste, and cook till mushrooms are just soft. Add the stock, stir, and cook for about 8 minutes.

Add the cream, bring mixture to the boil, and let cook, stirring, for about 2 minutes. Add the remaining butter and swirl till well blended.

Serve sauce very hot.

Wild Mushroom Sauce

Yield: About 1½ cups

Serve this earthy sauce with roasted meats, grilled fish or chicken, and even a roast rack of lamb. All sorts of fresh wild mushrooms are now widely available thoughout the country, but if you must use dried, soak 1 ounce of the mushrooms in ½ cup of warm water about 30 minutes and pick carefully for grit.

½ lb. fresh cèpe, chanterelle, or
   morel mushrooms
¼ lb. button mushrooms
Salt
3 Tb. butter

1 cup heavy cream
⅛ tsp. mace
Pinches of dried thyme and chervil
Freshly ground pepper

Rinse the wild mushrooms carefully and chop coarsely. Chop the button mushrooms coarsely. Place both varieties of mushrooms in a large saucepan, cover with water, and add salt to taste. Bring liquid to the boil, cook mushrooms for 3 minutes, and drain. Squeeze mushrooms dry in a clean towel, place in a blender or food processor, and chop finely.

Heat the butter in a large saucepan, add the mushrooms, and sauté over low heat for 3 minutes, stirring. Add the cream, mace, thyme, chervil, and salt and pepper to taste, increase heat slightly, and let sauce simmer for 5 – 10 minutes.

Mint Sauce

Yield: About ½ cup

I realize it's no longer fashionable in this country to offer mint sauce (much less mint jelly) with your *gigot* or "best end" of lamb, but no respectable restaurant in England would present roast lamb without also providing a fresh mint sauce, and I couldn't imagine savoring the pink, full-flavored slices carved tableside in my beloved Princess Grill aboard the *QE 2* without a spoonful of this modern equivalent of the medieval "verde sawse." Note that the sauce also goes very well with pork.

1 Tb. sugar	3 Tb. finely chopped fresh mint
½ cup water	¼ cup white wine vinegar

Combine the sugar and water in a small saucepan, bring to the boil, and stir till the sugar dissolves. Remove pan from the heat, add the mint, and let stand for 30 minutes.

Add the vinegar and stir. Covered in the refrigerator, the sauce keeps at least a week without losing its flavor. Serve very hot.

Hot Tomato Sauce

Yield: About 2 cups

4 Tb. (½ stick) butter	¼ tsp. sugar
¼ cup olive oil	1 Tb. minced fresh basil
1 medium onion, minced	2 cups canned tomatoes (with
1 garlic clove, minced	their juice)
1 celery rib, minced	¾ cup hot water

Heat the butter and oil in a medium saucepan, add the onion, garlic, and celery, and sauté over low heat for 2–3 minutes. Add the sugar, basil, and tomatoes with their juices, stir well, then add the water.

Bring liquid to the boil, reduce heat, and simmer, uncovered, for about 30 minutes or till sauce is reduced and slightly thick.

Cold Fresh Tomato Sauce

Yield: About 4 cups (enough for 1 lb. cooked pasta)

This thick, garlicky sauce can be served at room temperature with either hot or cold pasta. To render its full flavor, however, it must be allowed to marinate at least 2 hours — and preferably 3.

½ cup virgin Italian olive oil
¼ cup sherry wine vinegar
4 garlic cloves, minced
2 sprigs parsley, minced
1 cup packed shredded fresh basil
   leaves

½ tsp. salt
Freshly ground pepper
10 ripe medium tomatoes

*I*n a large glass or stainless-steel mixing bowl, combine the olive oil and vinegar, and whisk till well blended. Add the garlic, parsley, basil, salt, and pepper to taste, and stir.

Slice the tomatoes in half, squeeze slightly to extract as many seeds and as much juice as possible, and dice. Add tomatoes to the oil and vinegar mixture, stir, cover with plastic wrap, and let marinate for at least 2 hours.

Ravigote Sauce

Yield: About 1½ cups

Dress cold boiled shrimp with this sauce and you have the Creole classic shrimp ravigote. The sauce is also ideal for grilled or poached fish.

¼ cup red wine vinegar
¼ cup finely chopped scallions
¼ cup finely chopped parsley
2 Tb. finely chopped fresh tarragon (or 1 tsp. dried tarragon)

2 Tb. finely chopped chives
2 Tb. capers, drained and chopped
1 cup olive oil
Salt and freshly ground pepper

*I*n a mixing bowl, combine the vinegar, scallions, parsley, tarragon, chives, and capers, and stir. Stirring steadily with a whisk, add the oil gradually till well blended. Add salt and pepper to taste and whisk for a few seconds longer.

Fresh Mayonnaise

Yield: About 2 cups

Unlike Blender Mayonnaise (p. 542), this traditional mayonnaise is made with egg yolks only. I've always found that the mustard provides enough saltiness, but if you want a saltier flavor, sprinkle on a few grains after the oil is added. If the mayonnaise is not to be used immediately, beat in a tablespoon of water to stabilize the emulsion while stored in the refrigerator.

2 extra-large egg yolks
2 tsp. Dijon mustard

2 tsp. vinegar or lemon juice
2 cups vegetable or peanut oil

*P*lace the yolks in a mixing bowl, add the mustard and vinegar, and beat vigorously with a whisk or electric mixer till frothy.

Begin adding the oil drop by drop, beating continuously. Gradually add the remaining oil in a slow stream, beating all the time, till oil is used up. Do not continue beating after all the oil has been added.

Blender Mayonnaise

Yield: About 2½ cups

Since this mayonnaise must be made with whole eggs to assure the right emulsion, it is lighter than Fresh Mayonnaise (p. 541) and keeps longer in the refrigerator. The mayonnaise should not separate so long as you add the oil in drops at first and cut off the blender the second the oil is used up. If you do goof, however, simply blend 2 tablespoons of the separated mayonnaise with 1 teaspoon of prepared mustard in a large mixing bowl till the mixture is thick and very gradually blend in the remaining mayonnaise with a whisk.

2 eggs	*½ tsp. salt*
1 Tb. lemon juice	*¼ tsp. white pepper*
1 tsp. white vinegar	*2 cups peanut or vegetable oil*
2 tsp. dry mustard	

Combine the eggs, lemon juice, vinegar, mustard, salt, and pepper in a blender and turn machine on high. Add the oil in drops till sauce begins to thicken slightly, then add the remaining oil very gradually in a stream. Turn machine off as soon as all the oil has been absorbed and the mixture has thickened.

For Mustard Mayonnaise, stir in 2 tablespoons of Dijon mustard.

For Red Bell Pepper Mayonnaise, stir in 2 tablespoons of minced red bell pepper.

For Tarragon Mayonnaise, stir in 2 tablespoons of minced fresh tarragon or 2 teaspoons of dried tarragon.

Basic Vinaigrette Dressing

Yield: 2 cups

This basic dressing can be flavored further with a whole clove of garlic (removed when dressing is served), 2 tablespoons of mixed chopped fresh herbs (or 1 tsp. dried crushed herbs), or 2 tablespoons of minced shallots or scallions.

½ cup red wine vinegar

1 tsp. Dijon mustard

Freshly ground pepper

1½ cups top-quality olive oil

Combine the vinegar, mustard, and pepper to taste in a mixing bowl and whisk briskly till well blended. Add the oil gradually, whisking rapidly, till blended thoroughly.

Store the dressing for up to 24 hours in a tightly covered jar.

Vinaigrette aux Fines Herbes
(Mixed Herb Vinaigrette Dressing)

Yield: About 2 cups

Intended for use in the most delicate of salads, this vinaigrette is lightened with water and vegetable oil.

¼ cup tarragon vinegar

2 Tb. water

½ tsp. each dried chervil, basil, and dill

¼ tsp. dry mustard

½ tsp. salt

Freshly ground pepper

¾ cup vegetable oil

¼ cup olive oil

3 Tb. minced parsley

2 Tb. snipped chives

Combine the vinegar, water, herbs, mustard, salt, and pepper to taste in a blender. With the machine running, add oils in a stream till well blended. Stop machine, add the parsley and chives, and pulse machine for no more than 1 or 2 seconds.

Herb Dressing I

Yield: About 1¼ cups

¾ cup safflower or peanut oil
2 Tb. mixed minced fresh dill,
   tarragon, and basil
1 Tb. minced chives

1 tsp. minced parsley
Salt and freshly ground pepper
¼ cup wine vinegar

*I*n a small bowl, combine the oil, mixed herbs, chives, and parsley, cover, and let stand at room temperature for 3 – 4 hours.
    Add salt and pepper to taste and the vinegar, and whisk briskly till oil and vinegar are well incorporated.

Herb Dressing II

Yield: About 1¼ cups

2 Tb. finely chopped fresh
   tarragon (or 1 tsp. dried
   tarragon)
2 Tb. finely chopped fresh chervil
2 Tb. finely chopped parsley
2 Tb. finely chopped watercress

½ garlic clove, minced
½ cup sour cream
½ cup Blender Mayonnaise
   (p. 542)
1 tsp. lemon juice
Salt and freshly ground pepper

*C*ombine the herbs and garlic in a mixing bowl, add the sour cream, mayonnaise, lemon juice, and salt and pepper to taste, and blend thoroughly.

Avocado Dressing

Yield: About 2¼ cups

1 cup sour cream
1 cup plain yogurt
1 large avocado, peeled, pitted,
   and cut into cubes

2 Tb. lemon juice
2 garlic cloves, finely chopped
1 tsp. salt

Combine all the ingredients in a blender or food processor and blend till very smooth. Transfer to a tightly covered jar and store in the refrigerator for up to 24 hours.

Curried Chutney Dressing

Yield: About 2¼ cups

2 cups Fresh Mayonnaise (p. 541)
½ Tb. Dijon mustard
½ Tb. red wine vinegar
Pinch of powdered saffron
½ tsp. curry powder

½ Tb. honey
1 Tb. lime juice
Dash of Worcestershire
Tabasco
2 Tb. chutney

Combine all the ingredients except the chutney in a mixing bowl and blend thoroughly with a wooden spoon. Stir in the chutney, transfer dressing to a tightly covered jar, and refrigerate for at least 1 hour before serving.

Walnut Oil Dressing

Yield: About 1 cup

½ cup sherry vinegar
1 shallot, minced
¾ cup walnut oil

½ tsp. chopped chives
½ tsp. lemon juice
Salt and freshly ground pepper

Combine the vinegar and shallots in a small saucepan, bring to the boil, reduce vinegar by half, and let cool.
Pour vinegar mixture into a bowl and gradually whisk in the walnut oil. Add the chives, lemon juice, and salt and pepper to taste, whisk well, and store in a covered jar till ready to use.

Louis Dressing

Yield: About 1⅔ cups

1 cup Fresh Mayonnaise (p. 541)
⅓ cup whipped cream
⅓ cup chili sauce

1 Tb. grated onion
Dash of cayenne

Combine the mayonnaise and whipped cream in a mixing bowl and mix thoroughly with a rubber spatula. Add the chili sauce, onion, and cayenne, and blend well with the spatula.

Use dressing immediately.

Hot Bacon Salad Dressing

Yield: About 1¼ cups

6 slices of bacon
3 scallions (including some green
    tops), minced
½ cup white vinegar

½ cup water
2 tsp. prepared mustard
Freshly ground pepper

Fry the bacon in a large skillet till crisp, drain, crumble, and set aside. Pour the bacon grease into a saucepan, add the scallions, and sauté over moderate heat for 1 minute. Add the vinegar, water, mustard, and pepper to taste, stir well till mustard is incorporated, and continue cooking, stirring, for about 3 minutes.

Pour hot dressing over salads with bitter or robust greens and sprinkle with reserved crumbled bacon.

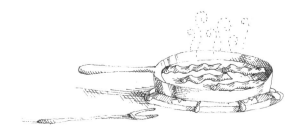

Poppy Seed Dressing

Yield: About 3½ cups

1 cup sugar
⅔ cup vinegar
1 Tb. finely minced onion
2 tsp. dry mustard

2 tsp. salt
2 cups vegetable oil
2 Tb. poppy seeds

Combine the sugar, vinegar, onion, mustard, and salt in a blender and blend well. Slowly add the oil and continue to blend till thick. Add the poppy seeds and blend for 2 minutes.

Transfer dressing to a tightly covered jar and chill for at least 1 hour before serving.

Salsa Dressing

Yield: About 1¾ cups

This tangy Mexican dressing that plays such an important role in the new style of California cookery can be made by simply chopping the ingredients, combining, and allowing the flavors to meld over the period of an hour. I find the dressing to be much more versatile when prepared in a blender.

2 ripe medium tomatoes, peeled
* and chopped*
1 medium onion, chopped
3 ancho or serrano chili peppers,
* seeded and chopped*
1 garlic clove, finely chopped

1 tsp. oregano
2 sprigs fresh coriander (also
* called cilantro and Chinese*
* parsley)*
1 tsp. salt

Combine all the ingredients in a blender or food processor and blend till very smooth. Transfer to a jar, cover tightly, and let stand for 1 hour before serving. Do not store longer than 1 day.

Yogurt Dressing

Yield: About 1¼ cups

1 cup plain yogurt
2 Tb. white vinegar
¼ cup skim milk
½ tsp. sugar

½ tsp. salt
2 Tb. minced chives
Dash of cayenne

Combine all the ingredients in a blender, blend just to mix thoroughly, pour into a jar, cover, and chill well before serving.

Mignonette Sauce

Yield: Enough for 4 persons

When you tire of serving standard red cocktail sauce with fresh oysters and clams, try this delectable, zesty combination.

5 shallots, minced
15 crushed peppercorns

½ cup top-quality red wine vinegar

Combine all the ingredients in a bowl and mix thoroughly. Serve the sauce in small individual dipping bowls.

Barbecue Sauce

Yield: About 3 cups

I've never been one to make a big to-do about red barbecue sauces used to baste meats and poultry grilled outdoors, since even the most complex ones always seem to resemble all those sampled before. This sauce, therefore, is no more and no less reliable than the next, and if you're really interested in great hot pepper vinegar sauces like those mixed with genuine chopped pork barbecue found only in North Carolina, write me a letter.

1 cup cider vinegar
1 cup warm water
3 Tb. dark brown sugar
3 Tb. dry mustard
1½ Tb. salt
2 tsp. freshly ground pepper
½ cup ketchup

¼ cup chili sauce
3 Tb. Worcestershire
1 garlic clove, mashed
3 Tb. minced onion
1 cup (2 sticks) butter
Tabasco

*I*n a large bowl, combine the vinegar, water, brown sugar, mustard, salt, and pepper, stir well, and set aside to steep for about 15 minutes.

In a large saucepan, combine the remaining ingredients and bring to the boil. Reduce heat, stir well, and simmer till butter melts completely. Add the steeped vinegar mixture, return to the simmer, stir well, and simmer for about 1 hour, stirring periodically.

Wild Game Marinade

Yield: Enough marinade for about 3 lbs. of game

4 cups dry red wine
2 Tb. red wine vinegar
¼ cup peanut or vegetable oil
1 medium onion, sliced
1 carrot, sliced
1 garlic clove, crushed

1 bay leaf
½ tsp. dried thyme
½ tsp. marjoram
4 juniper berries
1 Tb. salt
1 tsp. freshly ground pepper

*I*n a large mixing bowl, combine the wine, vinegar, and oil, and whisk till well blended. Add remaining ingredients and stir.

Marinade for Vegetables

Yield: About 2 cups

1 cup Chicken Stock (p. 521)
½ cup olive oil
½ cup dry white wine
2 Tb. lemon juice
2 Tb. chopped shallots
6 peppercorns
½ tsp. coriander seed

½ tsp. chopped garlic
Herb bouquet (¼ tsp. each dried
  thyme and fennel, 1 bay leaf,
  and 2 sprigs parsley wrapped in
  cheesecloth)
¼ tsp. salt

Combine all the ingredients in an enamel or stainless-steel saucepan, bring mixture to the boil, lower heat, and simmer for 5 minutes. Cool marinade and transfer to the glass or stainless-steel container used for marinating vegetables.

Caraway Seed Butter

Yield: ½ cup (8 tablespoons)

A tablespoon of this butter served atop broiled fish steaks or pork chops adds not only moisture but an interesting flavor.

8 Tb. (1 stick) softened butter
Salt and freshly ground pepper

1½ tsp. crushed caraway seeds

In a bowl, combine the butter and salt and pepper to taste and the caraway seeds, mash mixture with a wooden spoon till well blended, and store in the refrigerator till ready to use.

Hard Sauce

Yield: About 1 cup

This is the classic sauce for steamed puddings, and a small spoonful can also turn a slab of fruit cake into a very stylish dessert.

8 Tb. (1 stick) butter, room
   temperature
2 cups sugar

¼ tsp. salt
1 Tb. hot water
1 tsp. vanilla

*I*n a mixing bowl, cream the butter and sugar with an electric mixer till frothy, add the salt, hot water, and vanilla, and continue to beat till fluffy. Chill sauce slightly.

Crème Anglaise
(Light Custard Sauce)

Yield: About 2 cups

As far as I'm concerned, this is the ultimate dessert sauce — and a far more sophisticated one than all the *coulis* that have become so fashionable in recent years. It is the classic sauce for floating islands, but I love it also with any number of chocolate desserts and as the ideal pool for fresh fruit.

½ cup sugar
3 egg yolks
1 tsp. cornstarch

1¾ cups milk
1 Tb. rum
1 tsp. vanilla

*C*ombine the sugar and egg yolks in a large mixing bowl and beat with an electric mixer till pale and smooth. Blend in the cornstarch.

While beating egg mixture, bring the milk almost to the boil in a saucepan. Gradually add the milk in a thin stream to the egg mixture, with the mixer running all the time so the yolks do not cook.

Pour the mixture into a heavy enameled or stainless-steel saucepan, heat to moderate, and stir slowly but constantly with a wooden spoon till the sauce thickens enough to coat a spoon. Remove pan from heat, beat sauce for 1 – 2 minutes to cool it, strain through a fine sieve, and beat in the rum and vanilla.

Serve sauce immediately or keep warm over hot water.

Rum Sauce

Yield: About 1 cup

This sauce is good not only with a number of dessert mousses but also spooned over pies and glazed bananas.

2 egg yolks, beaten
¼ cup orange juice
3 Tb. lemon juice

¼ cup sugar
4 Tb. (½ stick) butter, softened
¼ cup dark rum

Combine the egg yolks, orange juice, lemon juice, and sugar in a saucepan and cook over moderate heat, stirring, till slightly thickened. Add the butter in pieces and continue stirring till well blended and glossy. Stir in the rum and heat for 1 minute longer.

French, 419–420
herbed toast, 447
limpa, Swedish, 426
orange oatmeal, 432
pita, 424
poppy seed, farmhouse, 429
soda, Irish, 423
sourdough, 421
tortillas, wheat, 417
walnut, 432–433
walnut pumpkin, 433
whole wheat caraway, 427
whole wheat pecan, 428
yeast, country, 418
Bread and butter pickle, 461
Brie with almonds on chicken sandwich, toasted, 125
Brioche dough, basic food processor, 414
Brioches, 434
Broccoli
and goat cheese soufflés, 95
and olive soup, chilled, 56–57
sautéed with peanuts, 337
steamed with foie gras sauce, 336–337
tuna, and tomatoes, pasta salad with, 138–139
Broth. See Stock
Brunswick stew, Georgia, 78
Bucatini pasta. See Penne
Buckwheat groats. See Kasha
Burgers. See Beef, ground
Butter, caraway seed, 550
Butter rolls, 430
Butter sauce, white (beurre blanc), 536
Buttermilk
biscuits, southern, 440
bread, 425
lemon cake, 494
scones, 442
Butternut squash. See Squash

Cabbage (red) and sausage, spätzle with, 392
Caesar salad with bulb fennel, 166
Cajun, eggplant Bon Ton, baked, 342
Cake
cheesecake, Lindy's original, 501–502
chocolate mousse with rum, 497
Dutch honey, 495
fruit, Dresden stollen, 503–504
fruit, white, Missy's, 505
lemon buttermilk, 494
Morjolaine (chocolate-nut), 498–499
pound, coconut, 496–497
pound, peanut butter, 496
Canapés, steak tartare and caviar, 16–17
Canard. See also Duck(ling)
aux olives chez Allard, 258–259

confit de, 264–265
Caneton au poivre, 260–261
Canning jars, how to sterilize and seal, 460
Cantaloupe(s)
chutney, 466
caraway shrimp stuffed in, 300
Caraway
seed butter, 550
shrimp stuffed in cantaloupes, 300
whole wheat bread, 427
Carmelized chestnut flan, 507
Carolina gumbo, 64
Carolina hush puppies, 437
Carrot(s)
and almond soup, chilled, 50
baked with horseradish, 338
flans, herbed, 37
glazed, and chestnuts, Bourbon chicken with, 247
honey-glazed, 338
potato and leek terrine, 14
tortellini, sausage-filled, salad with bulb fennel, 170–171
Cassata, Sicilian, 500
Cassoulet, lean, 333–335
Catfish Caribbean en papillote, 283
Cauliflower, baked with feta cheese, 339
Caviar
black, medallions of veal with, 190
golden, deep-fried new potatoes with, 25
jellied consommé with, 48
salmon dumplings stuffed with, 287–288
and steak tartare canapés, 16–17
Celeriac. See Celery root
Celery root
and endive, braised, 340–341
puree, 340
Cèpes. See Wild mushrooms
Cervelas aux cèpes (sausages with wild mushrooms), 212
Cervelas aux fruits de mer (seafood sausages), 36
Chanterelles. See Wild mushrooms
Charleston hobotee (curried meat custard), 13
Chawal Dhania Podina (lemon rice), 399
Cheddar shortbread, 446
Cheese. See also name of specific cheese
ball, herbed, 7
biscuits, 441
and eggs, spicy, 83
grits, baked, 403
soufflé, miniature, 101
and spinach pie, Greek (Spanakopita), 105
Cheeseburger in pita, club sandwich, 131
Cheesecake, Lindy's original, 501–502
Chestnut(s)
Bourbon chicken and glazed carrots with, 247
-chocolate log, 499

Cornbread. *See also* Johnnycakes
   corn sticks, 438
   crackling, Mrs. Wilkes', 435
   hush puppies, Carolina, 436–437
   jalepeño, 436
   southern, 434
Cornmeal, polenta with sausages and mushrooms, 408
Cornmeal pudding, Bourbon spoonbread, 405
Court bouillon, 524
   lobster with truffles, 70
   striped bass in, 280–281
Couscous, steamed, 406
Crab(meat)
   cakes
      with mustard sauce, 23
      Pawleys Island, 312
      spicy, 311
   and guacamole burgers, 132
   imperial, with coriander and capers, 310
   imperial, Creole (salad), 151
   and mushroom soufflé, 98
   and mushrooms, Japanese soba salad with, 171
   salad
      and corn, curried, artichokes stuffed with, 149
      Louis, 150
      with pink grapefruit and coconut, 152
   seafood sausages, 36
   soft-shell, with lemon-peanut sauce, 313
   soup
      with fennel, 48–49
      (she crab), 66
   and tomato bisque, 44
   trout sautéed with, in red wine sauce, 285
   and vermouth, eggs scrambled with, 84
Crackling cornbread, Mrs. Wilkes', 435
Cranberry
   -apple cobbler, 493
   conserve, 467
Crème Anglaise, 551
Creole
   crab imperial (salad), 151
   croque monsieur, 130–131
   marinated eggplant and peppers, cold, 21
   sauce, Commander's, 533
Crêpes
   basic, 416
   Roquefort, deep-fried, 102
Croque monsieur, Creole, 130–131
Cucumber vichyssoise, 53
Cumberland sauce, 528
Curry(ied)
   chicken, 237
      baked acorn squash stuffed with, 122–123
   chutney dressing, 545
   crab and corn salad, artichokes stuffed with, 149
   eggs with tarragon, hot, 89
   fish chowder, 58

fish sandwich, hot, 127
meat custard (Charleston hobotee), 13
mussels, creamed, 321
pasta salad with chicken and cashews, 173
pilaf with pine nuts, 395
potato and shrimp salad on avocado, 144
shrimp
   with coconut, Indonesian, 299
   with pumpkin seeds, cold, 120
tomato sauce for halibut steaks, 277
turkey hash cakes, 255

Daube d'oignons, 356
Desserts. *See* Cakes; Cobblers; Cookies; Ice Cream; Pies; Tarts
Deviled scallops with dill, 22
Dill(ed)
   asparagus, 326–327
   chicken, 231
   lobster mousse, 4
   sauce, 531
   sauce (cream), for lamb steaks, 200
   Scotch eggs, 94–95
   spanakopita, 105
Dough. *See also* Pastry, dough
   brioche, basic food processor, 414–415
   pizza, basic, 415
Dresden stollen, 503–504
Dressing. *See also* Marinade; Mayonnaise; Sauce
   avocado, 544–545
   curried chutney, 545
   ginger, 172
   herb, 544
   hot bacon, 546
   Louis, 546
   poppy seed, 547
   salsa, 547
   vinaigrette
      basic, 542–543
      mixed herb, 543
   walnut oil, 545
   yoghurt, 548
Duck(ling)
   canard aux olives chez Allard, 258–259
   caneton au poivre, 260–261
   confit de canard, 264–265
   with green olives, 258–259
   liver. *See also* Foie gras
      with hot vinaigrette sauce, 12
      with Madeira sauce, 261
      and walnut pâté, ramekins of, 17
   paella with olives and almonds, 262–263
   potted (rillettes de canard), 10–11
   preserved, 264–265
   and rice salad, 158–159
   roast, with black pepper sauce, 260–261
Dumplings, potato-spinach with Stilton sauce, 379
Dutch honey cake, 495

baked, stuffed fresh, Jean Anderson's, 305
à la Basquaise, 306
club sandwich, 129
and feta cheese, Mediterranean sandwich, 130
à la menthe, 15
sauce, garlicky, 534
sausage, and bean salad, 162
-stuffed eggs, 94
and tomatoes, gratin of, 307
and tuna tart, Moroccan, 308
Sauce. *See also* Butter; Dressing; Marinade;
   Mayonnaise
apple cider for swordfish steaks, 290
barbecue, 548–549
basil cream and mustard, 192–193
basil for salmon paupiettes, 286
Béarnaise, blender, 527
béchamel, 525
beurre blanc, 536
black pepper, 530
   for duckling, 260–261
choron, 528
crème Anglaise, 551
Creole, Commander's, 533
Cumberland, 528
curried tomato for halibut steaks, 277
dill, 531
dilled cream for lamb steaks, 200
fennel, 26
foie gras, 535
   for steamed broccoli, 336–337
garlic-mayonnaise for red snapper, 291
garlicky sardine, 534
hard, 550–551
Hollandaise, blender, 526
horseradish, 531
lobster, for poached eggs in potato jackets, 92
Madeira, 529
   for duck liver, 261
marchand de vin, 525
mignonette, 548
mint, 539
mornay, 526
mousseline, 527
mushroom, 537
mushroom cream for shad roe, 314
mustard, 534
   for beef rolls, 181–182
   for stuffed veal cutlets, 194
onion for braised veal fillets, 196–197
peanut butter-garlic for noodles, 389
peanut, spicy, 529
pesto, 532–533
   for pasta and ham salad, 168
Port for Smithfield ham, 216–217
pumpkin for veal cutlets, 195
ravigote, 541
rum, 552
shallot, 537
shrimp-tomato for fillet of flounder, 295

Stilton for potato-spinach dumplings, 379
tarragon-butter for sweetbreads, 221
tomato
   cold fresh, 540
   cold for rigatoni with olives, 383
   hot, 539
vinaigrette, hot, duck liver with, 12
vinegar-cream for ham, 219
watercress, 532
wild mushroom, 538
Sausage(s)
apricot, and prune stuffing for crown roast of
   pork, 204
and cabbage, spätzle with, 392
and chestnuts, goose stew with, 266–267
and chicken gumbo, 74–75
chipolata, lentils with, 350
-filled carrot tortellini salad with bulb fennel,
   170–171
Italian, creamed leeks with, 346–347
and mushrooms, polenta with, 408
poached, with wild mushrooms, 212
and potato gnocchi casserole, 393–394
seafood, 36
smoked, lima beans with, 329
spicy, lentil salad with, 141
spinach, sweetbread and, 222–223
white, with onions and apples, 251–252
Savannah red rice, 398
Scallion and white onion custard, 357
Scallop(s)
in Beaujolais sauce (coquilles St.-Jacques), 320
deviled with dill, 22
seafood sausages, 36
soup, cream of, with chives, 51
soused, and avocado salad, 143
soused, in romaine lettuce, 20
Scalloped oysters, 318
Scones
buttermilk, 442
lemon curd spread for, 473
Scotch eggs, dilled, 94 -95
Scrambled eggs. *See* Eggs, scrambled
Seafood. *See also name of specific seafood*
-fish cioppino, 77, 315–316
gumbo, 73
salad, mixed, 153
sausages, 36
seviche salad with avocado, 148
Senegalese soup, 54–55
Sesame seed (benne) cookies, 450
Seviche salad with avocado, 148
Shad roe with mushroom cream sauce, 314
Shad soup, Thai, 56
Shallot sauce, 537
She-crab soup, 66
Shellfish. *See also name of specific shellfish*
-fish stew (cioppino), 77, 315–316
Shiitake mushrooms. *See* Wild mushrooms
Short ribs of beef with olives, 179

Shortbread, cheddar, 446
Shrimp
  and artichokes, gratin of, 119
  asparagus, and cellophane noodle salad with
    ginger dressing, 172
  caraway, stuffed in cantaloupes, 300
  coconut beer, Paul Prudhomme's, 302
  and corn chowder, 70–71
  curry
    with coconut, Indonesian, 299
    with pumpkin seeds, cold, 120
  eggs, soft-boiled, with, 90
  with ham and straw mushrooms, stir-fried, 121
  Hong Kong crystal, 301
  oyster, and mussel gumbo, 73
  and oysters, creamed, johnnycakes with, 118
  pâté with gin, 18
  and pea salad with pork cracklings, 142–143
  pie, 304
  pilau, 303
  and potato salad, curried, on avocado, 144
  ravigote, 541
  soused and avocado salad, 143
  soused in romaine lettuce, 20
  -tomato sauce for fillet of flounder, 295
Sicilian cassata, 500
Simca's chilled sardines in aspic, 112
Singapore chicken, 234
Smelts. *See also* Sardines
  sautéed with dill, 309
Smithfield ham. *See also* Ham, country
  in pastry with Port sauce, 216–217
Snail(s)
  and mushrooms, skewered, 8
  and peas, fettucine with, 386
  in puff pastry, stuffed, 33
  quiche, 106
Snapper. *See* Red snapper
Soba (Japanese buckwheat noodles) salad with
    crabmeat and mushrooms, 171
Soda bread, Irish, 423
Sole. *See also* Flounder; Salmon, dumplings
  Provençal fish soup, 69
  stuffed with foie gras, 293
Sorbet, mango, 514
Soufflé(s)
  beet, 336
  chestnut, 341
  corn and bacon, 97
  crabmeat and mushroom, 98
  goat cheese and broccoli, 95
  Jerusalem artichoke, 96
  lemon, 509
  potato and feta cheese, 375
  prune and banana, 511
  raspberry, frozen (glacé au framboises),
    510–511
  squash, 361
  Stilton puffs, 101

Soup. *See also* Soup, cold; Stew
  bean with ham, Pecos, 41
  black bean, Coach House, 79
  Brunswick stew, Georgia, 78
  chestnut with ginger, 59
  chicken and sausage gumbo, 74–75
  cioppino (fish-seafood), 77
  clam and oyster bisque with orange zest, 68
  crab with fennel, 48–49
  crab (she), 66
  fish chowder, curried, 58
  fish Provençal, 69
  garlic (sopa de ajo), 54
  goulash (gulyás leves), 63
  gumbo, Carolina, 64
  lobster court bouillon with truffles, 70
  mussel (moules la Caravelle), 67
  onion, classic French, 45
  oxtail-barley, 65
  oyster avgolemono, 61
  oyster and spinach stew, 42
  pepper pot, Philadelphia, 72
  au pistou Vencienne, 76
  pozole (Mexican soup-stew), 60
  scallop, cream of, with chives, 51
  shad (red snapper), Thai, 56
  shrimp and corn chowder, 70–71
  shrimp, oyster, and mussel gumbo, 73
  Stilton with Port, 47
  tomato-avocado, minted, 46–47
  tomato, fresh, and snapper, 75
  tortilla, 62
  wild mushroom, 46
  zucchini, saffroned, 42–43
Soup, cold
  beet (chlodnik), 52
  broccoli and olive, 56–57
  carrot and almond, 50
  chicken gazpacho, 57
  crab and tomato bisque, 44
  cucumber vichyssoise, 53
  jellied consommé with caviar, 48
  lime glacé, 43
  mango, 55
  peach, gingered, 49
  Senegalese, 54–55
  tomato-avocado, minted, 46–47
Sourdough bread, 421
Soused. *See also* Marinated
  chicken in romaine lettuce, 20
  mussels and avocado, salad, 143
Southern buttermilk biscuits, 440
Southern cornbread, 434
Spaghetti
  pasta with chicken and vegetables, cold, 388
  primavera Le Cirque, 390–391
Spanakopita, dilled, 105
Spanish omelet, Sigred's, 87
Spätzle with cabbage and sausage, 392

Spiced, Spicy. *See name of food*
Spinach
    and cheese pie, Greek (Spanakopita), 105
    and flounder terrine with prunes, 27–28
    Moroccan, 358–359
    -pecan puree, mushrooms stuffed with, 351
    -potato dumplings with Stilton sauce, 379
    radicchio, and endive salad with avocado, 167
    and sweetbread sausage, 222–223
Spoonbread, Bourbon, 405
Squab(s)
    smoked, with Zinfandel sauce, 274
    braised with anchovies, 273
Squash
    acorn
        spiced, 359
        stuffed with curried chicken, 122–123
    butternut, with macadamia nuts, baked, 360
    pickled, 462
    relish, 464
    soufflé, 361
Steak tartare
    and caviar canapés, 16–17
    the Four Seasons', 110
Stew. *See also* Soup
    Bourbon beef and oyster pot, 182–183
    cassoulet, lean, 333–335
    chicken, Mexican, 249
    goose with sausage and chestnuts, 266–267
    gumbo, chicken and sausage, 74–75
    lobster with leeks, 297
    mixed meat (Alsatian baeckeffe), 188
    Moroccan onion kammama, 354
    oyster and spinach, 42
    shellfish (cioppino), 315–316
    vegetable ragout, 362
    venison ragout, 228
Stilton
    popovers, 446–447
    puffs, 101
    sauce for potato-spinach dumplings, 379
    soup with Port, 47
Stir-fried shrimp with ham and straw mushrooms, 121
Stock
    beef, 522
    chicken, 521
    fish, 524
    veal, 523
Stollen, Dresden, 503–504
Strawberry
    -peach cobbler, 492
    preserves, 468
    -rhubarb pie, 491
    tart, 480–481
Striped bass. *See* Bass
Stuffing, orange, prune, and chestnut, for turkey, 257–258
Sturgeon, smoked, pasta salad with capers, 140

Sugar cookies, Greek, 451
Sugarbush baked beans, 332
Swedish limpa bread, 426
Swedish meat balls with dilled sour cream sauce (frikadellar), 185–186
Sweet potato(es)
    and apples, maple, 381
    ham, and grapefruit salad, 161
    hash, ham and, 220
    pecan pie, 486
    and walnut pudding, 382
    yams baked with coconut, 382–383
Sweetbread(s)
    with orange in Chablis sauce, 233
    sautéed, with tarragon-butter sauce, 221
    soused, in romaine lettuce, 20
    and spinach sausage, 222–223
    and wild rice salad with grapes and coriander, 164
Swordfish steaks in apple cider sauce, 290

Tapenade, mushrooms, 6–7
Tarragon-butter sauce for sweetbreads, 221
Tart(e). *See also* Flan; Pie; Torte
    apricot tourte, 483
    au chocolat, froide, 488
    aux fraises, 480–481
    leek, 9
    lemon with orange (au citron Giradet), 479–480
    papaya with macadamia nuts, 478
    pear, red wine, with hazelnut ice cream, 477
    prune, glazed, 482
    sardine and tuna, Moroccan, 308
    strawberry, fresh, 480–481
Terrine. *See also* Pâté
    flounder and spinach with prunes, 27–28
    potato, leek and carrot, 14
Thai shad soup, 56
Three-fruit marmalade, 471
Timbales of zucchini and mushrooms, 364
Toast, herbed, 447
Tofu and vegetable brochettes, marinated, grilled over mesquite, 114
Tomato(es)
    -avocado soup, minted, 46–47
    and chilies, okra with, 353
    and country ham frittata, 86
    and crab bisque, 44
    fresh, and snapper chowder, 75
    green, and apple chutney, 465
    and sardines, gratin of, 307
    sauce
        cold fresh, 540
        cold for rigatoni with olives, 383
        curried for halibut steaks, 277
        hot, 539

sauce (*continued*)
    -shrimp for fillet of flounder, 295
    tuna, and broccoli, pasta salad with, 138–139
Torte. *See also* Flan; Pie; Tart(e)
    Huguenot, 484
    potato and salmon, 377
Tortellini, sausage-filled carrot salad with bulb fennel, 170–171
Tortilla(s)
    soup, 62
    wheat, 417
Tourte, apricot, 483
Tourtière Québecoise (Canadian meat pie), 210
Trout. *See also* Flounder, baby; Catfish, Caribbean
    sautéed with crabmeat in red wine sauce, 285
    smoked, pasta and vegetable salad with, 169
Truffled roast turkey, 256
Truffles, chocolate, 517
Tuiles (macadamia wafers), 453
Tuna
    broccoli, and tomatoes, pasta salad with, 138–139
    and sardine tart, Moroccan, 308
    sautéed with tarragon, 284
Turkey
    and ham casserole with water chestnuts, 254
    hash cakes, curried, 255
    roast
        with orange, prune, and chestnut stuffing, 257–258
        truffled, 256
    salad
        and chutney, James Beard's, 158
        with poppy seed dressing, 157
    scallops, creamed with chestnuts, 253
Turnips, potatoes, and ham, gratin of, 376
Twice-baked potato skins with cheese and bacon, 378

Veal
    birds, 191–192
    chops grilled with basil cream and mustard sauce, 192–193
    curried meat custard, Charleston hobotee, 13
    cutlets
        with pumpkin sauce, 195
        stuffed with mustard sauce, 194
    fillets braised with onion sauce, 196–197
    and herring salad with apple, 163
    kidney brochettes with fresh rosemary, 38
    medallions of, with black caviar, 190
    saddle of, stuffed, 189
    stock, 523
    tonnato. *See* Pork tonnato
Vegetable(s). *See also name of specific vegetable*
    and chicken, cold pasta with, 388
    hash, glazed, 363
    marinade for, 550

paella, 396–397
    and pasta salad with smoked trout, 169
    ragout, 362
    salad
        marinated, 167
        with yoghurt dressing, 174
    soup, au pistou Vencienne, 76
    spaghetti primavera Le Cirque, 390–391
    and tofu brochettes, marinated, grilled over mesquite, 114–115
Venison
    ragout, 228
    roast saddle of, with black pepper sauce, 226
    steaks with stuffed pears, 227
Vermicelli, pasta with chicken and vegetables, cold, 388
Vichyssoise, cucumber, 53
Vidalia onions. *See* Onions
Vinaigrette dressing, basic, 542–543
Vinaigrette
    dressing, aux fines herbes, 543
    sauce, hot, duck liver with, 12
Vinegar-cream sauce for ham, 219

Walnut(s)
    and apples, sautéed, 457
    bread, 432–433
    oil dressing, 545
    pâté and duck liver, ramekins of, 17
    pie, Greek, 487
    pumpkin bread, 433
Watercress
    apple and pecan salad, 165
    sauce, 532
Watermelon rind pickle, 460–461
Wheat tortillas, 417
White sausages with onions and apples, 251–252
Whole wheat
    caraway bread, 427
    pecan bread, 428
Wild game marinade, 549
Wild mushroom(s)
    Bourbon burgers with, 187
    chicken sauté with, 232
    cod poached with, 278–279
    and crabmeat, Japanese soba salad with, 171
    herbed, on pita, 18–19
    and leek quiche, 107
    pork chops stuffed with, 206
    and potatoes, gratin of, Alice Waters', 370
    sauce, 538
    soup, 46
    wild rice with, and pine nuts, 400
    woodland mushrooms with Port and cream sauce, 35
Wild rice
    and sweetbreads salad with grapes and coriander, 164

with wild mushrooms and pine nuts, 400
Woodland mushrooms with port and cream sauce,
    352

Yams. *See also* Sweet potatoes
    baked with coconut, 382–383
Yankee clam hash, 316–317
Yeast bread, country, 418
Yeast potato rolls, 431

Yoghurt
    dressing, 548
    pie, 489

Zucchini
    and fennel, glazed, 345
    and mushrooms, timbales of, 364
    moussaka, 365
    Provençale, cold, 24
    soup, saffroned, 42–43